Building the Primary Classroom

A Complete Guide to Teaching and Learning

Toni S. Bickart
Judy R. Jablon
Diane Trister Dodge

TEACHING STRATEGIES INC.
Washington, DC

Heinemann
Portsmouth, NH

Editor: Emily Kohn
Cover Photographs: Connie Reider and Andrew Edgar
Graphic Design: Winge and Associates, Inc.
Cover Design: Jenny Jensen Greenleaf
Illustrations: Jody Eastman

Co-published by:

Teaching Strategies, Inc.
P.O. Box 42243
Washington, DC 20015
www.TeachingStrategies.com

Heinemann
A Division of Reed Elsevier Inc.
361 Hanover Street
Portsmouth, NH 03801-3912
www.Heinemann.com
Offices and agents throughout the world

Publisher's Cataloging-in-Publication
(Provided by Quality Books, Inc.)

Bickart, Toni S.
    Building the primary classroom : a complete
    guide to teaching and learning / Toni S. Bickart,
    Judy R. Jablon, Diane Trister Dodge.
        p. cm.
    Includes bibliographical references and index.
    LCCN: 99-71242
    ISBN: 1-879537-38-9

    1. Education, Primary. 2. Teaching.
    3. Education, Primary--Curricula. I. Jablon, Judy
    R. II. Dodge, Diane Trister. III. Title.

    LB1507.B53 1999   372.24'1
                   QBI99-996

Printed and bound in the United States of America

First Printing: September 1999
Second Printing: October 2001

Acknowledgments

We have many people to thank for their help with this new edition of our work for primary grade teachers. *Building the Primary Classroom* is based on our earlier work, *Constructing Curriculum for the Primary Grades*. As teachers and learners we couldn't resist making changes based on what we learned from our teaching and staff development work during the last five years. This book has benefited from the major contributions of Cate Heroman, our colleague at Teaching Strategies, and the thoughtful comments and additions of Kathy Beland, Avril Font, Denise Gershowitz, Elaine Pierrel, Caitlin Pike, Monica Vacca, and Sybil Wolin.

We have added new information on social and emotional development, social problem solving, caring communities, and resiliency. We have included a new chapter on technology and updated all of the content chapters based on current research and standards in the field.

For their work on the original content chapters of *Constructing Curriculum*, we would like to thank again our contributing authors: Elizabeth Servidio, who drafted Language and Literacy; Wickes MacColl, for Mathematical Thinking; and Laura Thorpe Katz, for Scientific Thinking. We appreciate the work Charlotte Stetson and Pamela Becker did to review and comment on all chapters in the original book. We want to acknowledge our collaboration with the DC Public Schools. We deeply appreciate the support we received from the National Child Day Care Association and then-Deputy Superintendent Maurice Sykes and Austine Fowler, Early Childhood Specialist. We want to thank teachers in the DC Public Schools as well as those teachers in elementary schools participating in the Follow Through Project in Brattleboro, Vermont. We were influenced by the work of Samuel Meisels, Judy Jablon, Margo Dichtelmiller, Aviva Dorfman, and Dorothea Marsden, the developers of the Work Sampling System™ at the University of Michigan regarding performance indicators and domains of development.

We extend our appreciation to the many teachers who allowed us to take pictures in their classrooms that were used as the basis for the illustrations drawn by Jody Eastman.

And finally, we want to acknowledge the real life stories (including our own) of many teachers that are reflected in the examples throughout this book. To all of these people, we extend our deep gratitude and thanks.

Building the

Primary

Classroom

Introduction

Good teaching is hard work. Teachers make many decisions every day based on their knowledge of child development, the content of the curriculum, their own intuitive beliefs, and daily observation in the classroom. You have a major responsibility for shaping children's attitudes about school and learning—attitudes that can influence children's success both in school and in life. When children feel confident, competent, and accepted as learners, teachers know that they have made a difference. Our purpose in writing this book is to help you, as teachers, develop a vision of the possibilities in a classroom that is truly effective.

Who Should Use This Book

Building the Primary Classroom is for elementary school teachers who work with children in grades one through three. Its purpose is to provide a practical framework for making teaching effective and learning meaningful for children in these early grades. Although the book addresses classroom teachers, it also offers administrators and parents insight into high-quality teaching.

We strongly believe that teachers should be decision makers in their classrooms. Curriculum guides and performance standards offer direction about what children are expected to know and be able to do. But it is the classroom teacher, with the input and involvement of families, who knows the children well enough to make informed decisions about what each child needs to become a successful learner.

The teaching strategies described here build on approaches that teachers have found most effective for helping children develop social competence and become confident learners. Because teachers bring personal experiences, beliefs, and goals to the task of implementing curriculum, our framework allows teachers to construct and clarify their own ideas and beliefs about the teaching practices that work best for them and for the children they teach.

How Teachers Plan Instruction

Teachers make good decisions about curriculum and assessment when their decisions are grounded in a clear philosophy about teaching and learning. The philosophical framework that underlies this book is now called *developmentally appropriate practice*, but it is not new. It reflects what many primary grade teachers have intuitively known and believed but have not always been able to put into practice. It is based on the same philosophy John Dewey described at the beginning of this century, and that guided the work of Lucy Sprague Mitchell and Carolyn Pratt. Constructivist philosophers, including Jerome Bruner and Lev Vygotsky, have extended the knowledge base of early childhood education and therefore our ability to define appropriate practice.

Developmentally appropriate practice is based on information and knowledge in three areas (Bredekamp and Copple 1997):

- child development—what is age appropriate;
- the strengths, interests, and needs of individual children—what is individually appropriate; and
- knowledge of the social and cultural contexts in which children live—what is socially and culturally appropriate.

With knowledge of child development, teachers can plan a learning environment and experiences that address the normal sequences of growth for children at each stage of development. With information about individual children, teachers can address learning needs by recognizing the individual patterns of growth, and unique interests, experiences, and strengths that each child brings to the learning process. Knowledge of the social and cultural context in which children live helps teachers plan learning experiences that are meaningful for, relevant to, and respectful of each child and family.

Because expectations for what children need to know have greatly expanded in the last decade, developmentally appropriate practice is only the beginning of instructional planning. In order to help children acquire the knowledge and skills they need, classrooms have to function as "knowledge-centered environments" (National Research Council 1999) where children are actively engaged in the learning process. In such environments, teachers consider what children already know about a given subject and how to help them to construct new understandings based on that knowledge. They provide feedback to children throughout the learning process. Their goal is to guide children to make sense of new information, not just to memorize it.

Why We Need to Look at Teaching Practices in the Primary Grades

There is a growing consensus among educators today that a major reason why traditional teaching practices that emphasize drills, worksheets, and the teaching of skills in isolation have failed is that they are not based on a knowledge of what is appropriate or on the latest educational research on how children learn. Leading professional organizations dedicated to improving the quality of education for young children, including the National Association for the Education of Young Children (NAEYC), the National Association of Elementary School Principals (NAESP), the Association for Supervision and Curriculum Development (ASCD), the National Association of State Boards of Education (NASBE), the Carnegie Corporation of New York, and the National Research Council, have been directing and supporting efforts to identify more effective curriculum, teaching strategies, assessment tools, and staff development efforts.

For children to achieve grade-level expectations and become competent learners, professional practice must reflect what we know about how learning takes place. But teachers are frustrated by all the requirements placed on them. They try to engage children in meaningful learning but at the same time feel the pressure for children to succeed on tests. To further complicate matters, teachers may have personal concerns about the tremendous needs many children bring to school.

The goals, principles, and instructional approaches that emerge from a developmentally appropriate philosophy and an understanding of the subject areas give us a clear framework to help children acquire the skills and understandings they will need to function productively in the twenty-first century.

What Children Should Learn in the Primary Grades

Planning for children's learning should always begin with a vision of the purpose of education—the philosophy and values that guide decision making. We believe that the fundamental aims of education from PreK-12th grade are to enable children to:

- gain increasing self-awareness and a deeper understanding of the world around them.

- develop the dispositions to be learners—curiosity, independence, responsibility, initiative, creativity, willingness to take risks, to ask questions, and to persevere (Katz and Chard 1989).

- acquire the skills and knowledge they need to be successful learners in language and literacy, mathematics, social studies, science, technology, and the arts, and to apply these skills in everyday situations.

- function as contributing members of a community by developing social and emotional skills, such as self-control, cooperation, perspective taking, problem solving, and sharing responsibility.

The question that must be addressed next is, "What do we want children to learn during the primary grades that will enable them to become successful learners, lead fulfilling lives, and contribute to society?" To answer this question, we must consider both content and children's development. Most states now have standards in place identifying what children should learn in each subject area by grade level. These standards provide an overview of the content and skills children are expected to master. We feel strongly that teachers must also have goals for children's emotional, social, cognitive, and physical development.

Goals for Emotional Development

- To develop awareness of emotions in self and others.

- To regulate emotions and delay gratification.

- To acquire a sense of confidence about one's abilities.

- To take pride in one's heritage and family background.

- To experience a sense of belonging and learn to trust others.

- To be flexible and willing to take appropriate risks.

Goals for Social Development

- To develop positive relationships with peers and adults.
- To work cooperatively with others to achieve shared goals.
- To recognize and respect people's differences and perspectives.
- To contribute to establishing and maintaining rules for group living.
- To solve problems in nonviolent ways.

Goals for Cognitive Development

- To demonstrate curiosity and initiative in seeking out an increasing understanding about the world.
- To make increasing sense of the physical and social world through direct experiences and explorations.
- To express and communicate ideas and feelings.
- To read and write with understanding and increasing accuracy.
- To use mathematical thinking skills.
- To use the skills of scientific and social studies research.
- To identify, reason through, and solve real-life problems.
- To develop critical thinking skills.
- To question stereotypes based on various aspects of diversity (ethnicity, gender, age, ability, physical characteristics).

Goals for Physical Development

- To build and expand gross and fine motor skills.
- To show confidence in what their bodies can do.
- To value and promote personal health, safety, and fitness.

Given the emphasis in recent years on cognitive goals—the proliferation of testing programs and standards—we also assert the need for attention to social and emotional goals. Research indicates that children who are socially competent are more likely to succeed in school and in life (The Child Mental Health Foundations and Agencies Network 2000, 7). We also know that even those children who face major hardships in life—from abuse or neglect, poverty, family drug abuse, or mental health problems—can succeed because of particular social strengths called *resiliencies* (Wolin and Wolin 1993, 1995). This ability to show resilience—to be able to bounce back from hardship despite the wounds—can be supported by the school experience. Good schools, like supportive families, are one of the major institutions with the potential to foster resiliency in children (Benard 1999, Benson 1998).

"Bonding to school" is considered a major factor that contributes to resilience (Abbott et al. 1998). While we "are all born with innate resiliency" (Benard 1999, 5), teachers make the difference in whether a classroom will help children bond. What happens in the classroom influences whether this natural resiliency is fostered. In each of the six teaching strategies we suggest ways in which teachers can recognize and support children practicing behaviors that encourage the development of resiliency (Bickart and Wolin 1997).

How to Use This Book

Building the Primary Classroom is organized into two parts, one that presents the teaching strategies and one that describes subject areas.

Part One—Six Strategies for Building the Primary Classroom provides teachers with a practical framework for making decisions about their work with children.

- **Knowing the Children You Teach** means understanding developmental stages, individual characteristics, and the influence of culture. Because every group is unique, teaching and learning are dynamic processes shaped in part by the attributes and interests of each group of children.

- **Building a Classroom Community** involves having daily class meetings, helping children learn to work collaboratively, and teaching children social problem-solving skills. When a classroom functions as a community, children experience a sense of belonging and a sense of empowerment that are essential to their well-being and their academic success.

- **Establishing a Structure for the Classroom** involves organizing the classroom environment, establishing consistent routines and schedules, and conveying specific expectations for behavior. An explicit structure enables teachers to facilitate children's learning and helps children to become self-directed learners.

- **Guiding Children's Learning** describes how teachers create opportunities for children to acquire skills and content as children actively investigate, represent, and reflect on their increasing understanding of the world around them. Teachers organize the curriculum using an integrated approach that allows children to apply skills they are learning in reading, writing, math, science, social studies, technology, and the arts.

- **Assessing Children's Learning** occurs every day as teachers observe children and collect samples of their work. A comprehensive approach to assessment enables teachers to make informed decisions about curriculum, plan instruction, monitor, and share children's progress with families in a meaningful way.

- **Building a Partnership with Families** means taking time to learn about each child's family, involving families in the school community, establishing a structure for ongoing communication, sharing the curriculum, and involving families in the assessment process. When families are involved, children's achievement is enhanced, teachers obtain support, and schools become better places for learning.

Part Two—Curriculum Content describes the six subject areas that teachers address in the primary grades.

- **Language and Literacy:** As children develop their language and literacy skills, they learn how to communicate effectively through listening, speaking, reading, and writing. Teachers teach skills while they expose children to a wide range of literature and print materials, give children opportunities to write, and make conversations and discussions integral parts of classroom life.

- **Mathematical Thinking:** Math is defined as a way to organize information and represent relationships. Children learn about number concepts and operations, patterns, functions, and algebra, geometry and spatial relationships, measurement, data analysis, probability, and statistics. Through hands-on experiences, children develop problem-solving strategies and critical thinking skills.

- **Social Studies:** In social studies, children learn about people and places. As they pose questions, conduct research, engage in discussions, and present their findings, children begin to make connections between what they are learning and their own daily lives. Social studies experiences promote children's understanding of geography and culture.

- **Scientific Thinking:** Children wonder about and search for ways to explain the natural and physical world. By nurturing their excitement and curiosity about the world around them, teachers can guide children in the methods of scientific investigation and help them acquire knowledge and understanding of natural and physical phenomena.

- **Technology:** When children explore technology they learn to appreciate the tools and inventions we use every day. Teachers build on children's natural inclination to explore, invent, and make things. As they design machines or inventions, they handle tools and solve problems. Children use computers to support the writing process, solve problems in simulation exercises, communicate, and access information.

- **The Arts:** In the arts, children explore a variety of media. Teachers incorporate art, drama, music, dance, and construction to develop appreciation for different forms of expression and to support learning differences.

In each chapter we present an overview of the subject areas based on current national and/or state standards. We outline the skills and content children are expected to learn, and offer practical teaching strategies for guiding children's learning. The content chapters show how the six strategies provide a practical and focused approach to making learning meaningful for children.

We hope that this book will validate what teachers already know, help them construct a clear philosophy for themselves, and give them the confidence to follow their own beliefs.

References

Abbott, Robert D., Julie O'Donnell, J. David Hawkins, Karl G. Hill, Richard Kosterman, and Richard F. Catalano. October 1998. Changing Teaching Practices to Promote Achievement and Bonding to School. *American Journal of Orthopsychiatry* 68 (4): 542-52.

Benard, Bonnie. 1999. From Research to Practice: The Foundations of the Resiliency Paradigm. In *Resiliency in Action*. Edited by Nan Henderson, Bonnie Benard, and Nancy Sharp-Light. Gorham, ME: Resiliency In Action, 5-9.

Benson, Peter L., Judy Galbraith, and Pamela Espeland. 1998. *What Kids Need to Succeed.* Minneapolis, MN: Free Spirit.

Bickart, Toni, and Sybil Wolin. November 1997. Practicing Resilience in the Elementary Classroom. *Principal* 77 (2): 21-24.

Bredekamp, Sue, and Carol Copple, eds. 1997. *Developmentally Appropriate Practice in Early Childhood Programs, Revised Edition.* Washington, DC: NAEYC.

The Child Mental Health Foundations and Agencies Network. 2000. *A Good Beginning: Sending America's Children to School with the Social and Emotional Competence They Need to Succeed.* Bethesda, MD: The National Institute of Mental Health.

Katz, Lilian and Sylvia Chard. 1989. *Engaging Children's Minds: The Project Approach.* Norwood, NJ: Ablex Publishing Co., 30.

National Research Council. 1999. *How People Learn: Brain, Mind, Experience, and School.* Prepublication Copy. Washington, DC: National Research Council, 124-5.

Wolin, Steven, and Sybil Wolin. 1995. Resilience Among Youth Growing Up in Substance-Abusing Families. *The Pediatric Clinics of North America, Substance Abuse* 42 (2): 415-430.

Wolin, Steven, and Sybil Wolin. 1993. *The Resilient Self: How Survivors of Troubled Families Rise Above Adversity.* New York: Villard Books.

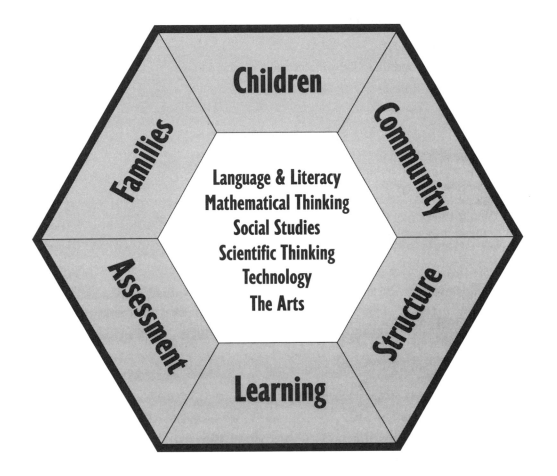

Children

Community

Structure

Learning

Assessment

Families

Language & Literacy
Mathematical Thinking
Social Studies
Scientific Thinking
Technology
The Arts

PART ONE

1

KNOWING THE CHILDREN YOU TEACH

The foundation for good teaching is knowing about children—developmentally, individually, and culturally. Teachers begin with a solid understanding of child development, and combine this with what they learn about the specific interests, abilities, needs, and experiences each child brings into the classroom. Because every group of children is unique, what is taught and how it is taught varies somewhat each year.

There are two reasons why knowing the children you teach is the first strategy for building the primary classroom. First, the developmental and individual characteristics of children influence the kinds of learning experiences you plan. Second, knowing children well makes it possible to build positive relationships with them, which is often the key to their success in school.

No matter how similar the children in your classroom may appear, every group is made up of individuals who bring their own set of experiences, interests, learning differences, and expectations into the classroom. This chapter describes how you can learn about the children you teach by focusing on:

- *developmental characteristics of children*—emotional, social, cognitive, and physical;

- *individual characteristics of children*—temperament, interests, talents, learning differences, life experiences, and special needs;

- the *cultural context* in which children have been raised and its influence upon their communication and interaction styles and on other expectations about their behavior.

We conclude this chapter with some specific suggestions for going beyond first impressions and initial expectations to learn about the children in your classroom.

Knowing About Child Development

Understanding child development helps teachers know how and why children behave as they do and what to expect of children within each age group. Child development refers to the generally predictable patterns of change that occur as children grow. An abundance of literature provides guidelines for the normal sequence of growth in all areas of development. The theories of psychologists Erik Erikson, Jean Piaget, and Lev Vygotsky have contributed to our understanding of children's emotional, social, and cognitive growth.

Curriculum is considered *age appropriate* or *developmentally appropriate* if it is based on knowledge of how most children grow and what they can do—socially, emotionally, cognitively, and physically—at a particular stage of development. This knowledge enables teachers to plan classroom activities that will be appropriate to children's developmental abilities. It helps teachers to anticipate children's behavior and have reasonable expectations about how children will respond to classroom activities.

Social development addresses how the child relates to others and the child's ability to make friends. Emotional development relates to feelings about self and others. Cognitive development refers to how the child thinks, processes information, solves problems, and uses language to communicate. Physical development includes growth in size, strength, motor skills, and coordination. Although we can look at each aspect of development separately, all areas of development are interrelated. By knowing the developmental characteristics of primary grade children, teachers can determine the kinds of experiences children are ready to undertake and how to support each child's growth and learning.

Differences in the Rate of Development Are Normal

While there are predictable patterns of development, children do not grow and develop at the same rate. Within any group of children the same age, a two-and-a-half-year span of development is perfectly normal. In addition, an individual child's development does not follow an even course across all domains: a six year old may have the fine motor skills of some seven year olds but the language skills of some five year olds. It is also important to remember that in September, a typical class of first graders will include some children who have not yet turned six and others who are approaching seven.

How Theorists Describe Primary Grade Children

Children in the primary grades tend to define themselves in terms of attributes and achievements.

"I wear glasses."   "I'm good at soccer."
"My skin is brown."   "I can read long books with chapters."

This period of development is characterized by a decrease in egocentricity and an increasing interest in others, especially peers. Children often express interest in and awareness of social issues as they read stories, observe local happenings, and hear about current events. They gain the capacity to infer another person's perspective (feelings, thoughts, intentions) with a good deal of accuracy. Establishing friendships takes on importance although children sometimes lack the skills necessary to do so. Many children this age think about how they look in the eyes of others and become increasingly self-conscious. A noticeable characteristic of children in the primary grades is the emergence of a sense of humor. Less dependent on adults and more dependent on peers, children are likely to question authority and test limits.

Theories of Erikson

Erik Erikson (1994) describes eight "psychosocial" stages; during each, a psychosocial strength is developed. As children move from one stage to the next, the strengths of prior stages remain and become related to the others.

Each stage is characterized in terms of a positive and negative attribute. According to Erikson, children between six and eight are in the fourth psychosocial stage, that of "Industry vs. Inferiority." Industry means that children become increasingly product oriented, want to do a job well, and want to feel competent. Competent children are sure enough of themselves to take risks and to struggle with challenges in order to reach a goal, solve a problem, or complete a task. When children do not achieve a positive sense of industry they feel inferior ("I can't do it."). Erikson's theories explain how important it is for teachers to provide children with appropriate challenges so they can feel successful.

Theories of Piaget

Jean Piaget (2000) describes how children's thinking changes as they progress through four stages. During each stage, children construct an understanding of their experiences with people and objects. Until about the age of twelve, children's constructions of reality are often distortions or approximations of how things actually are.

Between the ages of six and eight, children progress from what Piaget calls "pre-operational thinking" to "concrete operational thinking." Children at the pre-operational stage rely primarily on sensory experience for thinking and learning. They base their understanding of the world on what they learn from first-hand experience. The new set of mental abilities (concrete operations) that they acquire enables them to manipulate symbols in their minds, while a younger child can only manipulate concrete objects. This change in thinking affects many aspects of children's learning. Here are some examples of how their thinking changes.

- They can classify things in terms of hierarchical relationships (e.g., cats and dogs are all animals).
- They can explore something visually rather than only manually (e.g., looking at a set of Tangrams and mentally deciding on how they will fit into a pre-drawn shape, rather than having to push them around until they form the shape).
- They can follow a set of rules when playing a game.

Theories of Vygotsky

Lev Vygotsky (1999) emphasized the importance of the social and cultural context in shaping the development of thinking skills. He recognized that social interaction and the language that accompanies it are crucial for learning.

From his focus on social interaction, Vygotsky developed the theory (although not the name) of "scaffolding." In this model, children's learning is compared to a new building, temporarily supported by an outside structure as the construction progresses. Vygotsky noted how adults and "competent peers" support children's learning and that emerging abilities appear first in a context of support from others.

Through collaboration with others, children acquire new skills and gradually become successful at using these skills independently. Teachers must strive to find the right balance between engaging children at their existing level of competence and supporting them in reaching higher levels. The existing level and the new level is the "zone of proximal development" (Berk and Winsler 1995). Scaffolding supports children as they work on emerging skills. They assume more and more responsibility for their own performance as they learn (Bodrova and Leong 1996).

Developmental Characteristics of Primary Grade Children

In this section we describe some typical characteristics of children in first through third grades. Most children in these grades are between the ages of six and eight. However, many enter first grade having not quite turned six, and by the middle of third grade, some children have turned nine. In addition, more and more primary classrooms have mixed-age groups, including those that combine five and six year olds. For these reasons, we begin this section with a brief overview of five year olds and end by describing nine year olds.

Leaving Age Five

Five year olds revel in their newly acquired skills. Often emotionally solid and good tempered, they tend to be energetic and friendly. They can be overly confident about their abilities, having gained sufficient physical strength and control to have a sense of competence and power.

The egocentricity of five year olds is evident in the way they learn and relate to peers. Because they rely on their senses to take in new information, their questions about the natural and social world relate to what they see. They learn through their own direct involvement. Watching someone else have a turn doing something, or listening to a story about how something is done, does not help them learn as much as doing it themselves. Five year olds begin to make generalizations from repeated experiences, and their thinking depends on their actions. They frequently confuse fantasy and reality.

Five year olds are usually eager to please and to receive affection. It may be hard for them to share because they are so focused on themselves and have trouble understanding another point of view. However, while sharing may be frustrating one minute, the next minute a five year old may give up a turn or a toy to someone else as a way to please and make a friend. Although eager for friendships, five year olds may not have the skills to make and keep a friend. They often use language with ease and sometimes sound like adults, but they do not act or think like we do. Adult guidance and support is needed to help fives figure out what is fair when it comes to sharing materials, standing up for themselves, and negotiating friendships. As children turn six, they often move into a less stable phase.

Six Year Olds

Emotionally

The moods of six year olds can change abruptly from one extreme to another. One minute they may be friendly and enthusiastic and the next, they can be rebellious and irritable. Within a matter of seconds they can be best friends or worst enemies with the same person. The same six year old who acts silly and delights in a newly developing sense of humor may be prone to frequent tears and tantrums. They can identify and understand simple emotions (happy, sad, excited) but not complex ones (shame, contempt, embarrassment). Six year olds are gaining secondary coping skills—adjusting to a situation they can't change, such as not crying when getting a shot—but still use primary coping skills—attempting to change a situation, for example, by moving away from someone who is bothering them. Sixes generally enjoy routines. It is best to let them make transitions slowly, as they may be easily overwhelmed by excitement. It may be hard for them to make choices or decisions because they often want to weigh alternatives carefully and assess all of their options. Invested in doing things their own way, they may respond negatively to adult demands.

Socially

Eager to feel connected to their peers, six year olds work hard at making friends. However, because many have not yet developed the skills needed to do this successfully, social struggles are frequent. Sixes may be bossy in play activities and, like five year olds, demand their own way. Threesomes can be difficult for them. They need guidance on rules, cooperative play, and sharing. To make a situation come out the way they want, it is not uncommon for them to resort to changing the rules (cheating), or changing the story (lying). They can be very competitive and insist on being first (or last). They can begin to distinguish between intending an act—I meant to push you—and not intending a consequence—I didn't mean to hurt you. Although slowly moving away from dependence on adults, sixes still want adult approval and praise. When they tattle, it is usually to show adults they really know the rules. A supportive adult can provide the right words or a suggestion for a solution to a problem. Extensive social coaching and modeling teaches six year olds the skills they need to relate positively to peers. Easily discouraged and frustrated, sixes cope poorly with failure and do not take criticism well.

Cognitively

Six year olds are likely to be curious learners who are interested in both process and product. They learn best through their active involvement with people and materials. They are more like fives than sevens, however, in that process holds greater pleasure and importance than product. It isn't unusual for a six year old to rush through work, eager to move on to something new. Six year olds are beginning to think logically, and to organize concepts symbolically. For example, many understand that the number *three* can represent someone who is three years old, something that weighs three pounds, or three cookies. Unlike five year olds, whose thinking is based on what they see, six year olds are moving toward what Piaget calls "conservation." For example, many can recognize that two sets of ten cubes are equivalent, even when one is spread apart and the other is clustered together.

Physically

Six year olds seem to be in perpetual motion; they squirm as they sit, or gesture with their bodies as they talk. Although quite energetic, they can tire easily and benefit from activities such as listening to a story or quietly looking at books after recess. In the classroom, they need to be able to move around and have a variety of active and quiet activities. By six, most children are excelling at gross motor skills such as running and jumping, beginning to use a bat, throwing and catching with increasing skill, and doing somersaults. They are gradually gaining control of fine motor activities and can use tools such as scissors, pencils, markers, paintbrushes, saws, and hammers with increasing ease. Like five year olds, they gain confidence with their increasing physical competence.

Seven Year Olds

Emotionally

Emotional changes between six and seven are gradual and depend on the individual child and his or her own environment. Most seven year olds are able to regulate their emotions and control impulses in most situations. They are eager to master new skills and begin to demand perfection of themselves. Thus, they are likely to draw the same picture or write stories about the very same theme over and over, striving to achieve perfection. They can be highly self-critical, and more inhibited and worried about making mistakes than they were a year earlier. Seven year olds tend to take life seriously and often feel that things are unjust. Schedules and routines are important to them and they expect that these will be followed exactly. Like sixes, they often find transitions uncomfortable and benefit from having time to prepare for them.

Socially

At seven, children are evolving into capable social beings. They can appreciate situations from another person's perspective. They establish strong friendships and want to feel that they are part of the group. In group discussions and projects, sevens can listen to and appreciate the contributions of others. In their effort to feel a sense of security and belonging, they often imitate the actions of their friends. They will join in playground games and work with others in the classroom. Despite their interest in being with others, it is not unusual for seven year olds to want to work by themselves in a quiet space. They often begin to develop special interests such as collecting baseball cards, doing gymnastics, tap dancing, playing the violin, or playing soccer. Their tendency toward repetitive actions can be seen in their desire to play the same game over and over. While four to six year olds have a developing awareness of differences (e.g., gender, race, physical abilities), seven year olds can verbalize them and may even use them as a basis for exclusion.

Cognitively

Like six year olds, sevens continue to learn most readily through concrete experiences and active participation. They enjoy experimenting and have the intellectual capacity to organize their experiences mentally. Seven year olds are willing to take time to think and plan before they set out to work, and they are gaining the ability to reflect on what they have done. While sevens show an increasing ability to distinguish between reality and fantasy, they enjoy imaginative play and like to put on puppet shows and dramatize stories.

Physically

Seven is typically a period of slow but steady growth. Children this age have increased stamina, control, and balance, and a greater interest in team sports. Like the six year old, sevens are active and energetic and sometimes are unable to control their energy. Although their small muscles are still developing, their increased and improved eye-hand coordination enables them to draw and write with increasing facility.

Eight Year Olds

Emotionally

At eight, children gradually view themselves as individuals in the context of the larger world. They are keenly aware of the difference between the adult world and the world of children. Eager to be a part of the adult world, they are often frustrated by their limitations. As they begin to assert themselves, they can act rude and unreasonable or be easily disappointed when things do not go their way. Many will readily argue their point of view. At the same time, their increased ability to evaluate themselves and others makes them more self-critical than they were at seven. Although they still want praise from adults, they don't want to be told what to do and respond better to hints and cues than to direct orders. Reasonably consistent standards and demands from adults help them to successfully move out on their own. Because they can become overwhelmed and frustrated easily, they often need adults to help them come up with strategies for accomplishing tasks.

Socially

Eight year olds crave acceptance from their peers, and group membership grows in importance. They establish close friendships but are likely to struggle with endless disagreements. Some eights can be very moody about friends—close one day and fighting the next. Unlike many sevens, eights generally do not like to work or play alone. Eight year olds are very likely to form clubs and spend time planning who will be included and who will be excluded. They like team games and group projects and discussions. Trading and collecting is often a major social activity for eight year olds. They enjoy table games and are likely to invent their own. They look forward to roles, responsibilities, and even school traditions associated with being this age. For example, in some schools third graders are cafeteria monitors or perform in plays. Typically, third graders take pride in these special traditions and view themselves as especially important. While they can manage transitions more easily than at earlier ages, these times are liable to be busy and noisy because of the eight year old's desire to socialize.

Cognitively

Eight year olds have the capacity for abstract thinking as long as what they are thinking about relates to something they have experienced directly. As they begin to learn about what life was like long ago, they make comparisons to their own experiences. Maps capture their interest and they gain understanding of them by making maps of their own surroundings. Their work is more and more detailed. Although they continue to learn best through active, concrete experiences, they can use books as a source of information as well. By age eight, children have a longer attention span. Increasingly able to think and reason logically, they enjoy collecting, organizing, and classifying objects and information. Eight year olds like action. Their drawings often contain people and objects in motion. Imaginative play continues to be an important learning tool for them and they can become very involved in skits, role plays, and puppet shows.

Physically

The increased agility and high energy of eight year olds can make them seem restless and fidgety. Many enjoy rough and tumble play, as well as games and team sports (e.g., soccer or softball). Children this age take pleasure in the physical skills they have acquired and may be physically daring. They are also eager to learn new techniques for sports and other physical activities. They have increased speed and smoothness in fine muscle work as well as greater interest and control in skills that call for eye-hand coordination. Typically, the artwork of eight year olds becomes smaller and more detailed.

Becoming Nine

As children turn nine, you will see additional social, emotional, and physical changes too. They become more self-reflective and gain the ability to view their own behavior and motivation from outside themselves. They are capable of understanding complex emotions such as shame and jealousy, and of recognizing conflicting feelings such as sadness and relief. Nine year olds want to be independent and are strongly aligned with their peer group. They respond well to appreciation of their efforts. At this age, sex role identification becomes stronger. Like many eights, nines are easily embarrassed and can be very sensitive to teasing. They also tend to form clubs especially designed to include some peers and exclude others. Whereas eight year olds are still prone to tattling on peers, by nine, children are becoming more loyal to their peers and are less likely to do so. Nines often want and need the ear of an adult to talk over ideas and feelings. Adults can provide a cooperative setting in which children can share thoughts and feelings with peers and feel confident that they will not be "put down."

Nine year olds are intellectually competent in many ways. They can puzzle over problems mentally, whereas when they were younger they required actual objects to reach the same conclusions. Nines begin to see things from a variety of perspectives. Their attention span is expanding and they tend to enjoy projects that extend over a period of time. Even as they gradually move toward abstract thinking, they are still likely to rely on familiar experiences as a frame of reference.

Nines are becoming more and more competent physically. Most have good eye-hand coordination and enjoy detail work such as crafts, woodworking, drawing, and painting. They are becoming progressively more skillful in tasks that require motor skills.

Responding to Developmental Characteristics of Children

From these brief developmental descriptions, you can see that many characteristics recur between ages 6 to 8. The following chart summarizes those characteristics common to most children in the primary grades and suggests how an awareness of these developmental characteristics can help teachers plan an environment and experiences that will enable all children to feel competent.

Emotional Characteristics	How Teachers Can Respond
Act self-assured, but can still have many self-doubts (e.g., may overestimate abilities, don't want to fail, eager to do things perfectly)	• Allow children to take reasonable risks by providing clear boundaries and creating a classroom atmosphere where mistakes are accepted. • Provide reassurance and encouragement and convey confidence in children's abilities by being specific with praise. • Provide experiences in which children can be competent and then gradually increase the difficulty of tasks.
Beginning to see that rules are important and developing a strong sense of fair play	• Involve children in discussing the need for rules and establishing classroom rules. • Use meetings for discussions on necessary rules, problem solving, and conflict resolution. • Use role play, puppet plays, and stories to practice problem solving and conflict resolution.
Able to assume some responsibility for self	• Establish clear methods for storing belongings and bringing homework back and forth (e.g., a folder, a binder, a manila envelope). • Generate a list of jobs—with the children—for maintaining the classroom and discuss together how these jobs will be accomplished. • Help children set social and academic goals for themselves. • Model and provide skill practice in apologizing and making amends.
Sensitive to teasing, insults, and put-downs	• Lead class discussions on what constitutes teasing and put-downs. • Model and facilitate skill practice in how to respond to teasing and put-downs (ignore, use "I" messages, say "stop," seek support). • Cue, coach, and reinforce children's use of these skills. • Take a clear stand against bullying and explain why.

Social Characteristics	How Teachers Can Respond
Display strong likes and opinions	• Emphasize how children are similar in universal ways (e.g., everyone has feelings, wants to be included). • Provide opportunities for children to talk about and dramatize their feelings and express their ideas (e.g., debates) and reassure them that differences are okay. • If you see a child exhibit prejudice toward another person, intervene immediately by helping the child, and the class as a whole, understand why such behavior is hurtful. • Set up activities in which children can conduct surveys and make graphs regarding personal interests and opinions. • Read and discuss stories about issues and feelings typical of children this age.
Eager to be independent of adults and may challenge authority	• Provide choices for children each day, including activities they can do independently, so that they feel a sense of power and control. • Model and provide practice in interpersonal problem-solving skills (identifying a problem, generating solutions, predicting consequences, choosing and using a solution, switching to an alternative solution when one isn't working). • Give children positive feedback and point out the positive outcomes of working well together. • Let children select research topics within the context of a study. • Involve children in talking about rules and in resolving conflicts that arise. • Set reasonable limits and make sure children understand them.
Eager to make friends and be with peers but not always successful at doing so	• Plan a variety of small group activities and provide opportunities for children to pick their own work partners. • Discuss, model, and coach children in play entry skills (e.g., reading social cues, making positive comments and asking questions of their peers, switching to an alternative approach when necessary). • Plan time for children to discuss what does and does not work when two or more people work or play together. • Provide children with supportive social coaching (e.g., "Why don't you try saying it this way…?").
Enjoy working/playing with others as well as alone	• Set up the room so children can work collaboratively on tasks or on their own (e.g., different sized tables, moveable carrels, dividers). • Provide collaborative work activities as well as time for children to work alone.

Social Characteristics	How Teachers Can Respond
Developing a strong group identity	• Plan integrated, long-term studies as a way to foster a sense of community. • Organize cooperative games that help bond a group. • Use class meetings to address social issues and concerns (e.g., what to do about trash on the playground, how to share materials). • Encourage class spirit (e.g., doing group activities, projects, celebrations). • Establish some classroom routines (e.g., signals, greetings, goodbyes). • Display class projects in the classroom and in school hallways.
Like affection from adults though often embarrassed or uncomfortable	• Show children you care about them by offering personal greetings and by taking time to have individual conversations. • Use a sense of humor to convey certain messages and engage in casual joking. • Call attention to how children's efforts affect others (e.g., "When you included more people in your skit, they really appreciated it.").
Enjoy cooperative games and games with rules but may have difficulty coping with winning and losing	• Plan indoor and outdoor cooperative group games. • Have board and card games available in the classroom and allocate time in the schedule for children to play. • Use meetings for discussions and role plays about winning and losing.

Cognitive Characteristics	How Teachers Can Respond
Increasingly skilled and interested in reading and expressing themselves verbally and in writing	• Offer times for children to select and read their own books. • Give children opportunities to choose their own writing topics. • Expose children to a variety of writing and reading experiences (e.g., fiction, non-fiction, poetry, humor, mystery). • Engage children in discussions about reading and writing by asking extensive questions, encouraging personal responses, and letting them critique work. • Create opportunities for sharing jokes, riddles, puns, and imaginative language.
Able to work on long-term projects	• Provide opportunities for children to select, design, and carry out projects using a variety of media (e.g., puzzles, model making, cooking, weaving, planting). • Allow time for children to explore a topic in depth.
Developing the ability to hold more than one idea in their minds at a time	• Give multi-step directions and take time to go over them. • Use charts to list directions, choices, what to do when you're finished. • Encourage the use of self-talk to think through a social or academic problem.
Ask questions that begin with *how*, *why*, and *when*	• Begin long-term studies by having children generate a list of questions that are of interest to them ("What do you want to know about…?"). • Provide opportunities for research (e.g., interviewing, collecting data, going through books, studying maps and charts).
Acquiring the ability to see another person's point of view	• Facilitate role plays of common social situations and have children switch roles. • Point out how children's feelings may differ about the same thing. • Have discussions in which children express their ideas and hear opposing views about stories, current events, beliefs, interests. • Read books aloud and discuss how the characters have different points of view, relating the content to children's personal experiences. • Supervise opportunities for children to explore devices or equipment used by people with disabilities (e.g., wheelchairs, crutches, eyeglasses, braille books). • Introduce topics for study in which children learn about how others live, encouraging children to observe similarities and differences.
Like to use their imagination	• Provide opportunities for children to make up stories, skits, dances, plays, and puppet shows and then share them with others. • Offer opportunities for children to write and perform stories, poetry, and songs and to create artwork and music. • Set up opportunities for children to create inventions.

Physical Characteristics	How Teachers Can Respond
Very active and energetic (although they may suddenly get tired)	• Provide opportunities for movement throughout the day (e.g., variety in schedule, short indoor and outdoor breaks during the day). • Allow children to move about the room within reasonable limits during work times. • Have reasonable expectations for how long children can sit still.
Likely to become hungry in mid-morning and have low energy	• Provide time for mid-morning snack (either brought from home or prepared in the classroom). • Incorporate cooking experiences into projects.
Increasingly able to control and coordinate their actions	• Provide equipment such as balls, wifflebats, and jump ropes during recess so children can practice basic manipulative patterns. • Encourage children to use their bodies to express ideas and create (e.g., moving to music, acting out how a seed grows). • Provide activities that use fine motor skills (e.g., beadwork, construction, sewing, weaving, and building with a variety of manipulative materials). • Have reasonable expectations about quantity and quality of paper and pencil work.
Refining eye-hand coordination	• Provide opportunities for using these skills (e.g., woodworking, constructing models, cutting and pasting, mapping). • Provide alternatives to copying information from a blackboard.

Recognizing a Child's Individuality

In the previous section, we described the developmental characteristics of children between five and nine years old and offered some practical suggestions for responding to the developing skills and interests of children in the primary grades. Knowing these characteristics helps you to have reasonable expectations for children. However, each child is also an individual who brings a unique set of characteristics and experiences to the classroom. These characteristics and experiences affect how that child learns and relates to others. Careful observation will help you become more aware of the many influences that make each child unique.

There is no such thing as a homogeneous group of children. Even when all the children "look the same," every classroom contains a diverse group of individuals. The term *diversity* refers to the many factors that make people different, including gender, ethnicity, culture, religion, family structure, age, ability, physical characteristics, learning differences, language, economic position, and more.

For children to thrive as successful learners, the classroom has to be a place where each child feels comfortable and valued as an individual. This section will describe how temperament, interests and talents, learning differences, resiliency, life experiences, and the presence of a diagnosed disability all contribute to a child's individuality, and how these factors affect each child's self-confidence and response to learning experiences.

Temperament

Temperament refers to a person's mental outlook—the mood or spirit with which an individual approaches life. A few minutes in a classroom of busy children reveals how different children can be. Some may be shy, while others are outgoing. Some may be flexible, willing to go along with daily happenings, while others are more rigid, needing to stick to a tried and true approach or a personal opinion.

Often, children behave differently in different settings. A child who is reserved at school may be outgoing at home. A child may act one way around peers and entirely differently around adults. As you engage with and observe children in an effort to learn about their temperaments, it is important to notice how they behave in a range of settings and to confer with parents about what the child is like at home. This information can be very useful in understanding how a child goes about making friends, solving problems, and learning new skills.

Interests and Talents

Children bring their special interests into your classroom. Some children gravitate toward physical activities, others toward art. Some love the natural world and will delight in bringing all sorts of creatures and plant life into school. When you assess children to find out what they especially like to do, you can tap into these interests.

Children also have special talents, some learned and others innate. You may have a child who is a fine artist, an author, a gifted poet, a skilled soccer player, or a computer whiz. Sometimes a child's particular talent is obvious and other times it is not. For example, a child who studies violin or the drums after school and has become skilled at playing may not have an opportunity to exhibit this strength in the course of daily classroom life.

You can learn about children's interests and special talents by observing them and by talking with them and with members of their families. Encouraging children to interview one another will also help you get to know them. When teachers know children's special interests and what they are good at, they can more effectively support their growth and self-confidence.

Learning Differences

Because children approach learning differently and have particular interests that affect the content and products of their work, teachers have to think about how they can respond to these differences. Fortunately, new research on learning styles and multiple intelligences guides teachers in planning lessons.

We all have our own preferred ways of taking in new information. Think about how you approach learning. Are you aurally or visually oriented? Would you rather watch a demonstration, or study a chart or a diagram? Do you remember what a lecturer said by simply listening, or do you have to take notes? Perhaps you need to talk about what you heard to make sense of it.

In the classroom, teachers seek to recognize differences in learning styles by considering how each child best absorbs information, thinks about it, and reflects on what it means. Some children will need to handle concrete materials, ask lots of questions, test things out, or learn by talking. Others wait and watch before joining in. By observing children and getting to know them, a teacher is better able to find out how children go about the learning process.

In addition to recognizing children's different learning styles, teachers must also recognize children's special skills. Perhaps you know someone who can sketch a design for a room or repeat a line from a song heard once. Others can do mental computation quickly and easily or compose poems or skits for the office party. Schools have traditionally valued as smart those children who could demonstrate learning through oral and written communication or through computing.

As important as these language and math skills are, they are not the only ways of demonstrating what we know and can do. Research has expanded our views of learning and how important it is to recognize and use multiple learning models in the classroom.

Howard Gardner expanded our concept of intelligence and therefore our ability to recognize each child's unique strengths. According to Gardner, there are eight (Gardner 1999, 1993) different kinds of intelligence.

- *Logical-Mathematical Intelligence*—the ability to solve problems rapidly, often in one's head. Children who have strong potential in this area might solve difficult brain teasers, or easily calculate the solution to a math problem.

- *Linguistic Intelligence*—the ability to use words creatively and with ease. Children who have strong potential in this area might write poems and plays, include lots of detail in writing a story, report on an event with accuracy, use descriptive language, and acquire a large vocabulary.

- *Musical Intelligence*—the ability to produce and appreciate different forms of music. Children who have strong potential in this area might easily recognize the instruments playing a piece of music, sing in harmony with others, and enjoy many kinds of music, from classical to popular.

- *Spatial Intelligence*—the ability to form a mental model of the spatial world. Children who have strong potential in this area might be outstanding chess players, plan and create three-dimensional structures, or create and read maps with ease.

- *Bodily Kinesthetic Intelligence*—the ability to use one's body with great skill. Children who have strong potential in this area might excel in dance or gymnastics, take apart and rebuild a radio or clock, or invent a squirrel-proof birdfeeder.

- *Interpersonal Intelligence*—the ability to understand and work effectively with other people. Children who have strong potential in this area might be very aware of group dynamics, mediate conflicts between other children, or organize the group to perform a talent show.

- *Intrapersonal Intelligence*—the ability to recognize one's own strengths, weaknesses, desires, and intelligences and operate effectively. Children who have strong potential in this area might write an autobiography, set and pursue long-term goals, or give advice to a friend on how to handle a difficult personal problem.

- *Naturalist Intelligence*—the ability to recognize and classify living things and other features of the natural world, as well as objects in our man-made environment. Children who have strong potential in this area might be able to name and characterize a wide variety of dinosaurs, easily distinguish which sneakers are made by which brand, and readily perceive patterns.

Children who have strong potential in the first two areas—logical and linguistic thinking—tend to do well on standardized tests and are considered smart because these abilities are emphasized. Too often, children gifted in other areas are not recognized for their strengths and are even made to feel incompetent. Gardner points out that while everyone has some degree of each intelligence, certain individuals are highly endowed with the core abilities and skills of a particular type of intelligence.

How often have we judged children as not being very "smart" because they did not excel in linguistic or logical intelligence? Perhaps these children excelled in another way, but we failed to provide opportunities for them to practice and use their areas of strength. Rather than looking at each child and asking, "How smart is this child?" we should rephrase the question and ask "How is this child smart?" In so doing, we will discover new ways of appreciating each child's unique abilities and strengths.

Nancy Curry and Carl Johnson, in their book *Beyond Self-Esteem,* remind us that "middle childhood is an important period for developing a sense of industry or competence. Children need to experience themselves as growing, learning, and developing in valued ways" (1990, 130). By providing a variety of classroom experiences that enables all children to do well and learn in comfortable ways, we are more likely to help every child achieve a feeling of confidence and competence.

Life Experiences

Children bring into the classroom a range of life experiences that affect who they are and how they engage with other children, adults, materials and activities. These experiences contribute significantly to each child's individuality and ability to relate to others.

Some factors that may influence the child's outlook include:

- the child's position in the family—where the child fits in the line of siblings, or being an only child;
- the child's family structure (e.g., single-parent family, two parents, adoptive parents, grandparents or other relatives, foster care, two same sex parents, etc.);
- where the child has lived (e.g., in the same neighborhood since birth, having moved from another country, or having moved within the same city);
- whether the child's home language is English or another language;
- the living situation (e.g., urban, rural, house, apartment, shelter);
- the type of community in which the child lives;
- the kind of work family members do;
- the family's culture and religion;

- the economic situation and stability of the child's family (e.g., poverty, frequent family unemployment, middle or upper-middle class);

- whether the child has been exposed to violence or abuse;

- the existence of chronic health problems or drug abuse in the child's family; and

- whether the child has a physical disability (or a sibling or parent with a disability).

When teachers take time to learn about the life experiences of the children in their classroom, they can more effectively meet children's emotional and learning needs. Knowing, for example, that John has lived in numerous foster homes, helps his teacher understand why he acts out when everyone is making Mother's Day cards. When Jamal refuses to eat during snack and lunch, it is important to know that his family is observing Ramadan. If Cindy comes to school with suspicious bruises, teachers are required by law to report this to the school counselor or principal.

Children Experiencing High Levels of Stress

Many children have to deal with difficult family and life situations that profoundly affect their well-being and emotional stability. The stress that families experience today often shows in their children. If children are to learn, teachers must be alert to signs of stress and actively work to create a safe and comfortable place in the classroom. Recent brain research shows that persistent and high levels of stress caused by emotional or physical trauma produce a hormone called cortisol. This chemical actually kills off the connections between brain cells in the part of the brain that is important to learning and memory. When children are highly stressed, the brain literally shuts down (Hannaford 1995, Shore 1997).

A caring adult can help children deal with stress so they have the energy to learn. Children are usually willing to talk about their concerns and feelings if they trust that an adult will be open, caring, and accepting. You can let a child know you are aware and interested in his or her well-being by saying, "You look like something is troubling you. Would you like to talk about it?"

In a study of primary grade children dealing with separation and divorce, researchers found that children believe that they will do better work in school if their teachers understand what is going on in their lives. Children hope that teachers, knowing about the pressures the children are experiencing, will be more compassionate about occasional lapses in their school performance (Frieman 1993, 59). Of course, teachers need not excuse any behavior, but they must make clear that they care and are flexible about adapting the curriculum to meet a child's needs. For example, a child who cannot concentrate on a reading task might prefer to write in his journal about something that is on his mind.

Resiliency

You may have children in your classroom who come from families with severe problems. They may be struggling with drug or alcohol abuse, violence, poverty, or health problems. Children from multistressed families are often labeled "at risk" or "disadvantaged." These labels are neither useful nor accurate. They often lower our expectations of what children can accomplish because we view them as damaged. We focus on what they can't do. While children growing up in hardship conditions will experience problems, they need not be defined by those problems.

Recent research has shown that many children grow up to lead fulfilling lives despite the circumstances of their childhood. Wolin and Wolin (1993, 1995) have identified particular strengths or *resiliencies* in children who succeed against the odds. You can look for them in the children you teach.

- *Insight*—Children who are beginning to show this strength sense that something is wrong with their environment or home life and begin the process of asking questions to seek information about other ways to live.

- *Independence*—Some children in hardship conditions find ways to preserve their physical safety by leaving the home in times of trouble, going to a neighbor's, or hiding somewhere.

- *Relationships*—Young children who connect well with other people use this strength to form ties with adults who can help them overcome troubling situations and relationships in other parts of their lives. Many adult survivors say a relationship with a teacher was key.

- *Initiative*—This strength is demonstrated in children who like to explore and solve problems. They want to be good at doing something.

- *Creativity and Humor*—These strengths are apparent in children's dramatic play in the way they can take on other roles that make them feel powerful. They may create beautiful works of art, dance, or sing, or tell funny stories or jokes.

- *Morality*—As young children develop this strength they learn to make judgments about people and behavior. They are concerned about others, taking care of other children or animals.

While teachers cannot change the hardships children face, they can help children with a repertoire of instructional approaches that promote these strengths. In each subsequent chapter in Part I, we show how teachers can create a classroom environment that helps children practice behaviors associated with resiliency.

Special Needs

You may find that you have children in your classroom with special needs, including diagnosed disabilities. It is important to recognize that any individual teacher is not expected to possess in-depth knowledge about every type of disability. As a teacher, each year you meet new children and discover new challenges. Teaching children with special needs, like all teaching, builds upon the knowledge and experience you continually acquire. One person cannot become an expert on all disabilities, but it is possible to focus upon and learn a great deal about the particular special needs of individual children in your classroom.

Too often, children are labeled as having disabilities before a formal diagnosis has been made. A complete diagnosis involves thorough evaluation by specialists in the appropriate field, as well as consultation with the child's family. When the classroom encourages many different approaches to solving problems and completing tasks, children can work at their own pace and mislabeling is less likely to occur.

Diagnosed disabilities of children in your classroom may range from language impairment to physical disabilities. Gather information about the way the disability manifests itself in a particular child. It is also important to know that a child may have more than one disability. A child with a physical disability may also have perceptual difficulties. Another child may have a medical diagnosis requiring treatment (e.g., diabetes) but may not be eligible for special education services. Through conversations with parents, specialists, and other professionals, accommodations and modifications can be made that will overcome barriers to learning and full inclusion.

Laws and Regulations About Inclusion

The past several decades have seen a succession of federal, state, and local laws and regulations that require that children with disabilities be included in regular education settings. The Individuals with Disabilities Education Act (IDEA), amended and reauthorized in 1997, calls for a "free, appropriate public education" in the "least restrictive environment" for children with disabilities. IDEA-97 requires states to ensure that children with disabilities are provided "full educational opportunity." Under IDEA-97, Individual Education Plans (IEPs), required for students with disabilities, must now include goals that are linked to the "general curriculum."

Another federal law, Section 504 of the Rehabilitation Act of 1973, is a civil rights law prohibiting discrimination on the basis of disability in public and private programs and activities that receive federal financial assistance. Section 504 requires that students with disabilities receive an education comparable to that provided to students without disabilities. Students are guaranteed an appropriate special education as well as access to regular education programs.

The Americans with Disabilities Act (ADA) of 1990, also a civil rights law, extends the principle of non-discrimination to a wide variety of other settings with respect to people with disabilities. In schools, as in many other community settings, the ADA requires that reasonable accommodations be provided for individuals with disabilities. These laws make it clear that it is not enough just to include children with disabilities and hope for the best. These legal provisions reflect the importance of appropriate "supplementary aids and services" (e.g., classroom aides, consultations, or resource services) to achieve the successful inclusion of children with disabilities in regular classes. The laws require state and local regulations to ensure that teachers "are provided with the technical assistance and training necessary to assist them in this effort" (Individuals with Disabilities Education Act 1991). Seek the advice of specialists when addressing needs that may be beyond your experience or expertise. Even special education teachers are not always prepared for every kind of disability or every expression of a disability.

When successfully executed, including children with disabilities in the classroom can be a very rewarding experience for everyone involved. Inclusion provides an educational environment in which all children can succeed. It helps children with disabilities to gain independence and autonomy; enables all children to develop comfortable, fair relationships with others; and teaches all children to resist stereotypes, name calling, and other barriers when they appear (Derman-Sparks 1990). Children with disabilities are children first. They thrive in an environment that accepts differences and one in which adults strive to meet each child's individual needs.

Where to Start

Planning for children with disabilities requires good information and often the assistance of specialists. The first step in meeting the child's needs is to get to know the child and the family.

We have already stated that an individual child's development may vary greatly across domains, revealing greater or lesser degrees of skill in different areas. Within every category of disability, individual children will develop differently and the span of development will be even wider than in children who are not disabled. A nine-year-old child with Down's Syndrome may be very verbal, social, and able to read on a first grade level, or the child may be rarely verbal, or social, and unable to match picture cards.

It is very important to know the child's learning styles, likes, and dislikes, and how the specific disability may or may not affect the child's learning and activities. The following steps will help you to formulate the best plans for a child with a diagnosed disability.

- *Consult with the child.* Find out whether the child would rather talk with you alone, or with a family member present. Ask what has helped in the past and how you can best support the child now.

- *Consult with the family.* While this is important for all children, families of children with special needs may have extra information to communicate as well as specific suggestions to share.

- *Consult with a specialist.* Although the strategies for working with different disabilities may overlap, it is essential for teachers to have specific guidance on each type of disability. Advice should be sought from specialists (including the school nurse, school psychologist, or other resource personnel) to learn the most up-to-date instructional approaches.

- *Gather resources.* Resources might include a special education assistant or articles about special strategies to support the child's learning. Attending a workshop or asking your principal to provide an inservice event might help you to acquire new skills to meet a child's special needs. You are not expected to address every child's needs without support and resources.

The strategies presented in Part One of *Building the Primary Classroom* work to the advantage of all children, including those with special needs. Knowing the child means working with the family and specialists to gain a full understanding of the disability as one aspect of a child's identity. The classroom community creates a sense of belonging through which a child with special needs may contribute and flourish. A clear structure in the classroom helps a child with disabilities to feel safe and to focus. When teachers guide learning through investigations and representation experiences, individual needs can be accommodated. Assessment that is ongoing in the context of classroom learning informs teachers about a child's strengths by showing what a child with special needs can do.

Understanding the Influence of Culture

Ward Goodenough defines culture as "the set of standards or rules for perceiving, believing, acting, and evaluating others" (1971, 62). A person's culture is the product of many elements that have to be viewed and understood collectively. Too often, we give people cultural labels that only serve to perpetuate stereotypes. It is a misconception to think that all people from a particular group think or act in the same way. For example, a Latino child living in rural Mexico has a different cultural context from a Latino child living in inner city Los Angeles. Each of us is the product of many cultural influences. Race, ethnicity, social class, region, gender, religion, physical abilities, and sexual orientation are some of the dimensions of the human experience that define each person's culture.

Why is it essential to consider the culture of the child? Culture affects how we communicate and interact with others and the kinds of expectations we have. We are all influenced by the various cultures to which we belong. The greater the cultural differences between a teacher and the children, the more effort the teacher must make to get to know children to support their learning most effectively. A deeper understanding of children in the context of culture can have a significant impact on whether or not they succeed in school.

Each of us has a set of beliefs about ourselves as well as attitudes, assumptions, and expectations about people and events around us. These grow out of the culture in which we have been raised. An essential part of building relationships with children is being aware of and open to the beliefs, attitudes, assumptions, and expectations that children may have that are different from our own. Teachers cannot possibly learn about all of the cultural factors influencing the children they teach. But they can be open to the many ways in which children are influenced by culture.

Culture and Communication

Culture gives us our "communication framework"—our words, actions, postures, gestures, tones of voice, facial expressions, the way we handle time, space, and materials, and the way we work and play (Hall 1976, 42). Each culture has norms and rules for communicating and interacting with others. The meaning of each of these behaviors and actions may be different from one culture to another. What does silence mean? How are questions asked? What does it mean to interrupt? All children learn to understand these actions and behaviors from the beginning of their lives. By the time children enter school, they have achieved what researchers commonly term "communicative competence" within their own culture. However, every culture has its own definition of communicative competence.

Each of us interprets what we see and experience through our own cultural lens. In other words, we interpret what we see or hear from the perspective of our own beliefs, values, and experiences. Therefore, it is always possible to misunderstand or misinterpret the communication style of someone from a different culture.

I. K. Blake (1994), for example, noticed that "middle-class Anglo mothers" did a lot of naming of objects with their infants and toddlers ("Look at that red truck!"), whereas African-American mothers, who did the same amount of talking with their children, tended to talk about how objects made their children feel ("Isn't that a pretty toy? Doesn't it make you feel happy?").

Consider how this may affect life in the classroom. If children come from a culture different from that of the teacher, the teacher may have difficulty interpreting the children's ways of communicating. The reverse is also likely; some children may not understand the teacher's ways of communicating and interacting. When we fail to take into account the culture of each child we teach, we are in danger of reaching only those children who share our own ways of communicating and interacting. When communication between teachers and children fails, learning also fails.

It is easy to misinterpret the actions and behaviors of others. Was I being interrupted? Whose turn is it to speak now? Is my authority being challenged? What is happening now—aggression or enthusiasm? As educators, it is our responsibility to look for ways to understand the child's actions and perceptions of situations or tasks. The following examples illustrate how culture can influence children's responses to questions, their participation in group experiences, and their participation in sharing times.

Responses to Questions

Shirley Brice Heath (1982) examined the role of questioning in language and socialization to discover why a group of African-American children, from a working class community in a moderate-sized city in the Southeast, seemed unresponsive to questions posed by white teachers. Through her ethnographic study, Heath learned that the predominant characteristic of teacher questioning was the use of closed questions calling for a single answer. For example, (pointing to a picture of an apple) "What is this?" or "What is the name of the person who puts out fires?" In the children's community, questioning took a very different form. Here, people asked questions about whole events or about objects and their uses, causes, and effects. Examples of such questions might be: "What did you see at the firehouse?" or "What was happening at the firehouse while you were there?" or "What did you like about the trip?" Community members accepted many answers and ways of answering and their answers almost always involved telling a story, describing a situation, or making comparisons between the event or object described and another known to the audience.

Children were unfamiliar with the kinds of questions teachers asked. They perceived such questions as silly because the teachers already knew the answer, and therefore they did not respond. Because the children didn't respond, the teachers thought that they did not know the answers. Heath's five-year study documented how differently questions were used within the home and school communities, and identified additional cultural factors that influenced how children were taught to communicate, or not, with others.

Heath also described how the teachers in the study, determined to find ways of supporting children's success in school, made accommodations in their practice. First, they began using more open-ended questions such as those listed above. Second, in an effort to build children's repertoire of questioning strategies, they used tape recordings to accompany picture books of "closed questions," which children could use at a listening center.

Group Participation

Susan Philips (1972) studied ways people participate in groups, both in the classroom and in the community, on the Warm Springs Indian Reservation in central Oregon. By observing Indian children in classrooms with non-Indian teachers, she noted that the children were reluctant to talk during group lessons controlled by the teacher. However, the same children were extremely verbal when interacting with their peers.

Philips suggests that in the classrooms, a basic rule was established right from the start: the teacher controls the activity of the classroom and the student is expected to accept her authority. This includes controlling who will talk and when. However, within the community there is no context in which one person arbitrarily controls another person's actions, and certainly not his or her talk. Unfamiliar with the unspoken code of the classroom, the children withdrew. Their behavior was misinterpreted by teachers. It was assumed that they were unable to participate in the classroom activities. Misperceptions such as these lead to school failure and low self-esteem in children.

Many factors can affect group participation, including wait time and gender. *Wait time* refers to the interval between asking a question and calling on a child for an answer. Some children need more time to process information and organize their thoughts, differences that may be affected by culture. Others raise their hands to speak almost before the question is asked. By adding five to ten seconds of wait time to allow children to think to themselves, more children are likely to raise their hands.

Gender is another factor in group participation. Research shows that when hands are raised, teachers are more likely to call on boys than girls (Sadker and Sadker 1994). When teachers are made aware of this tendency to favor boys in discussion, they make a conscious effort to be more democratic in calling on children.

Participation in Group Sharing Time

Sara Michaels and Jenny Cook-Gumperz (1979) observed children's responses to sharing time in a first grade classroom where half the children were white and half African-American. A sharing time was planned by the teacher to offer practice in oral discourse, but the researchers observed significant differences in how children participated.

White children used a style termed "topic-centered" in which the stories were organized and centered on a single topic. African-American children used a "topic-chaining style," moving easily from topic to topic and focusing mainly on personal relations. It appeared to the teacher that these children were simply rambling on because she saw no clear beginning, middle, and end to their stories.

The teacher, who was white, was more familiar with a "topic-centered" style. When African-American children shared their stories, the teacher had difficulty understanding the topic and where the story line was going. Her questions often threw children off balance and stopped them in the middle of a thought. Because of the cultural mismatch between the teacher and the African-American children, white children were given more opportunities to share, got more practice, and received more positive feedback from the teacher. If the teacher had a better understanding of why children shared stories differently, she might have been more sensitive in her responses so that all the children felt comfortable sharing.

Culture and Expectations

What is acceptable behavior in certain situations? Should boys and girls engage in the same kinds of activities? What is appropriate dress for school? What kinds of activities should children be doing in school? What does it mean to work independently? Is it important to work independently? When you complete a project, how do you feel and how are these feelings expressed? Is waving a hand to get attention an indication of disruptive behavior or an expression of enthusiasm? It is natural to assume that our responses to these questions would be the same for all people. However, this is a misperception that often leads to misunderstandings.

Expectations for appropriate behavior, goals for personal achievement, and measures of success are developed within the context of culture and community. Therefore, an important aspect of knowing the children you teach is learning about what expectations the child and the child's family have. When the cultural background of the teacher, or that of the school community is not shared by the child and the child's family, it can result in misunderstandings of what is expected in terms of school behavior and success.

In a research study of classrooms of Hawaiian children, teachers were frustrated because they felt that children were not "doing their own work" (Gallimore, Boggs, and Jordan 1974). Teachers perceived children as cheating when they answered one another's questions or sought one another's assistance. In their home culture, this behavior was highly valued. Children were accustomed to helping one another and being helped by siblings and peers more than by adults. When the teachers changed the classroom structure so that collaborative work was encouraged, the children were more successful in their school work.

The following is an example of conflicting expectations between a third grade teacher and the parents of a child in her class.

> *Naoko, a Japanese-American child, is a very competent student, especially excelling in story writing. She has friends in the class and works quietly with them during cooperative activities. During class discussions, Naoko is an active listener, but rarely, if ever, speaks up. In the teacher's culture, verbal interactions are a dominant mode of expression. Her expectations for her students are that they, too, will use oral expression in group discussions as a means of sharing ideas and information. During the first parent conference, the teacher talks enthusiastically about Naoko's work in third grade, but notes her concern about Naoko's lack of oral participation in group discussions. The teacher explains to the parents that she hopes their daughter will become more outgoing in the classroom. The parents leave the conference very upset and meet with the principal. The principal helps the teacher understand how her personal expectations of what is appropriate and valued behavior are culturally biased. The principal suggests that in their next meeting the teacher should describe the child's classroom activities and ask the parents to talk about their expectations and goals for Naoko.*

In situations where the school culture is not shared by the child and the child's family and community, teachers have to work with the family and community to develop shared expectations and views of what it means to be successful in school.

The examples offered above are *not* intended to provide specific insights about particular cultural groups. As discussed earlier in the chapter, when we assign cultural labels to any group we risk promoting stereotypes. Rather, our purpose is to highlight how easy it is to misinterpret a situation because of one's own cultural lens. An essential first step in constructing curriculum that helps all children to succeed is to recognize that each child comes to school with a unique set of cultural and experiential influences that shape how the child learns.

Going Beyond First Impressions and Expectations

First impressions based on physical appearance and initial behavior affect how people relate to each other. Often first impressions are linked to expectations that are rooted in people's culture and experience. When we meet someone for the first time, many thoughts are likely to run through our minds as we react to physical appearance, ethnic/racial identity, or manner of dressing. Expectations and cultural biases, both positive and negative, are likely to determine whether and how we establish a relationship with that person. Of course, this applies to teaching children. First impressions can have a significant impact on how teachers get to know and develop a relationship with each child.

Teachers, however, must make a commitment to go beyond first impressions in order to help *all* children learn and to assess them fairly. Appreciating each child's individuality means recognizing differences and setting aside biases. Only when we acknowledge and accept differences and appreciate the ways they add richness to the classroom, can we develop a positive and supportive relationship with each child.

When you take the time to go beyond first impressions by learning about child development, the individual strengths of children, and the influences of culture, you have gone a long way toward getting to know the children you teach. Here are some things you might do at the beginning of the year to acquaint yourself with the children in your class.

- Begin by taking a walk in the neighborhood near your school with other teachers, and perhaps a parent or family member who lives in the area, who can point out interesting things or introduce you to people.

- Gather information by talking to family members about their children so that you will have more information about the particular children in your class.

- Talk to the teachers who had your children last year. Try to find out about the special interests of the children.

In the classroom, taking the time to observe and listen to children is both a way to get to know them better and the beginning of the assessment process. Here are some suggestions.

- Make time during the day for informal conversations with children—at arrival, at snack or lunch time, during reading or writing conferences, or at choice times.

- When you talk informally with children, ask about what they do after school; discuss the weekend; find out whom they plan to play with outside of school; find out about particular things they like to do.

- Spend time observing children at work and at play and make some notes about your observations.

- Be an active listener. Concentrate on listening and give children the time they need to construct answers.

If the content of the curriculum is culturally sensitive and diverse, children's self-image and confidence will be protected while they learn new skills and knowledge. There are also specific things you can do to help children feel comfortable no matter what their learning or interactive styles.

- If there are children who do not speak English, try to learn some phrases in the children's primary languages and use them in some classroom experiences.

- Vary the structure of classroom activities. For example, if very few children speak up during class discussions, suggest that children turn and talk with the person next to them to respond to the question. Then, after everyone has had a chance to say something, have a few children volunteer to share with the entire group.

- Vary the type of classroom activities. Some children are more comfortable working and sharing as part of a small group rather than responding to direct questions in front of the whole class. Provide different choices about ways to demonstrate what children have learned through writing, drama, art, music, or building.

Even when there is not much obvious diversity teachers can expose children to diversity by using books, posters, and videos, inviting visitors to the classroom, and discussing similarities and differences in an atmosphere that conveys acceptance and caring.

Closing Thoughts

Building the primary classroom and planning instruction is a dynamic process, ultimately shaped by the attributes and interests of the children you teach. You learn about the children by understanding child development, recognizing each child's individual characteristics, and appreciating the influence of a child's cultural background. The strategies that follow will help you to build from this base to develop a positive relationship with each of the children in your classroom and ensure their success.

References and Resources for Knowing the Children You Teach

Americans with Disabilities Act. 1990. *U.S. Code, Vol. 42*, secs. 12101–12213.

Banks, James. 1989. *Multicultural Education: Issues and Perspectives.* Boston, MA: Allyn and Bacon.

Berk, Laura E. 1996. *Infants and Children: Prenatal through Middle Childhood, Second Edition.* Needham Heights, MA: Allyn & Bacon.

Berk, Laura E., and Adam Winsler. 1995. *Scaffolding Children's Learning: Vygotsky and Early Childhood Education.* Washington, DC: NAEYC, 24.

Blake, I. K. 1994. Language Development and Socialization in Young African-American Children. In *Cross Cultural Roots of Minority Child Development.* Edited by P. M. Greenfield and R. R. Cocking. Hillsdale, NJ: Erlbaum.

Bodrova, Elena, and Deborah J. Leong. 1996. *Tools of the Mind: The Vygotskian Approach to Early Childhood Education.* Englewood Cliffs, NJ: Prentice Hall, 43.

Bowman, B., and F. Stott. 1994. Understanding Development in a Cultural Context: The Challenge for Teachers. In *Diversity and Developmentally Appropriate Practices: Challenges for Early Childhood Education.* Edited by B. Mallory and R. New. New York: Teachers College Press.

Bredekamp, Sue, and Teresa Rosegrant, eds. 1987. *Reaching Potentials: Appropriate Curriculum and Assessment for Young Children.* Vol. 1. Washington, DC: NAEYC.

Checkley, Kathy. 1997. The First Seven. . . and the Eighth, A Conversation with Howard Gardner. *Educational Leadership* 55 (1): 9–12.

Cohen, Dorothy. 1972. *The Learning Child: Guidelines for Parents and Teachers.* New York: Pantheon Press.

Cohen, Dorothy, Virginia Stern, and Nancy Balaban. 1996. *Observing and Recording the Behavior of Young Children.* New York: Teachers College Press.

Curry, Nancy, and Carl Johnson. 1990. *Beyond Self-Esteem: Developing a Genuine Sense of Human Value.* Washington, DC: NAEYC.

Derman-Sparks, Louise, and the ABC Task Force. 1989. *Anti-Bias Curriculum: Tools for Empowering Young Children.* Washington, DC: NAEYC.

Elias, Maurice J., et al. 1997. *Promoting Social and Emotional Learning.* Alexandria, VA: ASCD.

Erikson, Erik. 1994. *Identity and the Life Cycle.* New York: W.W. Norton & Co.

Frieman, Barry B. September 1993. Separation and Divorce—Children Want Their Teachers to Know: Meeting the Emotional Needs of Preschool and Primary School Children. *Young Children,* 59.

Gallimore, Ronald, Joan Whitehorn Boggs, and Cathie Jordan. 1974. *Culture, Behavior and Education: A Study of Hawaiian-Americans.* Vol. 11. Sage Library of Social Research. Beverly Hills, CA: SAGE Publications, Inc.

Gardner, Howard. 1999. Are There Additional Intelligences? The Case for Naturalist, Spiritual, and Existential Intelligences. In *Education, Information, and Transformation.* Jeffrey Kane. Upper Saddle River, NJ: Prentice-Hall, Inc.

Gardner, Howard. 1993. *Multiple Intelligences: The Theory in Practice.* New York: Basic Books.

Goleman, Daniel. 1995. *Emotional Intelligence.* New York: Bantam Books,

Goodenough, Ward. 1981. *Culture, Language, and Society.* Menlo Park, CA: Benjamin Cummings Publishing.

Greenspan, Stanley I. 1993. *Playground Politics: Understanding the Emotional Life of Your School-Age Child.* New York: Addison-Wesley Publishing Co.

Hall, Edward. 1976. *Beyond Culture.* New York: Doubleday.

Hannaford, Carla. 1995. *Smart Moves: Why Learning Is Not All in Your Head.* Arlington, VA: Great Ocean Publishers.

Heath, Shirley Brice. 1982. Questioning at Home and at School: A Comparative Study, Doing the Ethnography of Schooling. In *Educational Anthropology in Action.* Edited by George Spindler. New York: Holt, Rinehart, Winston.

Individuals with Disabilities Education Act. 1991. *U.S. Code, Vol. 20,* secs. 1412 (1), 1412 (5) (B), as amended 1997. Public Law 105–17.

Lee, Catherine. 1990. *The Growth and Development of Children.* 4th ed. New York: Longman Press.

McCracken, Janet Brown. 1993. *Valuing Diversity: The Primary Years.* Washington, DC: NAEYC.

Michaels, Sara, and Jenny Cook-Gumperz. 1979. A Study of Sharing Times with First-Grade Students: Discourse Narratives in the Classroom. Paper presented at the Education Research Forum at the University of Pennsylvania.

Northeast Foundation for Children. 1991. *A Notebook for Teachers: Making Changes in the Elementary Curriculum, Revised Edition.* Greenfield, MA: Northeast Foundation for Children.

Philips, Susan. 1972. Participant Structures and Communicative Competence: Warm Springs Children in Community and Classroom. In *Functions of Language in the Classroom.* Edited by Courtney Cazden et al. New York: Teachers College Press.

Piaget, J., and Bärbel Inhelder (Helen Weaver, translator; Jerome Kagan, introduction). 2000. *The Psychology of the Child.* New York: Basic Books.

Sadker, Myra, and David Sadker. 1994. *Failing at Fairness: How Our Schools Cheat Girls.* New York: Touchstone.

Schniedewind, Nancy, and Ellen Davidson. 1983. *Open Minds to Equality: A Sourcebook of Learning Activities to Promote Race, Sex, Class, and Age Equity.* Englewood Cliffs, NJ: Prentice Hall.

Shore, Rima. 1997. *Rethinking the Brain: New Insights into Early Development.* New York: Families and Work Institute.

Vygotsky, L.S., and Rieber, R.F. (ed.), Hall, M.J., (translator). 1999. *The Collected Works of L.S. Vygotsky: Scientific Legacy (Cognition and Language, 6).* Kluwer Academic Publications.

Vygotsky, L. 1962. *Thought and Language.* New York: John Wiley.

Wolin, Steven, and Sybil Wolin. 1993. *The Resilient Self: How Survivors of Troubled Families Rise Above Adversity.* New York: Villiard Books.

Wolin, Steven, and Sybil Wolin. 1995. Resilience Among Youth Growing Up in Substance-Abusing Families. *The Pediatric Clinics of North America, Substance Abuse* 42 (2): 415–430.

Wood, Chip. 1994. *Yardsticks: Children in the Classroom Ages 4–12.* Greenfield, MA: Northeast Foundation for Children.

BUILDING A CLASSROOM COMMUNITY

**E**very classroom, like every community, has its own distinct culture, values, and rules. Children belong to many different communities. By building a community in the classroom, teachers create a common and predictable cultural experience that helps children feel connected to others.

A community is a place where individuals share common values, goals, and activities. It is a place where each member takes on roles to provide sufficient services so that the community's goals are reached. In communities, everyone does not do the same thing at the same time, but groups work together to achieve common goals. A community is a place where social bonds are established and individuals can flourish (Bredekamp and Rosegrant 1992, 81).

Because a community is built around the shared interests, values, and goals of its members, the culture of your classroom community changes each year as children change and as you change. One year, you have a group that loves singing, and you make singing an important part of classroom life. Another year, the children become concerned about the welfare of a homeless person who has set up a tent on the street near the school, and the issue of homelessness becomes the focus of a long-term study. You can't tell from one year to the next what dominant interests or events will emerge and how they will define your classroom community and the content for studies.

Creating a classroom community is the second strategy for building the primary classroom. This chapter explains how creating a sense of community in the classroom enables teachers to address children's social, emotional, and cognitive development. It describes how teachers build community by making meetings a central part of classroom life, helping children relate positively to others, and teaching children to solve social problems peacefully.

The Value of a Classroom Community

Many of us grew up during a time when neighborhoods were communities that nurtured children and families. Families knew their neighbors and shared a common sense of responsibility for everyone who lived in the neighborhood. When children played outdoors, they were under the watchful eye of an adult who would not hesitate to keep them in line if their parents were not present. These caring communities helped children feel safe and gave them a sense of belonging.

Today, families from all socio-economic backgrounds are under varying degrees of stress. Children are the largest percentage of the poor in the United States today. An increasing number of children live in single-parent households, or in families in which both parents work. Many parents juggle hectic schedules that allow them little time or energy to be with their children. Television has become a babysitter for many children who come home to empty houses. Parents do not feel it is safe to let their children play outdoors. As a result, many children grow up lacking the social experiences that would help them develop the skills needed for cooperative living.

The opportunity to participate as a contributing member of a community is essential for children's well-being and academic success. A classroom community enables teachers to address children's basic needs, promote their resilience to hardship conditions, teach the values of respect and responsibility, and foster their social, emotional, and academic competence.

Addressing Children's Basic Needs

For children to participate in a classroom community—to relate positively to others and become successful learners—their basic needs for sustenance, safety, and belonging must be met. Abraham Maslow's "Hierarchy of Needs" (1987) illustrates that having one's basic needs met is the foundation for building "higher levels" of knowing and understanding. Only after basic needs are met can human beings crave more.

Physiological needs are the most basic needs of all living creatures. Children who are hungry think about their bellies instead of learning. Efforts to teach a hungry child are destined to fail. This is why many schools provide breakfast, snacks, and lunch for children who otherwise might not receive a balanced meal, or any meal, before coming to school.

Safety is the feeling of security, comfort, and being out of danger. For many children today, danger has replaced the sense of safety they need in order to thrive. These children may live in communities where violent acts happen every day, and they have had experiences that threaten their feelings of safety. Children need to feel that they will be safe in school and that no harm will come to them. When teachers create a safe classroom community, children are able to relate positively to others, explore their environment, and engage in learning.

Belongingness—feeling accepted and loved—is the third level of need. Children who do not experience a sense of belonging deem themselves unworthy of being loved or accepted. In an effort to seek acceptance and love from adults, these children often exhibit behavior that tests acceptance—acting out and attacking others because they are angry or hurt. They expect to be rejected and therefore behave in ways that prove to everyone around them that they are worthy of rejection. These children need adults who can create a classroom environment where everyone feels accepted and valued.

Self-esteem—a sense of one's own worth—is the fourth basic need. Children acquire self-esteem when they do things every day that make them feel competent. If the important adults in their lives regularly shame and belittle them in an effort to make them conform and behave, children hear the following messages.

> "You are a failure."
> "You can't do it right."
> "You will never be able to do it."

Young children are especially vulnerable to the messages they receive from others. Empty praise—such as "nice job" or "good work"—is not as powerful as messages that are specific—"You've really learned how to use quotation marks"—or ones that ask children for their opinions—"Tell me what you like best." It takes many positive experiences to build a child's self-esteem, but very few to undermine a child's confidence. Children who feel competent as learners are more open to new experiences, better able to empathize with others, and more willing to persevere in learning tasks than are children who consistently feel inadequate.

Maslow's Hierarchy of Needs

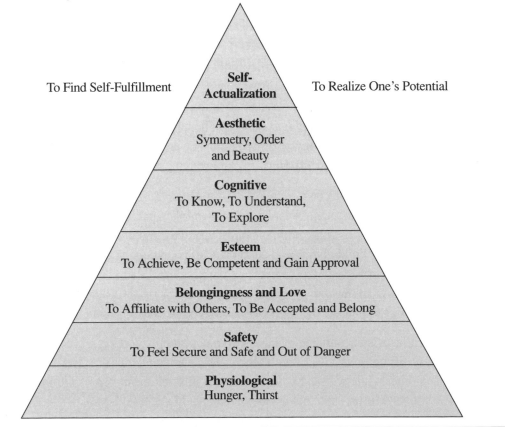

To Find Self-Fulfillment   **Self-Actualization**   To Realize One's Potential

Aesthetic
Symmetry, Order
and Beauty

Cognitive
To Know, To Understand,
To Explore

Esteem
To Achieve, Be Competent and Gain Approval

Belongingness and Love
To Affiliate with Others, To Be Accepted and Belong

Safety
To Feel Secure and Safe and Out of Danger

Physiological
Hunger, Thirst

Applying Maslow's Theory to the Classroom

When basic needs have not been met, children may have great difficulty learning and relating positively to others. Creating a caring community in the classroom is one of the most effective strategies for addressing children's basic needs for physical and emotional comfort so that they can be open to learning, feel hopeful about the future, and reach their full potential for knowledge and understanding, order and beauty.

Promoting Resiliency

You may have children in your classroom whose sense of security and safety is threatened. These children may live in chaotic and disruptive circumstances that jeopardize their emotional well-being. Some have had first-hand experience with violence in their neighborhoods or in their own homes. They may be neglected or abused.

While the wounds that hardship inflict on a child will remain, a caring and effective teacher can do much to strengthen behaviors that build a child's resilience. If you take time to learn about the life circumstances and experiences of the children in your class, you can more effectively address their fears and concerns and support them in developing coping skills. By creating a safe and caring environment in the classroom, children will be able to experience a positive and productive sense of their own power, a feeling that many children do not have in other life settings.

Supporting Children's Strengths in a Classroom Community

In the previous chapter (page 30) we discussed the strengths that are commonly found in children who show resiliency in the face of difficult life circumstances. Classrooms that function as caring communities where all children participate in and take responsibility for their learning, where children hear the message, "We are all here to help each other learn," provide opportunities during daily instruction for children to develop and practice behaviors associated with resiliency. As children use these strengths, they are more likely to be successful and "bond to school" (Abbott et al. 1998). Here are some examples (Bickart and Wolin 1997).

In a community, children solve classroom problems together. Difficulties arise in every classroom over being first at something, violating another child's "space," or taking someone else's belongings. When teachers use classroom meetings to solve these problems rather than rely on their own authority, they build *initiative* in children. Calling a meeting conveys the message, "In this classroom, we don't regard problems as stumbling blocks or as evidence that something bad is happening. We have the power to solve our problems." Classroom meetings give children opportunities to practice the skills of exchanging ideas and listening to one another.

Collaborative learning is encouraged in a classroom community. Children practice making and sustaining fulfilling *relationships* with others. These relationships develop as children learn from each other while working with a partner or in small groups. As children collaborate, they learn to take turns, share, give and get help, and listen to others.

Participating in a classroom community provides children with countless opportunities to be part of a dynamic group, letting them see how the behavior of one person affects others. They feel competent when they help a peer understand a math problem and feel comfortable when they ask for help. All children benefit from the experience of working together to create a safe, comfortable environment for all.

Teaching Respect and Responsibility

Schools of the past taught values and morals as part of the curriculum. The McGuffey Readers, for example, conveyed the values that underlie a democratic society: respect, responsibility, justice, and equality. Beginning in the late 1960s, and continuing in the 1970s and '80s, there was a debate about whether it was appropriate for schools to teach values. If schools teach values, it was argued, whose values should be taught? Many educators became uneasy about teaching morals and therefore schools tried to avoid the issue entirely.

Thomas Lickona, in his book *Educating for Character*, discusses the need for schools to return to teaching morals.

> Children learn morality by living it. They need to be in a community—to interact, form relationships, work out problems, grow as a group, and learn directly, from their first-hand experience, lessons about fair play, cooperation, forgiveness, and respect for the worth and dignity of every individual (Lickona 1992, 90).

This occurs in a classroom community where children engage in an ongoing process of thinking about moral behavior. Through their participation in a classroom community they learn two very important values: *respect* for self and for others, and a sense of *responsibility* for self, the community, and the environment. They discover why these values, central to a democratic society, are important.

Character education is not taught through canned curriculum, recitations about appropriate behavior, or rewards for good citizenship. In a classroom that functions as a community, children can learn to recognize and accept differences. They have countless opportunities to hear other points of view and to express their own ideas. They experience first-hand how a diverse group of people can work and play together harmoniously. The classroom community is a place to confront bias, teach respect, and demonstrate how differences can be resolved without resorting to verbal or physical abuse. They reap the rewards of learning and living together well.

Respect is best taught in an environment where children are treated respectfully. Similarly, in order to learn responsibility, children need experience making decisions and having responsibilities (Kohn 1998). Character education should be guiding children to discover how and why to be a moral person rather than focusing on teaching the right answers. The goal is for children to be able to distinguish among choices and make moral decisions. These values should guide all interactions with children, instructional approaches, and the content teachers address in the curriculum.

Promoting Children's Social, Emotional, and Academic Competence

A central concern for children six to eight years old is their relationships with peers. Children want to know that their peers find them competent and worthy of respect. Out of peer acceptance grows self-acceptance. Therefore, the children you teach are likely to be preoccupied with answering questions like these.

- Do I fit in with the group?
- Am I accepted by others?
- Do I have friends?
- How do I measure up to others?
- Am I competent?

To achieve acceptance, children must acquire social and emotional competence—the ability to identify and regulate emotions, to relate positively to others, and to make friends. Research points to the connection between social and emotional competence and academic success (Clark 1992; Pellegrini and Glickman 1991). Children who are aware of emotions in themselves and others, who work cooperatively with their peers, use adults and classmates as resources, and who have friends are more likely to succeed academically and lead fulfilling lives (Goleman 1997).

This connection between social competence and academic success is of critical importance to teachers who are held accountable for meeting curriculum goals established by the school system, and who find that they have to teach social skills first. Social skills directly tied to academic success include the abilities to:

- express feelings;
- recognize feelings in others;
- share ideas with others;
- listen when others are speaking;
- take turns and share;
- compromise;
- accept different points of view;
- negotiate in order to build consensus;
- take appropriate risks without fear of failure; and
- respect another person's belongings and physical space.

Social competence can be taught and nurtured most effectively when children are young, before negative behavior patterns become entrenched. Children who do not develop social skills in the early years are more likely to act out in serious ways that interfere with their learning: becoming disruptive in the classroom, attacking their peers, failing to do their work, and dropping out of school.

Supporting Inclusion of All Children

Building a classroom community is one of the most effective ways to fully integrate children with disabilities in the classroom (Jorgensen 1992). Membership in a classroom community involves inclusion in all aspects of the classroom—in responsibilities, jobs, projects with partners, special events, and in the use of the same equipment and materials. The teacher can make sure that every child feels involved in the life of the classroom.

Children with disabilities may have been treated differently in other settings and may even have come to expect rejection from a group. Barriers, exclusion, and teasing have a devastating effect on the child who is left out, and also harm the children who are excluding. The teaching of respect and inclusion is a central part of the curriculum. In a classroom community where meetings take place throughout the day, children have opportunities to learn about one another, to express feelings, to talk about differences, and to ask questions in a safe environment.

It is hard work for teachers to model respectful interactions and to demonstrate through their actions and words that all members are accepted and appreciated for their contributions. First of all, this kind of modeling requires an examination of your own feelings about including a child with special needs in your classroom. It may be new to you and you may be unsure of how to deal with a child's particular disability. Often, another child in the class becomes an unexpected resource and demonstrates how to relate to and support a child with disabilities. And, the child with a disability can often suggest ways he or she wants to be supported and included.

The approaches to building a classroom community that are described in the remainder of this chapter will help you to address the social and emotional needs of all children, including those with special needs, and to promote every child's academic success. Teachers build a classroom community by:

- welcoming children to the classroom community;
- holding daily class meetings to share ideas and discuss issues of importance to group living;
- helping children relate positively to others; and
- teaching children to solve problems and resolve conflicts peacefully.

Welcoming Children to the Classroom Community

Teachers start building a classroom community before school begins. Preparing for the children's arrival can give children consistent messages about what a teacher expects and values and can prevent many problems. Many teachers lament halfway into the school year, "I wish I could start over with my group and achieve a better sense of order in my classroom." Prevention is always the best cure.

Try to put yourself in the place of the children who will be entering your classroom for the first time. What are they likely to worry about before school starts? Typically, young children want to know the basics.

- Will I have friends?
- Is the teacher going to like me?
- How will I know what to do?
- Can I do the work?
- How will I find the bathrooms?
- When is lunch?
- Will I be comfortable and safe in school?
- Is the teacher going to take care of me?
- Will I lose the things I bring to school?

Try to anticipate children's concerns from the first day. If you address their concerns successfully, children will learn that the classroom is a safe place, that they belong, and that you are a person they can trust.

Planning for the First Days

In the days and weeks before school opens, you can take steps to begin building a classroom community. Contacting children and families, arranging the classroom and displays, learning children's names, and planning initial activities will set the stage.

Contacts with Children and Families

You can begin to build a relationship with children and their families by sending a postcard or letter introducing yourself and welcoming them to your classroom. You can also call each family or arrange a home visit, as discussed in the chapter on Families. If feasible, extend an invitation to visit the classroom when you know you will be there setting up so children and family members can meet you and see the classroom.

Some teachers give children an opening week assignment that fosters community building such as bringing an object to school in a paper bag that shows a particular interest they have. During class meetings they play 20 Questions to figure out what each child has brought. This builds a sense of belonging by enabling everyone to learn something significant about each member of the class.

Classroom Displays

How you set up the room will convey powerful messages to the children. There's no need to spend a lot of money or time on lavish bulletin board displays. A sparsely decorated room with lots of empty wall space conveys the message: "This is our classroom, and we will decide together how to decorate it." You might begin the year by displaying photographs of all the children in the class. Include your own picture and those of any other significant adults who will be involved in children's lives at school.

If you are not able to obtain pictures of all the children before school, you can take pictures of children as they arrive, or have them draw self-portraits. Each child can write some "interesting information" in response to specific questions.

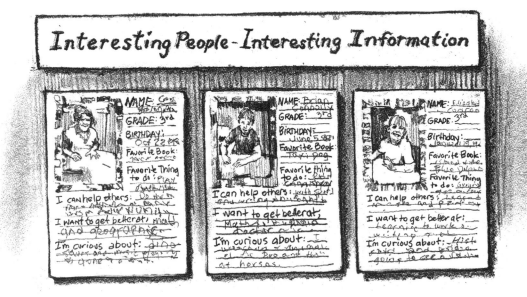

Children's Names

All of us are connected to our names; they are part of our identity and are often related to family history. Children with unusual names are often teased by their peers. They may become confused when teachers fail to pronounce their names properly. The importance of properly pronouncing children's names cannot be overstated. Before school begins, look over the class list and identify names that are unfamiliar and challenging to pronounce. The child's last teacher or school guidance counselor may be able to help you. Or, make a phone call to the child's family before school begins. Taking the time to learn the proper pronunciation of a child's name conveys to the child and family a positive message of respect.

Many teachers plan activities during the first weeks of school that help everyone learn names, such as these.

- Sing songs and play games during meetings that use children's names, such as "My Name Is" and "Cookie Jar."
- Have children create and decorate labels for their cubbies, journals, and message boxes.
- Have discussions on ways we are all the same and ways we are different. Charts generated from these discussions can be displayed in the classroom near the photographs.
- Assign each child to a partner and have them interview one another. After grouping their data, the children make graphs on topics such as favorite foods, colors, pets, TV programs. This activity encourages social interaction among classmates.
- Hang up the alphabet in the classroom and display the children's names next to the corresponding letter.

Initial Activities

It's very common for children to feel a little anxious the first few days of school. Getting them involved in non-threatening activities as soon as they arrive can help ease this anxiety. As much as possible, choose activities that the children can do independently or with one or more children, such as drawing pictures of themselves, exploring with manipulative materials, or playing a board game. This will keep children engaged so that you can take the time to respond to individuals or small groups.

Orienting Children to the Environment

To help children feel they belong, plan time to introduce children to the classroom environment, to teach them the systems for routines, and to show them around the school.

Talking About the Classroom Organization

In setting up your classroom, begin with basic materials that you know the children can handle successfully—art materials such as paper, markers, pencils, and glue, two or three kinds of manipulatives, puzzles, a few board games, and a selection of books. Children can easily become overwhelmed by a classroom that appears cluttered and offers too many choices.

At the very first meeting you might ask the children, "What do you notice about our classroom?" The question itself conveys that you care about their perceptions. To introduce the idea that the classroom organization is a shared responsibility, you might say to the children: "We can see how this arrangement works for us over the next few weeks. If you have ideas about any changes, we can discuss them and decide together." You can reinforce the principle that everything has a place by asking questions such as the following.

"Suppose I wanted to read a book. Where would I find one? Where could I go to read it?"

"What if I wanted to write a story or draw a picture? Who can show us where to find the materials I would need?"

Do not assume that children know how to use basic materials. Everything in the classroom should, therefore, be introduced to the children. In the beginning, this may be done during class meetings and involve the whole group. Take children's previous experiences with materials into account by asking what they already know about using a particular object. Teach the children how to store materials properly and how to care for them. Later on, you can introduce a new game or set of materials to a small group of children and ask them to teach the others. (Room arrangement and introducing materials to children are explained in detail in the next chapter on Establishing a Structure for the Classroom.)

Systems for Using the Bathroom

The location of the bathrooms and procedure for using them is likely to be a concern of the children. Like adults, children don't all have to go to the bathroom at the same time and they prefer to have privacy. If the bathrooms are not connected to your room, set up a procedure to keep track of who is out of the room and when.

One system for using the bathroom might be to have children go with a buddy and place their name tags in an envelope by the door indicating that they are out of the room using the bathroom. Teachers of older children find it's best to allow one child at a time to use the bathroom; otherwise there is a tendency for two friends to stay out together for long periods. Another idea is to hang two signs on the door—one for boys and one for girls. One side of each sign says STOP (to indicate the bathroom is occupied) and the other says GO. Children will feel secure if they know that they can comfortably use the bathroom when necessary.

Learning About the School

Children who are new to the school will have to learn where important places such as the cafeteria, the library, the gym, and the main office are located. You can pair these children with classmates who are familiar with the school until the newcomers learn their way around.

Introducing children to the classroom and school environment is an ongoing task. If you

try to accomplish too much in the first few days, children can become overwhelmed. Even after several weeks, expect children to still say, "Can I go to the bathroom?" or, "Where should I use this game?" or, "I forget how to find the library." A friendly reminder will be reassuring.

Teaching the Signal for Quiet

For many reasons including safety, you want to have a way of getting children's immediate attention and achieving order in the classroom. When the noise level becomes disruptive or you have a direction or reminder to give the class, you need some way to achieve quiet. Whatever signal you adopt—raising your hand, clapping a rhythm, ringing a triangle, turning off lights—take time to introduce it to the children on the first day.

Plan to spend time letting children practice responding to the signal. After introducing the signal and explaining its importance, you might say, "Now that you know the signal for quiet, we're going to see how it works. Whenever you see (or hear) the signal, stop what you are doing, look, and listen."

Positive reinforcement will go a long way, even if you don't achieve an immediate response in the beginning. Each time you use the signal, say something such as: "You remembered our signal. Let's see if next time we can stop a little more quickly." Let children know that you expect them to respond immediately and affirm them when they do. Don't hesitate to wait for every child to do what you are asking. This is particularly important in the beginning when you want to convey very clearly that this is an important rule and it must be followed by everyone.

Having welcomed children into the classroom community, you can introduce them to one of the most important components of classroom life—daily group meetings.

Using Meetings to Build a Sense of Community

The meeting area of your classroom is the center of community life. Participating in group meetings enables children to learn what it means to be part of a community where all members exchange ideas and listen to one another. The ability to speak and listen effectively, to make choices, and to settle differences when they arise, are critically important to the functioning of any community. There will always be issues that need to be addressed; people have different points of view and will sometimes disagree. By addressing differences in a group meeting, rather than imposing solutions and rules on children, teachers show that every member of the community has a right to contribute ideas, and has a stake in the outcomes. In accepting each person's contributions and working toward consensus, teachers convey the messages that there are many possible solutions to problems and that the group can make decisions together.

Meetings provide a forum for children to engage in group discussions on interesting topics. They also enable teachers to model and actively teach communication skills, such as how to speak so others will understand, how to listen respectfully when others are speaking, and how to solve problems and contribute to the group. All these skills are necessary for successful classroom life, collaborative learning, and social problem solving.

Types of Meetings

Teachers have class meetings whenever they want to talk with the whole group. Some meetings, such as the first meeting of the day, become part of the daily classroom routine.

Others are called for a particular lesson or event, or to handle a problem. Each type of meeting serves a different purpose and contributes to the establishment of a shared sense of community.

Meetings to Start the Day

The purpose of the first meeting of the day is to convene as a group and help children make the transition from home or child care to school. It's a time to welcome everyone, review the schedule, and reveal specific plans for the day. During this first meeting, children may share stories from outside of school and discuss ideas related to an aspect of the curriculum.

In some classrooms, a group meeting is the first event of the day. In others, especially where children do not all arrive at the same time, teachers set out small group tasks, such as math games or puzzles, for children to do during the first ten to fifteen minutes of the morning. Other teachers have a journal writing time, or encourage children to check homework with a buddy. Group tasks such as these allow children to ease into the classroom at their own pace and work with two or three classmates before joining the whole group for a meeting.

The first meeting is a time to set the stage for the day's work. Because children this age like predictability, many teachers follow a routine that children can look forward to each morning. Welcoming routines might include:

- greeting each child in the class;
- reviewing a morning message;
- reciting a poem the group has learned or singing a song; or
- introducing the next activity with a short lesson.

As children gain experience and skills, some teachers have the children take turns leading part of the morning meeting.

The morning message has become a tradition in many primary classrooms. Teachers write a different welcoming message each day, highlighting what will happen. During the meeting, the message is read by the teacher, or by the whole group together, or a different child may read each line, depending on the reading skills of the children. This can be a *shared reading* experience that allows the teacher to demonstrate that reading is purposeful, and also models journal writing. Children often use the message chart during the day as a resource, so it is a good idea to display it in a prominent place in the classroom. (The chapter on Language and Literacy describes shared reading experiences in detail.)

How the message is written and what it says depend upon the age of the children and what a teacher might want to emphasize during the meeting. In the sample messages that follow, the teacher has repeated several phases to help beginning readers identify some commonly used words.

> Good morning.
> Today is November 7, 1998.
> Today we will read.
> Today we will go to the gym.
> Today we will work on projects.
> Today we will plan our trip.

For an older group, the message would include more complex sentences. By third grade, the message might be in cursive.

> November 7, 1998
> Hello everyone!
> Check your homework with a partner before meeting.
> Think about this: What do you think our
>   neighborhood looked like 100 years ago?
> We will discuss this at meeting this morning.
> We will have music this afternoon.

The content of the meeting and the written message depend on the teaching goals for the day. If you intend to focus on patterns in math, the message might be written in a color pattern. After asking the children if they notice anything unusual about the message, you can then introduce the pattern activities. If a trip is planned for the next day, the message can remind everyone of the trip and the meeting might focus on where the group will go and what they have to do to get ready. The morning message can also be used as a springboard for a literacy lesson. You can ask children to find all the words ending in *ing* or search for rhyming words.

The first meeting of the day is an opportunity for substantive discussion around topics the children are studying. Part Two of *Building the Primary Classroom* offers many examples of using meetings to involve children in the intellectual content of discussions.

No matter how you decide to conduct your first meeting of the day, keep in mind that the goal is to come together as a group and set a tone of togetherness and purposeful work.

Meetings at Transition Times

During any school day there are numerous transitions—returning to the classroom after gym, preparing for lunch, concluding a work time, cleaning up, preparing for a trip, or simply moving from one activity of the day to the next. For some children, these are difficult periods because they lack a clear sense of direction. Brief meetings at transitions help provide a bridge, making these times of the day run more smoothly.

Teachers sometimes begin a transitional meeting before everyone is in the room or sitting down. This keeps some children from waiting endlessly, and gives the dawdler a reason to hurry.

Transitional meetings may be used to review what the children have been doing, to share results of their work, or to assign specific tasks for cleaning up the room. They can also be a time to share news, play a group game like 20 Questions, talk about a math challenge, or read a poem.

Meetings for Discussions

When teachers want children to participate in a group discussion, they convene the children in the meeting area. It is important to conduct discussions so that children can talk to one another rather than simply to you. Introducing a lesson in the meeting area reinforces the idea that you want children to express ideas and learn from one another. Returning to the meeting area after work time allows children to talk about what they have done and reflect upon their learning.

Discussions related to a study might include generating a list of what children already know about a topic and what they want to find out. Meetings throughout the study are opportunities for teachers to assess what children are learning. Children can use meetings to share stories they have written or discoveries they have made during an investigation.

Meetings can also focus on issues related to community life. Topics might include:

- planning jobs for the classroom;
- establishing rules;
- discussing a problem or issue and coming up with a solution;
- introducing, modeling, and practicing a social skill;
- introducing a new game or set of materials; or
- planning a classroom celebration.

Involving children in generating ideas and making decisions that affect the classroom community makes children feel respected and empowered.

Emergency or Impromptu Meetings

In any classroom, situations arise that need to be addressed immediately or that offer a wonderful teachable moment that merits interrupting work time to bring the group together.

If several children are breaking one of the class rules and their behavior is making it difficult for others to work, you might convene the group to discuss the problem.

> *In Ms. Crowley's second grade, several children are hoarding gold and silver colored pencils, keeping them in their cubbies. Two other children are looking for these pencils and can't find them. They complain to the teacher. She calls a meeting to discuss the problem. Leading a discussion on why these colors are most popular, and what the children's concerns are, she reminds them that classroom materials belong to everyone. She guides them to think about how it feels when you can't find what you need. She introduces the words "hoard" and "communal."*

Impromptu meetings may be called to share something exciting and important such as an unexpected visitor who has something interesting to share with the class, or a discovery made by a child.

> *During a work time in her K-first grade classroom, Ms. Hansen calls an impromptu meeting. She explains that Marcus is having a problem with his journal writing and asks him to describe the problem. "I keep trying to write the word 'made' but it keeps coming out 'mad' and I don't know how else to write it!" Ms. Hansen writes both words on a chart and shows the children the "silent e" rule.*

Impromptu or emergency meetings are called when a teacher feels that a topic is worth the interruption. If they are called too frequently, children will experience them as a nuisance and will be less enthusiastic. When used selectively, however, they can be very effective.

Children themselves can call impromptu meetings when they want to share an important discovery or resolve a common problem. You will know that children are becoming self-directed learners when they begin to take initiative in appropriately assembling the class for meetings.

Coming Together at the End of the Day

At the end of each school day, children leave the school community and return to another community. A group meeting brings closure to the day and allows children to leave the classroom on a positive note. Teachers can use this meeting to read aloud, review the day, discuss something important that happened, and talk about plans for the following day.

End-of-the-day meetings can also be used to review how children handled interpersonal issues throughout the day. Children recall instances of prosocial behavior. If the outcomes were not positive, children can discuss why and what they might do differently next time.

Talking about what happened in the classroom during the day enhances children's learning. It also gives children something specific to talk about when they get home. Classroom discussions can be documented, thus providing a history of the classroom community.

> *Ms. Nguyen's third grade ends each day by gathering in the meeting area and recording responses to the day in a "Class Journal." After clean-up, she and the children spend three to five minutes talking about what they feel was special about the day. Ms. Nguyen asks the children to decide on four or five ideas that they want recorded in the Class Journal. The Journal has become a popular independent reading book. When family members visit the classroom, children eagerly share its contents.*

Another way to keep a record of classroom life is on a calendar. Rather than discussing the calendar at the beginning of the day, it can become the focus of an end-of-the-day meeting to

record what was significant about the day. Younger children can draw a picture of something they want to remember; older children can write down their thoughts.

The end-of-the-day meeting is also a time to evaluate what members of the classroom community liked about the day and what they might want to change. Such discussions convey a commitment to continually work to make community life more comfortable and productive for everyone. Finally, teachers can preview what children will do the next day, thus setting the stage for returning to the classroom community.

Making Class Meetings Effective

The value of class meetings can be realized when teachers take the time to teach children how to participate effectively. How children gather in the meeting area and the length of the meeting are as important as helping children develop skills in speaking and listening. Teachers must also allow for individual differences in conducting meetings; not all children participate in the same ways.

Gathering the Children in the Meeting Area

One of the first decisions you will probably make in setting up your classroom is where you will have meetings. Since meetings involve exchanging ideas, a circle or square arrangement enables children to see and listen to one another. It conveys the message that each person is a part of the group and all contributions are valued equally.

It may be necessary to teach the children how to form a circle. If meetings take place on a rug, you have a natural boundary to guide children. In some classrooms, children sit on benches arranged in a horseshoe or square.

Who is sitting next to whom is an issue that will undoubtedly arise with six to eight year olds. Some children always sit together, and others tend to feel excluded. To address this issue, consider these suggestions.

- Make name cards (or have children make their own on the first day) and place them on the floor where you want children to sit. This gives you a chance to vary who sits next to whom.

- Draw a picture of the seating arrangement showing where each child is to sit, and post the picture in the meeting area. The arrangement can be changed at regular intervals. This also teaches children mapping skills.

- Establish different rules for seating arrangements. One week, have the children sit in alphabetical order by first names. Another time children might sit by last names. Invite the children to come up with their own ideas for how they might sit in the circle; they may surprise you with their creative responses!

Some teachers vary the seating arrangement when they read picture books aloud. Arranging the children in three rows—using masking tape on the floor to indicate where to sit—ensures that everyone can see the book.

Limiting the Time

One way to kill the effectiveness of meetings is to allow them to drag on beyond the children's ability to stay involved. A short, effective meeting is preferable to one that is too long and tries to accomplish too much.

In the beginning of the year, 15 minutes may be as much time as children can successfully sustain attention in a meeting. A great deal depends on children's experience, their age, and how engaged they are in the topic or activity. Observe children carefully to determine what works best.

Teaching Children to Speak and Listen Effectively

Speaking and listening are essential life long skills. Class meetings are an ideal time to teach these skills. By having daily opportunities to talk and listen to others, children can become effective communicators.

It helps to have a few simple rules about speaking and listening and to remind the children of these rules at the beginning of each meeting. You might spend one class meeting brainstorming ideas on what it means to be a good listener and speaker. As children volunteer ideas, list them on a chart. These rules might emerge.

- Raise your hand if you want to speak.
- Look at the person talking.
- Speak to everyone, not just the teacher.

Display the rules in the meeting area and reinforce the behaviors for effective listening by explicitly pointing out what you are doing so that children understand them.

When children feel they have been listened to and when they trust that they will get a turn, they become better listeners. At first, you may have to make this explicit by saying, "Jason will go first and then it will be Shontelle's turn." This helps Shontelle listen because she knows she will get her turn. The following chart presents some specific ways that teachers can promote children's speaking and listening skills.

What You Do	What You Might Say
Model what you want children to do.	*"Notice how I look in the direction of the person who is talking so I can hear better."*
Reinforce what you are doing by calling attention to it.	*"I'm using my loud voice so everyone can hear."* *"When I talk, I look at everyone."*
Remind children about using good listening skills.	*"It's now Nisha's turn. If you look in Nisha's direction, it will be easier to hear what she has to say."*
Give children guidance on what to do if they can't hear.	*"If you can't hear someone who is talking, raise your hand so they know to speak louder."*
When necessary, restate what a child has said to clarify.	*"Lonnie, Susan says she also thinks the Little Red Hen should share her bread. But she wants to know why you think so."*
Provide neutral responses.	*"That's one idea. Who has a different one?"*
Ask questions to encourage children to expand on what they are saying.	*"Could you say more about what you mean?"* *"Is there anything else you want to add?"*
Include everyone in the discussion.	*"Does anyone want to comment or ask a question?"*
Cue children when changing direction.	*"Here's another question…."*

Allowing for Individual Differences

Teachers must always be sensitive to individual and cultural differences that affect a child's level of participation in group meetings. Put any group of people together and some will speak up right away, dominating the discussion. The quiet people may be full of good ideas that rarely get shared. One of the responsibilities of teachers is to ensure that all children feel comfortable in a group meeting.

Cultural groups have various styles of communicating. Some families expect and encourage children to participate fully in discussions. Others expect children to listen and respond only when requested to speak. In some cultures, it is appropriate to talk about your personal characteristics (e.g., "I'm good at ____."); in others this is seen as bragging. Different cultures also have different modes of questioning and responding. (See the discussion on cultural differences in the previous chapter.)

Teachers must be knowledgeable about and respectful of many different styles of participation in order to nurture appropriate speaking skills in children and to communicate effectively with parents. Classroom goals may differ from home practices and these goals will have to be discussed with parents. Children who are reluctant to talk in a group may benefit from opportunities to practice one-on-one with their teacher or in a small group before they are encouraged to talk to the whole class.

Helping Children Relate Positively to Others

The ability to relate positively to others and to make friends is essential in a classroom community. A central approach to instruction is collaborative learning, and its success depends on the ability of children to work with their peers in ways that promote learning and self-confidence. Children whose lives are programmed with a regular series of activities, or who spend much of their time alone watching television, may have limited experience playing with peers and few opportunities to develop important social skills. Teachers can help children learn to relate positively to others by:

- modeling respectful interactions;
- promoting children's sense of competence;
- helping children make friends; and
- teaching children how to work collaboratively.

Modeling Respectful Interactions

Children learn from what they see. Caring, empathetic teachers set a powerful example. When children are treated with respect, they are more likely to treat others the same way. If children have a positive relationship with you, they will want to imitate you.

Teachers model respectful interactions as they welcome children each morning and send them home at the end of the day. In all their interactions during the day, they treat children with the same respect they give adults.

Greetings and Goodbyes

Your first and last contacts with children each day help set a classroom tone of warmth and acceptance. These contacts also establish a transition between school and home that gives children something to talk about.

Greet children by name when they arrive, and use a warm and welcoming tone of voice to convey that you are genuinely interested in every child. Try to think of something specific and personal to say every day.

> *"Good morning, Jeremy. I didn't realize until after you left yesterday what a good job you and Tyrell did organizing our writing tools. It will be so much easier for us all to find things. Thank you. You've both made this a better place for us all to work."*

> *"Welcome back, Cody. I know you're glad to be finished with the miserable chicken pox! We all missed you. Shannon said she wants you to join their project. She'll help you catch up."*

> *"Buenos días, José. I'm looking forward to reading the story you were working on yesterday."*

Dismissal time provides another opportunity to model the behaviors that you want the children to learn. Some teachers like to establish certain routines in their classroom, such as shaking hands with each child when saying goodbye. This ensures that they connect with everyone. Use children's names when you address them and try to mention something that you noticed, heard, or appreciated about each child.

> *"Tyrell, you really helped your reading buddy today. You have become a very good reader this year and now you're good at helping others."*
>
> *"Damen, I hope your Mom is feeling better. Let me know how she likes the card you made her today."*

When you say something encouraging and personally meaningful to every child at dismissal time, you send the child off with a positive message and a good feeling about life at school. Even if the day didn't go well for some children, you can offer a message of hope for the next day.

> *"Sonia, I know you were upset because you couldn't finish your project. Some things take longer than we expect. Tomorrow during choice time you can work on it."*
>
> *"Today was a hard day, wasn't it Crystal? We'll work together to make tomorrow better."*

If you don't have time to give every child a personal farewell you can praise the whole class for something they did well.

> *"I noticed the way you carefully listened to each other during our meeting today. I know our visitor tomorrow will appreciate your good listening skills."*

When children leave school every day feeling that they have accomplished something important, they feel competent. If they feel accepted and respected by their peers and teachers, children will look forward to coming back each day.

Treating Children with Respect

The way we treat other adults, especially our friends, is a good guide for our interactions with children. Sometimes adults treat children in less than respectful ways by using baby talk, ignoring their ideas, or saying things like the following.

> *"How many times have I told you ____?"*
>
> *"Can't you see I'm busy now?"*
>
> *"EXCUSE ME. I was talking and you rudely interrupted me."*
>
> *"I don't have time for this nonsense. Go finish your work."*

If we want children to use words such as "please" and "thank you" and "I'm sorry for interrupting," then we must remember to use these terms regularly in the classroom.

When you are talking to a child or a small group and another child interrupts, you might not be able to respond immediately. Instead, you could put your hand on the child's shoulder to indicate that you are aware of the child's presence and continue with your conversation. When you are finished, turn to the child and say, "Now I can help you." If the child has trouble waiting and interrupts again, you could say, "Excuse me Sara, I'm in the middle of giving this group directions. I'll be with you in a minute. What can you do while you are waiting?" Of course there are times when an interruption is necessary and appropriate. You can teach children how to do this politely by coaching them to say: "I'm sorry to interrupt but. . . . "

When another adult comes into the classroom and interrupts a teacher working with a child or a group of children, often the teacher immediately stops to respond. This conveys to the child that the adult's need comes first. If you feel the visitor can wait, you can say to the adult, "I'll be with you in a moment. I'm almost finished giving Allie my comments on her story." This response gives the message that your work with the child is important to you and also that you are polite to others.

Sometimes a visitor cannot wait. In this case, you can still model respectful interactions by saying something like the following: "Allie, would you hold our spot while I talk to Ms. Thompson for a minute? She doesn't have much time and I want to spend a bit longer with you." This lets the child know you believe her work matters a great deal and notifies the visiting adult that you can't take very much time.

Teaching Children What to Say and Do

Social skills are best taught formally because the emotions present in real situations often interfere with the learning process. Later, these skills can be reinforced informally. For example, students can learn specific social skills, such as how to interrupt politely, take turns, and enter social situations, in a brief lesson. Teachers can model the behaviors and then provide a time for students to practice them in pairs and receive feedback on their performance.

Sometimes modeling and practice are not sufficient; teachers need to be active in reinforcing the skills as well. You might take the role of a coach, pointing out why a particular interaction may have failed and giving an alternative suggestion on the spot.

> *Ms. Richardson knew that Carly was getting frustrated when she overheard her say to Michelle and Latitia, "You've had that game too long, I want it," and she was ignored. She took Carly aside and said quietly, "Go try that again. This time, instead of demanding a turn, try saying, 'I'd like to watch you play the game. When you're finished, I want to play.' See what happens."*

Direct teaching of respectful interactions helps children develop social skills. Teachers can also send positive messages through group experiences.

- They can read books to generate discussions on the topic of being respectful.
- Children can do role plays or puppet shows to illustrate disrespectful ways to talk to others or handle a conflict and respectful alternatives.
- Teachers can encourage respectful behavior when the group eats together by acknowledging the server, and making sure everyone is served.

Teaching children what to say and do can be very effective, but only when combined with modeling. Teaching children to interact in respectful ways is not a one-week course; all of these approaches continue throughout the year.

Promoting Children's Sense of Competence

Experiencing success in school work can help children acquire the self-confidence they need to relate positively to others. Children who are given tasks they don't understand may feel stupid and lose confidence in themselves. In a classroom where the curriculum and instruction are developmentally and individually appropriate, children are likely to experience success.

Treating Mistakes as Part of the Learning Process

Few of us are willing to take risks if we know we will be criticized or shamed for making a mistake. When teachers view mistakes as part of the learning process and a way to understand more about a child's thinking, children learn that the classroom is a safe place to take risks. In this environment, children are not afraid to volunteer their ideas, even when they are unsure of the answer.

There are many ways to handle a wrong answer in a positive manner. For example, suppose a teacher asks Sally how many tens are in 54, and she replies "Four." The teacher can respond in a variety of supportive ways.

> *"Did you mean there are four tens or four left over? Take another look."*
>
> *"That's part of the answer. Show me how you decided on four."*
>
> *"You're on your way to the answer. Would you like to try again on your own or have someone work with you?"*

These responses show that the teacher respects the child's thinking and is willing to offer a way for the child to continue working on the problem. When children engage in social problem solving and the solution they agreed to try doesn't work, help them to view it as a learning experience. Some solutions work well in one situation and not in another. Ask, "What can you do now?" or "What else could you do?" The ability to switch to an alternative solution builds perseverance and is one of the characteristics of a socially adept child.

Conveying High Expectations

Research studies and experience confirm that when teachers convey high expectations, children are more likely to be successful. This applies to promoting children's social skills as well as their academic success.

Teachers have countless opportunities to make comments or ask questions that help children see themselves as competent learners. A child who may have had a particularly frustrating time during one part of the day can be given a chance to succeed at something else later. For example, the child who was frustrated by an art project in the morning might be invited to share his story with the class during writing time in the afternoon. Children will begin to see that their teacher seeks to find and celebrate the strengths in everyone.

Teachers who convey to children that they fully expect them to be cooperative and caring with one another make their values and expectations clear. This message can be reinforced in the following ways.

- Acknowledge what children do: "Thank you for helping Sloan clean out the guinea pig cage. After the long weekend, it was too big a job for one person."
- State rules positively to give a clear message of what behavior is expected: "Be a friend" rather than "No fighting."
- Validate children's best intentions so they view themselves as people who have positive social skills: "You're the kind of person who likes to help others," or "It's just like you to be generous."

These kinds of statements will help make children feel competent and have positive interactions in the classroom.

Promoting Friendships

Peer relationships are a central social issue for children six to eight years old. Having friends can make the difference between a happy child and one who is lonely and ill at ease around others. Yet, despite the importance of friendships, many primary grade children are not skilled in making and keeping a friend.

Teachers know which children in their class make friends easily and which ones have difficulty establishing friendships. One way to objectively analyze friendships is through the use of a sociogram. Draw three stick figures and write a child's name on one. Interview the child and ask, "If you could only choose one friend to play with who would that be? If that friend couldn't play, who would you choose next?" Then make a chart of the children's names most frequently mentioned and also note the names that are never mentioned. This information can be used to help promote friendships in the classroom.

Children who do not have friends or who are repeatedly rejected by their peers are in a cycle of rejection that they often cannot break on their own. They may approach other children in ways that invite rejection: showing off, acting silly, playing too rough, bullying others, or being aggressive. The more they are rejected, the more they may exaggerate their negative behavior. Such children sometimes demonstrate violent behavior as they get older.

To break this cycle, children need the help of a caring adult. The younger the child, the easier it is to change the negative outcomes of being friendless. Failure to address the problem during the early years of school can lead these rejected children to engage in increasingly disruptive behavior in school and poor academic and social achievement.

Some children who are neglected by their peers tend to be quiet and unassuming. They too suffer but their plight often goes unnoticed by their teachers (Asher & Coie, 1990). These children need instruction and practice in group entry skills. Pairing them on projects with children who are friendly and outgoing can be helpful. Remember that children don't need lots of friends to feel content and secure; one quality friendship can be enough.

Children with disabilities may need extra help developing friendships if friendships do not form naturally. Like all students, children with disabilities will use friendships as the key measure to evaluate their inclusion in the community. They weigh informal time spent with children at school, after school and weekend visits, phone calls, and being chosen for teams to measure the degree of acceptance they have among their peers. Friendship-making skills will be particularly important to children with disabilities.

The skills children learn by participating in daily class meetings—talking and listening, taking turns, solving problems, respecting the ideas of others—will also help them in making friends. However, some children will need more specific guidance because they simply do not know how to approach others in ways that will gain them acceptance. It may be helpful to know the skills children need to make friends and to learn some specific techniques for promoting friendships among the children in your classroom.

Friendship-Making Skills

There are three types of skills that help children make and keep friends. They must know how to (1) establish contact with another child; (2) maintain a positive relationship with that child; and (3) negotiate when a conflict arises (Kostelnik 1990).

Establishing contact. To be accepted initially by a peer, a child learns which behaviors will be well-received. Behaviors such as smiling, asking questions, offering ideas, making positive comments, inviting someone to play, or offering to share something establishes contact.

Watch a child in your class who makes friends easily. What behaviors do you notice? Next observe a child who tends to be rejected by peers. In what ways does this child attempt to establish contact? What are the results? You will probably see substantial differences in approach. Children who are rejected at the initial stage in making friends often have not learned acceptable ways to establish contact with their peers.

Maintaining a positive relationship. To maintain a friendship, children must acquire skills in cooperating, sharing, showing empathy, expressing affection, offering ideas, helping, taking turns, and expressing enthusiasm. Children who have these skills are considered by their peers as fun to be with and reliable.

The behaviors that get children in trouble at this stage include aggression, unwillingness to cooperate, showing off, trying too hard, and acting in ways that annoy others. Notice the behaviors some children exhibit that turn other children off. Through coaching and specific teaching, you can help these children see how their behavior causes them difficulties and provide them with positive alternatives.

Negotiating a conflict. Disagreements will inevitably arise in any friendship, so children must acquire the skills to resolve differences. Children who resort to violent outbursts, physical or verbal, or who withdraw from the conflict entirely, fail to maintain and deepen their friendships.

Socially successful children express their ideas, explain how they feel, listen to another point of view, and work out solutions. The classroom community offers many opportunities to practice these negotiating skills.

Steps Teachers Can Take to Promote Friendships in the Classroom

Everything you do to build a classroom community in which children develop an appreciation for differences and experience a sense of belonging creates a social environment in which children learn friendship-making skills. Because friendships are essential to children's well-being, it may also be necessary to take specific steps to overcome the rejection some children encounter.

Establish rules for the classroom. Involve children in establishing the rules for the classroom to ensure that everyone feels safe and comfortable. (A process for rule making is explained in the chapter on Establishing a Structure for the Classroom.)

Initiate discussions about making and keeping friends. A group meeting can be a neutral time to discuss a topic related to making and keeping friends. Reading a book, such as *Tommy Goes to School* by Rosemary Wells, is a good way to introduce the subject and begin a discussion. Books such as *Leo, Zack, and Emmie* by Amy Ehrlich and *More Stories Julian Tells* by Ann Cameron can lead to interesting discussions about friends who have problems. After reading and discussing these stories, children can work in small groups to make up skits based on the plot and perform them for the class. Or children can draw a picture of one aspect of the story and write about it. Ask a librarian to recommend books on this topic that might especially appeal to the children in your class.

Model and practice friendship skills. Introduce, model, and practice specific friendship skills. Both neglected and rejected children have trouble with group entry skills. To remedy this, give children effective strategies for joining other children in play such as asking questions, making positive comments, and offering help. Other useful social skills that help build friendships include sharing, offering trades, taking turns, and making conversation. Children enjoy role playing these behaviors and trying them out in real life.

Highlight a child's strengths. Sometimes a child who has trouble making and keeping friends may have a special talent or particular knowledge about a topic or activity. By highlighting this child's strength, other children will gain respect and admiration for that child. For example, "Ted has figured out how to get the printer to work. If you are having a problem with the printer, you can ask Ted for help."

Pair children to work on a task. Partnering provides opportunities for children to work with peers they wouldn't normally choose. At the beginning of the year partner tasks should be simple and short. For example, partners can interview each other to find out something they each like to do after school. When they return to the meeting area, children introduce their partner to the group and describe what they learned. In completing these tasks, children relate to and develop a new appreciation for members of their class whom they might not befriend on their own. Additional ideas for partner activities are outlined in the following chart.

Partner Jobs	Partner Games	Partner Art	Partner Reading	Partner Math
Fixing a snack	Concentration	"Draw and guess"	Informally looking at books	"Mirroring" in which children work to manipulate, build, and match designs piece by piece
Washing tables	Puzzles	Posters for the classroom		
Straightening books	Dominoes		Paired reading in which children take turns reading to each other	
		Book responses		
Stacking chairs	Simple card games			"Checking partners" in which children check answers with each other and help each other when answers disagree
Hanging pictures	Checkers	Cooperative monsters or funny animals		

Interpret children's actions. Children sometimes do not know what they are doing to alienate their peers. By verbalizing what happens, teachers can help children become more conscious of and therefore able to change the behaviors that cause them trouble: "Jessica, I notice that you do most of the talking and directing when you work with Tiffany and Michael. If you give them more of a chance to make decisions, they'll want to work with you."

Use natural reinforcement whenever possible. Children are often praised for good behavior, but natural reinforcement can be a more powerful motivator. Natural reinforcement means you help children recognize the positive consequences of their behavior. If a child shares a possession with another child and enjoys the positive outcome of the act (the other child smiles, shows increased friendliness, shares something with them), then the behavior is naturally reinforced. You can help point out these benefits: "How do you think Rosa feels now that you've shared your markers with her?" "Do you think she might share with you in the future?" A child who recognizes these payoffs will be more likely to share in the future, not because she is seeking attention from an adult, but because the social skill worked!

Treat children's feelings with respect. Feelings invariably get hurt in the ever-changing dynamics of children's friendships. Often, in an attempt to be reassuring, adults trivialize a child's pain or upset: "Oh that's not such a big problem. He'll forget about it tomorrow." Children, just like adults, want to have their feelings acknowledged, not negated. When teachers listen to and accept children's feelings without making value judgments, they convey respect and understanding. "It's hard when your best friend is too busy to help you out. But it doesn't mean she's not your friend anymore."

In addition to these specific ideas for promoting friendships in the classroom, teaching children how to work collaboratively on their school work helps them acquire the skills for making and keeping friends and promotes their learning.

Teaching Children to Work Collaboratively

In the process of working with peers, children acquire both social and academic skills. Social skills that are strengthened through collaborative efforts include taking turns, sharing, giving help to others, and accepting help from peers. Rather than encouraging children to compete with each other for the right answers in order to "look smart," each child should have daily opportunities to contribute to the group and to learn from others. In this type of environment, children with limited social skills can still contribute their ideas to a group project and experience success. The underlying message of collaborative learning is that "in this classroom, we help one another learn."

Collaborative learning also improves academic success because children design their own questions, discuss and try out ideas, and explain their findings to others. In the process of sharing what they are learning, children clarify their own thinking and acquire a deeper understanding of the subject matter. Working together on real-life tasks improves communication among children, deepens their understanding of one another, and advances thinking.

Teachers' observations of the benefits of teaching children to work collaboratively are confirmed by research. Children's relationships with peers, especially those of different ethnic, socio-economic, and ability groups, are improved through collaborative learning (Slavin 1991). In classrooms where collaborative learning is successfully implemented, there is more prosocial behavior (Solomon et al. 1990). Teachers find they have fewer behavior problems and children are more accepting of differences.

Collaboration Fosters Learning

When instruction is teacher-directed, the teacher gives information, teaches skills, and asks questions of the whole group. Desks are traditionally lined up facing the front of the classroom so that all children can see the teacher and the chalkboard. After lessons are presented, children practice what they have been taught, working individually at their desks. Talking among children may be discouraged.

When collaboration is encouraged, children learn from one another as well as from the teacher. The teacher may introduce a task or concept to the whole group in the meeting area and help children plan their work. Children then work with a partner or small group, which allows the teacher to assess children's progress and provide guidance and support where needed. In this learning environment, classroom life is less stressful for children and teachers.

Collaborative learning takes place formally when teachers assign children to work with one or more classmates on a project or task with specific goals in mind. Informally, collaborative learning occurs throughout the day. When children working at tables turn to their peers for help or to share ideas, when they work together to solve a problem, or when several children make a discovery and want to explore it further, they engage in collaborative efforts. Building a choice time into the schedule several times a week provides many opportunities for children to work together on their own initiative.

How Teachers Facilitate Collaborative Learning

The meetings you have every day in the classroom help children acquire the skills they need to work with a partner or in small groups to accomplish a task. However, experiences in group meetings may not be sufficient to ensure the success of collaborative learning as an instructional approach. Even children who have engaged in collaborative learning before are likely to need time to refine their skills. As one teacher put it, "I have to teach sharing before I can teach mathematics."

To learn more about collaborative learning see the many excellent resources at the end of this chapter. Some specific steps teachers can take to facilitate collaborative learning are described next.

Consider your basic comfort level with collaborative learning. Who you are and how you teach will strongly influence the degree of collaboration among the children in your class. When a teacher shares the responsibility for learning with the children and is open to its many variations, the tone is set for collaborative learning to occur.

Organize the classroom for collaborative learning. The way you organize the classroom and materials can support collaboration. When children work at tables instead of individual desks, peer-conferencing becomes a natural part of classroom life and collaboration is the accepted style of learning throughout the day, not just at designated times.

Sharing materials can contribute to the feeling of community in the classroom. Supplies such as crayons, pencils, glue, scissors, and tape can be stored on shelves where children can easily find them and take them to tables. Some teachers place these materials in baskets, making sure there is a basket for every table. They find this procedure avoids the problems that can arise when a child loses a color or breaks a crayon from a personal set.

Other teachers feel that some supplies, such as crayons, lend themselves to individual ownership because children have strong preferences for maintaining these materials (e.g., some like them peeled of their wrappers and broken in half, others keep them neatly stored in their original boxes all year). These teachers encourage children to borrow and lend colors with a neighbor when needed. Other supplies in the classroom are shared.

Discuss ways to work together. Talk with the children about what it takes for people to work together successfully.

- Give everyone a turn.
- Listen when someone else is talking.
- Be responsible for your own behavior.

Some teachers find it helpful to post "respectful reminders" (Gershowitz 1999) and call attention to them before children go to work on a collaborative task. During class meetings, children can discuss what worked well and what didn't and develop new reminders as needed. (See the discussion of rules in Chapter 3, Establishing a Structure for the Classroom.)

Demonstrate collaborative skills using role plays. Use a meeting time to role play a collaborative task and illustrate the points you feel are important. For example, you could ask three children to volunteer to make a banner for the classroom. Explain that the purpose is to help us think about what it means to work together. Have a large sheet of paper in the middle of the circle and a set of markers. Ask the children to work on the banner. As they work, talk about what is happening.

> *Stefan immediately picks up the set of markers and begins to draw without consulting Meredith or Ron. The teacher says to the class, "What happened here?" One child volunteers, "Stefan just drew whatever he wanted. He didn't wait to see what the others wanted to do." The teacher then asks, "How could this have started in another way?" After discussing the need to share ideas first and then agree on what to draw, the teacher encourages the children to continue the role play. As they work out what they want to draw, share the markers, and listen to each other, the teacher invites the other children to describe what is happening.*

At the end of a role play it is important to summarize the key points about working together. List them on a chart as children volunteer their ideas. Then provide an opportunity for children to practice what they learned by working in small groups on a task.

Play collaborative games. Games reinforce a sense of community and allow children to experience the satisfaction of cooperating with others. Here are several suggestions.

- ***Musical islands.*** In this version of musical chairs, towels or rug samples are spread out on the floor as islands. When the music plays, the children can swim safely in the water. When the music stops, sharks appear and the children have to stand on one of the islands for safety. Each round, another island is removed, making the task more challenging. If a child falls off an island, the whole group is eaten by sharks, thus creating an incentive for everyone to work together to make a place for every child.

- ***Building a tower.*** In this game, each group of three or four children is given a set of blocks. The task is to see how high a tower they can make before the building falls. Children take turns placing the blocks on one at a time.

- ***Collaborative drawing in groups.*** Form teams of three or four children and give each a large sheet of paper and set of markers. Have children begin by talking about their favorite after-school activity and then agree on ways to illustrate their activities in a mural.

The resources listed at the end of the chapter provide additional suggestions of collaborative games.

Use collaborative learning for instruction. The opportunities for children to work together on academic tasks are endless. Once you begin using this form of instruction, you will find it easy to encourage throughout the day.

- During ***reading*** time, children read books together; write and illustrate a story; create a skit or puppet show about a book; critique each other's writing.

- In ***math,*** children work in pairs to collect, record, and share data with the class related to everyday life (e.g., weather, milk count, preferences for snack); estimate the number of beans in a jar and devise a way to record and report on their findings.

- In ***science,*** children study the stages of a caterpillar over several weeks, illustrating how it changes; research what they need to care for a new classroom pet; do research projects on different animals and then prepare a mural.

- In ***social studies,*** during a study of the school and its environment, groups of children make a map; create a book of information about the school that could be used to help newcomers feel at home; do research on the work of various members of the school community (e.g., the librarian, custodian, cafeteria supervisor).

A frequently expressed concern of teachers regarding collaborative learning is how to ensure that each child in the group actually learns the skills or content involved. This concern is reinforced when a highly competent or assertive child takes the lead. In responding to this concern, we refer to two important ideas.

First, learning is a cycle of four stages: awareness, exploration, inquiry, and utilization. (For further discussion of the learning cycle, see Chapter 4, Guiding Children's Learning.) In any classroom, it is rare for all children to be at the same stage in the cycle. For this reason, collaborative learning enables children at each stage to benefit from the presence and experience of others. The child at the awareness stage learns from the more experienced child. The child at inquiry or utilization consolidates learning and develops confidence by assuming the role of teacher-leader.

In Knowing the Children You Teach (Chapter 1) we discussed the concept of scaffolding. Vygotsky explained that that the less knowledgeable child benefits from working with a more expert child so long as the task is within the former's zone of proximal development. As teachers observe children working in small groups they can make decisions about which children need some separate direct instruction on a particular skill or how to help children learn to teach others appropriately. "Good helping behavior is not automatic; it needs to be defined, modeled, and practiced" (Graves 1991).

Part Two of *Building the Primary Classroom,* in which we describe each of the subject areas, includes many suggestions for using collaborative learning as an instructional approach.

Assign a role to each group member. If a few children tend to take over and assume all the roles for themselves, then assigning a role to each member ensures that responsibility is shared. This is particularly effective with older children. For example, if children are going to conduct interviews for a study, the jobs might include asking the questions, writing down the answers, and tape recording the interview. After completing the interview, group members discuss what they learned, record their findings, and present them to the rest of the class.

For true collaboration to take place, people have to feel equal in the roles they assume. This doesn't mean that the roles have to be the same. Different tasks lend themselves to different kinds of roles, so you will want to evaluate what is involved before deciding on the roles that need to be assigned. Not all jobs have to be active; you can help children see that observing and reporting is an important role.

Change group assignments regularly. Sometimes children choose a partner or form their own work groups. Because children tend to choose the same friends each time, it's wise to vary the make-up of groups on a regular basis. Children will be more apt to accept peers who are different from themselves if they have many opportunities to work together and to acquire an appreciation for each person's contribution.

Evaluate how collaborative efforts are working. Older children can evaluate for themselves how their group worked together—what went well, what problems they encountered, what they could do next time to improve their collaboration. Children can record their ideas on a sheet outlining these questions.

When the whole class periodically discusses the benefits and frustrations of a collaborative effort, it creates a greater awareness of the process itself. A general discussion might begin with the question, "What are some good things about working together?" The ideas could be listed on a chart.

A different approach would be to discuss, "What didn't you like about working together? What was frustrating?" To reinforce the positive, this discussion might also address what to do when frustrations arise. The children's ideas can be made into a chart to hang in the classroom as a reminder.

When you are in a group and you are frustrated, you can consider doing several things.

- Stop and talk about how everyone is feeling.

- Take a walk.

- Get a drink of water.

Since these discussions can raise a number of strong feelings, children may need to be reassured that working together is not always easy and that we all get frustrated sometimes. Your willingness to deal with problems and to teach children to resolve problems when they arise will help make collaborative learning successful in your classroom.

Promoting Social Problem-Solving Skills

Social problem solving is gaining increasing attention nation-wide from educators and parents. In some schools, children learn problem solving as a way of controlling their own impulses. In other schools, conflict resolution techniques are taught for resolving interpersonal problems. Both approaches can be effective, especially when the strategies are used on a school-wide basis and families are taught the approaches as well

When teachers are asked, "If you could teach only one thing, knowing that it would be learned, what would it be?" the most common responses given are: respect for others, communication skills, and the ability to solve problems non-violently. Given the importance of social competence, it is surprising how little time is allocated in the curriculum to teach children how to solve problems constructively.

"One more thing to fit into our already full day," many teachers say. The reality is that if you do not help children learn how to handle their anger without resorting to aggression, the disruptions that occur will occupy more of your energy and time than teaching children how to solve social problems in the first place.

The Value of Social Problem Solving

Helping children handle intense emotions, including anger, without resorting to aggression, and to resolve conflicts so that all those affected feel their views have been heard and agree to the solution, is a challenging task. Social problem solving is particularly appropriate in the primary grades for three reasons: it responds to important developmental issues, it is one way to reduce the increasing level of violence in today's society, and it gives children the skills to handle exclusionary behavior.

How Social Problem Solving Responds to Developmental Issues

Social problem solving addresses many important social and emotional issues of children six to eight years old. This is a particularly volatile stage of development. Children come to school with a mixture of feelings and they often react emotionally to what happens each day in the classroom and on the playground. When children's emotions are involved, they may lose whatever impulse control they have acquired and resort to striking out.

Many primary grade children are just learning to put their feelings into words—an essential skill in learning to handle conflicts. Even those who do have well-developed language skills may lose their ability to express themselves in the heat of anger or hurt feelings. While they are cognitively capable of seeing a situation from another person's point of view, this ability is often lost in the midst of a conflict.

The conflicts and developmental issues that children bring to the teacher's attention can be irritating: whose turn it is to be first in line; getting in each other's "space"; who is friends with whom; who took someone's belongings; who got something first. Such issues are important to children, and they want their teachers to stop everything and resolve the problem. It can be tempting to resolve problems for children: deciding who is right in a disagreement and dictating the solution, sending the offending child to a time-out chair, negating the seriousness of an issue or depth of a child's anger. A more enduring approach is to use problems as opportunities to help children acquire the skills to handle their conflicts independently.

A Way to Reduce the Level of Violence

We need social problem-solving skills today more than ever before. Statistics on the level of violence, the number of children involved in violent crimes, and the impact on communities and families are staggering. The United States is now the most violent country in the industrialized world, leading other nations in homicides, rapes, and assaults (Dodd 1993). Stand for Children sent out an alert stating that, "Every day more than 12 children die from gun violence" (Stand for Children 1999). An estimated 100,000 children bring guns to school every day, threatening the lives of peers, staff, and themselves.

In a national survey to determine the effects on children of violence in the media and toys, 91% of teachers who responded reported increased violence among children in their classrooms (Carlsson-Paige and Levin 1991). The message children receive every day is that violence is an acceptable response to perceived insults, conflicts, and any person who impinges on their space. By teaching children alternatives to violence, we can help reduce the level of violence in children's lives and in our country.

Addressing Exclusionary Behavior

It is not enough to simply value diversity. History has demonstrated that people's experience with diversity leads to conflict. This conflict may arise because people feel threatened by differences. For example, name-calling, overt or covert exclusionary behavior, teasing, and physical barriers may arise between disabled and non-disabled children, or among children from different ethnic or social groups.

One way to address exclusionary behavior is to confront it directly in the classroom. If, for example, a child with a disability is being teased, the teacher can intervene by supporting the child, assessing whether the child has internalized low self-esteem from current or previous conflicts, providing accurate and developmentally appropriate information about the disability to the class, having class discussions on how it feels to be excluded or teased, and clarifying or reminding children of the class rules on disagreements and respect.

It's also important to explore the ideas and feelings of the child who name-calls or excludes. While explaining how the behavior hurts the child in question, seek the underlying reasons for the behavior by asking, "Why do you think that?" or "Let's investigate that idea," "Let's ask the nurse/doctor/special educator about that," or "Let's ask Sarah's parents."

Incorporating Social Problem Solving into the Curriculum

Everything you have done to create a positive sense of community in your classroom also works toward minimizing conflicts and behavior problems. In a classroom where children experience a sense of belonging, where they know that their ideas and feelings are respected, and where collaborative learning takes place, children learn to handle disagreements before they escalate out of control. Yet even in these classrooms, conflicts will emerge and children will experience intense feelings of anger.

Social problem solving is not a quick fix; it's a process learned over time and enhanced by continual practice. Children can be helped to see that people have different opinions, that we have to listen to one another and learn to compromise, and that adults can help arbitrate when tempers flare. If teachers see problem solving as an opportunity to strengthen their classroom community, children will be more likely to approach conflicts with a healthy attitude.

Modeling How to Handle Anger

All of us feel angry at times; anger is a common human emotion. It's how we handle anger that is important. When we get angry, we have a choice to make. We can think of angry thoughts or we can think of calming thoughts. Angry thoughts tend to snowball inside us and make us lose control. By thinking calming thoughts ("I can do this. I'm not going to let Phillip get the best of me. I can help him.") we begin to gain composure and self-control. When we are in control, we have a better chance of helping children deal with anger.

Teachers can model for children ways to deal with angry feelings without resorting to aggression.

> *"I'm feeling really disappointed right now. I'm angry and I need some quiet time to collect my thoughts. Then I'd like to talk to the class about what just happened in the lunchroom."*

Occasionally even the best teachers lose their tempers in front of the children. When this occurs, it's best to acknowledge what happened and use the incident as a learning experience.

> *"I lost control when I shouted at you and I'm sorry. There was a reason I got angry, but I am sorry about how I behaved. Let's talk about what happened and why it made me so angry."*

Similarly, teachers can give children specific suggestions on what to do when they feel upset, frustrated, or hurt before these feelings turn to anger.

> *"When you feel yourself getting angry, stop and count to 10. Take 5 deep breaths. Think about what has made you upset."*

Using Class Meetings to Discuss How to Handle Conflicts

Class meetings are an excellent forum for teaching children the skills to manage conflicts. Discussions can take place when the atmosphere is calm. In the midst of a conflict, it is natural to fall back on old patterns and habits.

Role plays can be used to teach social problem-solving skills. When teachers participate, children are also willing to join in. You might take a real example of a conflict or one from a book you and the children have read together. To highlight the importance of listening to one another, you could establish the rule that each member of the role play must listen to the statement of feelings made by another member and restate it before explaining their own feelings. This can be done in a "fishbowl" with the rest of the class observing and discussing what they saw afterwards.

Puppets can also be effective for acting out a situation and generating discussion. Children's books with stories about feelings and conflict situations are excellent discussion starters. At the conclusion of a discussion, write the key points on a chart to remind everyone.

Some specific strategies and skills you can teach children in meetings to help keep conflict to a minimum are outlined below.

- Have periodic discussions about feelings, especially anger. Brainstorm a list of words that describe feelings and keep them on a chart so children can refer to them. This gives children the language to describe what they are feeling. During a writing time, you might use a mini-lesson to read a story about an emotion, and then encourage children to write their own.

- Have discussions about stereotypes, where they come from, and the impact they have.

- Teach children how to use "I statements" in describing a situation. "I feel ____when you ____ because ____." This changes the way they describe an event and helps avoid accusations and finger pointing. "I statements" can often help to defuse strong feelings.

- Introduce, model, and practice social skills that serve as solutions to conflict situations or help prevent conflicts from arising (sharing, trading, taking turns, apologizing).

- Generate, with the children, a simple set of steps they can follow when they are not happy with what someone says or does. Then when children come to you for intervention, you can refer them to these steps. Post them prominently in the room.

  If you don't like what someone does:

  1. Ask a question.
  2. Make an "I statement." (I feel____because____.)
  3. Make a reasonable request of the other person. (Will you please ____?)

You will have to discuss and practice these steps many times with the children until they begin to follow them independently.

Handling Conflicts Between Children

What children fight about tends to vary with their age (Carlsson-Paige and Levin 1992). The younger the child, the more likely the argument will be about actions or things: "He took my book," or "She pulled my hair." As children get older, their conflicts center more broadly on peer relationships: "They won't let me in the game," or "He always calls me a bad name." Few teachers have the time or patience for constantly arbitrating disputes between children.

Whenever possible, try to head off a conflict before it escalates. As soon as you hear voices rising, try to become a stabilizing force by getting close to the children involved. Ultimately, you want children to have the skills to resolve the situation on their own, but at first you will need to take an active role to help them learn the steps for conflict resolution described in the following paragraphs. By following these steps consistently, children will internalize them and apply them with increasing independence.

Help Children Calm Down

When emotions are hot, defuse the situation so children can hear one another. You might suggest a cool off time first, or describe what you think the children are feeling so that they know they have been heard and feel that their concerns are valid.

> *"I can see you're having a hard time waiting for your turn. It is hard to wait. You seem to be feeling impatient and angry."*
>
> *"This is hard for both of you. You're really upset right now."*
>
> *"Let's take a few minutes to calm down. Take a few deep breaths."*

If children are still intensely angry, it's too soon to try to identify the problem. Generally, it's not advisable to force the process before children are ready.

Several anger reduction techniques can be introduced and practiced during a class meeting. These include breathing deeply, counting backwards slowly, using positive self-talk ("Calm down. I can handle this."), and visualizing peaceful scenes. Later, when stressful situations arise, you can cue the children to use the techniques. Many people think that hitting a pillow is a good way to release anger, but it associates aggression with hitting, a bad combination.

Identify the Problem

Children will be more open to discussing solutions if they feel their views are understood. The goal of this stage is to give each child a chance to speak and be heard.

> *"We can hear better if one person talks at a time. We'll take turns. When Marcus is talking, Carrie will listen without interrupting. Then it will be Carrie's turn to talk and Marcus will listen without interrupting."*

Putting your hand on each child's shoulder or waist conveys that you will guide them and help them resolve the problem. Open-ended questions allow children to identify their view of the situation.

"What do you think happened?"

"Now tell us what you think."

"It looks like. . . Am I right?"

Children often have trouble hearing one another, or even looking at each other when they are intensely angry. The teacher's role is to help children hear each other's point of view. Many childhood conflicts arise out of confusion or misunderstandings.

"Did you hear what he said?"

"Do you need to hear it again?"

"Do you have a question to ask him?"

It's important to stay calm and neutral, even if you have strong opinions. Listen with your eyes as well as your ears and let children know that you want to hear both sides. Repeat what you hear so children know they have been heard and they have a chance to correct any misconceptions.

"So you're saying. . . ."

"And you're feeling. . . ."

"What I hear you saying is. . . ."

Have children restate what they heard. Then review each step of what happened, who did what, how each action made the other person feel, and what resulted.

Generate Solutions

If the children cannot come up with a solution, help them by asking questions.

"What can we do about this?"

"Do either of you have any ideas?"

Brainstorming is a valuable tool for problem solving. The goal is to come up with as many ideas as possible. One technique for encouraging many and varied solutions is to give neutral responses to children's suggestions, saying something like, "That's one idea. What's another?" This avoids a positive or negative judgment. Evaluation should follow brainstorming, not be part of it. Remember, it is helpful to get at least one or two inappropriate solutions so children can evaluate their effectiveness.

If the same type of conflict took place recently, or you have role played or discussed a similar situation during a class meeting, you can refer children to the solutions they generated.

> *"Remember last week when. . . ? Think about what you did then and see if that gives you an idea for solving your problem."*

If children are stuck, you might have to suggest some ideas, or ask if they would like help.

> *"What do you think would happen if. . . ?"*
>
> *"What do you think about. . . ?"*
>
> *"Do we need more information about. . . ?"*
>
> *"This is a tough problem. Would you like other class members to suggest things that have worked for them?"*

Evaluate Solutions and Choose One

During the previous phase, every idea suggested is accepted without judgment. During this phase, you encourage children to evaluate each idea and narrow down the choices to one that the children can agree has a reasonable chance of success.

> *"Would this idea be fair to everyone?"*
>
> *"Can you foresee any problems with this idea?"*
>
> *"Would another solution work better for you?"*

With younger children ask, "What might happen if you (cite a solution)?" Encourage older children to evaluate the effects of various solutions on those involved, safety issues, and workability. The goal is to arrive at a solution that everyone can live with, so all involved feel that their needs have been met.

This discussion can be time consuming, so to keep children's interest you might choose just three or four of the solutions to evaluate.

Implement and Evaluate the Results

One reason children may not act prosocially is because they don't know how to perform certain social behaviors. This can be problematic when solutions are composed of social behaviors for which they lack experience and confidence. To help children over this hurdle, discuss and practice how to enact solutions, such as apologizing, sharing, taking turns, and so on.

Once the agreed-upon solution is implemented, it's a good idea to check how it's working. If the solution isn't working well, help the children to switch to an alternative. Reassure them that they are experimenting to find the best solution—just as scientists do. If it's a particularly good example of problem solving, or you simply want to give the children recognition for their work in resolving a conflict, you might invite them to share what happened with the class at a meeting time.

Encourage Children to Resolve Problems on Their Own

As children acquire the skills to resolve problems, encourage them to work out solutions on their own. Sometimes you can't just stop what you are doing to mediate a problem between two children. You can make suggestions.

> *"I just can't help you right now. Think about it for a while and check with me in 15 minutes."*

> *"Go look at the chart about what to do when you don't like something someone does."*

> *"Remember this same problem came up last week? Try to remember what you did then. Go to the book area and talk about it. Report to me after you do."*

For older children, it often defuses the situation if they write down what happened or what they would like to have happened. Always remember to check with the children to see if they have resolved the issues. As children become increasingly able to handle conflicts on their own, the teacher's time spent resolving conflicts is minimized.

Provide a Place in the Classroom to Calm Down

Group life is demanding for adults as well as children. Everyone needs a break at times. Establishing one or two places in the classroom where children can go to cool off, relax, or take a break gives children a positive alternative to acting out or falling apart during a conflict.

A calm-down place might be the classroom library, the meeting area, a loft, or listening area. The designated area ideally will contain soft furniture: a rocking chair, bean-bag chair, rug, covered mattress, or pillows. Just flopping onto a bean bag chair, curling up with a book, staring at tropical fish, or listening to a favorite tape can be calming. Sometimes just being near a teacher is the best calming-down place.

Another idea is to set up a *peace table* in the classroom—a place children can go to work out a problem together. The steps for resolving a conflict could be posted nearby along with paper and pencils if children want to write down their ideas.

A place to calm down where children can choose to go is very different from a *time-out chair*. Children learn very little from sitting in a time-out chair and too often it is used punitively.

At first, you may have to tell children when they need to retreat and cool off. The goal is for children to recognize their own uncomfortable volatile feelings and know when they need to take a break in a quiet space. In this way, children become responsible for their own feelings and behavior.

Conflicts That Affect the Whole Class

Some issues affect the whole class and require problem solving as a group. Involving all the children in discussing the problem, generating solutions, and deciding on a plan teaches children that we are all responsible for each other and we can solve problems together. This is an important part of learning to function as members of a community.

The class meeting is an appropriate time for teachers to lead children in uncovering and resolving a problem. The following procedure, which may require several class meetings, can guide this process.

- Discuss the situation.
- Generate possible solutions.
- Evaluate solutions.
- Make a plan.
- Implement the plan.
- Assess progress.

To illustrate the steps in resolving conflicts that affect the whole group, we will use an example from a third grade classroom where recess has become unmanageable. Children fight continuously over game rules, some do not get involved in any activities, and after recess children complain and tattle endlessly. Many children have expressed the desire to stay inside during recess, rather than deal with the unpleasant atmosphere. Ms. Strickler, the teacher, decides that she will involve the children in improving the quality of the recess period.

Discuss the Situation

In the initial discussion, uncover the issues and have children describe the events leading to the problem. The tricky part of this discussion is to encourage children to describe the situation without resorting to blaming and fingerpointing.

Providing ample opportunity to discuss the situation, whatever it is, lets children know that their opinions are important. Because children at this age can be rigid about their opinions, discussions may become heated. The temptation may be to end a discussion by saying something like, "Unless you can talk calmly, the discussion will end." It's important to acknowledge the strength of children's opinions and remind them that the purpose of the discussion is to hear all points of view.

> *Ms. Strickler sets up a chart in the meeting area. On one side she writes, What's Good about Recess, and on the other she writes, What's Bad about Recess.*
>
> *"Everyone has strong opinions here and that's understandable. Let's work at taking turns talking and try very hard to listen to each other so we can see all sides of the issue."*

"Let's make a list of both the good and bad points of recess on this chart. Feel free to say whatever you wish about recess."

As the children express their opinions, she listens, modeling that this is what children should be doing as well. As each child finishes sharing, she asks, "What should I write on the chart?"

For about fifteen minutes the children brainstorm ideas; the list of bad points is getting quite long. Ms. Strickler acknowledges this, saying, "Hmm, I notice there are quite a few negatives. Does anyone have any ideas on what's good about recess?"

The process of engaging in discussion helps children both to clarify their thinking and hear the ideas of others. Sometimes it's helpful to review all the ideas so children hear them at one time.

Generate and Evaluate Possible Solutions

The next step is to brainstorm possible solutions to the problems raised. You may do this at the first meeting if interest is high and the children are still involved. Alternative approaches may also be useful.

- Categorize the problems, break into teams to address one problem, and then report back to the entire group.
- Ask children to write about possible solutions in their journals or for homework and then share ideas in a meeting the next day.

In this example, Ms. Strickler moves right into brainstorming possible solutions.

"Let's start brainstorming some solutions. I'll put up another chart. Who has ideas about what might make recess time more pleasant?"

A list of ideas is generated. Ms. Strickler decides that the children need more time for reflection and discussion before they can make a plan.

"You have done a lot of really good thinking. While you are out on the playground for recess today, think of yourself as an observer. Consider some of these ideas and whether you think they would work. See if you can come up with any others. We'll talk about this again at our meeting tomorrow."

During the second meeting on the recess issue, the children come up with a list of ideas for solutions, including having three organized games each day with a sign-up sheet for each game; playing one big organized game that the class votes on for a week; having a team of four children be recess mediators who serve in the job for two weeks; and dividing the playground into three sections for the different kinds of activities that take place, establishing a set of rules for each area.

After the list has been generated Ms. Strickler says, "This afternoon we'll break into small groups to discuss each of these ideas and begin to outline what each idea might be like if we did it. Your group can decide to evaluate all of the ideas or just pick one or two." Ms. Strickler assigns children to groups of four, tells each group to pick a recorder, and reminds them to collaborate in order to come up with the best plan. She encourages the recorder to take good notes to share in the discussion the following day.

Make a Plan

Discuss the alternatives and then either come to consensus or vote on a plan. A plan is most likely to be successful when children have a stake in making it work; ownership of the ideas leads to having a stake in the outcome.

Each of the four groups presents its ideas. There is a great deal of overlap. Ms. Strickler orchestrates the discussion to help children see how their ideas mesh.

"Let's take a minute to think about how the suggestion made by Jonah's group might work with the plan we heard from Ariana's group."

They formulate four possible plans by combining several ideas into one. Ms. Strickler suggests that they reflect on these plans for homework and decide which one they want to try. She reminds them that they can always change their plan if it doesn't work.

In anticipation of the next day's meeting, Ms. Strickler records the four options on a new chart. When the class meets again, they vote on the plans. The chosen plan is to have three organized game areas: two for big groups playing soccer and tag, and a third for kids who want to play 4 square, jump rope, or other games that involve only 3 or 4 children. Some children agree to design a sign-up sheet so that each morning before meeting children will sign up for their choice.

Implement the Plan

The next step is to allow children to try out their solutions. It can be helpful for the children to role play the plan prior to actually trying it out.

On the day the plan is to begin, Ms. Strickler hangs a chart describing the plan. She also has the sign-up sheet ready for children to use when they arrive. She reminds children of the sign-up sheet on the morning message.

"Today we will begin our new recess plan. Think about what you want to do at recess today. Talk your plan over with a friend. Once you have signed up, you have made a commitment for today. I am inspired by the new plan. You've done some excellent problem solving."

Assess Progress

Even in situations where it's obvious that the plan is working well, it's important to let children discuss how things are going at many intervals. Often when their plan doesn't work out immediately, children want to make drastic revisions or try something else. Teachers can help children modify the original idea and try it out again before abandoning a first attempt too quickly. Remind children that new ideas take time to work. Your patience helps children understand that results may not be immediately obvious.

Establishing a classroom environment where conflicts are kept to a minimum, and where children acquire the skills to solve social problems when they emerge, helps children feel that they are in control. They learn that their feelings and concerns are respected and that together, they can solve problems and make the classroom a peaceful place to work.

The School as a Community

Once you see children thriving in a caring classroom community, you may begin to look beyond the classroom to the school. It follows that classes can work together to make the school a caring community and that teachers would also benefit from belonging to a supportive, inclusive community. Ideally, the message everyone receives from the school community is, "We care about all members."

When the entire school shares the values and approaches described in this chapter, everyone benefits. The school principal or a school improvement team can promote a sense of community throughout the school. Just as the classroom teacher initiates the process of community building in the classroom, the principal can involve everyone in developing and achieving a shared vision.

Sometimes one teacher, or a small group, can begin the process of building a sense of community in the school by thinking of projects classes can do together or alone that will benefit the school as a whole. Here are some ideas.

- Plan a school beautification project and invite each class to make a plan (for example, maintaining the playground, planting flowers or bulbs, making signs, making maps for visitors, painting a number line on the floor of a hallway).

- Involve families in projects that classes do together. If there is a lunch program for seniors in your community, seniors may welcome visits from children who can share songs, poetry, or art projects.

- Set up partner classes and do special projects together. Older children can come and read to their partners, help them with projects, or go with them to the library to help with a research project. Singing is a wonderful joint activity.

- Think of a community service project such as making sandwiches once a month for an organization that feeds homeless people. Ask a local grocery store to donate the ingredients and organize a time when classes get together to make sandwiches.

Service to the community should be meaningful. When children are involved in a hands-on way in a project, they are likely to appreciate its impact.

Service learning is a way to address community needs and also meet the goals of the curriculum. For example, a first grade class might partner with a nearby senior assisted living complex and have an ongoing relationship with the residents. A project such as this is beneficial to both the children and to the residents. Here's how a teacher can link curriculum goals to service at the facility for seniors:

- **Language and Literacy:** Write letters and stories to the residents; read to the residents.

- **Mathematical Thinking:** Plan a party for the residents and determine the amount of refreshments and supplies needed, how much the party will cost; create subtraction problems by determining the age difference between the children and individual residents.

- **Scientific Thinking:** Plant a flower bed or a tree at the facility; share pets with residents.

- **Social Studies:** Encourage residents to share with children about their life in the past and the games they played as children.

- **Technology:** Write a letter or poem on the computer; look at the tools and technology that are used at the facility.

- **The Arts:** Perform a play for the residents; make painting for their rooms; have a sing-along with the residents.

Teachers also benefit from belonging to a supportive community. No matter how committed to the children a teacher might be, good teaching takes an enormous amount of energy, creativity, and knowledge. Teachers need opportunities to share their ideas, struggles, and solutions with one another.

Sometimes one teacher can begin the process of building a community of teachers. Here are some suggestions.

- Invite other grade level teachers to meet regularly to talk about curriculum issues and share ideas.

- Seek other teachers who can help you with a problem or share an approach they have implemented successfully. Ask for their help and advice. Offer to share ideas and resources with them.

- Suggest regular potluck get-togethers where staff can socialize. Take turns planning a topic for discussion.

Finally, take time for yourself. Your own professional development is as important as your health. Join professional organizations where you can meet other dedicated teachers and administrators. The conferences and resources you discover can provide a sense of renewal as you strive to implement curriculum that is meaningful for your children.

Closing Thoughts

When a classroom functions as a community, children can feel safe and accepted and make positive connections with others. The opportunity to participate as a contributing member of a community helps children to become successful learners, problem solvers, and decision makers. Teachers build a classroom community by welcoming children, using meetings to promote a sense of community, helping children to relate positively to others, and teaching them to solve social problems. In order for a community to work, a clear structure is essential.

References and Resources for Building a Classroom Community

Abbott, Robert D., Julie O'Donnell, J. David Hawkins, Karl G. Hill, Richard Kosterman, and Richard F. Catalano. October 1998. *American Journal of Orthopsychiatry*. 68 (4): 542–552.

Asher, S. R., and John D. Coie. 1990. *Peer Rejection in Childhood*. New York: Cambridge University Press.

Bickart, Toni, and Sybil Wolin. November 1997. Practicing Resilience in the Elementary Classrom. *Principal* 77 (2): 21–24.

Bredekamp, Sue, and Teresa Rosegrant, eds. 1992. *Reaching Potentials: Appropriate Curriculum and Assessment for Young Children*. Vol. 1. Washington, DC: NAEYC.

Carlsson-Paige, Nancy, and Diane E. Levin. 1998. *Before Push Comes to Shove: Building Conflict Resolution Skills with Children*. St. Paul, MN: Redleaf Press. (Goes with a children's book: *Best Day of the Week*. Nancy Carlsson-Paige. St. Paul, MN: Redleaf Press, 1998.)

_____. November 1992. Making Peace in Violent Times: A Constructivist Approach to Conflict Resolution. *Young Children* 48 (1): 7.

Carlsson-Paige, Nancy, and Diane E. Levin. 1991. The Subversion of Healthy Development and Play. *Day Care and Early Education* 19 (2): 14–20.

Charney, Ruth Sidney. 1992. *Teaching Children to Care: Management in the Responsive Classroom*. Greenfield, MA: Northeast Foundation for Children.

Child Development Project. 1998. *Ways We Want Our Class to Be: Class Meetings That Build Commitment to Kindness and Learning*. Oakland, CA: Developmental Studies Center.

Clark, Reginald. 1992. *African American Male Students in Bakersfield City Schools: An Assessment and Proposals for Action*. Claremont, CA: Reginald Clark and Associates.

Cohen, Elizabeth. 1986. *Designing Group Work Strategies for Homogeneous Classrooms*. New York: Teachers College Press.

Dodd, Senator Christopher. 1993. Testimony before the Joint Senate-House Hearing on Keeping Every Child Safe: Curbing the Epidemic of Violence, March 10, 1993.

Garbarino, James, Nancy Bubrow, Kathleen Kostelny, and Carole Pardo. 1998. *Children in Danger: Coping with the Consequences of Community Violence*. San Francisco: Jossey-Bass Publishers.

Gershowitz, Denise. 1999. Personal communication.

Goleman, Daniel. 1997. *Emotional Intelligence*. New York: Bantam Books.

Graves, Ted. April 1991. The Controversy over Group Rewards in Cooperative Classrooms. *Educational Leadership* 48:78.

Hill, Susan and Tim Hill. 1990. *Collaborative Classroom: A Guide to Co-operative Learning*. Portsmouth, NH: Heinemann.

Jorgensen, Cheryl M. 1992. Natural Supports in Inclusive Schools: Curriculum and Teaching Strategies. In *Natural Supports in Schools, at Work, and in the Community for People with Severe Disabilities.* Dover, NH: University of New Hampshire Institute on Disability.

Kohn, Alfie. 1996. *Beyond Discipline: From Compliance to Community.* Alexandria, VA: ASCD.

Kohn, Alfie. 1998. *What to Look for in a Classroom . . .and Other Essays.* San Francisco, CA: Jossey-Bass Publishers.

Kostelnik, Marjorie. 1990. Social Development: An Essential Component of Kindergarten Education. In *The Developing Kindergarten: Programs, Children, and Teachers.* Edited by Judith Spitler McKee. East Lansing, MI: Michigan Association for the Education of Young Children, 170–172.

Kriedler, William J. 1984. *Creative Conflict Resolution: More Than 200 Activities for Keeping Peace in the Classroom K–6.* Glenview, IL: Scott, Foresman and Co.

Lickona, Thomas. 1992. *Educating for Character: How Our Schools Can Teach Respect and Responsibility.* New York: Bantam Books.

Maslow, Abraham H. 1987. *Motivation and Personality.* 3rd ed. New York: Harper Row, 15–31.

McDermott, J. Cynthia, ed. 1999. *Beyond the Silence, Listening for Democracy.* Portsmouth, NH: Heinemann.

Orlick, Terry. 1978. *The Cooperative Sports and Games Book: Challenge Without Competition.* New York: Pantheon Books.

Slavin, Robert. February 1991. Synthesis of Research on Cooperative Learning. *Educational Leadership* 48 (5): 71–82.

Sobel, Jeffrey. 1984. *Everybody Wins: 393 Non-Competitive Games for Young Children.* New York: Walker & Co.

Solomon, D., M. Watson, E. Schagos, V. Battistich, and J. Solomon. 1990. Cooperative Learning as Part of Comprehensive Classroom Program Designed to Promote Practical Development. In *Current Research on Cooperative Learning.* Edited by S. Sharon. New York: Praeger.

Stand for Children. April 27, 1999. In Response to the Tragedy in Colorado. E-mail alert.

Werner, Emmy. 1990. Protective Factors and Individual Resilience. In *Handbook of Early Childhood Intervention.* Edited by Samuel Meisels and Jack Shonkoff. New York: Cambridge University.

Wolin, Steven, and Sybil Wolin. 1993. *The Resilient Self: How Survivors of Troubled Families Rise Above Adversity.* New York: Villard Books.

Wolk, Steven. 1998. *A Democratic Classroom.* Portsmouth, NH: Heinemann.

ESTABLISHING A STRUCTURE FOR THE CLASSROOM

Each community has its own structure—a set of rules, common understandings, and systems that all members agree to follow. Without a predictable structure, people often feel insecure and unsafe because they don't know what is expected or how to act appropriately. When the structure is clear, it is easier for everyone to work and to feel productive.

The kind of structure that is created in the classroom is based on your philosophy of teaching and learning. In a collaborative community where children are encouraged to become self-directed learners, all members of the community should contribute to creating the structure that governs community life. Six- to eight-year-old children, who typically need to feel autonomous and powerful, can become invested in building and maintaining the quality of community life. They can understand rules and systems when they help to create them, and they are willing to re-evaluate and change what does not work for the good of all.

Teachers create a structure in which children experience a sense of belonging and know that they are valued members of the classroom community. It is a structure in which children share responsibility for keeping the classroom neat and orderly, know how to get and use materials properly, and function with increasing levels of independence. The sense of order is not based on power, but on shared understandings. Structure comes from a well-organized classroom environment, a daily schedule and routines that are predictable, and clear expectations about behavior in the classroom. Making structure clear to the children is a critical step.

Why the Structure Has to Be Clear

The type of structure that helps children become self-directed learners may not be immediately obvious to children or to adults who visit the classroom. Therefore, teachers cannot assume that children will understand the classroom structure they have created unless they make the structure explicit to children. For example, although a well-organized classroom conveys the message that materials are valuable and everything has a place, children won't automatically use materials well and help maintain order. Teachers have to reinforce this message by systematically introducing the proper use of materials and explaining the systems for using and returning them.

In the classroom described below, the teacher has established a structure that the children understand. If you were a visitor to this classroom, here's what you might see.

> *When you enter the classroom, you hear a steady hum of activity. At first you don't see the teacher; she is sitting and talking with one of several small groups of children working on a variety of math activities at tables arranged in different areas of the room. Each group has three to four children and they seem intent on the materials they are using together. Children are talking in lively voices about what they are doing, explaining their ideas, giving directions, asking questions, challenging one another, and laughing. You sit down near one group of four children using geoboards and rubber bands. "Tell me something about what you are doing," you say. One child immediately volunteers: "We are finding out how many ways we can make different shapes. Look, we've made triangles, squares, and diamonds," he says, pointing to each one. Another child adds, "And I've made a hexagon. I know because it has six angles and six sides." You then ask, "How did you know what to do?" A third child explains, "We had a meeting and talked about different shapes we knew. Then each group got different things to use. We got the geoboards, that group got popsicle sticks, over there they have tangrams. Look around and you'll see." Just before you leave, the teacher calls the children together in the meeting area so each group can report on what they did and what they learned.*

To some, this classroom might seem noisy and lacking in structure. There's a lot of activity in all corners of the room—materials are out, and children's voices can be heard everywhere. But the noise and activity are not chaotic. Children are engaged in tasks that have meaning for them. They know what they are expected to do and are self-directed. The structure is clear; the teacher has planned it and children understand it.

The structure in this classroom has been established in three ways. First, the teacher has organized the physical environment so that children know where to find what they need and how to help maintain a sense of order. Second, the teacher follows a consistent schedule and set of routines so children know the day is predictable. They also know that they will have opportunities to make choices during the day about what they will do. And finally, there are clear expectations about behavior; the teacher has established these expectations by involving children in creating rules for the classroom, by identifying jobs for maintaining the classroom, and by introducing the proper use and care of materials.

The Physical Environment

The most obvious form of structure is the classroom itself—how you arrange the furniture, select and organize materials, and what you have on the walls. The physical environment conveys strong messages to children from the first time they enter the room. It can reassure them that their classroom is a place where they will be safe, comfortable, and where they will do interesting things.

Messages Children Receive from the Environment

A good place to start in designing your classroom is to consider what messages you want children to receive as soon as they enter the room. Think about some questions.

- How will children know that this is a place they can trust and that they will be safe here?

- How do I show children that the classroom belongs to them?

- How can I make it easier for children to work together and share materials?

The chart below offers some suggestions for communicating positive messages.

Positive Messages	How the Environment Conveys These Messages
This is a safe and comfortable place.	• Room dividers and shelves are at children's eye level; they can see everything and the teacher can see the children. • There are properly sized places to work, and rugs and comfortable furnishings for relaxing. • There is space to move around; the room is not crowded and congested. • There is a safe place for each child's personal belongings. • Children can see the teacher at all times. • The furniture is solid, clean, and well-maintained. The room has a clean, neat appearance.
I belong here and I am valued.	• Pictures and materials in the room reflect the children's families and communities. • The environment has been adapted for children with disabilities. • There is display space reserved for children's work. • Children can find their names posted in several places in the classroom.
I can make friends and share.	• Areas of the room are set up for small groups of children to work together. • There is a rug in a meeting area large enough to accommodate the whole class. • Materials are grouped for shared use (e.g., baskets of pencils, markers, and crayons for writing) and there are sufficient quantities. • There is a message board or mail boxes where children can leave messages for each other.

Think about how you react when you enter another person's home. You may make assumptions about how they live. Think also about how you have organized your own home. Each room serves a different function and is organized so that you can find what you need. Your home is a statement of who you are and what kinds of activities you enjoy. You can function efficiently and easily in your home because its organization makes sense to you. In the same way, the classroom's organization is most effective when it is well designed and makes sense to everyone.

Establishing

a Structure

for the

Classroom

Positive Messages	How the Environment Conveys These Messages
I know what I'm expected to do.	• Everything is neat and labeled so children can find things easily. • Materials are within reach. • There is a chart listing job responsibilities for the upkeep of the room. • The weekly and daily schedules are posted at children's eye level.
I can do interesting work here.	• The room and materials are organized in attractive ways. Everything looks inviting. • There are sufficient quantities of books, objects, games, and collections for children to explore and investigate—enough to go around, but not so many that it is over stimulating. • There are writing tools, blocks, art, and construction materials to encourage children to build, draw, write, and paint about what they are learning. • The displays change on a regular basis. • There are math and science tools (measuring devices, magnifying lenses, microscopes) for investigations.
I can find what I need and put things back where they belong.	• Materials are logically organized and labeled. • Games with small pieces and manipulatives are in containers so they won't get lost. • Shelves are labeled to show where materials belong.
I can make choices.	• Materials are placed on shelves where children can reach them. • There is a choice board and time in the schedule for children to choose their own activities.

Taking a Look at Your Classroom—First Steps

Begin with what you have. In your classroom you most likely have desks or tables, chairs, books, board or wall space, and different amounts of supplies. Organize what you have in ways that will make each day go smoothly. When possible, you can add materials to enhance your program.

Because the meeting area is the center of community life, it should occupy a well-defined place in the classroom. For children to work cooperatively on projects, and select and return materials, they will need tables for their work and convenient storage places throughout the classroom. Display space can serve many important purposes. And children, like all of us, want a safe place for personal belongings.

Meeting Area

The meeting area is where the class gathers to have discussions, listen to a story, learn about new materials, participate in a lesson, make a transition to a new activity, get directions, or summarize an experience. The meeting area should have a prominent place in the class-room—a place that says, "This is where we come together and do important work."

As you look around your classroom to select the best place for meetings, consider the following recommendations.

- Allow sufficient floor space in the meeting area to accommodate all the children and adults in a circle or square, on the floor, on chairs, or on benches. Using the floor means that chairs don't have to be moved every time there is a class meeting. Benches can define the area and also serve as cubbies or storage space.

- Make the space big enough so that children can wiggle without disturbing those around them.

- Define the meeting area and provide for children's comfort with a rug or sewn-together carpet squares to give every child a soft place to sit.

- Decide whether you will sit on the floor, a chair, or a bench. If you have a special chair, children can use the chair when they are conducting the meeting. Whoever reads aloud to the class can use it also.

- Include in the meeting area displays you will want to refer to, such as the daily schedule, morning message, choice board or list, job chart, and calendar.

- Locate the meeting area near a writing surface for group lessons, and have available chart paper and a sturdy stand or easel, magic markers, pocket charts to manipulate words and lines from a poem or book, and individual clip or chalk boards.

Arrangement of Furniture and Tables

In a classroom where collaborative learning is encouraged, tables that accommodate four to six children are preferable to individual desks. If you do not have tables, you can group individual desks to accommodate four to six children. Some teachers who use this approach still have assigned seats so children can store their personal supplies and books inside. If you want to be more flexible about where children work, then you can provide separate storage places for children's work and explain that all classroom materials are shared and accessible to everyone.

A few individual desks can be used as study carrels when children prefer to work alone, which is not unusual at this age. Providing other quiet places in the classroom such as bean bag chairs in the library or a loft with soft cushions also helps to address the need for privacy.

As you organize your furniture, keep these guidelines in mind.

- Separate noisier areas from quieter ones (e.g., blocks away from the library).

- Plan traffic patterns that will prevent children from interrupting one another as they move around the room, invite moderation in speed (no "runways"), and allow you to move freely between groups and individual children.

- Make sure you can see all areas without obstruction.

Organization of Supplies and Materials

In selecting supplies and materials for your classroom, a good rule to follow is "less is more." Classrooms that are cluttered with materials, walls completely covered with displays, and overflowing storage bins contribute to chaos. For some children, too much visual stimulation makes settling in extremely difficult and choosing activities and materials almost impossible. The task of cleaning up seems overwhelming when there are too many things to put away and it's not clear where everything should go.

Children are more likely to be responsible about caring for and returning materials if they understand the order you have established and if they have participated in establishing this order. When materials are arranged logically and in designated places, then children don't have to ask their teacher for everything they need. Because the organization is clear, children can take pride in helping to maintain an orderly classroom.

Consider these guidelines as you organize the materials in your classroom.

- Locate materials in logical places, as close as possible to where children will use them for their work (e.g., art materials near water, manipulative math materials near tables).

- Rotate materials periodically to attract or renew interest.

- Keep shared materials such as pencils, crayons, markers, erasers, and scissors in small baskets or plastic food containers—one for each table.

- Label all containers to indicate that there is a proper place for everything. When children help make these labels, they see the importance of labeling.

- Label shelves to show where containers belong.

- Keep materials within children's reach so they can use them independently.

Following these suggestions will enable you to establish a sense of order in the classroom from the very first day, thereby making the statement that everything has a proper place in the classroom. If it becomes evident that some of the arrangements are not working as well as they should, solicit the children's ideas for addressing the problem(s). Children who are invited to think of solutions to a problem are more likely to support its resolution.

Display Space

Classroom displays represent the children and what they are studying. When commercial materials or art projects that all look the same dominate the classroom, children receive the message that everything has to be done a certain way. In contrast, when children see their own work displayed, they learn that their creative work is valued and the classroom belongs to them.

It's a good idea to leave plenty of empty space in your room at the beginning of school. An empty wall tells children that there is more to come. Some teachers simply label the space to indicate what will soon be featured: "Pictures of Us" or "Who We Are."

Bulletin boards, shelf tops, easels, room dividers, and walls can be used to display children's work. Allocate special space for works-in-progress where children know their projects will be safe and accessible until the next day. Trays can keep projects organized and moveable.

Include in your classroom displays a variety of children's work such as writing, art, inventions or other constructions, math patterns, computer discoveries, and signs. Be sure to include the work of all students. In addition to individual work, you might display charts that have been developed in meetings with the children (e.g., "What We Noticed at the Construction Site" or a graph summarizing the children's findings after conducting a survey on favorite books).

Word walls that are developed with the children can be helpful in reading and writing. Add five new words a week that the children will need in their reading and writing as well as words that you have noticed are confused easily.

Not all displays have to be items made by the children, but they should reflect the interests of the children. Consider these ideas.

- Display books on various subjects (a book about ants in the science area, a book about numbers near where you store math materials).

- Show pictures that relate to a collection or project.

- Post newspaper articles on a community event or topic under study.

- Display objects that are relevant to a topic the children are exploring (shells if you are studying patterns, clocks if you are studying time).

- Collect materials children bring from home that relate to an interest or study.

Displays of children's work reflect what the class is studying and therefore should be kept current. Charts that remain on the wall too long are ignored.

Personal Belongings and Work

Finding safe and accessible places to store personal belongings is a concern in all primary classrooms. In allocating storage space for children's personal belongings, think about when and where children need access to their possessions. For example, if children leave the room to go to a cafeteria for lunch, then a good place to store their lunches might be on a shelf near the door. If your classroom has direct access to the outdoors, you will want clothing stored near the exit. Backpacks and special objects from home should be near work areas since children may need to retrieve items during choice time.

If children don't have assigned desks, then they need places to keep their work. Math journals, writing folders, and children's portfolios can be stored in plastic crates, library boxes, dish pans, or partitioned shelves.

Making Your Classroom a Place for Active Investigation and Representation

Children learn best when they can explore and investigate objects, events, and places. The classroom environment is enriched by allocating space and organizing materials that encourage these active investigations. If the materials in the classroom are well organized, attractively displayed, and labeled, children know where to look for information and locate materials to help them investigate and represent their learning.

In this section we offer suggestions on how to organize space and materials for:

reading	games	cooking, music, dance, and drama
writing	science	art and construction
math	social studies	block building
computers		

Setting Up a Library

When the classroom features an attractive library area filled with a collection of good books, the message is that literature and reading are valued. Children will be more likely to use the area if it also contains comfortable seating and if it looks attractive.

Organizing the Space

If you have moveable bookshelves, you may want to use them to define a library area. Try to allow sufficient room so children can read alone, with a partner, or with a small group of children. A soft carpet, a small (crib-size) mattress with an attractive cover, pillows, bean bags, or a rocking chair make the library area a restful retreat when children need a break from other classroom activities.

Walls or the top of a shelf can be used to highlight certain types of books or display children's work related to reading. Here are some ideas.

- Display books related to your social studies or science projects.
- Showcase books by a certain author or illustrator you are studying.
- Make a poster with suggested titles to read.
- Hang the artwork that books inspired children to create.
- Create an area devoted to books authored by the children.

Stocking the Library with Good Books

You can make your classroom library an interesting place for children by having a wide selection of books that will appeal to many different interests and reading levels. In selecting books for your library, be sure that they reflect ethnic, gender, age, and ability diversity. Consider the following categories:

poetry collections

picture books

chapter books

books related to a particular study

biographies and autobiographies

information books (e.g., sports, animals, weather, machines, solar system)

reference books (e.g., dictionaries, thesauruses)

magazines and newspapers

To help children find and return books independently, a library should be organized logically. You can group books by category in bins, buckets, baskets, or cartons, and label the shelves or mark the bindings with different colored tape for each category. How you plan to use books will dictate the way you want to organize them. Here are some possibilities.

- Categorize books by reading level (e.g., from easy to challenging).

- Group books by author.

- Create categories according to topics that interest your children (e.g., insects, mystery, sports, adventure, sea creatures, space).

To further encourage reading, invite children to write their name on a post-it and place it on their favorite books. This way, children can ask questions of the reviewer who posted a note. You will need multiple copies of books that you plan to use for small group or guided reading lessons. Many schools have created libraries of books that are stored in a central location for use in guided reading lessons. Because children's interests change and their skills improve during the year, new books should be added to the library throughout the year.

A nice addition to a classroom library is a tape recorder with headsets so children can listen to books on tape. If you have several sets of headphones, try to have enough copies of each book for every listener. Family members can create books on tape for the listening center.

To encourage children to care for books, include a first-aid kit for books in the library so that when a book is damaged, a child can easily patch it. A sturdy shoe box or pencil box works well for this purpose. Include transparent tape to repair torn pages, cloth tape to repair the spines of books, gum erasers to remove pencil marks, correction fluid to cover ink and crayon marks, and a pair of scissors. Children can be taught to make repairs themselves, thus learning the importance of caring for and maintaining books.

Displaying Books Throughout the Classroom

In addition to a classroom library, you may want to place book bins in other strategic areas of the classroom to further convey the message that books are important. For example, a few books about different kinds of buildings, cities, and bridges can be placed in the block area. Several books related to math concepts might be displayed with the math manipulatives. Books, magazines, and posters about science topics and inventors could be featured with a science display. How-to books and books about famous artists can be placed near the art supplies. The judicious placement of books in strategic areas inspires children and shows them how books are related to all aspects of the intellectual life of the classroom.

Storing Materials for Writing

Writers must have easy access to supplies for writing and illustrating their work. Because writing takes place throughout the classroom, the only space requirement is for storage. The designated space for storing writing materials can also be a place to display books, stories, or poetry the children have written.

Supplies for writing and illustrating work include items that are available in most classrooms:

standard pencils, colored pencils

color markers, crayons, paper, paint

erasers, pencil grips (especially helpful for children with limited fine motor skills)

stapler, staple remover

scissors, paste, tape, hole punch

paper—white, manila, construction, newsprint—in a variety of sizes

lined paper—one-half inch for younger children and regular-ruled paper for older children

computers with word processing programs

story paper with space for pictures

posterboard

a folder/file system in which to store finished and unfinished work

a date stamp and stamp pad

shelves, bins, or baskets to hold writing paper and writing tools

wastebaskets, recycle bins

book-binding materials (e.g., thread, yarn, needles, paper fasteners, a binder machine, cardboard)

Think about the messages you want to give children about writing. Children will be more likely to write independently when teachers take steps such as the following.

- Honor children's writing by displaying work on a book rack or on the bulletin board for others to read.

- Make sufficient quantities of writing materials available so children know there is enough for everyone.

- Display a chart that describes what happens at each stage of the writing process, so children can make decisions about what to do next.

- Provide reference materials such as alphabet charts, dictionaries (including electronic dictionaries), word lists, and (for third graders) thesauruses.

- Select and share library books for inspiration and clarification.

- Create a system for writing to one another—mailboxes, e-mail, message board.

Writing materials can be stored in plastic crates if shelving is limited. You can also use crates to store children's writing if you place hanging file folders in them.

Supplies and Space for Exploring Math

It is a good idea to put all math materials—manipulatives and games—in one place. This helps children to find materials efficiently. It also enables them to consider a variety of options for using materials. For example, a child who wants to measure the length of the classroom might go to the math shelf and decide to use cubes or colored rods. Board games, poker chips, dice (number cubes), and playing cards all encourage logical thinking and therefore could be stored together. Many manipulatives are available for use on the overhead projector and can be used by the children as well as the teacher.

Children are more likely to share, explore, create, and acquire skills and concepts with these materials if you take the following steps.

- Provide sufficient quantities for several children to work at a time.

- Display a range of children's work with different materials.

- Give each child a math journal to record ideas, questions, and problem-solving strategies.

- Keep the materials neatly displayed, organized, and available at all times.

As you expand the number and variety of materials, try to avoid cluttered shelves. Make sure children have enough room to use the materials comfortably. Sometimes large projects (e.g., measuring with links) may take up the entire classroom. Small projects that children want to preserve for a period of time (e.g., a pattern block design) can be safely stored on a tray.

Materials that invite explorations in math include collections and commercial manipulatives. Children also need supplies for recording information such as writing tools and paper.

Collections

Collections of household objects can be used for counting, estimating, and sorting. The children can help you gather these from their homes. Some suggestions are:

buttons	spools of thread
plastic bottle caps	screws, nuts, bolts
shells	patterned wallpaper or fabric samples
keys	ribbons

Children will use these collections to sort, organize, weigh, design patterns, trade in place value, estimate, and for many other math tasks. For storage, you can use dishtubs, shoe boxes, and plastic containers that can be purchased inexpensively at any variety store. For sorting, you can use trays, bowls, egg cartons, meat trays, and margarine tubs to hold sorted items.

Commercial Manipulatives

There are many excellent materials to inspire children to explore mathematical concepts. If you are just beginning to stock your math shelves and have a small budget, we recommend that you invest in the following materials:

colored links	colored cubes
Cuisenaire rods	pattern blocks
Unifix cubes	

Other basic and inexpensive materials for math that will enrich your program include the following:

beans and sticks	yard sticks, meter sticks, and clear plastic rulers
dice	playing cards
calculators	

When your budget allows, you can expand your supply of math materials. Many of the materials listed below can be found in school supply catalogs.

Blocks

attribute blocks	base ten blocks
multilink cubes	

Calculating and Counting Materials

play money	hundreds boards
plastic counters	dominoes
chip trading - tills and chips	

Drawing Tools and Measuring Devices

stencils	compasses and protractors
trundle wheel	even arm balance
deep dish simple scale	clear plastic containers with metric delineations
money stamps	measuring cups and spoons
clock stamps	clocks and stop watches

Geometric Materials

geoboards	tangrams
geometric solids	polydrons
pentominos	templates for tangrams and pattern blocks

Supplies for Recording Math Discoveries

To record discoveries in math, supplies such as the following can be used:

> pencils, markers, crayons
>
> graph, grid, and dot paper
>
> ruled, unruled, and colored paper
>
> chalk and 4 to 6 individual chalk boards
>
> adding machine paper
>
> tape, string, and rulers
>
> vinyl graphing cloth

Math materials and supplies, particularly those with small pieces, can be stored in dishtubs, buckets, or boxes and labeled with the name and picture. If you also label the shelf or table where each item belongs, children will know where to put things away on their own.

Collecting Games

Games can enhance learning in all areas of the curriculum, particularly math and reading. When children play games, they develop important social skills and practice winning and losing. Games are ideal for choice time. Because games may be played in many areas of the room, the only space required is a cupboard or shelf for storage.

Children enjoy both commercial and homemade games and puzzles. If you tape the corners of game boxes when they are new, they will last longer. You can store games in large self-sealing plastic bags, and type directions in large letters on the box cover or inside the bag. Sometimes children like to rewrite the directions given in commercial games. Directions can be preserved if they are pasted on cardboard and laminated or covered with clear contact paper.

Commercial Games/Puzzles

Many games promote mathematical and strategic thinking. They provide an enjoyable way to reinforce the acquisition of basic math facts in addition, subtraction, multiplication, and division. Some popular games for young primary age children are:

Uno	Connect Four	Sorry!
Rack-O	Dominoes	Twister
Stack	Checkers	Mancala
Chutes and Ladders	Parcheesi	Monopoly Junior
Battleship	Pictionary Junior	Guess Who
Chinese Checkers	Mastermind for Kids	Simon

For older primary grade children, the following games can be added:

Backgammon	Rummicub	Junior Boggle
Chess	Junior Scrabble	Othello
Yahtzee	Mastermind	

Playing cards can be used for all sorts of games that reinforce math skills (see Resources).

Jigsaw puzzles give children an opportunity to collaborate with partners. A sheet of cardboard, plywood, or a tray will make the puzzle moveable. Choose puzzles of interest to your class, including subjects that relate to social studies or science projects.

Homemade Games

Children take great pleasure in inventing their own games to practice skills such as times tables, addition and subtraction facts, and spelling. You and the children can make games with a few basic materials such as the following:

old workbooks to cut up

index cards of many colors

magnetic letters to manipulate for word construction

posterboard of various sizes and colors to make game boards

stickers to decorate boards

blank cubes on which you can write letters for spelling games or numbers
   for math games

one-inch ceramic tiles on which you can write letters, numbers, or symbols

rubber stamps

sticky-back velcro

magnetic tape

Invented games can be an excellent culminating project for a study. For example, after studying the neighborhood, children might replicate their community and make up a game similar to Candyland. It could incorporate what children learned about mapping, directions, keys and legends, and provide practice in reading and math. Work on regrouping might be encouraged by "trade-in" games like Race to 100 (also known as Win a Hundred). Other trading or renaming games can be devised to work in bases other than ten.

Organizing Science Materials and Tools

How you decide to organize science experiences in your classroom will dictate how you organize the science environment. You may have work times when all of the children are engaged in science activities. You may also want to have a shelf or an area equipped with tools for investigations in science and offer this as a choice activity. Since math and science materials are often used together (e.g., scales, measuring cups, rulers), consider storing these materials near each other. A table located close to the science materials may be sufficient for science explorations. If the whole class is involved in a scientific study, other work tables or the floor can be used.

Materials that will inspire scientific investigations include any of the following:

rocks and minerals	batteries, bulbs, and wires
magnets	plants
fish tank	shells
seeds and nuts	terrarium
meal worms	pets (guinea pig, bird, rabbit, hermit crabs)
ramps and balls	pendulums
straws and bubbles	

The materials in this area should be changed or additional materials included periodically to encourage exploration.

Tools for scientific investigations and for recording observations may include:

magnifying glasses	binoculars
microscopes	balance and bathroom scales
writing tools	medicine droppers
tweezers	measuring spoons and cups
drawing and graph paper	

Children will be more interested in using science materials and tools if they also see books, charts, diagrams, and posters relevant to the things they may explore. In addition, science studies for children will have more success if children:

- know how to handle the materials, insects, or other animals properly;
- understand and follow safety rules;
- have a place (e.g., Scientist's Journal) to record observations and questions; and
- see their work displayed.

While including materials and tools for science explorations will enrich your curriculum, don't ignore what's right outside your windows. Rocks, plants, bugs, construction projects, bodies of water, and weather can all be part of science.

Materials for Social Studies

Learning the concepts and content of social studies involves both active investigation and representation of new information. Here are some basics.

- Include books about people (including first person narratives) and places in the library or other areas of the classroom.
- Make art, wood working, and construction materials available for children to make models, paint pictures, and create murals of people and places.
- Provide blocks to recreate places children have visited; block building helps children develop geographic thinking and map-making skills.
- Have photographs of diverse people and places, as well as newspapers and magazines as needed.
- Include appropriate software for the computer for social studies research.
- Provide cooking experiences (e.g., making bread after a trip to the bakery, or preparing foods related to a study) to extend learning in science, social studies, math, and reading.

When thinking about social studies and the physical environment, also consider:

- space for displays of children's project work;
- space for the display of artifacts related to studies; and
- an area for dramatization (the meeting area is often sufficient) with props as needed.

Finally, taking trips to experience people and places first-hand is an essential aspect of the social studies curriculum. Trip boards (paper on clipboards, or paper attached to cardboard with binder or other clips) enable children to record their observations during trips.

Organizing Art and Construction Materials

Designate a place for storing art and construction materials so children have access to what they need. Depending on the project, children will use different kinds of work surfaces including tables, standing and wall easels, and, sometimes, the floor.

If you have a sink in the room, store the art supplies near it. Find space away from the line of traffic in order to avoid interruptions and accidents. Choose an area that is not carpeted and make that the main area for painting and other "messy" work. If the entire room is carpeted, a vinyl drop cloth or old shower curtain liner, taped to the carpet, creates a space that says, "It's okay to be messy here." Hang smocks or old shirts in the area for children to wear over their clothing.

A modest supply of basic materials will allow children to paint, draw, put things together, cut, mold, and clean up. Think about the clean-up supplies you want to have available such as a broom, dustpan, sponges, etc. Art supplies can be organized in three categories: painting materials, drawing and sketching materials, and construction materials.

Painting Materials

Liquid tempera lasts long and produces vibrant colors; however, it is costly. Powdered tempera is less expensive, but it must be mixed to the right consistency. If you choose to use powdered tempera, add a few drops of rubbing alcohol or oil of wintergreen to keep the mixture from spoiling. Water-color sets give children yet another painting experience.

The best brushes are those with metal bands and no seams. Large brushes are good for easel painting, murals, construction projects, and painting at the table. Smaller brushes are best for water colors.

Include a variety of types and sizes of paper as well as other materials:

manila paper	newsprint (18" x 24")	wood
butcher paper	construction paper	fabric
glossy fingerpaint paper		computer paper

An excellent alternative (or addition) to easels is using aluminum cookie sheets as paint palettes. "Tray painting" (originated by Lois Lord at Bank Street College of Education) allows each child to have an individual setup for painting. Supplies for tray painting can be stored on a shelf, preferably near the sink. Such supplies might include:

1 aluminum tray

5 plastic furniture coasters—each with a spoonful of red, yellow, blue, black, and white paint

2 bristle brushes (1" and 1-1/4" widths)

1 damp sponge

1 plastic water container

Painting Procedure
① Get a piece of newspaper and spread it out on the table.
② Set up your tray for tempera paints or a watercolor set.
③ Select the paper for your painting and sign your name and the date on back of it.
④ Paint!

white · blue · yellow · red · black · cup · brushes · sponge

If you don't have a sink in your classroom, have two buckets available, one with clean water and an empty one for dirty water. One of the advantages of tray painting or any palette painting, is that children need only the three primary colors plus black and white paint. They learn to create other colors by mixing the paints on the tray or palette and discover for themselves that blue and red make purple, yellow and blue make green, and so on.

Drawing and Sketching Materials

Children will draw pictures and sketch if you simply provide paper and writing tools. Sturdy manila paper is ideal. In addition, stock the shelves or place baskets on each table with the following materials: markers, crayons, chalk (white and colors), chalkboards (from the math area), and colored pencils.

Construction Materials

Materials for construction include: scissors (high-quality ones serving both left- and right-handed children), different kinds of paper, and glue (both white glue and glue sticks). Keep a supply of "junk" scraps for collages that you and the children (and their families) can collect, including fabric scraps, yarn, wallpaper, junk mail scraps, catalog pictures, and natural items (acorns, pine cones, seeds, etc.). Businesses in the community are often willing to donate materials that you can recycle into your art area.

Primary age children can use water-based clay and plasticine very effectively. Clay will last a long time and remain consistently soft and malleable if covered with a wet cloth and stored in a plastic container with a tight cover.

Block Building

Blocks provide opportunities for experimentation related to structure and design. Children can create three-dimensional representations of what they are learning, experiment with balance and weight, and measure and compare the size and shape of constructions.

First graders may use blocks to recreate their experiences—a trip to the zoo, the supermarket, or the harbor—and then use them for dramatic play. By second and third grades, buildings themselves interest children.

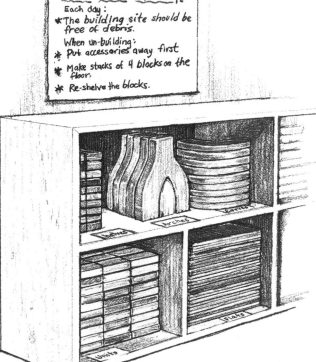

Block Area Clean-up.
Each day :
* The building site should be free of debris.
When un-building:
* Put accessories away first
* Make stacks of 4 blocks on the floor.
* Re-shelve the blocks.

Photographs or posters related to projects (e.g., bridges, buildings) posted in the block area often inspire block building. Children learn about mapping as they create representations of their neighborhood around school or the market they have been studying.

Unit blocks are wonderful materials for children of all ages. If space is limited, you can offer children building opportunities with smaller blocks that can be used on a table or rug.

Unit Blocks

Hardwood unit blocks are durable, have smooth edges, and are easy for children to manipulate. Unit blocks come in proportional sizes that help children acquire math concepts. There are at least 25 different sizes and shapes of unit blocks. A set of 390 unit blocks is recommended for one classroom. This total should include a wide range of sizes and shapes, such as ramps, curves, and cylinders. If you store unit blocks on labeled shelves and group them by size and shape, clean-up will be efficient.

The size and location of the area for unit blocks will affect how successfully children use them. Children need sufficient room to build, a clearly defined space, and appropriate flooring. The area for building activities must accommodate a small group and the building project itself. Tape on the floor, shelves, and/or a carpet can define the area. Large projects may sometimes be difficult to accommodate in the classroom. You may want to inquire about using a hallway occasionally, and then find ways to protect the construction from passersby.

Props and Accessories

While props and accessories for block building are essential in a preschool or kindergarten classroom, primary grade children are less dependent on commercially made props. Encourage them to develop their own props using art materials, manipulatives, and "junk."

When children are building and express a need for props, you can say to them, "Let's think about what we have in the classroom that you can use." Encourage them to solve the problem creatively, for example, by making fruits and vegetables out of plasticine, traffic signs from construction paper and sticks, furniture out of colored inch cubes, and so on. If you have organized your classroom materials so children know where to find and return them, using them temporarily for a building project will not be a problem.

Table Blocks

Many different sets of small blocks can be stored in plastic basins and used on tables or the floor. Among the most popular are Castle Blocks, Legos®, and construction blocks in logically ordered colors, sizes, and shapes. Children in the primary grades can spend hours using these blocks to construct elaborate buildings and designs. Often these constructions lead children into dramatic play.

Look through supply catalogs to find architectural blocks, dominoes, or unit block sets that are scaled down to be used on a table. Children this age love to build structures as tracks for marble runs or domino structures that tumble down when pushed.

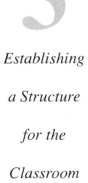

Providing for Cooking, Music, Dance, and Drama

It isn't necessary to have designated areas for cooking, music, dance, or drama in your classroom in order to offer these activities for children. Cooking can take place at a table; music, dance, and drama can occur in the meeting area or outdoors. These activities are not isolated but relate to the subject areas of your curriculum.

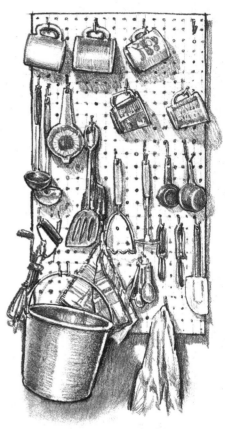

Since these activities take place in a variety of places, you need only a place to store supplies. Boxes with covers, laundry baskets, or buckets all serve this purpose.

Some teachers keep *cooking supplies* in the classroom; others bring supplies out as needed. A group of teachers can get together and share supplies such as these:

cookie sheets

measuring cups and spoons

muffin tins

bread and cake pans

electric frying pans

mixing bowls

cooking utensils

hot plate and toaster oven

pots and pans

sieves

simple recipes

recipe charts

children's cookbooks

For *music and dance,* you need only your voice and children who like to sing and dance. It is also helpful to have the following:

tape recorder and cassette tapes

CD player and CDs

musical instruments (e.g., bells, drums, xylophone, triangles, castanets, keyboard)

materials to make musical instruments

song books

strips of fabric and scarves

Again, these items can be shared among several classrooms.

For *drama,* children like to dress up when they act out scenes from books or those related to social studies topics. It's not necessary to provide many materials. Children can make them and bring in appropriate props and dress-up clothes from home.

Including materials in your classroom for writing, drawing, painting, constructing, cooking, music, dance, and drama will enable you to provide children with a wealth of opportunities to represent their learning.

Arranging a Computer Area

Computers can be tools for exploring, creating, solving problems, organizing data, reading, and writing in your classroom. They belong in your classroom, rather than in a computer lab, so that computer use can be integrated into your daily classwork. To ensure children's comfort, computers should be on low tables with keyboards at children's elbow level and monitors at eye level. Whether you have one or more computers in your classroom, try to arrange the space so two children can work together comfortably at each computer. If the monitors face outward toward the center of the room, other children can see what is going on and work can be shared.

Additional points to consider in locating your computers are listed below.

- Locate the computers away from water or messy activities.

- Avoid placing the computers where the lighting causes glare on the screens.

- Locate the computers near an outlet and use a power strip so all equipment can be turned on/off with a single switch.

- Place computers against a wall so that wires are not exposed.

- Provide storage space for printing paper.

- Use nearby wall space for displays of children's work and for information about how to use the area.

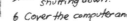

Computer Tips!
1. Use with clean hands.
2. Keep food, liquids and magnets away from computers.
3. Save your work.
4. Ask for help if you need it.
5. Exit the program before shutting down.
6. Cover the computer and put your disks away!

If your school is not wired for the Internet, then you will need a phone line to use your modem for e-mail or the World Wide Web. If your software is developmentally appropriate, computer use can be a shared activity that extends children's thinking and offers opportunities for children to solve problems together. Good computer programs also reinforce and extend math and reading skills in enjoyable ways. Other equipment to consider when funds are available includes a scanner and a digital camera. In addition, if you have children with special needs there are adaptive devices that can make technology more accessible to them.

The information in the chapter on Technology will assist you in thinking about how children might use computers and in making judgments about software that meets your goals.

Planning for Children's Physical Needs

Take the children's physical needs as well as your own into consideration in planning the physical environment of your classroom. If you have ever been to a workshop where you had to sit for hours on hard furniture sized for preschool children, you know how your discomfort can affect your learning!

Addressing Basic Needs

It's a great advantage to have bathrooms adjacent to your classroom. If you are not this fortunate, try to avoid the need for children to line up to go down the hall and use the bathrooms several times a day. You can do this by establishing a system for going to the bathrooms independently. See page 55 for some suggestions.

Children get hungry and thirsty during the day. If you do not have a drinking fountain or sink in the classroom, you can set up a pitcher of water and cups in a convenient place so children can help themselves. Alternatively, children can bring their own water bottles and drink whenever they are thirsty. Try arranging (with the school or with parents) to offer children a snack of crackers, fruit, raw vegetables, and juice to sustain them until lunch time. You can set up a "snack bar" in the classroom where children can help themselves if you do not have time in the schedule to stop. However, allocating time for a snack contributes to the feeling of community.

Creating a Comfortable Environment

Far too many classrooms contain only hard furniture. Sitting on hard furniture all day can be tiring and often causes restlessness by late morning or afternoon. When the environment offers more accommodating spaces and materials, children are more comfortable, better able to concentrate, and more likely to work cooperatively with others.

You can make your classroom more comfortable by including rugs or a small mattress covered with a colorful fitted sheet where children can stretch out. Adding large pillows, bean bag chairs, or an overstuffed chair to a reading or listening area provides a place for children to curl up with a book and relax when they need a break. Think about what you need to be comfortable, such as an adult-size chair and a safe place for your belongings.

The environment becomes more friendly when you have plants, a lamp in the library, and pets that children can hold and love. Living things also require care which generates jobs and promotes a sense of community.

Making Accommodations for Children with Special Needs

If you have a child or children with a diagnosed disability, you may need to make changes to the physical layout of your classroom to ensure accessibility and comfort. If, for example, you have a child confined to a wheelchair, you will need to look at traffic patterns to determine if the child has access to materials and working spaces. At least one table in the classroom should be at an appropriate height to accommodate a child in a wheelchair. An alternative is to provide trays for the chair. Some children may need adaptive equipment for standing, or bolsters for floor work.

It is not the classroom teacher's responsibility to obtain any special equipment needed or to make structural changes to the physical environment. Teachers who include children with disabilities in their classroom are entitled to support from a specialist who is knowledgeable about the particular disability.

Offering Places to Be Alone or to Calm Down

Get-away places within the classroom can provide a respite when tempers flare or children just need to be alone for a few minutes. These areas might be designed for other purposes but can double as neutral territory when two children need to work through a disagreement in a quiet place. The library, for example, could be a place where children can go to discuss a problem and resolve a conflict.

Privacy in the classroom can be achieved by building lofts, filling an appliance box or an old bathtub on legs with pillows, or using shelves and furniture to define a space where children know they can go to be alone.

Providing Space and Time for Large Motor Movement

Children's physical development should not be taken for granted; its benefits are far too important. The Surgeon General's Report on *Physical Activity and Well-Being* (1996) states that physical activity makes a significant difference in personal health and well-being. Physical education in the early grades contributes to children's academic achievement, general health, self-esteem, stress management, and social development. And recent brain research confirms what adults have often experienced, that physical activity literally wakes up the brain.

During the primary grade years, children's gross movement skills expand dramatically. They benefit from daily opportunities to practice locomotor skills such as running, jumping, galloping, climbing, skipping, and sliding. A good physical education program teaches children the manipulative patterns for throwing, catching, striking, dribbling, kicking, and punting.

These patterns are critical to future development because they form the basis for more complex movements required for sports and dance.

If your school does not offer a well-rounded physical education program, you may need to make time for gross motor movement activities either in the classroom or outside. Store equipment in a laundry basket or large cloth bag that can be taken outdoors easily during the day. Collect jump ropes, balls, wiffle bats and balls, bean bags and cardboard frames, and hoops. Do some research on games that involve children in practicing physical skills. You will find that promoting children's physical development has a very positive effect on their academic work.

Creative Solutions to Common Problems

Very few teachers start with everything they need. If you are committed to enriching your classroom but your resources are limited, here are some solutions to common problems. You can probably add many of your own ideas.

What if you have individual desks in your classroom and no tables?	• Four desks can be grouped together to make a table. You can turn the open ends toward the center if it doesn't hinder seating, and provide other places for children to store their work. • Let administrators, custodial staff, and other teachers know that you are interested in obtaining tables whenever they become available. • Provide spaces where children can work on the floor.
What if you do not have any bookcases or shelves in the room?	• Boards and bricks or cinder blocks can be used, but need to be safe and stable. • Check with a high school shop program to see whether they could make bookcases for you. • Scout yard sales and search second hand furniture stores. • Use plastic stacking bins or milk crates. • Ask parents for donations. • Check discount or used furniture stores.
What if the shelves in your room are too high for children?	• Lay them on their sides and find bins to use in vertical spaces. • Cut them down if this is possible. • Create shelving using milk crates and boards. • Use window ledges.

What if you don't have a rug for a meeting area?	• Ask people you know if they are replacing carpets in their home. • Visit carpet stores and seek donations. • Ask for discontinued books of carpet samples and sew squares together. • Call people who install carpets and ask them to save any used carpeting for you. • Check thrift or discount stores.
What if you don't have the materials suggested?	• Save common household junk objects (buttons, bottle caps, keys, plastic bread tabs, seeds). • Take pictures that show ethnic/disability/gender groups. • Purchase at yard sales. • Ask for donations from community groups, friends, and parents. Holidays are an especially good time to ask for donations. Children can bring a "present" for the class (new or old) and open it at a class meeting. • Become a partner with a school or another teacher who is willing to share. • Put a notice in a school or community newsletter. • Approach shopkeepers in the neighborhood to help. (A hardware store might have lots of discarded keys they could save for you, and a wallpaper store will have discontinued books of wallpaper samples.) • Get a teacher's library card and ask the librarian to help select books for your class. • Find out whether there is a teacher resource store in your area. • Use your budget to purchase manipulatives and other materials that will last for many years.
What if you don't have enough display space in your classroom?	• Cover the chalkboard with paper and use it for display. • Ask permission to hang art in the hallways, cafeteria, or administrative offices. • Hang displays from the ceiling or tape them flat on the ceiling. • Display art on "laundry lines" strung across the classroom. • Use ends of shelves or dividers. • Drape paintings across windows.

The Daily Schedule and Routines

The schedule and routines reflect the way you want children to spend their days. A predictable schedule and clearly understood routines help children feel safe and become independent, confident workers in the classroom. Just as a properly designed physical environment is conducive to learning, a well-planned schedule gives children a sense of order and makes the day run smoothly.

Considerations in Planning the Daily Schedule

An appropriate schedule is based on an understanding of child development and the specific needs of a particular group of children. Eager for increasing independence from adults, children six to eight years old benefit from having informal, social times during which they can make independent choices. They are active and energetic, yet they tire easily. Therefore, it is a good idea to plan for variety in the day—times to sit quietly and times to move around—and opportunities to run around outdoors.

The amount of time you schedule for activities will vary. For example, meeting times will last longer with older children and their ability to sustain reading and writing times will also increase.

The schedule should include blocks of time for meetings, writing, math, reading aloud, silent and small group reading, choice time, projects or studies, outdoor time, snack, and clean-up. Some of these activities might be grouped together, for example when children are working on projects or a task that involves several content areas.

In planning your daily and weekly schedule there are several issues to consider. What factors must you include (e.g., school or district requirements)? What are your priorities? How will you balance children's need to make choices with your knowledge about what they need to learn? What are the difficult times for children (and you) each day? And finally, in the best of all possible worlds, can you arrange common planning time with colleagues at the same grade level? Once you have answered these questions and planned your classroom schedule, think about how you will make it clear to children.

Starting with Fixed Times

There are some times during the day over which you have little control or choice. These include:

- arrival and departure times;
- mealtimes (lunch and sometimes breakfast);
- special classes (physical education, music, art, library);
- recess;
- individual children's schedules (special services); and
- assemblies and other required school functions.

A good way to start is to make a chart of the week and fill in the times of each day that are fixed. By doing this you can see where you have big blocks of time and consistent time slots each day.

Sometimes, even the fixed times of the day are not carved in stone. For example, if special classes or the time allocated for recess don't work for you, try trading times with another teacher. Or invite art or music teachers to come into your classroom and help with projects, rather than having the children go out. Another alternative is to have half of your class join another for special classes, thus giving each of you more time to work with a small group in the classroom.

Determining Your Priorities

Your priorities may change from one year to the next but they are important factors in determining a workable schedule. Consider these questions.

- How do I balance the importance of consistency with the need for flexibility?
- When will meetings take place?
- When will group lessons and work times be scheduled?
- When can I schedule large blocks of time for projects?
- When will the children have outdoor time?
- How can I schedule time for a snack?

Consistency vs. Flexibility

An effective schedule is one that allows for both predictability and variety, but is also realistic. Because you want to help children become increasingly independent, it is a good idea to schedule some activities at the same time each day.

When you know what experiences you want children to have on a regular basis, you can put those into the schedule. For example, if children know that they have writing every day after lunch, or math in the morning, or a free choice time every Tuesday and Thursday before lunch, they can anticipate those activities and prepare for them independently. If you have several special classes each week in which the children have to leave the classroom, it may make sense to schedule reading, writing, and math times only four times each week.

Rather than attempting to fit everything into every day, you can schedule several substantial work times a week. For example, if children have physical education two days each week, you may decide to schedule outdoor times on the other three days.

Meetings

Different types of meetings occur in the classroom—some that are scheduled every day and others that are called for a specific purpose. It may not be possible to have a meeting first thing every day. For example, if your class is scheduled for music or has to attend a school assembly every Thursday morning, you may want to schedule a meeting later in the day.

If you decide to end each day with a fifteen-minute meeting in which you read a story to children, and you want children to spend about ten or fifteen minutes each day cleaning up the room, then you have to anticipate that the work of the day will end a half hour before school does. The kinds of decisions you make about scheduling meetings are based on your priorities and your goals for the children.

Different Kinds of Work Times

Within the course of each week, there will be a variety of work times. They often begin with a group meeting where the teacher introduces something new to children and then has them work independently or in small groups on a task. For example, Monday's math time may be an hour long. For the first 15 minutes a new concept is introduced to the children in the meeting area. For the next 30 minutes children work in small groups on tasks related to the new concept. Then the children regroup in a meeting for 15 minutes to share what they have done. Subsequent math experiences during the week may be scheduled, integrated into other curricular areas, or completed during a work time in which children work on a variety of tasks.

Introduce a new concept or skill in one subject at a time. When you decide to teach something new, think about whether it would be best for the whole class to be together or if children would be more successful learning it in small groups.

Projects require large blocks of time because children often have to set up and clean up materials when they are finished. We recommend selecting one or two times during the week for longer, uninterrupted periods (about an hour or an hour and a half) during which children can work on projects in science or social studies.

Outdoor Times

Unless it is raining hard or the temperature is severe, children need outdoor play time every day. Even when the weather isn't perfect, a five- or ten-minute break outdoors in the middle of the morning and again in the middle of the afternoon can refresh tired children and increase their ability to concentrate on classroom tasks.

An increasing number of children in the primary grades return to empty homes where they must stay indoors until family members return. They have little time to play outdoors. This makes it especially important for teachers to provide outdoor time for the children on a daily basis.

While many schools have scheduled recess times for an entire grade or several grades after lunch, having class times outdoors is also desirable. During these times the rules of your classroom community are taken outside. Children have the opportunity to play in groups with your guidance and support. Lessons can also take place outdoors. Social studies trips or science expeditions provide an outdoor break. Art projects or measurement activities can also be done outside. As children explore and make discoveries outside, or play games, they continue the classroom lessons of establishing rules, solving problems, cooperating, negotiating, and talking.

Snack Times

Whether and when you schedule a snack time will depend upon your children's arrival and departure times, and lunch time. In addition to providing important energy, snack time can also be used to reinforce social skills and build community. Healthful snacks may be brought from home or provided by the school. Snack time can be combined with outdoor time in nice weather or used to celebrate a birthday or other special event.

The Difficult Times of the Day

In planning your daily schedule, give some thought to the difficult times during each day and how you can make them less stressful. Major transitions include arrival, going to and returning from lunch, and departure times. Additionally, there are numerous smaller transitions during the course of the day as children change from one activity to another: from writing time to recess, snack to a group lesson time, choice time to clean-up.

Many children lose focus and purpose during times of change. This can be especially true for children with certain kinds of disabilities. If you establish a clear transition process, it will be helpful for all children. For example, some teachers have short meetings in the meeting area to wind up the last activity and prepare for what comes next. Involving the children in planning what to do often leads them to have a greater investment in the procedures. Ask children for their ideas about what they might do while waiting for another activity to begin.

Transitions work more smoothly if set procedures are followed consistently. When children have helped to create the procedures, they are more likely to follow them.

Arrival

In some schools, children gather on the playground first and then go to their classrooms as a group. In others, children may ride the bus and arrive earlier or later than children who walk or who are driven to school. In some schools, children may attend a breakfast program before classes begin.

Whenever the children arrive, they each come from a different setting and have to make the transition to school. First thing in the morning is probably not the best time to teach something new or even to expect all children to sit still and focus on a morning discussion. Having a fifteen-minute transition time in which children can play quiet games, draw, or write in a journal enables children to settle down, socialize, and adjust to the classroom community. It also gives you a chance to talk individually with children as they go about their transition activity. Try not to plan something that children have to make up if they are too late to participate.

Lunch Time

Hungry children do not learn well. Right before lunch may be a good time to read aloud, offer a *free choice* time, have children write in journals, or finish up work. Having children gather in the meeting area prior to lunch provides a time to help them get settled, remember cafeteria and recess rules, and think about what will happen when they return to the classroom.

After lunch can be equally difficult. Children may have just had to negotiate all the issues that are hardest for them: socializing, fairness, games with rules, cheating, and aggression. When they return to the classroom, they are almost always filled with energy. If tempers are hot, you may need to have a discussion to address social problems. This is also a good time to plan a calming activity such as read-aloud or independent reading. Children can reconnect with the positive feelings of their classroom community. You will have to observe your group's temperament to determine the most suitable activity for the period after lunch.

Clean-up

Clean-up after a choice or project time can be challenging. It's important to give children a warning. Give the class signal for quiet and tell children how many minutes remain so they can mentally prepare themselves for closure. If children have assigned jobs for clean-up, you can remind them at this time.

Some teachers find it helpful to allow children a little time between work and clean-up. They call a brief meeting where children can share what they have been working on, and then make plans for clean-up.

Departure

If you want children to leave feeling good about the day, try to arrange some time for them to wind down. Gather the class together in the meeting area to talk about the day, participate in an activity, read from a chapter book, and/or distribute papers.

Making the Schedule Clear to Children

Children often ask, "What's next?" A predictable daily schedule minimizes the need for this question and helps children feel secure. If you can refer children to a written schedule to figure it out for themselves, it reinforces their independence. When children can read the schedule and use it as a guide, they are more likely to feel a sense of control over their day.

A good place to post the daily schedule is in the meeting area, where you can review it with the children each morning. You can make daily schedule cards in five different colors (for each day of the week) to distinguish the days of the week. These cards can record the unchangeable elements of each day. The special activities for the day can be written on the morning message and read with the children during the first meeting of the day.

Settle in

Morning Meeting

Writing Workshop

Outdoors

Snack

Book Clubs

Morning Work Time

Lunch and Recess

Story and Quiet Reading

Math or Science Activity

Choice Time

Jobs

Meeting

In summary, the day's structure needs to include sufficient time for active learning, teacher-initiated activities, and children's self-directed activities. An effective schedule for children in the primary grades offers a balance of large group activities, small group activities, individual work times, outdoor and snack times, quiet and noisy times, and active and sedentary times.

Establishing Classroom Routines

Routines are procedures that ensure the effective use of time and space. The regular daily routines, as well as those special routines and events that are particular to your class, help establish a structure for classroom life, and contribute to the positive sense of community. Routines give children the message, "This is our way of doing things."

The routines of your class are often what make the year special for children. They help create bonds within the classroom community. Special routines might be a particular way you start and end the day, the songs you sing, or an activity that is unique to your class such as a special snack on Fridays or being reading buddies with the kindergartners. Knowing that third graders love to tell jokes, one teacher scheduled a ten-minute joke time every Friday after lunch. Often teachers don't know something is a ritual in the class until the children ask, "Why aren't we doing it anymore?"

What Routines Are Needed

In planning the routines for your classroom, think about all the things you want children to do, and how you can establish procedures that will enable them to work with increasing independence. These may include:

- putting away and later retrieving coats and lunches;
- getting quiet;
- going to the bathroom;
- coming to meeting, sitting, and taking turns talking;
- cleaning up after work times and at the end of the day;
- lining up;
- getting and eating a snack;
- doing something constructive during arrival time in the morning;
- putting away finished work and works in progress;
- turning in and receiving homework;
- working in groups;
- using and cleaning up art and construction materials;
- storing journals;
- following procedures for math, writing, reading, and computer activities; and
- collecting and dating samples of work for portfolios.

As you review this list, you better understand why it may be difficult for many children to negotiate their day, especially at the beginning of the year. It's also a challenge for the teacher, especially a new teacher, to create the necessary routines and communicate them to the children! Clearly defined routines, however, are an extremely important aspect of the classroom structure. When children know in advance what is expected of them, they feel in control.

Once you have identified the routines you need, think about what must be in place so children can be successful in following the procedures you establish.

- What will children need for the routine (e.g., folders, signs or charts with instructions, bathroom passes, meeting seat chart, attendance cards)?

- What do I have to collect or do to get ready (e.g., for writing workshop I have to have folders, boxes to store the folders, and labels on the boxes)?

- How can the children help (e.g., label their own folders, suggest where to display the books they write)?

For example, if you are using storage boxes for the children's folders (for math, writing, reading, or homework), you can label the storage boxes in advance. If there are written directions for a project, review them with the children at a meeting and then post them near the storage boxes as reminders.

Teaching Routines to Children

Routines will truly become routine if they are made explicit to the children. You may help children learn routines by introducing them at a meeting, helping children remember by reminding and practicing, and giving children reasons for following them.

Using Meetings to Introduce Routines

When you introduce children to a routine such as your procedure for going to the bathroom or lining up, you will need to explain it clearly and model the steps to be followed. You can introduce it by asking children for their ideas on how best to form a line. A simple role play can add humor: have the children watch you proceed to the door by running, pushing chairs aside, in order to get there first. Ask the children to assess what was wrong and why it might be dangerous. After the discussion, ask for volunteers to show the group a better way to form a line.

Open-ended questions are an effective way to begin a discussion on a new procedure. For example, suppose you are going to introduce homework to children. You might begin by asking children what they know about homework. Depending on their age and experience, children will have a variety of thoughts. Some might say, "My sister does homework every night for hours," or, "We had homework last year on Wednesdays."

A discussion about a routine serves many purposes. It enables children to express concerns and expectations. It allows you to get to know the children better. And it is likely that children will say things you can build on.

"Jason, you mentioned that you had homework on Wednesdays. Now that you are in third grade, we will have homework on two nights. One will be the same, Wednesdays, but we will also have it on Mondays. Who remembers how you brought homework back and forth from school last year?"

Children this age often say things with great bravado such as "Ugh, I hate homework," or "Do we have to have homework two nights? Second graders are so lucky." Comments such as these are typical. Most children are both excited and a little afraid about whether they can meet the expectations of a new grade. They need opportunities to express these feelings.

Whether or not you are going to tell children what is expected or invite them to participate in establishing the method, it's a good idea to take time for discussion. Once the routine has been introduced, children will need regular reminders to conform to it.

Helping Children Remember

Of course, taking time to discuss the routine doesn't mean that everyone will remember it. Children need a great deal of practice and reminding. If they sense they are being criticized, they will often resist doing what they are asked or told. The following examples illustrate how teachers can help children remember what to do in a positive way.

"We're going to get in line now for lunch. Close your eyes and think about what you have to do. Get a clear picture in your mind. Are you ready? Okay. If your birthday is in a month that begins with J, please get your things and get in line."

"Who can demonstrate for us how to set up for writing workshop? Debra? Okay. Let's all watch closely. She's going to the folders. She finds hers in the box that has her name on it. She goes to the pencil can. She takes some yellow lined rough draft paper. She goes to a seat. Good job, Debra. Is everyone else ready? The people sitting from Janet to Shana can go get their writing folders."

"We are about to get ready to go home. Tonight is a homework night. Let's brainstorm all the things you have to do to get ready to go home. Think about what you will need. Who wants to start?"

Each of these ideas requires taking some time to discuss and practice the routine. However, it is time well spent. Everyone is involved. Of course some children will still have difficulty and need a friendly reminder from time to time: "Nina. Do you have your backpack? Is the note about the PTA meeting in it? Do you have your homework folders?"

Providing Reasons

Children in the primary grades often have difficulty waiting for turns or doing things an adult tells them to do. The minute the adult gets impatient, the child may become increasingly stubborn. Rather than waiting for a conflict to arise, explain your thinking in simple ways.

"I know that you are really thirsty and it's hard to wait to get a drink. But if everyone rushes to the water fountain at once, what will happen?" Provide children with time to respond. "Yes. There will be pushing and shoving and someone is likely to get hurt. So the reason I am calling only three people at a time is to avoid an injury."

Children may not agree with our reasons, but they are more likely to cooperate once they understand them.

You may think that the reason for something is obvious, but it is sometimes not obvious to children. Often, the actions of adults can seem arbitrary and confusing. Offer an explanation like: "Not everyone can use the papier maché materials at once because it is messy. I decided that five children would work with papier maché today. Everyone will have a turn sometime during the next two weeks. I realize that this is frustrating. Papier maché is a wonderful but very messy material." Explaining your reasoning to children helps them become logical thinkers. It also enables them to move from self-centeredness to cooperation. When you explain your reasoning and children see that you will let everyone have a turn, they grow to trust you. Teachers have to try to be fair. For children, wanting and waiting can be the hardest part of school.

Evaluating the Effectiveness of Routines

Sometimes even when you have thought through the routines for your classroom, things don't run smoothly. A procedure may work for one group of children and the next year be totally ineffective. Do not assume rules and routines can be carried over year after year. If a particular routine is not working, try to pinpoint where the problem is. Ask yourself the following questions.

- Do the children understand what they need to do?
- Are there too many steps involved?
- Am I sending too many children at one time so that things get chaotic?

Once you have located the problem, try to identify two or three ways it can be addressed. Pick the one you think will work the best. Explain to your class why you are changing the routine and why you think the new one will work better. After you have tried the new routine for a few days ask your class whether they notice a difference.

Ms. Pope was feeling frustrated because at the start of every writing time her students were falling all over one another as they reached for their supplies. She decided a change was needed. The next day she carefully observed this writing time. She noticed there were too many children going to the supply shelf at one time. She also saw that if she moved the paper supplies away from the writing tools it would naturally divide the writers. The next day Ms. Pope explained what she had observed and what she decided to change. She asked her class to observe how the beginning of writing time felt and to plan to talk about it tomorrow.

Involving children in the evaluation process helps them understand why you want to make a change. It is also more likely to engage their support.

Offering Children Choices

When children have choices in school, they are likely to feel competent and independent about their work. Whether the choices are small—what snack to eat, which game to play—or large—selecting a topic for a story, planning a skit about a study—children are more motivated to pursue a task or idea they have chosen. Teachers who provide genuine choices on a daily basis convey an important message: "I respect your ability to make decisions about what you will do and how you will do it." In these classrooms, children feel empowered to pursue something of interest to them, to take on a project because they have questions to explore, and to be in charge of their learning.

Giving children choices also enables them to practice behaviors associated with resiliency. Whether choices involve simply selecting a book to read or topic to write about, they can also allow children to decide how to express themselves through their work. After reading a book or studying a topic, for example, children might make charts or graphs, draw pictures, paint a mural, create a computer design or game, build a model, put on a skit or puppet show, or write a report. Often these artistic expressions mingle personal aspects of a child's self along with the newly learned material. Such choices allow children to be *creative* and demonstrate *independence*, two of the strengths highlighted in the resiliency research (Wolin and Wolin 1993, 1995). (See also Chapter 1, page 30.)

Choice times are a wonderful opportunity for teachers to assess children. By noticing and documenting what kinds of choices children make, the children they work with, what materials they gravitate toward, and how they complete a task, teachers learn a great deal about individual children that helps them in planning the instruction. Choice times also allow teachers to interact one-on-one with an individual child, either by playing a game or talking informally.

Teachers who find ways to provide children with daily opportunities to make choices soon find that some of the behavior problems they experienced in the past—short attention spans, children who act out and disrupt the class—are minimized. Children interested in what they are doing are less likely to be bored and disruptive.

Types of Choices

There are countless opportunities for children to make choices during the day. Choosing a book to read, the type of manipulative to use to solve a math problem, or whom to sit next to at lunch are all meaningful choices. When you talk with children about the rules or jobs needed in the classroom (described in the next section), you are offering them an opportunity to make choices. When you plan a lesson in which children work in groups of four to investigate a topic, children feel that they have a choice in deciding how they will proceed with the task.

There may be specific times during the day when you offer children open choices. Some teachers call this *choice time* or *free choice* and offer a specified number of options: painting, games, blocks, computers, cooking, and so on. Open choices allow children to apply the skills they have learned to tasks and projects that particularly interest them. When children are encouraged to pursue their own interests, teachers can learn a great deal by observing them.

A particularly good time of day to plan an open choice time is in the afternoon, toward the end of the day, when children may be getting restless. In the beginning, you may decide to have every child try each activity at least once so that they understand their options.

Helping Children Make Choices

If children are not accustomed to making choices, they may need specific guidance in the beginning. At a meeting, teachers can introduce the choices that are available.

> *"Today during choice time, you have five options. As I name them, think about what you would like to do. I'll be asking you in a few minutes for your choice. The choices are: games, tray painting, computers, drawing and writing, and working on social studies projects. When you have decided what you want to do, raise your hand so I know you have a plan."*

Before children leave the meeting area, the teacher hears from each child or small group about their plans. Thus, a clear structure for making choices is established.

It's very important to respect the choices children make during an open choice time. Many teachers wonder if they should be concerned if a child always selects the same activity. It's tempting to say this.

> *"You've chosen games every time we have choice. Why don't you try something new?"*

This statement, however well intentioned, belittles a child's selection. Try a more respectful response.

> *"You really like games. I guess you like them better than anything else in our classroom."*

This validates the child's choice, and lets the child know that you are aware of this personal preference. It also reinforces the idea that other choices are available.

If you determine that a child is stuck, and perhaps uneasy about trying something new, you may want to be a little more forceful. You could say something like the this.

> *"It's wonderful that you have a favorite choice, but part of school is trying new things. Next week, try a different activity. I'll help you get started."*

> *"Who has not tried the Tangram puzzles? I would like the three of you to try them today. Tomorrow you can make a choice again."*

Inviting children to talk about what they have done during choice time at a meeting will often inspire reluctant children to try something new.

Listing Choices

To further structure the process of making choices, some teachers find it helpful to have a choice board in the meeting area. The board lists the activities that are open and tells how many children can be involved in each activity. Children state their choices and indicate on a choice board where they intend to work. Choice boards can be made in a number of ways.

- Turn a chalkboard that attracts magnetic tape into a choice board. You will need cards for each of the choices, and name tags for each child with magnetic tape on the backs.

- Use a peg board with cards to indicate the choices for that day. Next to each choice card, place a specific number of pegs to show how many children can select that activity.

- Insert hooks into piece of plywood and use it as a peg board. Write children's names on round tags with holes.

- Hang library pockets on hooks to show which choices are available. Children put their names in the pocket of their choice.

A choice board must be introduced to the children. At a meeting you can discuss the system: how the number of pegs or hooks indicates the number of children who can choose each activity; where children put their name tags; and how they can change their choice if they decide to try another activity during choice time.

Keeping track of choices reveals children's preferences. A class list on a clipboard can serve this purpose. Older children can be responsible for recording their own choices on a monthly record sheet.

A form for recording choices makes a good portfolio item to share with parents to illustrate a child's interests. Children can also observe their own patterns, which helps them to gain greater self-awareness.

If you have not tried including a choice time in your schedule, you may want to plan it one day a week, perhaps on Friday afternoons, and see how it goes. The children's enthusiasm for this opportunity may inspire you to offer choice time more often.

Choice Record

Name: _____

Week Of	Monday	Tuesday	Wednesday	Thursday	Friday

Clear Expectations About Behavior

The third way that teachers establish structure in the classroom is by establishing clear expectations about behavior. Children feel safe when they know how they are expected to behave, when they understand the reasoning behind classroom rules, and when rules are consistently enforced. Teachers develop these expectations from the first day of school by:

- involving children in creating classroom rules;

- taking care of the classroom; and

- introducing the proper use and care of materials.

Involving Children in Creating Classroom Rules

You may feel that you already know the rules you want for your classroom and you don't want to take the time to involve children in the process. There are, however, compelling reasons to give children a say in determining the rules for their classroom community.

One very compelling reason is that children are more likely to follow rules they generate. Discussing rules invites children to weigh the effects of certain behaviors and to reflect on concepts like fairness, the reasons for rules, and the instances when they apply. Creating their own rules helps children not only develop responsibility for their own behavior, but also for one another, and for the group.

Establishing rules for community life is a good social studies lesson and teaches children what living in a democracy involves. At the same time rule-making is a way for children to practice *morality*, another of the array of strengths found in children who are resilient (Wolin and Wolin 1993, 1995). Finally, as Alfie Kohn suggests, the "ultimate reason to give children a say is that it can help them to make their own good decisions, to grow into ethical and compassionate people. . . ." (Kohn 1996)

Although you may begin involving children in creating classroom rules on the first day of school, that is not the end of the process. Throughout the year it is necessary to revisit the list of rules, have discussions about how they are working, and modify them as necessary.

Generating Rules

When we invite children to create rules, we have to accept the fact that they may not come up with the exact rules we have in mind. The process of creating, however, is more important than the specifics generated. It is through the process of thinking about the need for rules and how to apply them that children learn the most (Kohn 1996). And, we may even find that some of the rules we thought were so essential are really not that important! There are a number of ways to introduce the idea of having rules and to involve children in deciding what rules are needed to make the classroom a hospitable place for everyone. You can use the suggestions that follow to design an approach that is comfortable for you.

Introduce the need for rules at a meeting. "I want to welcome all of you to our classroom. We will be together for the whole year. This is our classroom community and it's important for everyone to feel safe and comfortable here." The Child Development Project suggests that the class discuss the "ways we want our class to be" (Child Development Project 1996).

Lead a discussion about why we have rules. "We will need some rules for our classroom community. Let's think about how we define the word rule. Any ideas? Does anyone know what a rule is? What kind of rules do we have for crossing the street? Why are those rules important? What might happen if we don't follow the rules about when to cross the street safely?" Relate the discussion to children's experiences. "What would happen if we wanted to play kickball and there were no rules?" Discuss issues of safety, fairness, and comfort.

Ask children for their ideas. "I want you to help me decide what our rules will be. If we make the rules together, it will be easier for all of us to remember them. Because we want our classroom to be a safe place, we'll start with rules that will help us feel safe. Let's take a few minutes for each of us to think about what would make us feel safe here." Invite children to raise their hands when they have an idea. As they share their ideas, write them on a chart, repeating each word as you write it. You may need to ask more probing questions such as, "How do you want people to treat you?"

Help children be specific. A child may suggest the rule, "Be nice." This would be a hard rule to follow because it is not specific. It doesn't let children know what to do. To help children focus on behavior, you might say, "Let's think about that rule. What does it feel like when people are nice to one another? Can anyone think of an example of being nice?"

State rules positively. This increases the likelihood that children will follow the desired behavior. When we say "Don't run," children tend to focus on the word "run" rather than the desired behavior. If we state the rule positively, "We walk when indoors," then children have a positive image of what is expected.

Give examples to illustrate your points. "Let's pretend that someone just shared an idea in one of our meetings and another person said, 'That's a stupid idea.' How would the first child feel? What rule do we need to make sure everyone feels comfortable sharing their ideas in our classroom?" Guide children in developing a rule such as, "We help each other."

Summarize a group of ideas that are related. Children may have offered a series of ideas such as, "Don't push. Don't hit. Don't pinch." Read these back to the children and ask, "How can we say this positively in one rule?" The children might come up with a rule such as "Don't do anything to hurt anyone." Encourage them to say it positively, for example: "We treat each other kindly."

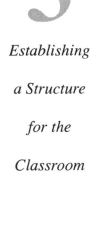
Discuss where the rules should be posted.
After you have a list of rules, explain that
you will put all their best ideas on a chart
and bring it to the next meeting. Ask the
children where to keep the list so everyone
can refer to it. One teacher made the rules
into a classroom pledge (Stetson 1994). The
children read it together most mornings and
have discussions about what each rule
means. Another teacher developed "respectful reminders" with the children and posted
those (Gershowitz 1998).

> Raise your hand when you wish to
> speak.
>
> Don't interrupt.
>
> Be a good sport.
>
> Include everyone.
>
> Treat others the way you want to be
> treated
>
> Always be willing to help a friend.
>
> Listen carefully while others are speaking.
>
> Respect classroom materials and clean up after yourself.
>
> Share with others.
>
> Be polite:
>
>> Say please and thank you.
>>
>> Say hello to teachers and children in the hall.
>>
>> Hold the door for the next in line.
>>
>> Remember to say, "Good game."

You may not be able to get through the whole process of generating rules in one meeting.
This will depend on the age of the children and how familiar they are with participating in
a discussion. For some groups, you will need several meetings before you complete your
classroom rules.

To further clarify the meaning of each rule, you can ask the children to draw pictures of what
each rule means. The children can also make up skits to show what it would look like if each
rule was followed.

Our Classroom Pledge

Because our classroom needs to be
a safe, peaceful, and comfortable place,
I will do my best to:

1. Be helpful to others.

2. Solve problems with words.

3. Keep the room neat and organized.

4. Move slowly.

But most of all, I will try to
follow the golden rule:

Treat others the way you would like
them to treat you.

Reinforcing and Evaluating Rules

The philosophy behind the structure of the classroom becomes most apparent in the way the teacher acknowledges children who follow the rules and handles children who make mistakes. In a caring democratic community, the goal is not automatic compliance (except where safety may be a factor), but a group and individual understanding. After all, it's not the rule itself that is important, but the purpose of the rule—"to make the classroom a safe, happy place for everyone" (DeVries and Zan 1994). When children follow the rules, rather than getting individual or group rewards, children should be encouraged to see and feel the benefits of adherence to a rule. "We had a great discussion today because we took turns talking." Similarly, when rules are broken, rather than punishment or "logical consequences," which are punishments by a different name (Kohn 1996), the key is to figure out what went wrong and why.

You can expect that rules will sometimes be broken, and that everyone will need reminders. In fact, one community-building rule might be, "We remind our friends if they forget the rules." This keeps the responsibility for order within the group and not just with the teacher.

Sometimes it may be worth discussing the rule at a class meeting to evaluate why the rule isn't being followed. The children may decide to modify the rule, discard it, or in talking about it come to value it more highly. Some children may need help in following a rule and other children can assume responsibility for helping them. If Petey forgets to move slowly and bumps into other children frequently, maybe Alonzo can be a buffer and slow him down.

Sitting alone with a child and discussing why the rule was developed and what it means can help. "Do you remember why we have that rule? How can we help you remember it?" Sometimes a child needs to spend time practicing and role playing the helpful behavior if she has wasted class time and upset the constructive atmosphere of the classroom.

When you stay calm and speak in positive terms to children about breaking the rules, you show them that you dislike their behavior but you will provide time for them to practice more positive behavior. Public embarrassment or ridicule makes children feel bad and does not help them change their behavior. Instead, it is best to speak to a child privately. This gives children the message that you care about their feelings and that you want to help them to keep trying to be successful in following the rules of the classroom.

Taking Care of the Classroom

While it is important to have the room organized with a clear plan in mind for the first week of school, there are compelling reasons for leaving some things until after the children arrive. You don't have to spend your summer vacation making beautiful labels for everything in your classroom and preparing elaborate job charts and bulletin boards. You can involve children in making labels for materials, and in deciding on what jobs are needed for the classroom. The process of involving children in these tasks sends a very important message: "This classroom belongs to all of us and we will decide together how to take care of it."

Generating Jobs for the Classroom

Sometime during the first week of school, a class meeting can be used to discuss the need for classroom jobs. You may begin this discussion by asking children:

"Why do we need a neat classroom?"

"What would happen if we left the classroom a mess every day?"

"What are some of the jobs we need to keep our classroom clean and neat?"

List the ideas children offer on a chart. You can include the name of the child who offered each idea.

If children are not thinking of all the jobs you know are needed, you can ask leading questions.

"Let's suppose we were finished painting and there were dirty brushes and paint holders on the table. What would we need to do?"

"If no one was responsible for watering our plants, what might happen?"

"What kind of job do we need to make sure the tables are cleaned before snack time?"

Recognize, however, that if the children do not list a job that you believe is needed and you let them discover this on their own, you allow them to learn from the process. Once you have a list of the jobs, you can have the children vote on how many children it will take for each job. Job-sharing is a good way to have children get to know their peers and learn to collaborate.

In making the job chart, try to have everyone's name on the chart all the time. If there are not enough jobs to go around, you can have a category called "Substitute." These children fill in for anyone who is absent or take on special tasks during job time such as helping the teacher file work or prepare for the next activity.

Jobs We Need to Do in Our Classroom

Danna — We clean up rubber bands.
Arben — We clean up blocks.
Franny — We clean up markers with the tops facing up.
Shantelle — We clean up the paints.
Pavel — We clean up crayons and markers.
Bailey — We need to take care of frogs and hermit crabs.
Zara — We have to clean up paper.
Tommy — We clean up our books.

Classroom jobs need to be re-evaluated periodically. After trying the agreed upon jobs, the class can discuss questions.

- Are the jobs being done well?
- Do we have the right number of people assigned to each job?
- Are other jobs needed?

Once children have had the experience of deciding on jobs for their room, they are likely to think of new responsibilities and roles. Some of the most popular jobs involve leadership roles. For example, one class decided to have a "Meeting Starter." The job entailed giving the class signal for quiet, gathering the children in the meeting area, and having the class read the morning message. In another class, the children decided in the middle of the year that they needed a "Clean-up Manager" to keep everyone on task. Another year, the children decided to have a "Floater" who circulated during clean-up time asking if anyone needed help and offering assistance if needed. One teacher established a "Math-board Data Collector" to record daily counts for the class. The possibilities are endless!

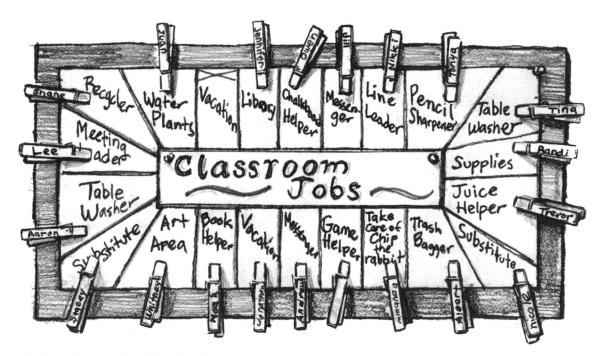

Making Signs and Labels for the Room

Some teachers prefer to make all the signs, charts, and labels themselves because they want everything to look attractive and neat. This is a perfectly valid reason and may be particularly appropriate if you teach younger children.

If you teach second or third grade, consider having the children make some of the signs and labels for your classroom. Even first graders can write their names and label their own cubbies. It won't look as neat, but children learn that the classroom belongs to them.

Introducing the Proper Use of Materials

In the previous chapter on Community, we suggested that at the beginning of a new school year, teachers should limit materials to ones that children are able to handle. To establish a structure for the use of materials, it's important to give some thought to how you want children to use the materials, where you want them stored, and how you want them maintained. Children will then learn that you want them to be responsible for their own actions, and that they are trusted members of the group.

Using Meetings to Introduce Materials to the Class

Meetings are an ideal time to introduce classroom materials to the entire class. Present the material in an interesting way by hiding part of it, giving a clue about it, and asking the children to guess what it is. Engage the children in a discussion about the material and its use in the classroom. Next, invite several volunteers to make something with the material and talk about the uses children can invent for the materials. Discuss all the safe and purposeful ways to use the material in the classroom. Ask children for their suggestions about the care of the materials.

Each time you introduce new items, take time to talk about them with the children. Encourage children to think of new ways to use and care for all materials. Listed below are the kinds of questions you can ask children when you introduce new materials. Taking time to have children share their responses to these questions helps to insure satisfying learning experiences as children begin to work independently in the classroom.

- What materials do you see?
- How many objects look the same? How many are different?
- Can you name all the things that you see?
- Do you see something you have never seen before?
- Do you see anything that looks like something you used at another time?
- What could you do with this. . . ?
- What would happen if. . . ?
- Do you see something you would like to try to use?
- Where can we keep these materials?
- Where can we put your finished work?
- How will we know whose work it is?

Give children an opportunity to ask questions themselves, and keep instructions simple. Here is an example of how you might introduce tray painting to the children during a meeting time.

Before the meeting, prepare an aluminum tray as a paint palette as previously described. Place the tray where everyone can see it and spark the children's curiosity by saying, "I've collected all these things on the tray from our art area. Can you tell me what you see on the tray?"

After the children name the items, continue with a series of questions to extend their ideas.

"How many paint colors do you see? Can you name them?"

"What if we need a color that's not here? Does anyone know how we can get colors we don't see?"

"How can we keep the colors from getting all mixed up?"

"Can you think of why there are different sized brushes here?"

"Why do we need a container of water?"

"What ways will we be able to use the sponge?"

"When you are finished, how do you clean up? Where do the materials belong?"

Each question encourages the children to consider ways in which the painting tray can be used as an independent classroom art activity, while it also anticipates their needs.

Introducing all classroom materials in this way generates interest and teaches children how you expect them to use materials. By inviting children to think about all the ways they could use the materials and by accepting their suggestions, you model respect for ideas, encourage logical thinking and problem solving, and help children learn to use materials thoughtfully. If you have begun the year without introducing materials to the children and you find that you are unhappy with the way they are using and caring for materials, you can remove the materials that are being used poorly or abused. At a class meeting, introduce each set of materials to the children as described above.

Involving Children in Introducing New Materials

Once you have introduced all the basic classroom materials and discussed their use, where they go, and how to keep them orderly, it may not be necessary to introduce every new addition to the classroom during a class meeting. An alternative is to teach a small group of children how to play a new game or use a new set of manipulatives and then have these children teach the others.

Suppose, for example, you want to introduce a new card game. You could offer this as an option during choice time by saying, "I have a new game and it's called Uno. I can teach it to four children today. Who is interested?" If some children already know the game, you can have them help you. In this way, the teacher's job is made easier and children reinforce the proper use of materials for one another.

Whether the teacher introduces materials or children teach one another, it is important to convey the message that materials are valued and must be used with care. The benefits of introducing all materials are well worth the time involved.

Closing Thoughts

An explicit classroom structure enables teachers to teach more effectively and children to become self-directed learners. Children who know how to use and care for materials, who create and understand the rules of the classroom, and who are able to make choices experience the power of being in control of their learning. It then becomes the teacher's job to guide the learning process.

References and Resources for Establishing a Structure for the Classroom

Bickart, Toni, and Sybil Wolin. November 1997. Practicing Resilience in the Elementary Classroom. *Principal* 77 (2): 21–24.

Bronson, Martha B. 1995. *The Right Stuff for Children Birth to 8, Selecting Play Materials to Support Development*. Washington, DC: NAEYC.

Child Development Project. 1996. *Ways We Want Our Class to Be: Class Meetings That Build Commitment to Kindness and Learning*. Oakland, CA: Developmental Studies Center.

DeVries, Rheta, and Betty Zan. 1994. *Moral Classrooms, Moral Children: Creating a Constructivist Atmosphere in Early Education*. New York: Teachers College Press.

Gershowitz, Denise. 1999. Personal communication.

Golick, Margie. 1973. *Deal Me In! The Use of Playing Cards in Teaching and Learning*. New York: Jeffrey Norton Publishers, Inc.

Kohn, Alfie. 1996. *Beyond Discipline: From Compliance to Community*. Alexandria, VA: ASCD, 83.

Stetson, Charlotte. 1994. Personal communication.

U.S. Department of Health and Human Services, Centers for Disease Prevention and Health Promotion, and The President's Council on Physical Fitness and Sports. 1996. *Physical Activity and Health: A Report of the Surgeon General*.

Wasserman, Selma. 1990. *Serious Players in the Primary Classroom: Empowering Children Through Active Learning Experiences*. New York: Teachers College Press.

Wolin, Steven, and Sybil Wolin. 1995. Resilience Among Youth Growing Up in Substance-Abusing Families. *The Pediatric Clinics of North America, Substance Abuse* 42 (2): 415–430.

Wolin, Steven, and Sybil Wolin. 1993. *The Resilient Self: How Survivors of Troubled Families Rise Above Adversity*. New York: Villard Books.

GUIDING CHILDREN'S LEARNING

All teachers want children to become confident, competent learners. A competent learner understands the processes of learning: how to define a problem, find information needed to solve problems, put ideas together in an organized way, and apply knowledge to new situations. The most important message children can receive from adults is "I have confidence in you. You can learn. Trust yourself."

> The elementary grades constitute a defining experience for children— one that will heavily influence the life course from middle childhood to adolescence and beyond. The importance of success in school is profound. A child's fundamental sense of worth as a person depends substantially on the ability to achieve in school. A child who is faced with low expectations for performance or who is not supported in meeting high expectations sets in motion self-defeating attitudes that can lead to education alienation and diminished prospects over the entire life span (Carnegie Task Force 1996, xvii).

Because the early elementary years establish a foundation for lifelong learning, teachers have the responsibility to provide challenging but attainable projects and goals and then help children to succeed. Therefore, **how** teachers guide children's learning is as important as **what** children are learning.

The fourth strategy for building the primary classroom describes the teacher's role as a guide in the learning process. Underlying this approach is an understanding of how children learn best and a set of principles that guide teachers in planning instruction that is meaningful to children. Teachers design classroom activities so that children can construct their own knowledge by actively investigating real problems, representing their growing understandings in a variety of ways, and reflecting on what they have learned. They use an integrated approach that allows children to apply skills they are learning across the curriculum in math, reading, writing, science, social studies, technology, and the arts.

How Children Learn

To plan instruction that is responsive to the needs and interests of a group of children, teachers base their decisions on a well-defined philosophy of education. This philosophy emerges in part from a teacher's own experiences, and also relies on the work of psychologists and learning theorists.

In the first chapter, Knowing the Children You Teach, we provided an overview of what several respected theorists have taught us about how children learn. Piaget observed that children's thinking changes over time and that they continually construct their own knowledge. Vygotsky emphasized the influence of social interaction on children's development and learning. Erikson explained how children in the primary grades are at the stage of Industry during which they enjoy the challenge of new ideas, are capable of collaborating with peers, and like to use tools to produce products. And Gardner's work alerts us to consider all types of intelligence in planning learning experiences so that every child can feel confident and experience success.

Confidence and success also relate to research about resiliency. In each chapter thus far we have tried to demonstrate how teachers recognize and support children in practicing behaviors associated with resiliency, such as *independence*, *initiative*, *creativity*, and *insight*. Key to each of these strengths is self-confidence. In school, self-confidence comes from feeling competent—knowing that you can do the work of school well. Thus, in guiding children's learning, we need to think about how we promote children's "cognitive competence" (Werner 1998). While high expectations are important, those expectations have to be realistic if children are to experience success.

Based on the work of these theorists, we highlight four concepts about how children learn: (1) children actively construct an understanding of knowledge; (2) children learn by interacting with others; (3) play engages children in active learning; and (4) learning takes place in stages in which children move from a concrete, personal understanding to a symbolic and more conventional one.

Children Construct Understanding

Children are doers—they explore the world around them to learn how things work, and what will happen if they try an experiment. They strive to make sense of their experiences, to relate new information to what they already know, and to acquire understanding.

Children's natural tendency to explore and figure out how things work is active, not passive. Using all of their senses to examine and work with objects and materials, children form understandings of the physical properties of things: hard or soft, flat or bumpy, rough or smooth, straight-edged or round. They learn about relative sizes and weights, cause and effect, and that different objects behave in different ways. A trip to observe first-hand how pizza is made—the tools, ingredients, and techniques used—gives children a chance to think about all the processes needed to create a product. When they return to the classroom and follow a recipe for making pizza, or paint a mural of what they saw in the pizzeria, they make their own meaning from the experience. Children learn by doing, not simply by listening or looking.

Learning is a process of building new and deeper understandings about the world, and acquiring and refining skills. The human brain strives to make sense of experience, to find patterns and construct meaning. When children actively engage in the learning process, they "construct knowledge." This means that children apply information they already have in order to interpret what they observe and make sense of the new experience. They revise their theories and form a clearer understanding based on their previous experiences and observations.

> *Six-year-old Petey looks at the fish tank in the classroom and announces, "We have to put more water in the fish tank because the fish are drinking the water." His teacher asks how he knows this is happening, and Petey replies, "Two reasons. First, they keep opening and closing their mouths. And second, the water used to be up here," pointing to the water line at the top of the fish tank, "now it's down to here," pointing to the current water level.*

Petey makes his best guess as to why the water level is decreasing. The teacher could use this observation to explain evaporation, or, preferably, encourage Petey to begin an investigation that would help him to construct new understandings of the phenomenon he has observed. For example, by observing the water level in another tank or jar without fish, Petey can see whether the level stays the same or changes. Other experiments might include painting on the blackboard with water and making chalk lines around puddles after a rain. Based on these experiments, the teacher can guide Petey in developing new theories about what happens to the water.

> *Eight-year-old Simone is adamant that she can explain why the stars shine brightly at night. "The earth is like a ball and we live inside the earth. When it is dark inside the earth, it is light outside. There must be holes on the outside of the earth that let in the light and that's what we see when we look at the sky."*

Simone has some information about day and night—that when it is night where she is, it is day somewhere else. Although she seems to know that the earth is round, she has not yet grasped that people live on its surface. Using the information that she has, she is thinking hard to find an explanation. A skillful teacher observes how Simone thinks and recognizes that Simone needs additional information, experience, and time in order to acquire understanding. Given Simone's explanation, simply telling her the facts is not likely to increase her understanding. Discussion and a variety of appropriate experiences can provide the scaffolding she needs to construct an increasingly accurate explanation. Observing the night sky, making maps of imaginary places, working with a globe, reading myths about the earth, and writing some of her own stories will stimulate continued and revised thinking about her theory.

The process of forming and revising explanations based on experience is the way that children (and adults) learn—we construct understanding. As children gain a larger repertoire of experiences, they move toward more logical explanations. Listening closely to children as they describe their thinking enables teachers to perceive how children understand their world. Teachers also learn about the types of experiences that can lead children to more accurate understandings.

Children Learn by Interacting with Others

Learning is a social experience. Most of us are eager to talk with someone else when we learn something surprising, read an interesting book, or acquire a new skill. Children also like to share what they know with others.

Just as children construct knowledge as a result of their active explorations with materials, they also learn by interacting with adults and other children. From infancy children interact with their caregivers. The give and take of sounds, facial expressions, and body language is the beginning of communication. Long before they use words, children understand their meaning. With language comes the ability to put thoughts and feelings into words and to communicate effectively with others.

In a classroom where children are encouraged to work collaboratively to solve problems and to create representations of what they are learning, there are countless opportunities for children to learn from others—their peers as well as adults. As they work with their classmates, children are exposed to ideas that may be unfamiliar to them. They acquire new concepts and understandings when they have opportunities to share information with others, ask questions, and work together to achieve new insights.

> *Ms. Sanders' class is studying the river in their city. As part of the investigation, the children explore bridges, mills, and dams. Ms. Sanders organizes many research materials for the children to use. Today, at an early stage in the research process, the children work in small groups, organized by topic, to locate the materials they will use. Gina's topic is the Memorial Bridge. She finds pictures of it in several books. Hannah, who is researching the 14th Street Bridge, finds a book on the Arlington Memorial Bridge. She calls to Gina saying, "I found something on your bridge." Gina argues that it's not the same bridge, because the name isn't exactly the same. Together they look at pictures of the bridges in both books and determine that sometimes this bridge is referred to in one way, sometimes in another.*

In the process of talking about what they know, children unravel problems they encounter together and clarify their own thinking. As a result, they acquire a greater comprehension of the concepts and contribute to others' understanding.

Play Engages Children in Active Learning

Children learn naturally through play. Their play is often spontaneous, imaginative, and engaging. Block building holds children's attention and offers endless opportunities for creative problem solving. Spontaneous and planned dramatization in response to literature or a trip enables children to develop language skills and express feelings. Card, board, computer, and dice games help children develop logical thinking and mathematics skills.

Sara Smilansky identifies four different kinds of play: functional play, constructive play, sociodramatic play, and games with rules. Each type of play contributes to children's growth and learning (1990).

Functional play occurs when children explore and examine the functions and properties of objects and materials. By handling, experimenting, observing, listening, and smelling, children make discoveries. As children express what they are doing in words or pictures, they both recognize and articulate what they are learning. Working with pattern blocks, for example, leads to numerous discoveries—they are flat and can be stacked, when placed on edge they form walls, and they fit together in different ways to make stars, flowers, towers, and tunnels.

Constructive play involves using materials to shape a representation of something—either real or imagined. To study the neighborhood around the school, some children construct a map of the area using blocks, or create a model out of boxes and collage materials. In constructive play, children represent their understandings concretely and, in so doing, reveal their interpretation of their experiences.

Socio-dramatic play entails pretending or make-believe. When children engage in socio-dramatic play, they re-enact experiences they have had, observed, or imagined. When first graders recreate a trip to the restaurant by building a restaurant with blocks, and then use the block people for different roles—cook, server, cashier, customer—they are engaged in a cognitive task.

- They must remember the actions of workers and customers.
- They select relevant details of particular events to incorporate in the scene.
- They use real or imaginary props.
- They display in gestures and words that they are playing the roles appropriately.

Children in a third grade class who act out different scenes about life in early America based on museum trips, books, and discussions are using dramatization to construct an understanding of a time and way of life that is unfamiliar to them. The act of dramatizing helps make the newly learned content personally meaningful for them.

Socio-dramatic play is important for children in the primary grades because it supports the development of abstract thinking. When children engage in socio-dramatic play, they develop the ability to substitute symbols for real objects and events. When they dramatize a story they have read, their play may have imaginary qualities, or it may serve as a means for children to express their understanding and interpretation of the story.

Dramatizing stories leads to many valuable problem-solving tasks: who will play each part, what props will be used, how to summarize the story, and how to remember cues. By replaying experiences with others, children gain new understandings about a topic they are studying.

Games with rules are board games, many computer games, sports, or any type of play governed by a set of rules that everyone understands and follows. In board games such as checkers or Connect Four, children have to keep the rules in mind as they invent strategies to win. Children practice math skills in games that require dice-rolling or score-keeping. By playing card games, children compare quantities and apply mathematical thinking skills.

Playing games with rules provides opportunities for children to learn how to deal with competition and the feelings generated by winning or losing. Teachers can help children learn to cope effectively with competition if this occurs in the context of a supportive community with clear rules and expectations for behavior. Providing a safe setting for competitive play helps children learn to handle feelings of anger, aggression, and competition (Greenspan 1993).

Many different factors can affect the level of children's play and what they gain from play activity. These factors include family background, individual personality, environment, and

gender. Children with learning disabilities or a physical handicap may play differently—their ability to use play to learn new skills or to generalize new concepts may be restricted. They may need to be taught specific play skills such as where to find materials, how to play with them, and how to involve other children in their play, before they begin to learn through their play (LAUSD 1990, II-1).

Learning Takes Place in Stages

Reaching Potentials (Bredekamp and Rosegrant 1992) describes learning as a four-stage process in which children move from a concrete, personal understanding to the conventional understandings of society. All learning begins with awareness and exploration and moves to the stages of inquiry and utilization.

- Children must be exposed to concepts and ideas *(Awareness)*.

- Children need opportunities to interact with these concepts and ideas on a personal level *(Exploration)*.

- Children require support in their efforts to achieve mastery *(Inquiry)*.

- Children must use and refine their skills and understandings in real situations *(Utilization)*.

All learners, regardless of age, go through these stages when learning something new. And in any classroom, there will be children at different stages in the learning process.

Exposure to Concepts and Ideas (Awareness)

The best time to teach children something new is when they are ready to understand the concept or value the skill. This is why it is important to select content for study that is relevant to children. Content should relate to their own experiences so that they can make connections with what they already know.

The teacher's role is to observe what children already know and set up an environment in which children are exposed to concepts and ideas that are important for them to learn.

- To foster language and literacy learning, teachers fill the room with a variety of interesting books, read stories and poetry to children daily, record children's words and ideas on charts, and put a selection of writing tools and paper on shelves accessible to children.

- To foster mathematical thinking, teachers make materials such as scales, rulers, measuring tapes, thermometers, calculators, and various kinds of graph paper accessible to children. They encourage children to explore with different kinds of dice, a variety of manipulative materials, and measuring tools. They use meetings to discuss mathematical problems. They provide time for children to play mathematical games.

While some children are ready to use the materials a teacher sets out, others may not be. Children who have been read to at home or who have seen older children and adults reading and writing are often eager to become readers and writers themselves. Similarly, children who haven't been read to, or haven't had occasion to observe people reading, may not seek out books. Lacking first-hand experience, they may not understand why it is worthwhile to become a reader. Although they may gradually recognize letter-sound relationships, or learn sight words by rote if teachers require it, they are unlikely to feel a sense of purpose and motivation in the process. Hearing stories read aloud and watching a teacher write on charts is a first step to help children with little experience gain awareness of the value of literacy skills. Learning to read is made purposeful when the learner has an awareness of the advantages of reading and writing.

Interacting with Ideas on a Personal Level (Exploration)

Once children have been exposed to new ideas or skills, their natural curiosity usually takes over. During this stage in the learning process, they seek understanding by exploring and investigating on their own. At this stage children don't want to be told how; they may not be aware that there is a "right" or conventional way of doing something. They want to jump in.

Theresa takes an unfamiliar book and studies the pages using pictures as cues. While she does not yet recognize all the printed words, she is using the strategies she knows about text to get an idea of what the story is about before actually attempting to read it.

Early in the year Jesse draws a picture of his cat who is quite fat. On the bottom of the page he writes "mi kt s ft." He reads his story to his teacher: "My cat is fat." Jesse is inventing his own way of spelling and demonstrating an awareness of the sounds letters symbolize. He has no trouble reading his own story perfectly.

Adult encouragement during this stage of exploration is essential for children to acquire their own understanding of skills and concepts.

Efforts to Achieve Mastery (Inquiry)

In the third stage of learning, children gradually realize that conventional methods may differ from what they are doing. They want to know the "right" way and often ask for help. Sometimes they may be ready to learn a more effective technique, but don't know it exists. Because children are motivated at this stage, it is often the optimal time to teach new concepts and skills directly. Teachers can sense when children are ready to learn conventional techniques by carefully observing and listening to children as they work. Knowing when to introduce new ideas and skills is part of good teaching.

After Jesse has had some time to experiment with invented spellings for simple words, Ms. Lane has a conference to show him some conventional spellings of words. She uses a book she has just read aloud to the class and points out the correct spelling of the word cat. *Ms. Lane asks Jesse to observe the difference between the two spellings—his in the story and the one in the book. Jesse writes "the book spelling" in his word list to use the next time.*

In Mr. Cory's first grade class, Mei is trying to figure out how many unifix cubes there are in a bucket. Mr. Cory notices that while she has formed stacks of ten cubes, she starts at one to count the whole amount. Having observed previously that Mei knows how to count by tens, he shows her how to apply this strategy to a new problem.

In each example the teacher uses careful observation to assess when the child is ready to learn a new skill. Jesse and Mei are both ready to respond to some simple direct instruction from their teachers.

Skillful teachers continually assess the skills and understandings each child has acquired in order to avoid trying to teach something that may be beyond a child's ability to understand. When teaching matches a child's readiness to learn, that child is likely to experience success and develop self-confidence.

Using and Refining What They Have Learned (Utilization)

Once children (or adults) have acquired a new skill, they want to use it. When children apply what has been learned in an authentic context, they refine their new skills and understandings. Because primary grade children are increasingly interested in creating products (Erikson's Stage of Industry), the classroom can be a place where children become productive, purposeful workers, using skills and tools in meaningful ways as they engage in the learning process. The following examples illustrate how children use and refine what they have learned.

- Reading books for pleasure and information involves children in practicing their reading skills. Doing research reports provides children with a focus for reading for information.

- Writing stories, messages, charts, notes, letters, and scripts helps children become competent writers. Publishing stories, collections of poetry, or a class newspaper enables children to feel a sense of accomplishment at creating a written product.

- Working with patterns, shapes, and measuring tools to solve interesting problems helps children become mathematical thinkers. Children utilize mathematical thinking by recording strategies in a math journal, creating graphs, making up games that incorporate skills, or designing LOGO inventions on the computer.

- Collecting specimens, using scientific tools, making observations, and sharing what they've learned all involve children in the work of discovery. When children work like scientists, they have to use the process of scientific inquiry as they go about their work.

- Participating in a classroom community and acting as a responsible member of that community helps children to increase their social awareness and social competence. Applying these skills and knowledge to larger communities by participating in a recycling project or helping to put up a handicap access at school enables children to expand their sense of community responsibility.

- Drawing, painting, and sculpting enable children to refine their artistic skills and to demonstrate concepts learned in other areas. Children demonstrate their learning by setting up art exhibits, or producing a play.

Teachers should be aware that the learning of a child with disabilities may require compensating strategies to "go around" a deficit. Technology, a peer, or a classroom assistant may be helpful. Most children with disabilities learn according to the same developmental stages as other children, but be aware that you may have to teach something in a different way if a deficit prevents a child from participating in certain learning experiences. Sometimes significant growth in a skill area can occur after some specific coaching and instruction has been given.

The more teachers know about the children they teach, the better they can plan experiences that support each child's learning. Because in any classroom children bring diverse experiences, have a wide range of interests, and learn at varying rates, you can assume that their receptivity to learning will also be different across all areas of the curriculum. When learning experiences are interesting and leave room for children's input and interests, children can participate in ways that have personal meaning. In the process, children begin to see themselves as successful and competent learners.

Principles That Guide Teachers in Planning

Teachers constantly make decisions as they plan instruction. Some decisions are made in advance and involve scheduling work times for various subjects or long-range planning for studies; other decisions are made on-the-spot as a "teachable moment" arises in the classroom. Whether the decisions are about teaching a specific skill, a new concept, or introducing a long-term study, you can most effectively guide children's learning if you apply the following four principles in your planning: (1) learning should be purposeful and relevant to children's lives; (2) meaningful learning is integrated; (3) communication is central to learning; and (4) learning takes time.

Learning Should Be Purposeful

Think of a time when someone was trying to teach you how to do something in which you had very little interest. Despite an energetic manner, what the person said probably went in one ear and out the other. In contrast, recall a time when you either wanted or had to know something and you eagerly sought the answer yourself. Perhaps you looked in a book, or struggled with the ideas until finally they made sense. Having a reason and desire to find something out increases our willingness to learn.

Children are more motivated to learn when they are challenged to solve real, interesting problems. When children pursue answers to questions of interest to them and apply their learning to something they care about, they are more likely to remember what they have learned than if they are taught skills out of context. As you think about the new skills and content you want to introduce, look for ways to build on children's interests and help them to see the relevance of what they are learning to everyday life.

Responding to Children's Interests

Children's personal observations and interpretations of an experience can be a marvelous stimulus for introducing new information. A teacher who takes advantage of a child's interests by encouraging further investigation helps that child clearly understand the purpose of the task.

> *After a ferry trip to a nearby island, Sherri, a second grader, asserts the theory that islands float in the water. Some of her classmates agree while others argue that this isn't so. Ms. Kallen asks them how they could find out and the children offer many suggestions. They form groups to test out their ideas. Sherri's group suggests using plasticine and a tub of water to test the theory that islands float. Repeated experiments lead to many sinking balls of plasticine. When finally the ball is big enough to stick out over the top of the water, Jeremiah points to the top and exclaims, "Is this part the island?" Following this, Ms. Kallen sets up other activities for the children to continue their explorations of land forms.*

The teacher could have responded to Sherri's statement by giving her the information that islands do not float. Instead, Ms. Kallen builds on Sherri's curiosity about islands. She encourages exploration that can lead to answering Sherri's question and simultaneously captures the interests of other children. She allowed the children to construct their own understanding by encouraging them to generate and test their theories. It didn't take much encouragement because the children were investigating a topic of genuine interest to them. Because they made their own discoveries and came to their own conclusions, they are likely to retain what they learned.

Teaching Skills in Context

Most children are practical: when they learn something new, they want to use it. When children use newly learned skills in practical ways, they are more likely to remember them.

> *Committed to capturing the excitement he is feeling about a camping trip with his family, eight-year-old Brian makes several revisions to the rough draft of his story before deciding he is ready to "publish" it. In the final editing stages of his writing, Ms. Asche observes that his story contains lots of dialogue. She shows him how to use quotation marks and why they are important. Brian readily uses them because he wants to make his story perfect for publication.*

Skills taught in isolation usually have little meaning for children. Skills taught in context—where children can immediately use what they learn—make sense to learners. When Ms. Asche told Brian that quotation marks help the reader know who is talking, she made the purpose of Brian's learning explicit. Giving a reason to learn a new skill that made sense to Brian motivated him to learn it.

Teachers can use moments such as the one with Brian to present new information to everyone in the class. Brian might share his writing with the class during story sharing, at which time Ms. Asche can point out to the class how Brian incorporated quotation marks into his story to make it clear to the reader who was talking. At first, she may use the term, "talking marks," until she is sure the children understand what a quote is. Using chart paper, she might write a part of Brian's story large enough for the entire class to see. In this way other children can learn from Brian's experience.

Meaningful Learning Is Integrated

Integrated curriculum means planning activities that enable children to gain knowledge and apply skills across many disciplines. Teachers have long recognized that children are more likely to learn and remember new skills and concepts when they use them in a meaningful context. Because children in any classroom are at different stages in the learning process, integrated learning experiences offer a wide range of possibilities so that all children may participate successfully.

An Integrated Approach Reflects Real-Life Experiences

In our everyday lives we do not have experiences that are "math experiences" or "literacy experiences" or "social studies" experiences. We utilize a broad range of knowledge and skills from many disciplines. Shopping in the supermarket is an example of this process: we may select items to buy based on our knowledge of nutrition and good health; determine quantities to buy based on knowledge of weights, measures, and costs; move throughout the store guided by our understanding of categories of organization; and speak with store clerks using our language skills. Shopping is an integrated experience—we use skills and knowledge from many different disciplines to accomplish our goals.

Curriculum is naturally integrated. For example, language and literacy includes speaking, listening, reading, and writing. We teach these skills in an integrated way all the time. Children listen and speak as they discuss stories they have read and math problems they solved. In exploring who works in the community, or investigating the life cycle of a butterfly, children use speaking, listening, reading, and writing skills. Mathematical skills are used to answer science and social studies questions: "How many of the eggs in our incubator will hatch?" or "What are the different jobs in our school and how many people do each job?"

Integrated learning experiences already take place in most classrooms. For example, after reading a story, a teacher may have children draw pictures or make puppets of the characters, create maps of the setting, write about a character, or create a sequel. In each of these choices, children use a range of skills. When curriculum is integrated, children can see connections between the skills they are learning and how to use them.

- To follow a recipe, children realize they have to measure and therefore need a measuring cup and a teaspoon.

- To send a letter to the senior citizen center arranging a visit, children appreciate the importance of writing neatly and using a business letter style.

- To build a model of the city, children measure, consider scale, draw a plan, and research what to include.

Organizing instruction around real topics and problems enables children to make connections, which are a critical part of learning.

Integrated Curriculum Facilitates Planning

Teachers often feel pressured because there is so much to teach and not enough time. Finding ways to integrate curriculum effectively addresses a range of curriculum objectives at once. In thinking about the possibilities for integrating your curriculum, ask yourself some questions.

- Do children use math skills as they work on science or social studies projects? Could they?

- During math and science lessons, do children read, write, and discuss? Could they?

- Are children using dramatics and art to represent their interpretations of literature or what they are discussing in social studies? Could they?

Long-term studies are an effective way to integrate curriculum because a teacher can use them to teach skills, process, and content.

Communication Is Central to Learning

Communication—the exchange of knowledge, ideas, and opinions with others—reinforces children's understanding. As children investigate problems or topics of interest, teachers encourage them to talk about what they are learning. In doing so, children learn to value their own thinking as well as to respect the ideas and opinions of others. Effective communication is an important feature of a learning community.

Talking Clarifies Thinking

When children try to put their ideas into words to explain them to others, they must describe, explain, evaluate, and clarify their own thinking. Informal talking around learning tasks takes place in classrooms all the time.

> *Mei and Ben, two first graders, work together on a math problem. Mei, having just learned to count by tens, makes a suggestion: "Let's make stacks of ten, like this [pointing and counting] so we can count by tens." Because Mei attaches words to her thinking, Ben learns a new strategy for counting.*

A more formal way for children to talk with others takes place in meetings. Group discussions promote the development of critical thinking skills as children express their own thoughts and evaluate the thinking of others. For example, before a work time, several children talk about the model they are going to make. They discuss what size the people will be and therefore how tall the buildings should be, how many buildings to include, the size of doors, and so on. In the process of describing the model and making their building decisions, they organize and clarify their thinking and learn to make decisions as a group. Another example of how teachers encourage children to talk about their work is to call a meeting after a writing time so children can share their stories and ask for the questions and comments of their peers.

Just as children bring their individual learning styles and differences to investigating and representing information, they also bring varied comfort levels and habits of speech. Some children readily speak in discussions while others prefer to listen. Some have learned how to engage in discussions at home while other children may have been taught not to express their opinions or ideas in a public setting. By offering options—working in pairs, small groups, one-on-one conferences, or group meetings—teachers demonstrate respect for children's individual preferences and learn more about what each child knows. Based on their observations, teachers can ask questions and offer information to extend children's thinking.

Open-Ended Questions Extend Thinking

Teachers use questions to find out what children know and to encourage children to reflect on their ideas. Depending on their goal, teachers ask one of two types of questions: closed and open-ended.

Closed questions have only one right answer. They simply tell us whether or not a child knows a fact: "How many sides does a triangle have?" or "What is the main idea of the story?" In closed questions, the teacher knows the answer and the child's response is either right or wrong.

Open-ended questions enable children to respond with many possible answers. Rather than asking how many sides the triangle has (a closed question), a teacher might ask, "What do you notice about this shape?" This way, the teacher will find out whether or not children know the number of sides of a triangle as well as their other thoughts and observations.

You can use open-ended questions and comments to help children:

- *label and organize their thinking*—"Tell me how you estimated the number of jelly beans in the jar," or "What would you like to happen to the character in your story?"

- *describe what they already know*—"What do you already know about the public library in our town?" or, "What do you know about caterpillars?"

- *anticipate and wonder about what they will see or do or what might happen*—"Let's think about what we might see when we visit the telephone company," or "Based on the picture on the cover of this book, what do you predict this story will be about?" or "What will happen to each of these fruits if we slice them and leave them on the windowsill for the weekend?"

- *reflect on an experience*—"What did you see on our visit to the court house?" or, "Tell us about the part of the story that you remember," or "Tell us more about how the machines worked at the bread factory."

- *think about possible ideas or solutions to problems*—"What jobs will we need in our classroom for it to remain clean and orderly?" or "Let's make a list of the ways we can represent a favorite part of the story we just read," or "Tell us how you solved the problem. That's a good approach. Can anyone think of another way?"

By listening to children's responses to open-ended questions and comments you get vital assessment information that helps in planning appropriate next steps. For example, after asking children what they expect to see when they visit the harbor the next day, a teacher realizes from their responses that several children have not visited a harbor before and have no idea what to expect. She decides to read *Harbor* by Donald Crews, to prepare children for the upcoming trip.

Keep in mind that children react differently to different kinds of questions, depending on the experiences with questions they have had previously. Many teachers find that children not familiar with open-ended questions may be hesitant to respond because they wonder what answer the teacher really wants. With experience, these children will become more comfortable as they realize there are no "wrong answers" and the teacher is genuinely interested in their ideas. With open-ended questions, children have room to interpret the question their own way.

Learning Takes Time

Meaningful learning can't be rushed. It doesn't always fit into fifteen- or thirty-minute time slots. Frequently, the necessity of scheduling the day into brief time periods arises from pressures to "cover the curriculum" and manage the schedules of specialists and resource teachers. Many teachers complain about not having enough time and feeling pressured by scheduling demands. Scrambling from one activity to the next increases the level of stress in the classroom for everyone and is not conducive to learning.

Three ways teachers can allocate time for learning are: (1) scheduling extended work times each day so children can become involved in tasks; (2) recognizing the importance of giving children time to revisit concepts that have been taught; and (3) giving children time to think about and play with ideas.

Schedule Extended Work Times

Each day, try to schedule work times of at least 45 minutes to an hour so children get involved in an activity. Once or twice a week, it's beneficial to plan even longer periods for projects such as model making, murals, or working on skits. Combining subjects means you don't lose time making the transition from one work time to another.

This may sound impossible at first, but it can work if you adjust your schedule by rethinking time allocations. For example, if a work time will involve children in exploring more than one subject (e.g., math and science, or language and math), try allotting an hour for one activity rather than 30 minutes for two separate ones.

Children, like all of us, become frustrated when they are busy at work and we expect them to stop and quickly make a transition to the next activity. When you have no choice but to end a work time when the children are engrossed in what they are doing, it helps if you say something like, "I know it's really hard to stop what you are doing when you're so close to finishing. We just don't have a choice today. You can put your things on this tray and get back to work first thing tomorrow morning."

Encourage Children to Revisit Ideas and Concepts

Simply because you have presented a concept or skill to children does not mean that everyone will now understand and be able to use what you have taught. Some children may already know what you introduced; others will have varied levels of understanding. Like adults, children often need time to come back to an idea, to revisit it in other contexts, and to construct their own understanding.

> *During a discussion about birthdays, Ms. Wong talks with the children about their birthdays. Jenny says, "Tomorrow is my half-birthday." Several children ask her what she means. Ms. Wong asks the class if they know why Jenny says it is her "half-birthday." One of the children volunteers that there are 12 months in a year and 6 months in half a year. The children use the calendar to figure out when their*

half-birthdays occur. The following week in the midst of a math activity related to money, Ann-Marie says to Ms. Wong, "I just figured out that my quarter birthday is next week. I'm going to ask my parents to give me a quarter for my quarter birthday." Ms. Wong realizes that Ann-Marie has continued to mull over the discussion from the previous week. She applied what she learned to solve a problem of interest to her that relates to money, time, and fractions.

This example provides insight into the importance of allowing children to stay with topics over time and to revisit them.

Give Children Time to Think

Group discussions highlight children's individual differences. In response to a question or statement, some children will immediately raise their hand, bursting to share their thoughts; other children will ponder the question or the concept presented, trying to assemble their thoughts before raising their hands. The eagerness of their classmates often interferes with their ability to think. As a result, they may lose their own train of thought and therefore the opportunity to contribute to the discussion.

Allowing children time to "think about their thinking" is a teaching technique that addresses children's individual learning styles and makes it possible for all children to participate equally. Here are some ways to provide children with thinking time.

- After posing a question during a discussion, say "Take a minute to think of an idea. Don't say anything yet. Close your eyes and just think."

- Before inviting children to share their ideas in the group, invite them to share with a neighbor. "Turn to the person next to you and talk about what you are thinking."

- Model your own ways of taking time to think before talking. "That's an interesting question. Give me a minute to think about it. I have lots of ideas and I need to sort them out."

- Prior to sending children off to work after a meeting, check to see if anyone needs more time or help. If so, encourage those children to stay for a minute or two, to talk with each other or with you, until they are ready to get to work.

When you model the importance of slowing down to think, you reinforce the value of careful thought as part of the learning process.

In this section we have discussed the importance of making learning purposeful, integrating the curriculum, fostering communication, and providing ample time for learning. These four principles can be applied to planning learning experiences that enable children to construct their own knowledge.

Ways Children Construct Understanding

For learning to be meaningful for children, they have to be given time and materials to construct ways to understand knowledge so they can make sense of their experiences. To do this, teachers plan experiences that allow children to investigate a problem, represent their thinking, and reflect on what they are learning.

Active Investigations

Learning experiences that enable children to question, explore, and research respond to how children naturally learn. Investigation allows children to see, hear, touch, smell, and therefore extract personal meaning from their experiences.

Investigation experiences can take many forms. Children investigate when they:

pose questions	explore problems using computers
explore materials	study pictures, maps
conduct interviews	form hypotheses
have discussions	create experiments
observe objects/events	take trips
watch videos, slides	listen to speakers, tapes
read books, articles, diaries	

Not all children participate in investigations in the same way and with the same enthusiasm. Depending on their individual styles, some may eagerly ask questions and rush to gather information. Other children may be more watchful, carefully taking things in before getting involved. Teachers who offer a range of investigation experiences allow for these differences. As children participate in investigation activities, teachers can observe their responses and learn more about the children's individual learning styles.

The examples you will find in the content chapters of *Building the Primary Classroom* emphasize engaging children in investigations. Active investigation can take place as part of a scheduled work time in any subject or in the context of a study.

Active Investigation During a Work Time

In planning a work time, think about ways children can investigate a topic. Open-ended tasks have many possible outcomes as opposed to lessons limited to a single objective. Open-ended tasks increase the chances that all children will learn something and be able to contribute.

In the two examples that follow, teachers use geoboards so that children can explore concepts in geometry. However, there is a difference in the kind of investigation each teacher promotes.

Ms. Parker, a second grade teacher, shows the children how to construct triangles and squares using rubber bands and a geoboard. Then she has the children practice making triangles and squares of different sizes on their geoboards following the instructions she has written on task sheets.

Ms. Hernandez introduces geoboards and rubber bands to her second grade class. They discuss the attributes of the materials and how to use them carefully. She assigns the following: "Work with a partner to see how many shapes you can make and how many different ways you can construct them. Keep a record of the shapes you make in your math log."

In the first classroom, Ms. Parker has a clear sense of her objectives and expectations for the children. The structure of the lesson allows little room for free exploration and discovery. The children who understand and follow her directions exactly will succeed, while others may be confused. Children who already have knowledge of simple shapes may get bored quickly and ask, "What should we do now?"

Ms. Hernandez encourages the children to be active investigators. She, too, has clear objectives, which include recognition of shapes. However, the way she has organized the lesson encourages children to learn different things, depending on what they already know and what they learn from their investigations. Children can continue their investigations, inventing their own next steps. She builds the possibility of surprises into her lesson structure. She observes what each child takes from the experience so that she can plan additional challenges or extra support. Ms. Parker's lesson might be more appropriate as a follow-up to an open-ended investigation for a small group of children whom she observed needed some direct instruction.

Active Investigation in a Study

Making active investigation a central part of learning content and acquiring skills means that teachers encourage children to wonder about something, to generate their own questions, and to seek the answers. The two teachers in the following examples take different approaches to a social studies project.

Ms. Jones' third grade class studies immigration using their social studies textbook as the primary source of information. The chapter they read describes the reasons people leave their homelands to move to a new place. The children answer questions at the end of the chapter. Ms. Jones suggests that the children draw pictures of something they remember from the chapter.

Ms. Parks approaches the study of immigration with her third graders by first reading Letters from Rivka *by Karen Hesse, a story about a family who leaves their homeland. The children tell and write personal stories about moving to a new house, going to a different school, and moving to a new city, state, or country. Ms. Parks asks the children to think about people they know who are "experts" on the subject of moving from a birthplace. The children decide to interview people in the community, including family members, who immigrated to the United States. They form small groups to plan interview questions.*

Children in the classroom described in the second example are actively investigating the topic of immigration. Ms. Parks allows ample time for the study. She structures the experience by:

- sparking children's curiosity;
- encouraging children to think about what they already know; and
- getting them to generate questions that will guide the investigation.

Ms. Parks involves children in research so that they can extract personal meaning from their experiences.

The process of investigation can encourage children to be active and purposeful as they seek answers to interesting questions. When given opportunities to represent new information and ideas, children begin to internalize what they learn.

Representing Ideas

When we learn something new and then describe it in our own words, draw a picture of it, or act it out, we solidify our understanding of the concept. Offering children a variety of ways to represent their learning contributes to the effectiveness of guiding children's learning. As children investigate and make discoveries, they process new information and relate it to what they already know. When children represent their ideas in drawings, constructions, writing, or clay models, they internalize the information.

Vehicles for children to represent their learning include:

drawings	puppets	writing (stories, letters, journals)
constructions	murals	diagrams or charts
skits or plays	graphs	dioramas
songs	dances	clay models
models	mobiles	

In the previous example with geoboards, Ms. Hernandez suggests that the children use the rubber bands to construct shapes on the geoboard and then record what they make in their math logs. She recognizes that by having the children record or represent their work, they can learn the symbolic representations of the shapes and the shapes' attributes as well as the differences between shapes.

Children grasp complex concepts and gain new understanding by representing newly acquired information.

> *Following a trip on the commuter train, first graders construct a model that includes the two train stations, the tracks, the bridge they traveled over, and the train. The construction of the model engages them in learning how trains can go in two directions on one set of tracks, how the bridge is constructed, and how the train cars connect.*

Encouraging children to record and represent what they are learning gives teachers another source of information about each child's thinking. These insights help teachers ask appropriate questions, give clarifying information, and guide children's thinking to a higher level.

Allowing for Differences in Interests and Learning Styles

Because children have different ways of expressing and representing their learning, it is essential to offer a range of possibilities for children to represent their ideas. Some children may be more comfortable writing while others more readily express their thinking through artwork. Similarly, children personalize the meaning they get from experiences. When offered choices about what to describe and how to do it, children often surprise us with what they have learned and the aspects of a topic that interest them most.

> *In studying bridges, Delante expresses his understanding of the function of bridges by building with blocks. Cynthia achieves a similar understanding by painting a picture in which two cars move across a bridge while a boat passes underneath it.*
>
> *After a trip to the science museum, Roger writes about seeing the diorama of underground life, describing in detail the roots, worms, and different colors of soil. Eli is enchanted with the architecture of the museum and uses Lego® blocks to reconstruct the arches and ramps of the main lobby.*

The first two children have different ways of revealing what they understand about bridges. The second two children have extracted different meaning from similar experiences.

Children are the best source of ideas about ways to represent what they are learning. Asking them in a group discussion how to proceed puts children in charge of their learning. You might ask, "How can we show what we saw at the museum?" or, "How can we record our observations of the chameleons?" or "How can we show our interpretations of the story we just read?" If children have choices about how they want to show what they have experienced, they will have more of an investment in their work than if they are told what to do.

Reflecting on Learning

An important but often overlooked part of the learning process is reflection—stepping back and thinking about what has been learned and evaluating the process itself. Children become thoughtful learners when they are encouraged to ask themselves questions.

- What did I learn?
- What do I know now that I didn't know before?
- What questions do I have?
- Am I confused? About what?
- What do I think of the work I've just done? Is there something more I want to do? Do I like it? Was it hard? Why?

Allowing time for reflection doesn't come naturally to many teachers, particularly at first. However, once you make it a part of learning experiences, either after a work time or as part of a study, it will be easier to see how to include it as an ongoing part of classroom life.

Reflection After a Work Time

In the section on investigation, we provided an example of a geoboard lesson in Ms. Hernandez's classroom (page 167). In that example, reflection could be included in the following way.

After the children complete the activity, Ms. Hernandez has them come to the meeting area to share their work. Using their math logs for reference, and drawing on chart paper, the children take turns describing the discoveries they have made. At the end of the meeting, Ms. Hernandez asks the children to think about the discussion, look over their work in their math logs, and then write down something they have learned or understood in a new way.

Reflection as Part of a Study

Recall the example, described in the section on representation on page 169, of the class that took a trip on the commuter train. The teacher encourages reflection at several stages during the study.

After the children return from the trip, the teacher asks them to think about what they saw. As a group, they share memories and information, which the teacher records on a chart. She helps them plan their model by asking them to think about what they need to include in it. While the children build, they continually reflect on what they saw and grapple with concepts—how the trains fit on the tracks, how the tracks form curves, how the bridge is constructed. Throughout the building process, the teacher listens to what children say and do. She asks questions to help them reflect on their learning. When the model is completed, the teacher photographs it with the six builders standing next to it. She has each child write about the experience of building the model, which she attaches to a photocopy of the photograph. These reflections and representations of the work are excellent examples of children's learning for their portfolios.

When children reflect on their learning they become aware of what they have learned and how they learned it. Including time for reflection helps children become self-directed learners.

Putting It All Together: Organizing Your Curriculum

How can you put all these ideas and principles together in an organized way? We have talked about how children learn, and proposed four principles that guide teachers in planning curriculum: learning should be purposeful; meaningful learning is integrated; communication is central to learning; and learning takes time. We suggested that to help children construct knowledge, teachers provide experiences that allow children to investigate actively, represent, and reflect on their learning. The missing element is how teachers apply these principles as well as what they know about child development and individual children in order to meet curriculum guidelines and standards. Teachers need a plan.

In planning your instruction—how you will address the content and skills for all subjects—you will probably rely on one or more resources. They may include:

- the curriculum guides of your school district;
- textbooks that outline the goals for learning in each discipline;
- assessment tools that outline what children can be expected to understand and learn at a given age;
- local, state, or national standards; or
- resource books (such as those listed at the end of each chapter in Part Two).

These resources can help you think about reasonable expectations for children's learning at a given stage. They can provide some direction for planning what you will introduce to the children during the year. When and how you will address the curriculum content is organized in three ways.

Many teachers find that planning long-term studies first is a good way to organize instruction. Studies integrate many different subjects and allow children to acquire skills and content as they explore a topic for an extended time. Second, teachers schedule daily work times. Work times often begin with a mini-lesson followed by time for children to explore a topic or practice a skill in one or more subjects. Finally, recognizing that learning occurs all day long, teachers use *teachable moments* to address various components of their curriculum.

Planning Long-Term Studies

Long-term studies enable teachers to guide children's learning of skills, content, and processes across various subject areas in the primary grades. Studies can make instructional planning efficient and more interesting for teachers and children. Instead of striving to explore a wide range of topics during the year, a few well-selected studies allow children to uncover and explore aspects of the topic that are beneath the surface. Within any broad topic, children can explore many smaller topics.

The content for a long-term study often comes from the social studies and science curriculum. These content areas provide appropriate topics for studies because they address real people, places, objects, and events that children can investigate first-hand. For example, a second grade class in a rural community studies how foods are grown and/or raised in their community. Their research includes in-depth investigations of an apple orchard and a dairy farm. In the process of their study, children explore questions that address both social studies and science concepts.

- What jobs do people do at each of these places?
- How do apple orchards and dairy farms affect our community?
- How do these foods get transported to stores?
- How do apples grow and change?
- What is the life cycle of cows?
- How is fruit preserved?
- How is milk pasteurized?

During a study, teachers encourage children to develop questions, theories, and explanations. They conduct research, try out their ideas, and evaluate them. As children learn more about the topic, they are able to revise their theories. They begin to see themselves as competent learners and budding "experts."

The Length of a Study

The length of a study depends on the age and interest level of children as well as the scope of the topic. A teacher may plan a month-long study, but in the process of investigation, children come up with a slightly new direction, so the study goes on longer. On the other hand, sometimes a study is initially intended to last for several months, but for whatever reason, the topic doesn't click and so it is best to end it sooner.

This approach has advantages for teachers and children. When children explore a topic over time, they can gain a broader understanding of the world around them. Studying a few topics in depth also enables teachers to address objectives in all curriculum subjects within an interesting context. The more time allocated to explore a topic, the more likely that teachers learn along with the children. And when children work together to become experts about a topic, it strengthens the sense of community within the classroom.

A Sample Study That Integrates Curriculum

The following example illustrates how one teacher, Mr. Phillips, plans a long-term study that permits enough flexibility to accomplish many areas of study outlined in the school's standards for social studies (e.g., people, work, geographical relationships), science (e.g., water, machines, pollution), math (e.g., measuring, graphing, patterns, geometry, problem solving), literacy (e.g., reading, writing, researching, speaking, listening), technology (e.g., use resources to collect information, exchange information, use writing and/or drawing tools, create products), and the fine arts (visual arts, music, dramatics). Mr. Phillips allows children to explore their own interests within the structure of this study. He creates a broad plan for the study that includes several trips. Class meetings are used for discussions and planning sessions with the children, thus supporting the goal of building a classroom community.

As you read the example, note the variety of investigation, representation, and reflection experiences. Think about how you might adapt a study like this to the neighborhood in which you work.

Mr. Phillips' class of first and second graders is doing a study of their city, a capital located on a coastline with a large harbor. He divides the study into three parts: the harbor, factories, and public buildings.

He begins the study with a trip to the harbor, a place where people work and spend leisure time. He talks with the children about the trip by posing open-ended questions in a meeting to find out what children already know and what questions they have about the harbor. They generate a list of questions they want to answer on the trip.

Mr. Phillips assigns the children to research groups. Each group will investigate specific aspects of the harbor. The children have some choice in selecting the focus for their group project. He gives each child a "trip board" made from a sturdy piece of cardboard with paper stapled to it so the children can record what they see. They can choose to sketch or write about points of interest to them.

During the study, children take additional trips and interview people who work at various jobs at the harbor. They represent their findings in many ways:

building with blocks   *making milk carton constructions*

drawing and painting   *reading and writing stories about harbors*

making graphs   *engaging in continual discussions*

creating skits   *making a map of the harbor area on the computer*

Throughout their work on these projects, Mr. Phillips uses open-ended questions to engage the children in critical thinking and problem solving.

"Why would people want to build factories close to water?"

"Why would our city be selected the capital of our state?"

"What problems might result from having so much industry along the waterfront?"

The children regularly share their thinking with one another and also with other children in the school. The research skills they develop during the first part of the study are used again as they move through the study of factories and other public buildings in the city. The children make maps of the places they visit. During the study of factories, they learn about machines, creating some of their own.

By continuing the study over an extended period of time, children are able to ask questions, come up with explanations, and revise their thinking based on new information. The study described in this example draws on the children's immediate environment. They study a harbor because a harbor is in their city. They study the public buildings in their community as a way to think about community workers and city government.

Once the children become experts about their immediate surroundings, they can begin to think about life in other places. What if they didn't have a harbor? How would their city be different? What are harbors like in faraway cities? Literature, videos, and computer resources can extend children's thinking about differences and similarities between their lives and the lives of other people in other places.

Steps for Planning Studies

A good study takes both advance and ongoing planning. The teacher provides the overall framework for a study and gives some thought to the content, experiences, and materials needed. Once a study is underway, the teacher involves children in the planning process by asking them what they already know about a topic and what they want to find out.

As you read the following ten steps for planning a study, think about how they apply to a topic that would be of interest to you and the children you teach. Consider the environment right around your school and what's available for children to see and investigate.

1. Select an Appropriate Topic

As stated earlier, the science and social studies curricula are excellent sources for long-term studies. The topics children can explore in these subjects relate to the physical, natural, and social world and address questions such as:

- why things are the way they are;
- how events happen;
- how and why people live as they do;
- how things work;
- who performs a certain job and how; and
- how things change.

Studies related to self, families, and the community can provide rich content for social studies. Science topics can be drawn from natural and physical phenomena immediately observable in the children's environment. This allows children to engage in investigation, representation, and reflection on topics that they already know something about.

For example, if the second grade science curriculum in your school calls for a study of water, habitats, and living things, ask yourself, "What nearby body of water can children observe and study over time?" If there is a lake close by, then organize all three of these topics around the study of a lake. If there is a stream or pond, then make this the focus for learning about your required topics. If there isn't a body of water close by, begin with habitats of living things that children can observe. Then think about how to set up a water environment for snails, fish, or hermit crabs in your classroom.

Guidelines for Determining Suitable Topics

- The topic permits children to think, question, and solve problems as they investigate.
- The topic allows me to teach the required objectives of my school's curriculum.
- The skills and knowledge that children acquire from studying the topic can be applied to future living and learning.
- The topic is real, relevant to children's experiences, and is age-appropriate. The topic begins with phenomena that children can observe directly.
- Resources and materials related to the topic are readily available. They might include people to talk to, places to visit, books to read, and artifacts to examine.
- A wide variety of skills can be applied to the topic.
- The topic can be explored in various ways over an extended period of time.

---

2. Brainstorm Ideas About the Content of the Study

Once you have selected a topic that meets the criteria above, take time to brainstorm the possibilities the topic offers. Ways to begin brainstorming a study include talking with colleagues, making lists, webs, or calendar plans. Looking at books and web sites on the subject or taking a field trip by yourself may spark more ideas. If you can interest a colleague in collaborating with you, the planning and implementation will be easier to manage and more enjoyable.

Some teachers find it useful to begin with a web to map the possibilities for a topic. As they learn more, they add to the web. The web on the next page shows how Mr. Phillips organizes his thinking about the harbor, one topic in his class's year-long study. By making this web, he generates a range of possibilities for the study and extends his own thinking. The children will not actually investigate all of the concepts.

3. Become Familiar with the Subject

Brainstorming gives you a sense of the directions the topic might take. You may decide that you have to learn more about the subject. This might involve taking preliminary trips, locating books and materials, and talking to people. Exploring the topic on your own helps you anticipate children's interests and questions. It enables you to plan how to guide children toward their own discoveries by organizing investigation experiences.

Imagine that you selected machines as the topic. You have visited several factories in your community where workers use different types and sizes of machines. Now you have to decide where to take the children. Should all of the children see all of the machines? Can you arrange small group trips? Which places can best help children answer their questions? You can answer such questions most effectively after you have familiarized yourself with the subject.

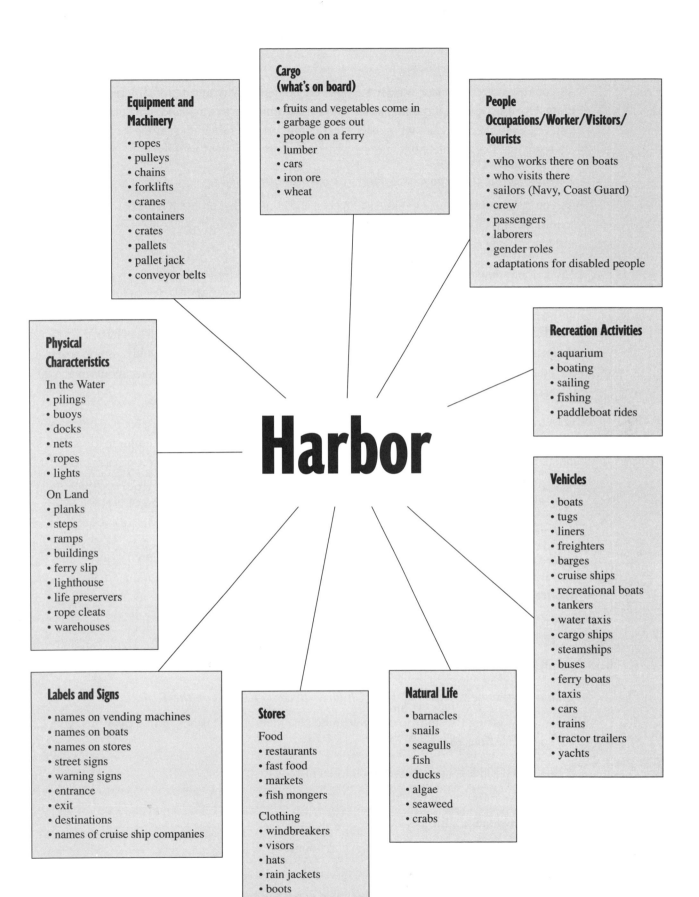

Cargo
(what's on board)

- fruits and vegetables come in
- garbage goes out
- people on a ferry
- lumber
- cars
- iron ore
- wheat

Equipment and Machinery

- ropes
- pulleys
- chains
- forklifts
- cranes
- containers
- crates
- pallets
- pallet jack
- conveyor belts

People Occupations/Worker/Visitors/ Tourists

- who works there on boats
- who visits there
- sailors (Navy, Coast Guard)
- crew
- passengers
- laborers
- gender roles
- adaptations for disabled people

Physical Characteristics

In the Water
- pilings
- buoys
- docks
- nets
- ropes
- lights

On Land
- planks
- steps
- ramps
- buildings
- ferry slip
- lighthouse
- life preservers
- rope cleats
- warehouses

Harbor

Recreation Activities

- aquarium
- boating
- sailing
- fishing
- paddleboat rides

Vehicles

- boats
- tugs
- liners
- freighters
- barges
- cruise ships
- recreational boats
- tankers
- water taxis
- cargo ships
- steamships
- buses
- ferry boats
- taxis
- cars
- trains
- tractor trailers
- yachts

Labels and Signs

- names on vending machines
- names on boats
- names on stores
- street signs
- warning signs
- entrance
- exit
- destinations
- names of cruise ship companies

Stores

Food
- restaurants
- fast food
- markets
- fish mongers

Clothing
- windbreakers
- visors
- hats
- rain jackets
- boots

Natural Life

- barnacles
- snails
- seagulls
- fish
- ducks
- algae
- seaweed
- crabs

As you research the topic, consider the open-ended questions you can ask children during the study. Open-ended questions and statements enable children to think and wonder about a subject. For example, a teacher who visits a textile mill prior to taking the class on a trip might say to them, "Let's think about reasons why the factory is located on a river."

4. Think About How You Can Address Curriculum Objectives

As you review the long list of skills, concepts, and content that children are expected to acquire during their year in your classroom, it is helpful if you can assemble it in an organized and logical way.

Think about how the topic you selected can address a broad range of curriculum objectives. If your district or state has specific standards or benchmarks, see which ones can be addressed through the study. The web of the harbor gave you a sense of the many directions a study could take. Focus on the directions that relate well to other learning areas. The Harbor Study chart (on the following page) shows the range of possibilities. During the study, as you work with the children and incorporate their ideas, you will make specific decisions about time, materials, and different ways to explore the topic.

With the list of ideas for a harbor study, Mr. Phillips can prioritize activities. He can begin to find books to read aloud as well as books with a range of difficulty for the children to read independently. He can ask other teachers for ideas about books, songs, and computer programs; he can collect tape recordings of songs, look for jigsaw puzzles about sea animals, and think about the materials, books, and supplies he wants to organize for classroom resources.

5. Begin Collecting Materials Related to the Topic

Gather pictures, books, and artifacts to stimulate discussions and elicit children's questions. Children's individual interests and learning styles will lead them to different materials, so try to offer a variety of choices.

Children, as well as their families, may contribute materials relevant to the topic. When you establish a partnership with families and keep them informed about classroom life, you will greatly expand the resources available for your study.

6. Plan Experiences That Will Help Children Become Experts on the Topic

Before introducing the study to children, anticipate their questions and draft a plan. Ask yourself some questions to prepare.

- What kinds of questions will children have at first?
- What information will help them ask in-depth questions?
- Can we take a trip?
- Can we invite an expert into the classroom?
- How can children represent the information they are learning?

Review the goals and objectives of your curriculum for all subjects. Think about the activities and experiences you can plan so children will develop and practice skills across a variety of

Harbor Study

Social Studies	• Location of the harbor • Different kinds of work/jobs • Goods that meet people's needs • Unloading and transporting cargo • Rules for harbor use—quarantines, dumping, safety	• Different kinds of cargo ships • The harbor today and in the past • Skills and tools used • Issues related to the environment—transportation, housing • Area around harbor—mapping
Science	• Sea gulls, snails, barnacles, fish • Cycle of the moon • Boats • Sounds of the harbor • Machines, ramps, pulleys	• Water, currents, tides, pollution • Why objects sink, float • Inventions • Water • Concept of leverage
Math	• Notice patterns, textures • Classify boat sizes • Depth of water • Number of workers • Recognize shapes • Things that float, sink • Graph types of people, cargo, boats	• Describe boats • Count things around the harbor • Amounts of cargo • Length of boats • Notice symmetry, water reflections • Nautical time—24 clock hours • Make predictions about cargo
Language and Literacy	• Poetry to read aloud • Letters home from a long trip • Journals, diaries about life at sea • Spelling words • Vocabulary words • Interviews of workers	• Books: read aloud, picture, non-fiction, fiction • Read and write advertisements around harbor • Poems about sounds, smells of the harbor • Research projects about workers, machinery • Research skills needed to get information • Letters to companies for more information
Technology	• Use computer for data collection, statistics, writing, and research • Pulleys, simple technology • Design machines	• Building small boats that float • Navigational instruments like depth sounders, radios, and latitude and longitude
Arts	• Water colors of harbor • Fish prints • Songs about the sea • Perform a play about going to the sea	• Act out observations • Mural scene of harbor • Skits on different harbor scenes/workers

domains. For example, after reviewing your math curriculum, consider whether children's investigations can involve measuring, recording patterns, and preparing graphs. Can you fit these experiences into the study in a logical way?

During the study, children share their knowledge and raise new issues they want to explore. You may find that scheduling an additional trip or inviting a local expert to visit the class can respond to the growing interests of children. In order to involve children in continually evaluating their learning, teachers have to remain flexible in their thinking and planning.

7. Introduce the Study to Children

Introduce studies by finding out what children already know and what they want to learn. You can inspire children's curiosity by putting a few hints around the room: books, a chart, a question, a few interesting pictures. In an introductory meeting, ask children if they noticed something new in the room that might indicate what the next study will be. Then ask some questions.

> *"What do you know about [the topic]?"*
> *"What do you want to find out?"*
> *"How can we find answers to these questions?"*

When you record children's ideas on a chart you validate the knowledge and experience they bring to the study. If they have misinformation, you may say something like, "That's interesting. We may find more information about that. Let's put a question mark next to it to remind us that we want to know more about it." Although you may teach the same topic for several consecutive years, each group of children will have their own unique set of questions that interest them.

Very often children need time to think about their questions. Give them time to talk with peers or ask them to write down questions for homework. Encourage them to talk with family members about the topic, too.

Invite children to contribute materials related to a study. Suggest that they get books from the public library or bring in books, pictures, or other artifacts they may have at home that are related to the study.

8. Invite Families to Participate in the Study

Parents and relatives can be wonderful helpers and resources. Family members can participate in trips, talk with the class about their work, assist with projects, or share a special skill.

Sending home brief newsletters or notes describing the study and inviting participation keeps family members up-to-date on classroom activities. Throughout the study children can involve family members by bringing home surveys, interview questions, opinion polls, or work they have created in class.

9. Listen to and Learn with Children

Throughout the study, pay close attention to what children say and how they respond. Observe and record children's comments and questions. Note the level of their involvement with projects, their successes, and their confusions. Think about the amount of time you allot to activities. Finally, pay attention to the level of children's enthusiasm for the study, as well as your own.

Allow time in the study to help children reflect on their learning. Refer to the questions they raised at the beginning of the study. Identify those that have been answered and those that merit further investigation.

Include children's representations—dioramas, models, writing, drawings, paintings, graphs, or photographs of their work—in their portfolios. Encourage children to evaluate their learning regularly.

Documenting the activities of the study along the way can be invaluable for future planning. Take notes about what you might do differently next time. Keeping a journal or log in which you record books read, trips taken, and people contacted will enable you to repeat the study with another class with greater ease.

10. Think About Concluding the Study

Some investigative studies last for a month and some for several months. The length of time depends on the nature of the study, the age of the children involved, and the level of interest the children exhibit.

Marking the end of a study with an exhibit of the children's work, a play, a class book, or a breakfast with parents provides closure to a study. A culminating event unites all the parts of the study, enables children to see how much they have learned, and promotes children's growing awareness of how much they learned together.

These steps can serve as a beginning guide for planning studies. Remember that it is not possible to teach everything through a long-term study. Many times, material that must be taught does not fit into the study. You can plan work times to focus on particular skills or content using the principles and processes presented earlier in this chapter.

Scheduling Work Times

Scheduling work times each day enables teachers to address specific content or skills related to one or more subjects. Most teachers schedule times for math, small group reading, independent or silent reading, reading aloud, writing, and sometimes an open choice time when many different activities can take place. Work times will vary depending upon whether you introduce something new or continue a previous investigation.

Introducing Concepts or Skills

In order to pursue certain activities related to a study, children may need to be introduced to particular skills that have not yet been taught. Thus, a study can help you think about what new concepts or skills to address during work times. For example, in his study about the harbor, Mr. Phillips considers that children will see many kinds of vehicles and that collecting data about various types can lead to making graphs. He may plan a work time in which to introduce graphing as a way of organizing and comparing collected data.

Teachers often begin a work time with a brief lesson. At a meeting, the teacher introduces a new skill or a concept that the children will explore in small groups immediately afterwards. Here are some examples of topics for brief lessons.

- Talk about a spelling rule (e.g., how to add "ing" to words).

- Introduce the concept of paragraphs before a writing time.

- Demonstrate a technique for using a piece of science equipment prior to an activity.

- Teach a strategy for counting or measuring that children will use in solving a problem.

Once children begin working, the teacher may assist a group with a specific reading strategy or reinforce a math skill. If it's a silent reading time, the teacher might listen to individual children read aloud or may talk with children about their reading. Using work times to address curriculum objectives allows teachers to reinforce skills or teach a specific lesson to a small group or to one child. Children who have acquired the skill or concept don't have to listen to a whole class lesson on something they already know.

For children with a diagnosed disability, tasks and skills may need to be carefully analyzed and broken down into sequential steps. It is very important, as it is for all children, to identify the child's most effective modes of learning and to teach to the child's strengths. For example, one child may need visual cues to get information, another may need extra time and several practice sessions to master a skill.

Addressing Multiple Objectives in a Work Time

When children engage in active investigations, teachers can address multiple objectives within one subject or across subjects. The whole class may be involved in the same subject, but the teacher's objectives for different children vary. For example, during a writing work time, some children might compose letters, some edit a story, while others talk to the teacher about what makes an effective story ending. The teacher has considered what each child knows and has identified different objectives and activities based on individual needs.

The following example of a work time shows how a lesson on using the dictionary can address multiple objectives within one subject area—language and literacy. The teacher structures an activity to allow children to actively investigate, represent, and reflect on what they learn.

> *Ms. Richards wants to introduce dictionary use to her third grade class. She observes that the few children who have attempted to use a dictionary ignored the guide words at the top of the page. She constructs a lesson that involves children in learning more about the dictionary and how to use guide words. She reviews the skills from her third grade benchmarks that could be addressed in an investigation about dictionary use, including:*

> *alphabetical order*   *using the dictionary as a resource*
>
> *syllabication*   *guide and entry words*
>
> *spelling rules*   *suffixes*
>
> *vocabulary words*

To begin the lesson, Ms. Richards brings a large dictionary to the class meeting. She poses several open-ended questions and statements, allowing time for children to respond to each one and share their knowledge.

"Let's think about how this book is used."

"What do you know about dictionaries?"

"When have you used a dictionary?"

"Let's consider some ways dictionaries can help you."

Ms. Richards records the children's ideas on a chart. Following the meeting, the children work in teams of three or four as "dictionary detectives." Each group has its own dictionary. She gives the following directions.

"Study the book. Record what you observe about how the book is organized, and what it has inside it. Notice as many details as you can. Pick one person on your team to record your observations and your questions on paper. Later we'll share what each team learns."

As they examine the book, the children record the items they find interesting. Working in small groups, each child has a chance to discuss something and to share information. Ms. Richards moves around the room, listening to and observing the children at work. She asks open-ended questions to find out what they are learning and to extend their thinking. At the end of the work period, they report their findings in a class meeting. This allows Ms. Richards to further assess each child's learning and gives the children an opportunity to learn from each other.

Following this exploration time, the teacher incorporates dictionary use as part of everyday life in the classroom. She places one in the meeting area and suggests that children take turns looking up unfamiliar words they find during discussions and stories. She plans other investigations during work times to focus on particular aspects of dictionary use: she sends the children on a dictionary scavenger hunt for four-syllable words, and asks the children to see if they can discover rules for how words are divided.

Ms. Richards could have taught a lesson on guide words by demonstrating their location using a dictionary, and asking the children to complete a practice worksheet of duplicated pages from a dictionary. Instead, she presents the task in a meaningful context, structures it so children investigate the topic and record what they learn, and allows time for them to talk about and reflect on their discoveries.

> **Questions to Consider in Planning Work Times**
>
> - Keeping the key objective(s) in mind, what investigation task can children do that requires them to explore, experiment, collect data, or gather information?
> - What other skills/concepts might children use/acquire (within and across subjects/disciplines)? In what ways can I extend the task to foster the use of these skills/concepts?
> - How can children interact with one another most effectively in this task? As a full group? In pairs? In small groups?
> - In what ways can the task be constructed so that children invent and design their own strategies for gathering information?
> - How can children record and represent their process of thinking and their work?
> - How can children reflect on their work?
> - How can I encourage children to talk with others to organize and clarify their thinking?
> - How can children apply what they learn to real-life or simulated situations?

By asking yourself these questions as you review your objectives for children's learning, you may begin to see natural connections within and across disciplines. Carefully structuring work times will allow children to explore extensively, think deeply about ideas, invent solutions, and record what they have learned. These experiences help children become successful life long learners who can think, solve problems, and work independently or collaboratively with others.

Using Teachable Moments

Children learn all the time; not everything that happens in the classroom is planned. The whole day is full of opportunities to teach because there is always something happening, whether it's serious investigations, telling jokes, playing a game, or transitioning to another part of the day. Here are some examples.

- After having a conference with a child who uses dialogue in a story, a teacher writes part of the child's story on a chart and uses it to teach the class about quotation marks.

- In the process of cutting oranges for a snack, a teacher conducts a mini-lesson on fractions.

- In reading the morning message, "We will share stories after lunch. . . ," one child points out that the word "stories" is missing a *y*. The teacher uses this observation to teach the spelling rule about changing the *y* to *i* and adding *es*.

- While reading a story to the class, a teacher points out how the illustrator used borders. Later that day, several children use this technique in illustrating their stories.

- A child brings in baseball scores from the newspaper and the teacher suggests making a class graph.
- When a child makes a clothespin person and it's bigger than the door in her diorama, the teacher conducts a lesson on scale.

Teachers can use *teachable moments* effectively if they keep in mind the various components of each subject and observe skillfully. We teach some of our most successful lessons on the spur of the moment, or as a follow-up to a child's question or need.

Closing Thoughts

Teachers are constantly making decisions about instruction. Sound decisions are based on knowledge of how purposeful learning occurs. Teachers guide children's learning by designing classroom experiences that are integrated and allow children to construct knowledge by actively investigating, by representing their understandings, and by reflecting on what they have learned. By observing and listening to children, teachers modify instructional experiences to respond to individual children's needs and interests. When children learn by doing, the process of assessing learning takes on broader and richer dimensions.

References and Resources for Guiding Children's Learning

American Association for the Advancement of Science. 1993. *Benchmarks for Science Literacy, Project 2061*. New York: Oxford University Press.

Bredekamp, Sue, and Teresa Rosegrant, eds. 1992. *Reaching Potentials: Appropriate Curriculum and Assessment for Young Children*. Vol. 1. Washington, DC: NAEYC.

Bredekemp, Sue, and Teresa Rosegrant, eds. 1995. *Reaching Potentials: Transforming Early Childhood Curriculum and Assessment*. Vol. 2. Washington, DC: NAEYC.

Carnegie Task Force on Learning in the Primary Grades. 1996. *Years of Promise: A Comprehensive Learning Strategy for America's Children*. New York: Carnegie Cooperation of New York, xvii.

Chard, Sylvia C. 1998. *The Project Approach: Making Curriculum Come Alive*. Books 1 and 2. New York: Scholastic, Inc.

Gamberg, Ruth, et al. 1988. *Learning and Loving It: Theme Studies in the Classroom*. Portsmouth, NH: Heinemann.

Greenspan, Stanley I. 1993. *Playground Politics: Understanding the Emotional Life of Your School-Age Child*. Reading, MA: Addison-Wesley Publishing.

Katz, Lilian G., and Sylvia C. Chard. 1989. *Engaging Children's Minds: The Project Approach*. Norwood, NJ: Ablex Publishing.

Los Angeles Unified School District (LAUSD), Division of Special Education. 1990. *Special Needs Supplement to The Creative Curriculum for Early Childhood*. Los Angeles, CA: LAUSD.

McCracken, Janet B. 1993. *Valuing Diversity: The Primary Years*. Washington, DC: NAEYC.

Ramsey, Patricia G. 1987. *Teaching and Learning in a Diverse World: Multicultural Education for Young Children*. New York: Teachers College Press.

Short, Kathy G., and Carolyn Burke. 1991. *Creating Curriculum: Teachers and Students as a Community of Learners*. Portsmouth, NH: Heinemann.

Smilansky, Sara, and Leah Shefatya. 1990. *Facilitating Play: A Medium for Promoting Cognitive, Socio-Emotional and Academic Development in Young Children*. Gaithersburg, MD: Psychosocial and Educational Publications.

Wasserman, Selma. 1990. *Serious Players in the Primary Classroom: Empowering Children through Active Learning Experiences*. New York: Teachers College Press.

Werner, Emmy. 1990. How Children Become Resilient: Observations and Cautions. In *Resiliency in Action*. Edited by Nan Henderson, Bonnie Benard, and Nancy Sharp-Light. Gorham, ME: Resiliency in Action, Inc.

Wolk, Steven. 1998. *A Democratic Classroom*. Portsmouth, NH: Heinemann.

ASSESSING CHILDREN'S LEARNING

ssessment is the process of gathering information about children in order to make decisions about guiding their learning. Teachers obtain useful information about children's knowledge, skills, and progress by observing, documenting, and reviewing children's work over time. Ongoing assessment that occurs during classroom activities can provide an accurate, fair, and representative picture of children's learning and progress. To get a well-rounded picture of each child's growth and development, the materials used for assessment must be comprehensive.

> The root of the word evaluation is "value," and authentic assessment includes understanding what students value and then building from there. Authentic assessment is inside-out rather than outside-in. It is an attempt to get away from sorting a mass of students and closer to the teacher's question: Given what I know now, how should I teach this particular student (Ayers 1993, 113)?

Assessment is the fifth teaching strategy. When teachers devote time to observing children carefully and have a method for collecting information on children's development and learning, they can plan effective instruction so that every child experiences success. This chapter discusses the different purposes of assessment, explains classroom-based assessment and standardized tests, and describes how assessment can support instruction. It focuses on methods of assessment that inform instruction and describes specific approaches for assessing children's progress.

Understanding Assessment

Assessment includes the tools and processes used to answer questions. Assessment is comprised of two processes: documentation and evaluation. The first process, documentation, means gathering data. The second, evaluation, is comparison to a standard. There are several purposes and types of assessment. To determine the type that is most appropriate, it is essential to know the purpose and how the results will be used (Hills 1992).

Purposes of Assessment

Two critical and interrelated purposes of assessment are to guide instruction and keep track of children's achievement. Observing and documenting children's work in the classroom is one way to obtain this information. Traditionally, schools have relied more on paper and pencil methods of assessment—graded worksheets, end-of-unit tests found in textbooks, or standardized tests.

A third purpose of assessment is to identify children with special needs who may require additional educational services or interventions. Observations of the child, input from family members, and the use of screening instruments and diagnostic tests are appropriate for this purpose. Developmental screening instruments identify children who may be at risk for school failure. Screening instruments do not identify the nature of a problem, but rather, indicate whether it is necessary to seek additional information. Diagnostic tests are designed to confirm the presence and extent of a disability.

Finally, assessment is used for program accountability and evaluation. Assessments designed for this purpose attempt to determine whether educational programs achieve their goals. For administrators, program accountability is often judged by children's performance on standardized tests. Later in the chapter we address some of the concerns associated with standardized tests.

For teachers, the primary purpose of assessment is answering questions about children's knowledge and skills in order to understand and plan for strengths and needs. In addition, teachers want to be sure that their program is effective. Classroom-based assessment is the best way for teachers to learn about their students and determine program effectiveness.

Classroom-Based Assessment

Appropriate classroom-based assessment provides teachers with information they can use to shape instruction to meet the strengths and needs of each child. One type of classroom-based assessment is performance assessment. Performance assessment involves assessing children as they work each day—writing stories, making maps, solving math problems, and creating paintings. Sometimes performance assessments are conducted in test-like settings. Authentic assessment is a type of performance assessment that occurs as part of actual classroom experiences.

Teachers assess learning daily by observing what children do and say, reviewing their work to determine strengths and weaknesses, and keeping track of progress made over time. To assess children accurately and fairly in the classroom, assessment procedures should be aligned with curriculum, ongoing, in context, and comprehensive.

Assessment Is Aligned with Curriculum

Assessment should be aligned with curriculum that is based on reasonable and age-appropriate expectations for children. What teachers assess should reflect what they teach.

Today, curriculum in many schools is based on standards designed at a local, state, or national level. Unfortunately, the quality of standards varies greatly from place to place and the application of standards is often misguided. For example, in an effort to ensure that children know certain material by the end of third grade, first and second grade teachers may be pressured to teach material to children before they are ready to learn it or in ways that are not responsive to how children learn.

Standards are written in many different ways. Sometimes they state broad goals such as "Students will use the reading process effectively." Other times, they specifically state the knowledge and skills students should master. Kendall and Marzano (1997) refer to the former as curriculum standards and the latter as content standards.

How standards are written can affect their usefulness regarding assessment. For example, a curriculum standard such as "Students will use the reading process effectively" is an exemplary goal but does not provide teachers with information that helps with assessment. It would be more helpful to have greater specificity such as "Students can read text and identify the main idea and supporting ideas."

Teachers can use two techniques to help them apply standards effectively. One is to discuss them with colleagues in order to understand and interpret what they mean. Together they can generate meaningful learning opportunities that promote children's learning specifically toward the standard. Another technique is to translate them into age- or grade-appropriate content and examples. For example, many standards are written in terms of grade clusters such as kindergarten through third grade. It is useful to think about what should be taught at each grade so that by the end of third grade children will achieve the standard. This involves reflecting carefully about the steps along the way to the third grade standard.

Although standards are designed to provide consistent expectations for all children, instruction has to be tailored to children's individual strengths and needs.

Assessment Is Ongoing

Ongoing assessment guides instruction. Teachers begin assessing children's learning and development at the outset of the year so that they understand what children already know, their interests, strengths, and approach to learning. They also gain insights into the child's needs. The knowledge teachers acquire from early assessment serves as the basis for shaping instruction. As they observe children at work, they modify learning experiences to meet the individual needs of their children.

Teachers share assessment information with children so that the children know how they are doing and can trace their own progress. An assessment strategy that is ongoing and involves children in monitoring their own performance is the use of rubrics.

A rubric is defined as a scoring tool that lists the criteria for a piece of work and describes gradations of quality for each criterion, from excellent to poor (Goodrich 1997). Rubrics can help teachers and children have a clear and shared understanding of quality work and expectations for performance.

Assessment Is in Context

Current thinking about assessment emphasizes finding out what children know and can do, rather than what children do not know. This positive approach promotes children's sense of competence and provides teachers with clues about what and how to teach. Watching children work in a familiar setting is more likely to give an accurate picture of what they know than assessing them in a contrived or unfamiliar setting.

For example, asking a child to solve a math problem using subtraction on a paper and pencil test may not show whether or not the child has problem-solving skills or can use the operation of subtraction to solve a problem. Perhaps the child doesn't feel well, had a bad morning, or doesn't understand the meaning of the problem. In contrast, observing him each day as he solves many different types of problems alone and with others enables his teacher to find out what he understands about subtraction, problem solving, as well as other mathematical ideas.

Assessing children in familiar settings provides more reliable information than tests, which give only a single snapshot of children's abilities (Meisels 1993). Ongoing assessment in the context of daily classroom life allows children to reveal their knowledge, skills, and abilities in many different situations and over the course of time.

Assessment Is Comprehensive

Comprehensiveness refers to both the range of information teachers have and the types of data collected. To get a fair and accurate picture of each child's growth and development— a picture of the whole child—teachers assess children's social, emotional, cognitive, and physical development.

Too often, when children move into the first grade, assessment focuses primarily on the cognitive area. However, children's success in school is dependent on all four areas of development. For example, a first grader's success as a writer is tied to his fine motor skills. A third grader's success working collaboratively with a team of four other children on a math problem depends on both social and cognitive skills. Teachers need information about children's strengths and weaknesses in all areas to inform their decision making and guide their instruction.

Moreover, it is important to collect information on all subject areas within the domain of cognitive development. Collecting samples of work in only a few subject areas (e.g., children's writing or their work in math) does not provide a full picture of what the child has learned. Children who are talented artists or strong scientific thinkers may not have documentation of their special strengths if only written work is collected.

Comprehensive assessment also means that teachers collect many different kinds of data and use a variety of approaches.

> Assessment utilizes an array of tools and a variety of processes, including, but not limited to, collections of representative work by children (artwork, stories they write, tape recordings of their reading), records of systematic observations of teachers, records of conversations and interviews with children, and teachers' summaries of children's progress as individuals and as groups (Bredekamp and Rosegrant 1992, 10).

Systematic observation of children as they go about classroom tasks gives teachers information about how children think, what they know, what they are confused about, and how they approach learning tasks. Reviewing samples of children's work reveals the quality of children's thinking and learning. Comparing children's work over time enables teachers to evaluate progress. Summarizing the collected data gives teachers a way of sharing information with parents. Appropriate assessment that is aligned with curriculum, ongoing, in context, and comprehensive both supports instruction and enriches curriculum planning.

Standardized Tests

A standardized test is one administered under controlled conditions. There are many kinds of standardized tests used for different purposes. Some are administered to students individually, sometimes to determine the presence and degree of disability. Most of us are familiar with tests that are given to a group of children at the same time and designed to provide information about student achievement. Standardized tests can be norm-referenced or criterion-referenced. Norm-referenced means that children's performance is compared with the performance of other children. Criterion-referenced means that performance is compared to a fixed standard or criteria for measurement. Although there are many problems associated with standardized tests, they are a reality in most primary grade classrooms. Thus, it is necessary to have a plan for how to prepare children to handle them successfully.

Understanding Problems

Many standardized tests are problematic because they raise issues of fairness, they have a narrowing effect on the curriculum, and the consequences associated with them make them "high stakes" (Meisels 1992, 1993; Sheppard 1989).

When children take norm-referenced, group administered, multiple choice, objectively scored tests, two issues of fairness arise. First, the experiences of the children taking the test are often very different from the experiences of the children on whom the test has been "normed." Children from diverse backgrounds often interpret questions and express their knowledge differently. Second, experts have raised concerns as to whether or not group administered achievement tests are, in fact, "standardized" tests. Research has demonstrated that such tests often are not administered under standard conditions. Teachers provide children with unequal amounts of preparation time and different verbal cues to help them perform successfully.

Standardized tests often dictate and narrow the curriculum. In an effort to ensure that children perform well on tests, teachers may stop teaching meaningful material and resort to teaching only those basic skills likely to appear on a multiple choice test. Multiple choice tests cannot measure some of the most important goals and objectives of the primary curriculum, such as critical thinking, self-confidence, problem solving, and cultural awareness and pride. In some parts of the country, new performance-based standardized tests are being used. They are intended to also measure thinking and problem-solving skills. Although the purpose and design of these tests is more appropriate, the pressure for children to do well still sometimes results in inappropriate curriculum practices.

Finally, standardized tests are often used for "high stakes" purposes, such as to make important decisions about student promotion and retention, teacher salary increases, or the allocation of resources to schools. The pressure to perform well on the tests creates stress on teachers and children. The high-stakes consequences of these tests often lead to negative feelings and lost confidence on the part of both the test giver and the test taker.

Recognizing Realities and Preparing Children

Despite the problems, standardized tests are usually a given in the primary grades. For this reason, it is essential to ensure that what you teach meshes with (but is not limited to) the curriculum goals evaluated by the tests and that you provide opportunities for children to gain familiarity and practice with the tests.

Become familiar with the tests and think about when they are given in relation to the outline of your curriculum. Consider this example from a third grade classroom.

> *Ms. Kidd, a third grade teacher, knows from last year that the statewide math test she will administer to her students in January will include questions about fractions. Her curriculum plan doesn't address fractions until the spring. She decides to adjust the plan so that children will have some experience with fractions in the fall and then revisit the topic again later in the year. She plans several activities that enable the children to solve meaningful problems using fractions: dividing into teams, making pizza, solving word problems. Knowing that she wants to build children's comfort level with the concept of fractions, she makes notes to herself to incorporate discussion of fractional parts into future math projects related to measurement, patterns, and geometry. In addition, she develops a few practice worksheets with test-like questions to help children get comfortable with the test language and format.*

How Assessment Supports Instruction

Most primary teachers have a state or local curriculum they are expected to teach. How they teach the content—the specific instructional methods used—and when they teach certain elements—the timetable for the year—are shaped by the individual teacher. Assessment guides the decisions teachers make about instructional methods and timing. The foundation for good teaching is knowing the children you teach. The more information teachers have about what each child knows, the more effectively they can plan instruction that builds on children's strengths and addresses individual learning needs. Effective assessment provides this information and helps to promote children's success as learners by involving them in the assessment process. When assessment is tied closely to curriculum and instruction, the information teachers and children collect and share with families offers an in-depth portrait of what the child is learning in school and how the child is progressing.

Using Assessment to Plan Instruction

Assessment is a critical first step in planning instruction. If the assessment approach you use is compatible with the goals and objectives of your curriculum, then information obtained from assessment helps you know what to teach, when children are ready to learn particular skills and concepts, and how to structure learning experiences.

Assessment at the beginning of the year provides preliminary information about each child. Ongoing assessment enables you to determine how children are growing and developing and when to modify instruction to meet individual needs.

Assessment at the Beginning of the Year

The assessment teachers do at the outset of the year helps them know children, develop relationships with them, and use the knowledge and relationships to guide instruction. Assessment early in the year provides answers to questions such as these.

- What skills do children already have?
- What are children ready to learn?
- What are the interests, experiences, and learning styles of this group of children?
- What are the special strengths and needs of each child in this class?

The first four to six weeks of school can be viewed as a time to get to know each child well. Conversations with children, family members, and the child's former teachers can help you learn about each child's special strengths and talents.

Assessment at the beginning of the year provides baseline information and later helps you evaluate children's progress. Having appropriate and realistic expectations about what each child can do helps teachers craft successful learning experiences. Recognizing that uneven development is normal and expected also allows teachers to assess children fairly.

How Ongoing Assessment Informs Instruction

Teachers observe how certain children respond to particular learning tasks and use that information to structure new experiences. Sometimes teachers plan an activity thinking that children already have had certain experiences and understandings. Once into the activity, they realize their assumption was wrong.

> *Mr. Johnson's third graders are learning to solve problems with two- and three-digit numbers using estimation and counting strategies. He places a jar filled with buttons on a table and suspends a clothesline with clothespins across the blackboard. On the left he places the numeral "0" and on the right the numeral "500." The morning message tells the children to estimate the number of buttons in the jar, write their estimates on a card, and hang the card along the number line in numerical order. Mr. Johnson assumes that the children understand the concept of numerical order—greater than and less than—because they have worked on it before. However, as several children begin hanging numbers incorrectly (e.g., 230 after 320) he senses that he has to make some adjustments in his lesson plan. First, he decides to postpone the next step of having children count the buttons in the jar. Instead he will have the children work in their groups to review the number line and identify places where numbers are out of order. Each group is encouraged to offer an explanation of why a number is out of order and where it belongs. Later, they will resume the estimation activity.*

By observing children during the activity, this teacher realized that some children were not secure in their understanding of the content. The "scaffold" he had set up required too big a leap for them. He had to modify his plan. By having them work in small groups on reasoning and proof, he provided a way for everyone to participate with more competent peers supporting others along the way. In addition, careful observation enabled him to identify who was still confused about numerical order so that he could plan a small group lesson to teach this skill.

Individualizing Instruction

Individualizing instruction means making modifications in method of presentation, content, and timing so that each child can continue to make progress on the learning continuum. Observation in a variety of situations often leads to ideas for individualizing.

> *Because Jeremy, a third grader, struggles as a reader, he dislikes quiet reading time each day. Other than relying on picture cues, he has very few strategies for getting meaning from print. During a choice time Ms. Keats observes him looking at a baseball magazine. She notices that he studies each picture carefully and tries to read the captions beneath the picture, pointing to each word with his finger and mouthing the sounds quietly. The next day she brings in a biography about Jim Abbott, the baseball player, by Greg Lee. Although she senses that the text will be challenging for him, she suspects that the content will sustain his interest so that she can continue to work with him on acquiring reading strategies.*

Observing children in a variety of settings gives teachers many occasions to look for children's strengths. A child who isn't able to demonstrate knowledge in one situation may do so easily under different circumstances.

> *The class is studying the night sky. Following a trip to the planetarium, Janine barely writes one sentence during a writing assignment. Ms. Bernard wonders if Janine learned anything from the trip. The next day during a work time, she suggests that Janine draw a picture of the constellations exhibited at the show the day before. By looking at the details in Janine's picture, Ms. Bernard discovers that, in fact, she learned quite a bit during the trip but needed another way to demonstrate her knowledge.*

Individualizing means paying attention to children's learning differences, rates of learning, cultural influences, and fluency with English. During the course of the year, you may find that you are having difficulty meeting the needs of certain children. If attempts at alternate teaching strategies are not effective, it may be helpful to talk with parents, consult the previous year's teacher, or obtain the advice of a specialist. For a child with a diagnosed disability, refer to the child's Individual Education Plan (IEP), which outlines specific goals for instruction.

Promoting Children's Success as Learners

Parents and educators become concerned when children lack motivation and do not seem involved in their work. Involving children in assessment can take many forms and enhance motivation and achievement as well as strengths associated with resiliency.

Independence and *insight* are fostered in a classroom where children participate in developing standards for their work and receive feedback. Working hard and mastering something new is often frustrating for children. Success requires *independence*, the ability to distance oneself from difficult feelings. How often we hear children say, "But I didn't know that neatness (or handwriting or length) counted!" Teachers can prevent such excuse-making by discussing the characteristics of a good project from the outset. When children see models of excellent work and are given the chance to participate in establishing standards, they know how their efforts will be evaluated and are more easily able to overcome frustration.

Constructive feedback helps children to consider the quality of their work, think about what has been learned, and understand how they performed in relation to expectations. As their *insight* develops, children can begin to evaluate their own work, guided by teachers who ask, "What was easy (or difficult) for you?" or "What might you do differently next time?" (Bickart and Wolin 1997). Children's investment in their learning and the quality of their work increases when teachers involve them in setting personal goals and evaluating their own progress.

Helping Children Set Goals

Children want to know the expectations and standards their teachers and parents have for them, how they are being evaluated, and how they are doing. Encouraging children to set their own goals helps them become self-directed learners. By modeling the language and process of setting and striving for personal goals, teachers foster self-directed learning.

Goal-setting activities occur throughout the year in different ways. At the beginning of the year, teachers can help children think about questions such as these.

- Which of my skills improved last year?
- What can I do very well? What are my personal strengths?
- Which skills can I improve?
- What is one thing I really want to work on this year?
- What do I hope to learn this year?

When teachers pose such questions, children become involved in self-assessment. By recording their thoughts and goals in a journal, children can return to them later in the year and reflect on their progress. This also gives children an opportunity to re-examine their goals and set new ones.

Consider these opportunities for children to set personal goals.

- Before beginning a long-term study, encourage children to write in their journals in response to the question, "What do I really want to learn during this study?"

- Before editing a story, ask a child: "What editing skill do you want to work on? What do you want to get better at as a result of editing this story?"

- At the outset of a week, ask a child, "What do you want to work on this week?"

- Before a field trip, have children respond to the question: "What do you hope to see and find out?"

- To focus positive attention on a difficult time, ask a child, "How would you like to act during this activity (e.g., in the lunchroom, at recess, during music or physical education) and what will help you to be successful?"

Using Rubrics with Children

Rubrics are intended to help teachers and children have a clear and shared understanding of quality work and expectations for performance. One reason children lack motivation is that they don't know the criteria being used to evaluate their work.

Classroom rubrics are powerful learning motivators that make explicit goals and expectations and enhance fairness and objectivity in assessment (Guthrie and Wigfield 1997). Consider this example of a rubric from a first grade classroom.

It is early in the school year and Ms. Jones has just read a big book to her first graders during a shared reading lesson. At the conclusion of the story, she gives them an assignment to illustrate their favorite part of the story and then write about the illustration. Before sending them off to work, she says, "Let's take a few minutes to think about your illustrations and writing. If you were going to do a really good job on this assignment, what would you have to do? What would a really good piece of work look like? Let's brainstorm some ideas." Ms. Jones called on several students and recorded their ideas on a chart. As each idea was listed, the class discussed it and determined if they wanted to keep it on the list. They generated and agreed upon a list of 5 ideas.

1. Use lots of color.

2. Include many details in the illustration.

3. Include a background.

4. Be neat.

5. Make sure the words you write match your picture.

Ms. Jones explains that as they work, they should review the list to determine whether or not their work is complete.

The rubric described in the example above is called a *coaching rubric*. Coaching rubrics do just what their name implies. They guide children toward quality work by providing them with a clear understanding of the expectations for performance. This type of rubric allows children to reflect on and evaluate their own work. Currently there is pressure on teachers to promote high standards of achievement. Rubrics can be an effective way to help children have a clear understanding of high standards.

Another type of rubric is called a *scoring rubric*. Like the coaching rubric, it delineates criteria and also describes different degrees of quality. When the rubric is developed as part of establishing the assignment, it serves to inform instruction or coach children. The same rubric is then used by the children and teacher to evaluate or *score* the work. The following example comes from a third grade classroom.

> *Ms. Charles' third graders are reading biographies and autobiographies. This week they will work on writing their own autobiographies during writing workshop and at home for homework. During the mini-lesson prior to writing workshop on Monday, Ms. Charles develops a rubric with them to help each child be successful on the assignment. First, they determine that their autobiographies will include an introduction, a body, and a conclusion. The class has established that they have three levels of performance for their rubrics: minimum, excellent, and exceptional. Next, they brainstorm what would be included in each part in order to meet the expectations for each rating. Because they are working on improving the mechanics of their writing, they add two additional categories: punctuation, capitals, and spelling and complete sentences.*

The chart on the next page illustrates the rubric they developed.

The children rely on the rubric to guide their writing process. They use it to help them develop their stories and when they conference with each other. Ms. Charles has them rate their final product prior to her evaluating their work. When her rating and the child's differ, they have a conference using the rubric and discuss reasonable goals for the next assignment.

Creating rubrics with children supports teachers' efforts to build a community of learners in the classroom. Children enjoy debating criteria and expectations for performance. Many teachers report that when they incorporate rubrics in their classroom, they find that the children are harsher critics than they are. Some teachers present models to children showing examples of each level of the rubric.

Children are motivated to work hard when they are involved in establishing the expectations and when the expectations are clear. Rubrics are one way to help children reflect on and evaluate their work. However, not every assignment or activity lends itself to creating a rubric. Moreover, in addition to evaluating childrens performance, you want to provide opportunities to reflect on what they have learned, their process, and the progress they have made over time.

Autobiography Rubric

Parts of Autobiography	Minimum	Excellent	Exceptional
Introduction	Your name When you were born Family members	Your name When you were born Family members Places you have lived	Your name When you were born Family members Places you have lived A description of yourself

Body	School
	Summer
	Places you have been
	Friends
		School
		Summer
		Places you have been
		Friends
		Details about your
		  family members
		House
		What you do for fun
		What you are good at
		Your pets
			School
			Summer
			Places you have been
			Friends
			Details about your
			  family members
			House
			What you do for fun
			What you are good at
			Your pets
			What you are afraid of
			A special event

Conclusion	The job or career you
	  want
		The job or career you
		  want
		How you want to live
			The job or career you
			  want
			How you want to live
			Details about your
			  dreams for the future

Punctuation, capitals,
  spelling
	two or more mistakes
	  of each
		one spelling mistake
		one punctuation mis-
		  take
			no mistakes

Complete and interest-
  ing sentences
	Subject, verb in each
	  sentence
	At least two descriptive
	  words
		Subject verb in each
		  sentence
		Some compound
		  sentences
		Many descriptive
		  words
			Subject, verb in each
			  sentence
			Some compound
			  sentences
			Descriptive words in
			  each sentence

Reflecting on and Evaluating Their Learning

Children become aware that they have accomplished something—that they know something now that they didn't know before—when teachers provide opportunities for them to think about what they have learned. In the process of reflection, children may observe that they have tried something for the first time. When they review samples of their work over the course of the year and see the progress they have made, they have concrete evidence of their growing competence.

Too often, teachers and children focus on "best work." However, there are many ways to evaluate work besides "best" and "worst." In the beginning, children need help from their teachers about how to reflect on and evaluate their work. Their first and most natural responses are likely to be "I like this" or "I hate this" or "This was so easy." You can guide children to evaluate their work more critically by asking specific questions.

"What do you like best about your drawing?"

"How do you decide if you like a story you write, or a picture you draw?"

"What did you enjoy most about this project?"

"Which math problem was frustrating? Why?"

"What was most difficult for you to do? What was easy to do?"

"Did you try using a new technique in writing your story?"

"What's the hardest part of working in a group?"

The more practice children have in setting goals, discussing, and evaluating their work, the more they take responsibility for their learning. When children are involved in the assessment process, they learn to think critically about their work and take pride in their accomplishments.

Communicating with Families

All families want to know what their children are doing in school and how they are progressing. Although all families do not convey their expectations and dreams in the same way, they all want their children to become competent learners.

When family members attend conferences or receive written reports about children's progress, they have questions.

"How is my child doing?"

"What are you teaching my child?"

"What can I do to help my child?"

Family members appreciate specific examples of children's progress. It is more meaningful to see their child's work than to receive a grade of "B+" or "Satisfactory." Showing actual examples of work collected over time enables parents to personally assess their child's progress: "Oh. She can write sentences now. Earlier this year she could only write single words."

When presenting assessment information to families, it is essential to tell them the "whole story." The whole story means giving answers to two different but related questions.

- Has the child made progress? In other words, given where he or she began the year, has there been growth?

- How does my child's performance compare to expectations for children of the same age or grade level?

If only the first question is answered, families can be left with a misleading impression. For example, during a conference with a family, a teacher might report that a second grader has made great progress with reading. At the beginning of third grade, the new teacher tells the family that the child is reading below grade level. This occurs when teachers report information about progress but omit information about performance. Talking with families about standards, using rubrics in conferences, and differentiating between performance and progress are some ways to avoid this confusion and to ensure that families get the whole story about assessment.

A comprehensive approach to assessment that is tied to your curriculum enables you to share children's performance and progress in a meaningful way. Parents will have a much better picture of the child's learning when they see concrete evidence of the child's work.

How Teachers Assess Children's Learning

Every day teachers talk with children about their work, observe children interacting with others and materials, and study the products children create. Teachers often express frustration that although they continually monitor children's growth and learning informally, they have difficulty knowing what to observe for and how to keep track of what they see. Having a structure for assessment that includes ways to focus observations, document what you see, and organize information helps teachers manage the assessment process.

A framework for assessment or a formal tool can help to ensure that observations are focused and that all areas of a child's development and learning are assessed. Such a framework should outline developmentally appropriate expectations for children and be linked to the goals and objectives of your program. Many schools as well as individual teachers use published assessment instruments. We list a variety of instruments in the resources section of this chapter. Whether you use a commercial assessment instrument or organize your assessment independently, there are several components that should be part of a quality assessment framework:

- observing children and documenting your observations;
- collecting, reviewing, and evaluating children's work; and
- sharing with families.

Observation and Documentation

Observation is the best way to get to know children, the first strategy discussed in this book. Teachers watch children all the time. Some observations are informal while others are focused to determine whether or not a child has acquired specific skills. Together, informal and formal observations of children give teachers a more complete picture of each child.

How does a busy teacher find time to observe all the children in the class and to document these observations? Establishing a routine for observation and documentation makes this process manageable. It's not necessary or possible to observe and record everything that children say and do. Organizing a plan for what and how to observe and record, and then spending a few minutes a day doing so, yields a wealth of valuable information.

Making Observations Part of Daily Classroom Activity

Observation is part of everyday life in the classroom. During work times, when children are engaged in investigation and representation activities, teachers move around the room watching what children do, listening to what they say, and talking with them about the products they create. When children work collaboratively with others, teachers learn about children's thinking by listening to what children say to each other. By asking children questions teachers also gain information about children's thinking.

In the chapter on Guiding Children's Learning, an example of a geoboard lesson (page 167) showed how children use active investigation, representation, and reflection to construct knowledge. Their teacher, Ms. Hernandez, has opportunities to assess individual children in the context of that lesson. She notes what children say in the introductory meeting; their comments about shapes and their attributes give her some ideas about children's prior knowledge and experience. As she moves about the room during the work period, she carries a clipboard with her. On it is a photocopied paper with each child's name on the left-hand margin. At the top of the page she writes the date and next to it, "Shapes and Attributes." Occasionally she jots down a note or two to help her remember what children are doing. Later, she will review the children's math logs and add to her list of notes.

Conferences with children offer another way to observe them. For example, during writing workshop a teacher might have two- or three-minute conferences with children to discuss what they are doing and observe how they are working. These conversations between teacher and child usually provide insights about the child's thinking. Regularly scheduled reading or math conferences enable teachers to gather information and individualize their instruction.

Week of: 10/14	Shapes and Attributes
Amy	explored variety of triangle shapes.
Arona	
Brendan	in mtg. said " two triangles can fit together to make a square."
Brian	
Chris	
Celia	
Denise	made trapezoid - divided it into square + 2 triangles.
Elisha	made triangles of various sizes
Greg	
Gerard	check whether knows diff. between sq/rect
Hector	
Kim	resumed geoboard work at choice times
Leonard	
La Shon	
Nathanial	
Raashon	working w/ blocks - used "square, rectangle, triangle."
Richie	
Rondelle	
Sherise	
Steven J.	created parallelograms - looked in book for name
Steven R.	
Tony	used dot paper to transfer designs to log.
Vanessa	
Zack	

Many teachers find it helpful to inform children that part of a teacher's job is to observe them at work. At a meeting, you might pose the question, "What are some ways I find out what you are learning?" Give children time to think about the question and share their ideas. As children often do, they may surprise you with some thoughts that you did not expect. Explain that one of the ways you learn about them is to observe them carefully. Tell them that sometimes you may want to observe them without being interrupted. For example, you might say, "When I carry my clipboard it means I need a few minutes to observe. Ask someone else if you need help. If it is an emergency, of course you can interrupt me."

And, while observation is a key assessment strategy, it has other benefits as well. Through careful observation, by watching, listening, and talking to children, you discover special qualities about a child. For example, you may find out that the child has a special talent, a favorite relative, or a new computer. Teachers can use this information to show children respect and appreciation, the key components of effective relationship building. When teachers have a good relationship with a child, that child is more likely to be successful in school (Jablon, Dombro, and Dichtelmiller 1999).

The Importance of Documentation

Collecting observations made at various times of the day, over time, and in many situations gives you a great deal of data for reflection. Although one observation may not be typical of a child's skills or behavior, you may get a clue about how to support a child's learning after reviewing written notes from several observations. The documentation you have from ongoing observations helps you to make instructional plans for children and gives you information needed to report to families and complete school reports.

Documenting observations enables you to detect patterns in a child's behavior. For example, by recording the choices children make, whom they choose to work with, the books they select, or the topics they write about, you may discover that certain children are stuck. You can make suggestions to expand their choices and ideas: "You spent each choice time last week building the city with Legos. Today you might want to use the drawing program on the computer to design a model city." Or "You have written several stories about your dog during writing workshop. Would you be interested in reading a book about a dog? I know a chapter book that I think you'll really enjoy."

When teachers take the time to document their observations, they can often detect the source of a problem, devise a plan, and then monitor the plan's effectiveness. The examples that follow show how two teachers were able to pinpoint and appropriately address problems based on their documented observations.

> *Ms. London observes that after meetings, while other children readily start their work, Kim invariably wanders around the room. Noting this same behavior on several occasions, she wonders whether or not Kim understands the directions she gives to the whole group. She decides to have a one-minute conference with Kim at the end of each meeting to help Kim get started on her work. To her surprise, Kim tells Ms. London exactly what is expected of her. In fact, she listens carefully during the meeting. However, it helps Kim to say the words back to Ms. London as a way to get focused on the next task.*

> *Observing that Janet is consistently unable to settle down during morning work time, but does so easily after lunch, leads Mr. Sparks to investigate whether Janet is eating breakfast in the morning. He learns that Janet's bus is often late and that she misses the school breakfast program because she doesn't want to come into the classroom after meeting has started. He arranges to have another child pick up Janet's breakfast and bring it to the classroom. After a few days, there is a noticeable improvement in Janet's ability to settle into her morning work.*

Documented evidence of children's development is important because it is often difficult to remember what a child was or was not able to do earlier in the year. Having recorded observations can be invaluable in cases where a child may need additional support.

Recording Actions Not Impressions

One of the hardest aspects of observing children is documenting their actions and words, rather than our impressions of them. It is normal for our interests, culture, beliefs, and experiences to influence our observations. However, when we observe children for the purpose of assessing them, we need to make every effort to guard against our biases by focusing on actions and avoiding judgments about behavior.

To illustrate the difference between an objective and biased observation, consider these two examples of anecdotal records about Natalya. In each, the anecdote was written while observing the child, and the teacher used abbreviations.

Example 1

March 6; 1:15 p.m.

Natalya is reading on the rug with Cherise. Cherise is trying to concentrate for a change, but N is bugging her. C is reading aloud. N looks down at the book for a second and then starts talking to C again. N is fiddling with C's hair. N seems bored by the story. She is more interested in socializing.

Example 2

March 6; 1:15 p.m.

It is read-with-a-partner time. Natalya is sitting next to Cherise on the rug. C is holding the book. C is reading. N looks down at the book, touches the corner of the page. She puts her hands in her lap. She looks at C. She says something to C (which I can't hear). She touches C's hair for a few seconds, then looks at the book. She says something else. C keeps on reading. N puts her arm around C.

Take a moment to think about your reactions to these two records of the same observation. In Example 1, the teacher's irritation and judgment of Natalya is very apparent. She interprets Natalya's actions as "bugging Cherise." She labels the touching of Cherise's hair as "playing with it." After reading the first anecdote, one would probably conclude that Natalya is misbehaving.

In the second anecdote, we may have several interpretations of the incident. Perhaps Natalya is listening to the story and taking pleasure in Cherise's reading. Or possibly Natalya is unhappy about something and needs the comfort of being close to Cherise.

When only the child's actions are recorded and judgments are omitted, it is possible to consider a variety of explanations for behaviors and to be open to different ways of interpreting a child's motives. Therefore, in recording and observing, try to write down only what you see and hear. Questions and concerns can be documented separately.

Techniques for Recording Observations

It is easy to understand why many teachers say, "I watch my children all of the time and I know what they can do. I just don't have the time to write things down. There's too much else going on in the classroom." Classrooms are busy, hectic places with constant demands for a teacher's attention. Some practical techniques for observing and recording children's work make this task more manageable: creating a system for recording observations, allocating time to document observations, and using a checklist to structure your observations.

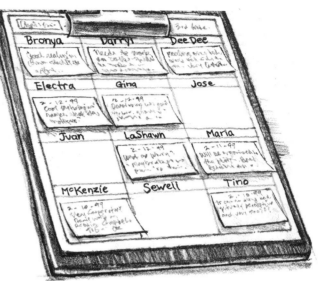

Creating a System for Recording Observations

Different types of records serve different purposes. Systems for recording observations include anecdotal records, running records, and quick classroom notes.

- *Anecdotal records* are descriptive reports of behaviors recorded after the event has occurred. They can provide rich and detailed descriptions of the child's abilities and approach to learning.

- *Running records* are actual accounts of what a child says or does, recorded at the time of the action. When used to observe reading they help teachers analyze specific reading behaviors (Clay 1993).

- *Quick notes on a class list* are made during a busy work time to keep track of what children do. Teachers review these periodically to complete checklists or to write more detailed anecdotes or narratives about a child.

Post-it notes, sticky mailing labels, or index cards are useful for collecting records. Some teachers carry a clipboard with dated class lists on it.

It helps to review periodically the records you collect. Some teachers have a file folder for each child or a section of a looseleaf binder in which they gather all of their notes. This can make it easier to review information prior to conferences or when writing final reports.

Allocating Time to Record Observations

Observing and recording take time. To ensure that these processes happen regularly, identify periods of the day when you can set aside a few minutes for the task. Ideas include:

- 10-15 minutes during a project or work time, 2 or 3 times a week;

- half of each silent reading period, 3 times a week;

- during a time that children share stories after writing workshop;

- during reading and writing conferences;

- 1 or 2 times a week as children arrive in the morning;

- once every two weeks during a special subject class; or

- once a month during P.E. or recess.

Having a realistic schedule helps make the job of observing and documenting systematic and manageable. Some teachers find it helpful to spend twenty minutes immediately after school once a week writing down one thing they have noticed about each child.

Using Checklists

Checklists can provide a structure for observing children by identifying the range of specific skills, knowledge, and behaviors that children may be expected to acquire at particular ages. Many curriculum guides list discrete skills for children to learn within a particular subject area. It is both challenging and limiting to try to piece these together to create a comprehensive checklist.

Useful checklists reflect the development of the whole child by including personal, social, and physical development, as well as all aspects of cognitive development. It is also important that the checklist show a continuum of development because children's growth and development does not proceed at fixed intervals.

Collecting, Reviewing, and Evaluating Children's Work

The work children create each day in the classroom as they investigate, represent, and reflect on their learning provides concrete evidence of what they are learning. Collecting, reviewing, and evaluating children's work on a regular basis is important for three reasons.

- Children are more motivated when they receive specific feedback about their work.

- Studying the products children create helps you learn about how children think, what they know, and what they are ready to learn next.

- Samples of children's work can be organized into a portfolio to create a portrait of the child's growth and progress.

Giving Children Feedback

Feedback is more than evaluation. All teachers—including the best ones—occasionally give children's work a quick glance and write the words "Good Job" at the top of the page. But children need more than that. The type of feedback children receive about their work can significantly affect their attitudes toward their learning. They may say things like, "Well, you didn't say it had to be my best work" or "It doesn't matter if my homework is neat. The teacher doesn't look at it anyway." Constructive and supportive feedback often leads children to a stronger ownership of and commitment to learning.

How, when, and in what form should feedback be given? The answers to these questions depends in large measure on the nature of the work. A story that a child spends several days writing, a model of the neighborhood that a group of children work on for two weeks, or a first attempt at painting a mural deserve a different type and amount of feedback than a series of math problems solved for homework. Children can get feedback on their work by:

- reading a story they wrote and inviting other children to give comments and ask questions at a meeting;

- getting comments from an audience after dramatizing a scene from a book;

- having a conference with the teacher to make a plan for next steps in a story or to review a book report;

- receiving written comments and/or questions on a journal entry, a collaborative social studies project, or on a science observation;

- comparing strategies used to solve a math problem with a peer; or

- discussing their work with a peer using a rubric created by the class.

Sometimes the feedback comes directly from the teacher; at other times children receive feedback from peers as they collaborate on a project. There may be times when more than one type of feedback is appropriate. For example, children may share strategies for solving math problems in a group discussion and get feedback from both the teacher and their peers in the process. However, the teacher may also want to review children's math logs to find out more specifically how they handled the task. In reviewing the work, a teacher may make a comment or pose a specific question that validates the child's work or helps to extend the child's thinking. For example, next to Jason's math journal entry his teacher writes: "Jason, it was a good strategy to group the Unifix cubes by tens before you counted. You got the right answer."

Studying Children's Work

Observing children in the process of creating representations and then reviewing their work informs teachers about children's skills, knowledge, and approach to learning tasks. It helps teachers know what children are ready to learn next.

Different types of representations reveal different aspects of children's thinking and learning.

- José's block building of the hospital shows how well he observed during the class visit to the hospital. His building includes an underground garage, signs showing patients and visitors where to park and how to get to the emergency room, and stretchers to carry the patients through the halls. The building also reveals José's spatial thinking; his construction is symmetrical and includes doors and windows.

- Theresa's story has no clear beginning or end; it is mostly a string of conversations. She uses lots of dialogue but does not know how to include the transitions that show who is talking or how the action got from one place to another. If she could focus more on how to convey who is talking, what leads up to the conversation and how it ends, she will be more aware of the concept of sequence.

- Yana's painting of sea creatures is incredibly detailed. She has included both fish and plants. She obviously remembers a great deal from the fish study earlier this year. She used some books about sea life from the class library to make the creatures look realistic. Her painting reveals that her fine motor skills are well developed and she has learned to mix paints to make a wide variety of colors.

- A third grade class has been collecting information to determine which grade in the school has the most children. Working in teams, they add long columns of two-digit numbers. The teacher uses this activity to assess whether children demonstrate number sense, recognize patterns, and see combinations of ten.

Sometimes teachers observe children's work as they are creating it. They notice aspects of children's learning and take notes. At other times teachers reflect on children's work during a conference with the child. In both of these cases teachers talk with children about their thinking. Studying children's work when the child is not present also gives teachers opportunities to be reflective. They can take time and learn a great deal from the work as they begin to consider appropriate next steps for the child's learning.

Portfolios: Portraits of Children's Growth and Progress

Portfolios are purposeful collections of a child's work. They tell the story of a child: what the child can do, the child's special interests, and how the child thinks and solves problems. A portfolio is not simply a scrapbook or folder of children's work. It is a tool that is organized in such a way that the teacher, the child, and the child's family can learn about the quality of the child's work and observe progress over time.

Because a portfolio is a collection of a child's work that reveals its quality as well as the child's thinking, it should include a range of samples, including some that the child feels were hard, easy, enjoyable, frustrating, and successful. Examples of work in a child's portfolio might include the following:

- samples of writing (e.g., stories, poetry, journal entries, reports, letters, signs for projects, scripts for puppet shows);

- examples of solutions to mathematical problems (e.g., diagrams with written descriptions, photographs with narratives, drawing and writing, pages from a math journal, charts or graphs);

- documentation of science observations (e.g., stages in the transformation of a caterpillar to a butterfly, findings from a study of shadows);

- drawings, paintings, collages, or photographs of three-dimensional constructions; or

- photographs of a project (e.g., skits, models, presentations) with written narrative.

Portfolios can be a valuable assessment tool when they are organized according to a plan. While some teachers collect samples of children's work only in math and writing, others strive to create a comprehensive portrait of the whole child by including work samples across all aspects of the curriculum. When you structure portfolio collecting so that similar types of work samples are collected at intervals during the year, you will observe growth and change in children's thinking and skills. There are many excellent resources available to help you learn how to incorporate portfolio collection into your classroom. Several are listed at the end of this chapter. A few important logistical techniques to help you get started are: determine methods for work collection, review, and evaluation; schedule time for children to review their work; provide storage for portfolios; and be sure to send work home periodically.

Methods for Work Collection, Review, and Evaluation

The process of collecting, reviewing, selecting, and storing work in portfolios is only manageable if you have a well-organized system. Teachers cannot do this alone; children must be involved. Teachers do the initial planning and then engage children in discussion to get their ideas as well.

Establish a Place to Collect and Date Work

A place to collect work that may eventually be placed in the portfolio is essential. Some teachers have collection bins with a section for each child's work. Children should have easy access to collection bins so they can place work in the folder regularly.

In order to use collected work for assessment purposes, each item should be dated. You can help children get in the habit of dating work by making date stamps available in the classroom.

Schedule Time for Children to Review Their Work

To provide children with feedback and encourage them to reflect on their work, teachers must allocate time in the schedule. Some teachers like to do this at the end of the week and allot 45 minutes every Friday for a work review period. One way to introduce a work review session is to invite children to talk about the projects and activities they have been doing as a class. As children begin to go through their collections of work, you might suggest they sort items into categories: *easy* and *hard*.

During the work review time, you can move about and conduct individual conferences with children as they select the work they want to save for their portfolios. Older children can write comments on their work to explain the reasons for their selection. Creating a comment sheet that children can attach to each sample of work helps to focus children's thinking. They can answer questions such as these.

- What was the assignment?
- Why did I select it?
- Did I work alone or with others?
- What did I learn from doing this work?

Provide Storage for Portfolios

The portfolio itself can be an accordion folder, a large sheet of construction paper folded and stapled, or pocket folders. Some teachers find it beneficial to divide the portfolio into sections according to subject areas. The portfolio can be stored in milk crates or in a filing cabinet. Unlike the collection bins, children do not need to have daily access to their portfolios.

Send Work Home

When children review work at the end of the week, they can take home the work that is not being saved for portfolios. Having an organized method for children to take work home helps family members feel connected to the child's life at school. When primary grade children take work home every day, it often arrives crumpled in a back-pack and families never get to see it. Saving it in the classroom and then sending it home in a folder often helps children take pride in their work because they see it is valued.

Sharing Assessment Information with Families

When families have a clear understanding of what their children are learning and what the expectations are for performance, the job of presenting assessment information becomes easier. Keep families up to date on curriculum and instruction by sending newsletters home regularly that describe topics and activities going on in the classroom. Be sure that families understand your expectations for children's performance. Sharing rubrics with families is one way to provide them with concrete information about what you expect.

When teachers have conducted observations in an ongoing way and collected samples of children's work over time, they have extensive assessment information to share with families or others who need to know about children's learning. Reviewing the notes collected about a child and examples of the child's work helps you to think carefully about your work with children. What do you know about the child? What are the child's primary interests? Strengths? Weaknesses? Who are the child's friends? What materials does the child particularly like to use? What part of the long-term study interested the child most? Reflecting on individual children also influences how you think about your own work as a teacher. Have you provided each child with sufficient challenges and opportunities for success? Are there children with whom you are having trouble connecting? What other ways might you try to reach the child? What information might you try to obtain from the family?

Many teachers find it useful to have conferences with children prior to writing reports and having conferences with families. They encourage children to reflect on the goals they have set for themselves, review work together, and discuss progress. Children describe ways they feel they have grown and what new goals they have. Teachers explain the information they will be sharing with families so that children are not surprised by what their family members hear.

More and more teachers are including children in their conferences with families. It is an excellent way to encourage family members to attend and it helps children develop a sense of responsibility for their school work. During the conference children can use the work in the portfolio as the basis for discussing strengths, areas of concern, progress, and goals.

Written Reports to Families

Most, if not all, school systems send written reports home to families. In some instances the written report accompanies the conference. In others, a written report is sent home three or four times during the year. Written reporting methods differ from one district or school to the next.

Some school districts are moving away from using grades to report the growth and learning of young children. Letter grades and ratings such as "Very Good," "Satisfactory," "Unsatisfactory," or "Needs Improvement" do not provide sufficient information for families about children's growth and progress.

If you are tied to a reporting system that requires you to use summarizing words that you feel are not supportive of children's growth and development, or the categories that you have to rate do not reflect the goals, objectives, and instructional techniques you are using, consider writing an addendum to the report form, offering parents a brief explanation of terms. For example, if one of the categories on the report card for first graders is "Spelling" it might be helpful to clarify your expectations for children's spelling.

Because we want first graders to become confident writers, we encourage them to use what they know about letters and sounds to spell a word the way it sounds. We call this sound or invented spelling. This helps children be independent as writers and helps us see how their knowledge of phonics is put to use. Gradually children's spelling progresses to look more like conventional spelling.

Or for "Science" you might write something like this.

During the last two months we have been studying insects. The study has helped children learn to observe, write about what they are seeing, and make predictions about living things. Children have learned about different kinds of insects, the body parts of insects, and how and where insects live.

In addition to sending home copies of this addendum, you can add a specific comment about the child's progress. For example, "Larry worked particularly hard on his model of a cricket. The details on his model show what good observation skills he has acquired."

Whatever system of reporting you use the information you have to share with families will be broad and detailed if you have been observing children carefully and documenting your observations, as well as collecting, reviewing, and evaluating children's work during the course of the year.

Closing Thoughts

Knowing children well is the first strategy for effective teaching. Assessment helps you learn about children—who they are and how they learn best. Assessing children over time and in the midst of daily classroom activities gives you information about children's interests, strengths, and areas of concern. You apply this valuable information each day by tailoring instruction to support each child's continued growth and learning. Involving children in assessment promotes self-reflection and increased motivation. A comprehensive approach to assessment enables you to share children's performance and progress with families so that they can work with you to ensure their child's success in school.

References and Resources for Assessing Children's Learning

Almy, Millie, and Celia Genishi. 1979. *Ways of Studying Children.* New York: Teachers College Press.

Ayers, William. 1993. *To Teach: The Journey of a Teacher.* New York: Teachers College Press.

Beaty, Janice. 1990. *Observing the Development of the Young Child.* 2nd ed. New York: Macmillan Publishing Company.

Bickart, Toni, and Sybil Wolin. November 1997. Practicing Resilience in the Elementary Classroom. *Principal* 77 (2): 21–24.

Bredekamp, Sue, and Teresa Rosegrant, eds. 1992. *Reaching Potentials: Appropriate Curriculum and Assessment for Young Children.* Vol. 1. Washington, DC: NAEYC.

Bridges, Lois. 1995. *Assessment: Continuous Learning.* York, ME: Stenhouse Publishers.

Clay, M.M. 1993. *An Observation Survey of Early Literacy Achievement.* Portsmouth, NH: Heinemann.

Genishi, Celia. 1992. *Ways of Assessing Children and Curriculum: Stories of Early Childhood Practice.* New York: Teachers College Press.

Goodrich, Heidi. December/January 1997. Understanding Rubrics. *Educational Leadership.* 54 (4): 14–17.

Guthrie, J. T., and A. Wigfield. 1997. Reading Engagement: A Rationale for Theory and Teaching. In *Reading Engagement: Motivating Reading through Integrated Instruction.* Edited by J. T. Guthrie and A. Wigfield. Newark, DE: International Reading Association, 1–12.

Hanson, Jane. 1998. *When Learners Evaluate.* Portsmouth, NH: Heinemann.

Herman, Joan, Pamela R. Aschbacher, and Lynn Winters. 1992. *A Practical Guide to Alternative Assessment.* Alexandria, VA: ASCD.

Hills, Tynette W. 1992. Reaching Potentials through Appropriate Assessment. In *Reaching Potentials: Appropriate Curriculum and Assessment for Young Children.* Vol. 1. Edited by Sue Bredekamp and Teresa Rosegrant. Washington, DC: NAEYC, 43–63.

Jablon, Judy R., Amy Laura Dombro, and Margo L. Dichtelmiller. 1999. *The Power of Observation.* Washington, DC: Teaching Strategies, Inc.

Jablon, Judy R., Margo L. Dichtelmiller, Dorothea B. Marsden, Lauren A. Ashley and Samuel J. Meisels. 2001. *The Work Sampling System Omnibus Guidelines: Kindergarten through Fifth Grade.* 4th ed. Ann Arbor, MI: Rebus, Inc.

Johnston, Peter H. 1997. *Knowing Literacy: Constructive Literacy Assessment.* York, ME: Stenhouse Publishers.

Kendall, John S., and Robert J. Marzano. 1997. *Content Knowledge: A Compendium of Standards and Benchmarks for K-12 Education.* 2nd ed. Aurora, CO: McRel and Alexandria, VA: ASCD, 20.

McAfee, Oralee, and Deborah Leong. 1994. *Assessing and Guiding Young Children's Development and Learning*. Des Moines, IA: Allyn and Bacon.

Meisels, Samuel. 1993. Doing Harm by Doing Good: Iatrogenic Effects of Early Childhood Enrollment and Promotion Policies. *Early Childhood Research Quarterly* 7:155–174.

Meisels, Samuel. 1993. Remaking Classroom Assessment with the Work Sampling System. *Young Children* 48:34–40.

Schipper, Beth, and Joanne Rossi. 1997. *Portfolios in the Classroom: Tools for Learning and Instruction*. York, ME: Stenhouse Publishers.

Sheppard, Lorrie A. April 1989. Why We Need Better Assessments. *Educational Leadership* 46 (7): 4–9.

Shores, Elizabeth, and Cathy Grace. 1998. *The Portfolio Book*. Beltsville, MD: Gryphon House.

6

BUILDING A PARTNERSHIP WITH FAMILIES

amilies and educators share the same goals: to help children become successful learners and socially competent members of their community. The primary educational setting for children is the family. In the home environment, children first develop language, the ability to relate to others, and attitudes about learning and school. When children see that their teachers and families share common goals and can work together in positive and mutually respectful ways, they feel more comfortable at school.

Research and anecdotal evidence convincingly show that parent involvement in their children's school life benefits everyone.

> When parents… become actively involved in their children's education at school and in the community, their children earn higher grades and higher scores on achievement tests than do those whose parents are uninvolved (Carnegie Task Force 1996, 35).

Children improve their performance and continue to achieve in school when a family member becomes involved. Parents who develop a partnership with their children's teachers feel accepted in the school community and more confident about their parenting. Teachers gain needed support and respect from parents and find that children are more cooperative. Schools that view families as partners in the educational process become better schools (Henderson and Berla 1994).

The sixth strategy for building the primary classroom addresses the importance of partnering with families to help children succeed. Throughout this chapter we refer to parents and families interchangeably. While most children live with one or both parents, other family members may be primary caregivers and therefore most involved in the child's school life. The critical factor is that someone of importance in the child's home life—a parent, relative, or another significant adult—develops a positive relationship with the child's teacher, and that this person supports and feels supported by the school community.

Setting the Stage for a Positive Relationship

People build relationships based upon trust. To establish trust we sometimes have to begin by eliminating fears. Many parents have expectations, and often fears, about school. These may be based on their own experiences or the ways they have been treated in the past by teachers and administrators. If these experiences were not positive, families have no reason to trust that you will be open to building a different kind of relationship with them.

Teachers also have past experiences that affect both their openness to building relationships with families and their expectations of what can be accomplished. If previous efforts to involve families have failed, making new efforts may seem futile. It's easy to get discouraged when parents seem unresponsive or negative.

Perhaps the best place to start is to consider the perspective of a parent. As one teacher said, "I was always a good teacher, but now that I'm a parent myself, I've become a great teacher." Setting the stage for a positive relationship with the families of the children you teach means understanding parents' feelings and the influence of culture, and developing the ability to communicate effectively.

The Parent's Perspective

James Hymes captured the parent-child-teacher relationship well when he said:

> . . . parents are your friends. Show your interest in a child and parents are on your side. Be casual, be off-handed, be cold toward the child and parents can never work closely with you… To touch the child is to touch the parent. To praise the child is to praise the parent. To criticize the child is to hit at the parent. The two are two, but the two are one (1974, 8-9).

James Comer reinforces this view when he describes a child as a "parent's handiwork" (1989). Teachers who keep these views in mind tread carefully and respectfully in all their contacts with parents. They are more willing to give up old ideas about parent involvement and adopt new beliefs to guide their interactions with families.

All parents want their children to succeed. They care about what happens while their children are at school. Parents, however, have different ways of conveying their expectations and becoming involved in their children's education. Not all parents will attend school events or participate in their children's classroom activities. Many are raising children alone. For some families, coping with everyday life is a struggle, and basic responsibilities—getting their children up, dressed, fed, and to school—represent major accomplishments. These parents are involved in their children's education to the greatest degree they can achieve at the time. Their efforts need to be appreciated and acknowledged as sincerely as the efforts of parents who participate in the PTA, in decision-making, or in classroom activities.

As educators, we have a responsibility to find ways to help all families feel that they can contribute to their child's education. Parents tend to respond positively to a teacher who conveys respect and appreciation for *whatever* they do to support their child's life at school.

Changing the Focus of Parent Involvement

The traditional view of parent involvement focuses on getting parents to participate in school activities or fund-raising efforts. Success is often measured by how many parents attend a school event or donate their time and resources. However, not all parents have the capacity or desire to be involved in traditional ways. Given the number of working parents and non-traditional families in today's society, these measurements fail to assess family involvement realistically. Consequently, we may be discouraged by the failure of our efforts to achieve a high level of attendance and may blame families for a lack of interest in their children's education. A promising alternative focuses on collaboration and outreach rather than on "educating parents" and "getting them into the schools."

Teachers can involve parents in the educational process of their children at many different levels. A range of involvement is possible.

- Parents meet the child's needs for safety, security, nutrition, health care, and discipline.
- Parents consistently respond to school notices, invitations, meetings, forms, and progress reports.
- Parents or family members assist classroom teachers and/or school administrators with school tasks and attend events and/or workshops.
- Parents help their children at home with learning activities coordinated with the children's classwork.
- Parents are involved in school governance and advocacy through the PTA/PTO, advisory councils, school board, or other decision-making committees or groups.

As with many critical aspects of school life, administrators play a key role in supporting positive school-home relationships. The value of parent involvement must be conveyed by all school personnel: the principal, vice-principal, counselors, office staff, custodians, and health staff. By creating a school atmosphere that welcomes parents and all family members, and by recognizing the importance of effective relationships with parents, administrators enable staff to feel positive and enthusiastic about involving parents.

Understanding the Influence of Culture

Understanding cultural influences helps teachers build strong relationships with families. Children define themselves in relation to their families, and culture plays an important role in how families raise their children. A failure to understand and respect parents ultimately affects a teacher's relationship with the child.

As defined in Chapter 1, Knowing the Children You Teach, culture is that which forms the knowledge, perceptions, and understandings each of us brings to a situation. Culture, language, and ethnic origins are a major part of our identities. The foods we eat, the ways we celebrate holidays and life events, and our child-rearing attitudes and practices reflect our cultural heritage. Regardless of how long ago our ancestors came to the United States, our cultural roots influence our attitudes, thoughts, and behaviors.

When the culture of the school is entirely different from the child's culture at home, the child may be confused and uncomfortable at school. It is too much to ask children to bridge the gap between these two very different cultures. What often happens is that these children identify most strongly with their home culture and reject the school culture because it is so unfamiliar. In so doing, they also reject the goals and values of the educational setting. The teacher must take the initiative to bridge the gap between home and school (Lightfoot 1978).

Cultural Differences that May Affect Relationships with Families

When working with families from diverse cultures and backgrounds, it is extremely helpful to know something about traditional values and attitudes that may influence your interactions. Cultural values and norms can vary greatly along many dimensions, including the following:

- orientation to time
- importance of individualism and privacy
- attitudes toward competition/cooperation
- degree of formality in interactions
- respect for adults/authority
- reflecting on questions before answering
- orientation toward work, achievement, and materialism
- spirituality and religious orientation
- gender roles
- child-rearing practices
- comfort with physical proximity
- expectations for the future

Family cultural values may conflict with school expectations. For example, some families have a relaxed attitude toward time and do not view punctuality as especially important. The teacher may view tardiness as a sign of disrespect.

Ms. Wheelock prepares for conferences with family members. In order to see all the parents, she has to schedule conferences twenty minutes apart. She knows that some family members may not be comfortable with this schedule and want a more relaxed or informal way to talk. To help her keep on schedule and to alert families to the need to keep to a schedule, she posts a chart on the door to her classroom listing conference times. She addresses the issue early in the conference by saying, "I wish we had more time to get to know one another and talk about Hannah. If we don't get a chance to talk about everything that's important to you today, we'll schedule another time to get together."

In some cultures, a fatalistic acceptance of life circumstances may mean that special help or assistance for a child with special needs is unlikely to be pursued. A willingness to accept "what is," including the possibility of a limited future for a child, does not mean that the parent does not love the child and want the best life possible for the child, but that the parent views the situation differently.

Mr. Sherwin is concerned that Anthony's language development may be delayed. He wants to get some additional information by scheduling an evaluation with a specialist. When he speaks with Anthony's parents about this, they are resistant to the idea of involving a specialist. Based on their response, Mr. Sherwin realizes that the intervention he proposes is offensive to Anthony's parents. He decides that a better approach for now is to encourage them to play a game at home that will enhance Anthony's language skills. He offers to send home the materials and suggests that the parents let Anthony teach them the game he learns at school.

These two examples highlight the importance of understanding and respecting cultural values and norms in order to communicate effectively and build positive relationships with families.

Self-Awareness Is an Important First Step

An understanding of culture begins with gaining awareness of our own cultural background and influences. Listed below are questions about messages you may have received, and experiences you may have had when you were growing up. Take some time to think about the impact they may still have on your attitudes, assumptions, and expectations about children's families. Ask yourself, "What stayed?" "What changed and why?" and "What do I wish would go away?"

- How was your racial/ethnic identity described to you? Were there any characteristics of your group that were described as special?

- What were the early messages you received about other ethnic/racial groups?

- How have the media's labels of different groups influenced you at different times during your life?

- What messages did you receive about your family's socio-economic position?

- What types of exposure did you have to people with mental or physical disabilities? What were you told about these people? How did you feel when you were around them?

- What messages did you receive about "being smart"? Were certain groups of people smarter than others?

- How important was the ability to express yourself verbally? Was it acceptable to interject your opinion when others were speaking?

- Was it okay to be noisy and physically active in your home/community?

- Were you exposed to families that did not have a traditional familial structure (husband/wife)? What were you told about non-traditional family structures?

It is helpful when teachers know something about the specific cultures represented in their community and among the families in their class. At the end of this chapter and Chapter 1, we list resources that can help you learn about the influences of culture. Remember that no family will necessarily share every belief and value attributed to its cultural background. The length of time the family has lived in the United States, the family members' social class (in their country of origin), and various other influences can all affect the family's values and practices. Each family should be viewed as unique with its own personal history and background and treated accordingly.

Communicating Effectively with Families

Transmitting information accurately is an essential component of building relationships with families. Communication involves both the sending of messages and the understanding of messages received. Though fundamental to human understanding, communication is often fraught with misunderstanding. Many factors influence the effectiveness ofcommunication: language, literacy levels, listening skills, voice tone, cultural expectations, values and beliefs, and body language.

Schools traditionally rely upon written communication in the form of letters, memos, and newsletters sent home with the children. Written communication is not the most effective way to exchange information. This is true for all families but especially for those with poor literacy levels or stressful living conditions. Written forms of communication should be reinforced with personal contact.

Personal contact—through home visits, conferences, or visits to the school—promotes good communication and relationships with families most effectively because body language and voice tone usually communicate more powerfully than words themselves. But, as with written communication, one-on-one communication is being filtered through the receiver's and the sender's values, beliefs, past experiences, and expectations.

Effective honest, respectful, and open communication takes time. The following suggestions may be helpful.

- Give total attention to the communication process when interacting with parents. Look directly at the person, smile, nod, and use body language to convey your interest and respect.

- Make sincere attempts to understand the parent's point of view. By listening carefully, restating, clarifying, and checking what you've heard, you demonstrate a genuine desire to understand. Listen carefully to the stories parents want to tell you.

- Suspend judgment about what the parent says. Although you may disagree with the parent's viewpoint, avoid making quick judgments about whether you feel the parent is right or wrong. Recognize how much you can learn from parents.

- Use simple, clear language and avoid educational jargon. Keep in mind that most parents have not been trained as educators, so words that have a specialized or professional meaning may be foreign to them and interfere with good communication. Avoid trying to "educate" the parents.

- Convey respect for other cultures. Parents' views about child-rearing or school involvement may differ from yours. By communicating an open mind and a willingness to listen, you convey respect.

- Always leave parents with a sense of confidence in their child. Avoid saying anything that will undermine a parent's sense of hope for a child's future. Close a conference by telling parents about their child's recent accomplishments.

When you do send home written notices, make sure parents will be able to understand them. Literacy organizations make the following recommendations (Weinberg 1990).

- Use short, easy, familiar words.
- Avoid long introductions—get to the point.
- Keep sentences short (no more than 20 words) and try to avoid words with multi-syllables.
- Write in logical order (who, what, where, when, why, and how).
- Be direct—use "you" instead of "parents."
- Use the active voice—"Please join us" rather than "Your participation is encouraged."
- Avoid jargon or abbreviations that parents might not know.
- Use pictures and headings to break up text.
- Have written communication translated for families who do not speak English.

Acquiring the skills to communicate effectively both within one's own culture and across different cultures is a lifelong process. The trust that good communication with families builds makes it worth the effort.

Eight Approaches to Involving Families

In this section we describe eight approaches to involving families. We have focused on those approaches that an individual teacher can implement. However, we recognize that much more can be accomplished when everyone in a school believes in and promotes a partnership with families.

Before-School Contacts

The unknown often makes us feel uneasy. Before entering your classroom, parents wonder if you will like their child, recognize their child's special talents and interests, and if you will be a good teacher. You may wonder if parents will like and support you. Will they respond to your efforts to communicate? Follow through on requests for assistance? Convey appreciation for your efforts to help their child succeed in your classroom? A friendly contact before school begins frequently puts everyone at ease and starts the year on a positive note. Here are some suggestions.

- Write a brief note or postcard to each child and family welcoming them and conveying your enthusiasm about the coming year. School administrators can support this effort by providing stamped and addressed postcards or envelopes, or at least the names, addresses, and phone numbers of the children and families in your class. (Try to have all school-home communication translated into the family's primary language whenever possible.)

- Make a phone call to each family the week before school starts. This personal contact allows you to begin the partnership on a one-to-one basis. You can use this call to introduce yourself, talk a little about your program, and find out if the parents have any questions or concerns. If language will be a barrier, ask someone to help you who can translate the conversation.

   "Hello, Ms. Carter? My name is Margaret Eliot. I will be Latita's teacher this year. I just wanted to tell you personally that I am looking forward to having Latita in the third grade and getting to know her family. I understand from Ms. Smith, her teacher last year, that Latita is quite an artist. Has she done any drawings this summer? Ask her if she would like to bring some of her art work to school to share. If you have any questions please feel free to leave a message for me at school and I'll get back to you."

- Have an informal open house prior to the beginning of school so families can stop by with their children. This friendly gesture helps reassure both children and their families that they are welcome at school.

- Arrange a home visit to each child's family. A half-hour visit is usually sufficient to go over some of the plans you have for the year and ask about the parent's expectations and hopes. You will learn a great deal by observing how the child and family members interact with one another. Parents who might feel uneasy in the school setting often are relaxed and more open at home. On the other hand, if families feel they are being judged, the visit will be uncomfortable and unnatural. Therefore, be careful not to infer too much from this brief glimpse of family interactions. If the families do not want you to come to their home for any reason, it's important to respect their decision and suggest an alternative place to meet.

- Visit the community where your children live, particularly if you are from a different community. Walk through the neighborhoods, visit cultural institutions, businesses, and recreation facilities. Learning about the community provides valuable insights into the cultures and life circumstances of the children in your classroom. It will also be helpful in planning your social studies and science curriculum.

You may think of other ways to establish contact with children's families. Talk with colleagues to find out what works for them. These initial contacts are so important because they set the stage for all future interactions between you and the families of the children you teach.

August 19, 1999

Dear Families,

Welcome to Second Grade! I look forward to meeting you and getting to know your children. Because families are so important, we plan to begin the school year by learning about families. Please have your child bring a picture of your family so we can include it on our bulletin board. If you don't have a picture available, I'll have a camera ready on the first day of school and will be glad to take a picture of you with your child.

I will send home bulletins every two weeks to tell you about life in our classroom. Your questions and concerns are very important to me. I encourage you to come by the classroom, call, or write to me at school. I will be in our classroom, Room 123, all day on September 1 and on the afternoon of September 2. Please feel free to stop by with your child to say hello.

You are an important member of our classroom community. I look forward to working with you and your child to make this a successful school year for everyone.

Sincerely,

Informal Contacts

Every day you have many opportunities to communicate informally with families. You can use the times when children are brought to or picked up at school by a member of their family to build relationships.

Some parents avoid coming to school because of their memories of unpleasant school experiences. Other parents avoid coming into the school building with their children because they aren't treated well. They feel that administrators and teachers ignore them or convey the impression that they are too busy to talk. Many parents feel unwelcome and out of place.

Teachers who take the time to greet each family member with a smile and a friendly welcome can often put even the most wary parent at ease. You may be too busy to talk at length, but in just one minute, you can convey a positive message to anyone who enters your classroom.

> *"Good morning, Mr. Washington. I bet Lionel wants to show you his caterpillar diary. Please come on in and spend some time with us this morning. Lionel, you know where we keep the science journals. I'm sure your grandfather will be interested in what you recorded yesterday."*

> *"I'm so glad you stopped by, Ms. Morales. Let's set up a time when we can talk. I have free periods on Tuesdays and Fridays from 2:00 to 2:45. Would you be able to meet with me at one of those times, or would you prefer a time before or after school? I'd welcome the opportunity to talk to you about Miguel."*

A smile, a handshake, and a brief communication can go a long way toward making family members feel welcome.

In schools where children arrive and leave by bus, you have fewer opportunities for informal communication with families. The telephone is the next best means for communicating on a regular basis. Once a month you might call each family to chat informally about school life and say something positive about the child's progress. Not all teachers are willing to give out their home phone numbers, but those who do find it helpful to identify specific times when parents may call and discuss any questions or concerns they have. Some schools set up a dedicated phone line so parents can call anytime, day or night, to get a brief message on current events or announcements. E-mail is also becoming an effective way for parents and teachers to communicate.

Informal, positive contacts—whether in person, on the phone, via e-mail, or through brief notes—build trust and keep parents informed.

Back-to-School Night

Most schools have a back-to-school night so parents can visit their children's classrooms and hear about the curriculum. This is an excellent opportunity to give parents a tour of the classroom and to share the highlights of your curriculum and instructional approach. If your school does not have a back-to-school night, you may want to find a few interested teachers and collaborate on a plan to have one.

Attention to logistics makes a big difference in attendance at these events. Schools located in neighborhoods where people don't feel safe coming out at night sometimes schedule the event in the late afternoon or on a weekend. The school could also arrange for extra security in the parking lot and neighborhood and publicize the measures taken to promote everyone's safety.

The availability of child care often has a major impact on attendance. Many parents can't attend events because they have no one to look after their young children. Ensuring accessibility for disabled parents and arranging for a sign-language interpreter for deaf parents conveys the message that all families are welcome. An evening potluck meal or coffee and dessert at the school also increases participation in school events.

Prior to the event, send home an announcement and a brief agenda so parents know what you plan to discuss. Arrange the chairs in a circle or horseshoe to convey that you want everyone to feel part of the group. Be sure that what you display in the classroom includes samples of every child's work.

Here are some suggestions for conducting a meeting with parents on back-to-school night.

- First, give everyone a warm welcome. Then, begin with the parents themselves. Help them get to know each other. Suggest that everyone turn to the person next to them and introduce themselves. Ask them to think of their own school experiences, such as a time when a teacher really helped them to feel successful and competent as a learner, or a time when they were truly happy in school. Invite them to share their experiences with their partner. Then ask for volunteers to share what they discussed. Make a list of the key characteristics that are identified. Use this list to explain your approach. (If you try this introductory exercise, limit the time to approximately 10 minutes so you have ample time to talk about your program.)

- Share some information about yourself. Parents want to know about your education, your background and family life, and perhaps, some personal interests.

- Provide a brief overview of child development, focusing on a few typical behaviors of children in your grade level. You might begin by asking parents about developmental characteristics they've noticed. (You can base your presentation on the characteristics we discussed in Chapter 1, Knowing the Children You Teach.)

    "I enjoy working with seven year olds because they are such social beings and get so serious about their work. Because each of you lives with a child this age, you are also experts on what they are like. Let me read to you some of the typical characteristics of sevens. Think about whether this fits with what you know about your child."

    Usually parents can relate well to what you have to say about developmental characteristics. It is immensely reassuring to parents to know that the behavior of their child is not unusual.

- Highlight key points about curriculum. Share your approaches to teaching reading, your views on invented spelling, hands-on math, and any other aspects of the curriculum you want parents to understand. Reinforce the importance of parents reading with the children every evening, if possible, instead of watching television.

- Explain the classroom procedures about materials, jobs, and routines. Explain how they were developed by the children. Some of the issues you may want to discuss are whether children should bring personal supplies from home, what happens on the days children go out for special classes, when they need to wear sneakers, and whether they need smocks for art.

- Discuss homework—its purpose, how it's assigned, how long it should take, and how you want to involve parents. Ask about the best days to send work home. Invite parents with older children to share what has worked for them in the past.

- Give parents a picture of what has happened in your classroom to date related to organization and curriculum. Give lots of examples. Show slides or a video of children working at school. Point out how children work collaboratively, how they use and care for materials, and how they acquire skills and concepts as they investigate, represent, and reflect on what they are learning.

- Develop a handout on the topics you will explore in long-term studies. Talk about the activities you plan for the year and when you expect to take trips. Invite families to contribute their talents and ideas.

- Share your commitment to establishing good communication with families and invite input on how to make this happen. Invite parents to let you know if they welcome phone calls, prefer notes, want to volunteer in the classroom, and so on.

You probably have many tried-and-true approaches of your own. Other teachers in your school can provide additional suggestions. Also, keep in mind that not all of these suggestions will be appropriate or successful for every group.

Bulletins/Newsletters

Regular written communications keep families in touch with classroom life. They need not be elaborate or beautifully typed and formatted; a simple handwritten newsletter or brief, one-page bulletin can accomplish much with very little time or effort. You can print a supply of "Good News Bulletins" with space to write a personal message to each child's family. (Again, have these messages translated into the family's home language if possible.)

Good News Bulletin

Date: *October 12, 1998*

Dear *Mr. and Mrs. Riley,*

Timothy **and I have some good news to share with you**.

This week Timothy completed a final draft on his story and he will bring it home on Friday with his work folder. I think you will enjoy reading it together. He also helped two other children edit their stories. He is learning a lot about good writing.

Timothy and I have selected samples of his work for his portfolio. We are looking forward to portfolio night when we can show you how much he has accomplished this year.

Sincerely,

A general message that goes to everyone in the class might address specific aspects of the curriculum.

November 12, 1998

Dear Families,
We are studying time. In order to help the children become more aware of when things happen, I have asked them to choose 5 activities that they do in a typical day. These could be: waking up, brushing teeth, eating breakfast or dinner, homework time, bedtime, or doing a particular chore. I have enclosed a chart for the children to use to write the activities and keep track of when they happen each day.

Please help your child fill out the chart for any two days next week. I'd like to have all the charts back by the end of the week. Thank you for your help.

Sincerely,

Some teachers find it helpful to send home bulletins/newsletters on a regular schedule so parents know when to expect them. If you number these bulletins, parents know if they receive all of them.

Invitations to Participate in the Classroom

There are many ways in which having families participate in the classroom can be an asset—for the child, for the family member, and for the teacher. Children love to have someone from home see what their life is like at school. When a Cambodian child's grandmother comes to school and two other children who speak Cambodian have a chance to speak their language with her, they feel that a special part of their life experience is valued. At the same time, the grandmother makes an important connection with her grandchild's world. And for the teacher, involving families in classroom life provides extra help.

Families can participate in the classroom in a variety of ways: as the audience for a play or assembly, as guests at a holiday party, as assistants on trips, or as volunteers to share their talents and skills. An extra hand to help a group with a project, listen to children read, play games, or assist writers can free a teacher to work with individual children or a small group. Several adult volunteers on a trip can help supervise children to ensure their safety.

Dear Families,

Our classroom community includes children's families. We hope you will be able to volunteer your talents and services. Please indicate any areas that interest you.

Name: _____

Phone Number: _____

❑ Assist children in working on tasks during choice time (Mondays, Tuesdays, Wednesdays, Thursdays, or Fridays)

❑ Volunteer occasionally for special projects (e.g., visits to stores in the neighborhood)

❑ Help on field trips

❑ Share a special hobby or area of expertise with the class
Please indicate area(s) _____

❑ Interested in reading to the class or telling stories

❑ Available for home assignments such as sewing costumes (if we have a play), or book binding

❑ Willing to bake for classroom celebrations, or to supply juice and snacks

❑ Other? Please indicate: _____

Please return this to me by: _____

Thank you very much!

Sincerely,

In any group, you will find family members with special skills and talents to share with the children. An open letter offering a range of options for participating in the classroom may inspire some volunteers.

When you send home an invitation to participate, explain to the children what the letters say so that they can help convey the message to family members. Have the letters translated if you know the family has limited English proficiency. Always follow up when a parent responds to your request for volunteers. Parents get discouraged when their offers to assist are ignored.

Although there are many benefits to encouraging this kind of family involvement, there may also be worries or difficulties associated with opening your classroom to family members. Some teachers are uncomfortable asking for help, or they worry about being watched and not looking good. Others are concerned that parents might not do something correctly. Teachers who are helping children to become more self-sufficient may worry that having family members around encourages children to be clingy. While there are no easy answers to these concerns, the benefits of making your classroom an inviting place for families are worth trying to overcome these difficulties. It may be helpful to reframe your idea of parent involvement. Parents can be partners and collaborators in teaching children.

Conferences with Families

Individual conferences with children's families provide time for an in-depth exchange of information. Teachers can explain aspects of the curriculum of interest to a child's family, and ask questions that solicit valuable information about a child's special interests and family background. Parents frequently have specific questions and concerns to raise with their child's teacher.

The best use of the first conference of the year is to discuss goals that you and the parents have for the child. Let parents know ahead of time that you hope to use the conference to learn more about their child, discuss the expectations they have for the year, and respond to their questions. Then parents can think about what they would like to learn and discuss during the conference.

Conferences later in the year can focus on reviews of children's work and progress. You'll want to have actual examples of children's work to share and discuss (e.g., the portfolios discussed in the previous chapter on Assessing Children's Learning).

In planning for conferences with families, consider the following suggestions.

- Schedule conferences at convenient times for families and for you, so no one will feel rushed.

- Make sure you have adult-sized chairs for parents. Having to sit on child-sized furniture does not give parents confidence or help them become comfortable in the school environment.

- Make a plan for conducting the conference and outline a few specific questions you want to ask. Send home a form listing your questions so parents can prepare as well. In this way you will be able to use the time most efficiently and effectively.

- At the start of the conference, establish a relaxed and comfortable tone. Allow time for social conversation and a tour of the classroom if parents have not been there before.

- Ask for parents' opinions about how their child likes school and the changes they have seen in their child.

- Make positive statements about the child. Try to know a particular strength, talent, or special interest that you can share with parents. Convey sincerely how much you like having their child in your classroom. Parents tend to like and support a teacher who genuinely likes their child.

- Discuss social as well as academic progress.

- Share examples of the child's work such as a book the child can read, paintings, math work, journals, or a computer program the child enjoys.

- Discuss parents' goals for the child, share your goals, and develop a plan identifying what each of you will do to help the child achieve these goals.

- End by discussing with the parent how you will maintain communication.

It is quite normal to feel somewhat anxious about an upcoming conference. Some conferences are more difficult than others. If, for example, you are planning to meet with the parents of a child who is having a particular difficulty, or you know a parent tends to be defensive and argumentative, try to be especially positive in your approach.

> *"I'm a parent myself so I can sympathize with what you are going through. My oldest son was just like Patrick. I want you to know that I am absolutely committed to Patrick's success. I know that you are committed as well and that's why you are here today."*

An approach like this reinforces for the parent that you share the same goals—to help their child learn and experience success.

Prior to a conference you expect to be difficult, it may be helpful to discuss your concerns with another teacher, preferably someone who knows the family, or with your principal. Ask yourself, "What's my biggest fear?" Then develop some strategies for handling what worries you so you feel more prepared for the conference. Role playing how you plan to handle a conference can also help.

Parent Meetings and Workshops

Schools and individual teachers sometimes plan meetings or workshops for parents about the curriculum. For example, if you have started a new math program in your classroom, introduced a writing workshop, or added computers and want to share new software with families, you might plan a workshop to talk about these approaches.

Rather than conducting these meetings on your own, consider collaborating with other teachers in the same grade to conduct a series of workshops. When child care is a consideration, some teachers may offer to share this responsibility during a meeting so that more parents can attend.

In addition to meetings in which you discuss particular instructional approaches or materials, some schools offer Family Math, Family Science, or Family Literacy nights. In these sessions, children come to school with their parents and work together to solve problems. A leader, or teams of leaders, facilitate the group as they learn some math, science, or literacy activities that can be done at home. These "courses" usually last 6-8 weeks so that families can learn a few activities, try them out at home, and return to reflect and learn some more.

In planning and running parent meetings and workshops, consider the following suggestions.

- Arrange for simple refreshments for the meeting. This sets a friendly tone and makes parents feel relaxed.
- Survey families about the topics they would like to hear about (e.g., drug education, sex education, literacy) and then work with your principal or PTA to try to accommodate their interests.
- If a parent asks too many questions and dominates the meeting, you may consider saying something like, "You have so many ideas to share with me, I'd like to set up an individual conference with you."
- If parents ask no questions, it may be useful to say, "Last year many parents wanted to know. . . ." or "A frequently asked question is. . . ."

It's very likely that some parents who have an interest in the topic being presented simply cannot attend. If possible, make an audio or videotape of the presentations and lend copies to parents who express an interest.

Workshops or seminars on a school-wide program such as conflict resolution can involve parents and staff learning together. Getting support for such programs at home and school promotes teamwork and increases the chances for a successful program.

Family Gatherings

In addition to meetings and workshops for parents, family gatherings involve both the children and their families. At the end of a project, such as the study of machines, the children might want to invite their families to come see the machines they created in the classroom and to celebrate the conclusion of their study. Some teachers have an "Authors' Breakfast" when children share their published work with family members. Family meetings can be held during the school day, in the afternoon or evening, depending on when most families can attend.

If you only have one conference each year, consider planning a family gathering mid-year. You might plan a family portfolio night, for example, where children can share their school work with family members. You can talk about how children have been saving work samples and how they reflect the work you have been doing together. While children share their portfolios with their families, you can move from one group to another and answer questions or make comments.

How Involving Families Supports the First Five Strategies

We recognize that building relationships with families takes a great deal of time and effort. Most teachers find, however, that when they are successful in building relationships with families and involving them in the educational process, it makes their job easier and more rewarding. In addition, supportive families, like good school experiences, have the potential to foster resiliency in children. Thus, anything you do that encourages supportive families is good for children socially and academically (Benard 1999, Benson 1998).

We conclude this chapter on families by showing how developing a partnership with families based on trust and mutual respect supports each of the strategies described in the previous chapters: knowing the children you teach, building a classroom community, establishing a structure, guiding and assessing children's learning.

Getting to Know the Children You Teach

In the first chapter we stated the dimensions to knowing the children you teach: who they are developmentally, individually, and culturally. You can learn about child development from books and your own teaching experience. In order to learn about each child as an individual and about how culture and family background influence the child's communication and interaction styles, your greatest resource is the family.

In parent conferences, home visits, or informal conversations at school or on the phone, you can ask for information that will be helpful in understanding your children. Let parents know that you are always open to hearing what their children say about school, concerns they have, and insights they wish to share with you.

Talking with Parents About Their Child

You may want to begin these discussions by sharing a little about yourself, such as why you went into teaching, what you enjoy most, your own experiences as a child in school or as a parent. When teachers share something personal, parents are more likely to share a little about themselves.

You might explain that each year you adapt and build instruction around the specific needs and interests of the children. Therefore, you are eager to know as much as you can about each child so that you can best meet his or her learning needs.

To learn more about the child's position in the family, temperament, talents, and interests you might ask some questions.

- Does your child have siblings?
- How does your child help at home?
- When are you most proud of your child?

- How does your child respond to new people or situations?
- Does your child have any special interests (e.g, sports, games, nature, art, music, dance, computers)?
- Do you have any concerns about your child or about school?
- What kind of school experiences do you wish for your child this year?

Another area in which parents can provide useful insights is in defining their children's preferred learning styles and strengths. In the first chapter we described Howard Gardner's expanded view of intelligence, and how we have often judged children as not being very "smart" because they did not excel in language or math skills. It can be very reassuring to families to learn that their child, who may excel in other areas such as music, art, physical skills, and relationships, has special strengths that you appreciate and will build upon.

To learn more about each child's learning and interactive styles, you might pose a few of these questions.

- What is your child's favorite activity?
- Does she like to have friends over or to go to other children's homes?
- How does your child approach other children? Does he hang back and watch a while, or does he join right in?
- What kinds of activities does she enjoy doing for extended time periods?
- Have you ever seen your child take things apart and put them back together to figure out how they work?
- Do you have to repeat directions several times or does your child understand them the first time?
- How does he respond to books and stories?
- How do you know what your child is thinking or feeling?
- Does your child watch television? Do you notice any ways in which television affects her positively? Negatively?

Understanding Cultural Expectations

As previously stated, culture has a profound influence on children. The greater the difference between the teacher's cultural background and those of the children in the class, the greater the effort the teacher must make to understand children's behavior and expectations. Your contact with families can help you learn what they value most, the expectations they have about school, and the behavior considered appropriate and respectful at home. This understanding can give you valuable insights and keep you from seeking changes that would be inappropriate in the child's culture. Consider the following story.

Ms. Robinson, a teacher who values choice time and encourages children to work collaboratively at tables, is concerned about Lee Ming's behavior in the classroom. He constantly runs in the classroom, picking up toys and materials and dropping them everywhere. When he paints he spatters all over the table. At a parent conference, Ms. Robinson describes Lee Ming's behavior at school and the problem it is causing. She learns that at home, the child is expected to be very quiet and to respect his father's need to study and read. The parents explain that they give Lee Ming coloring books and workbooks, which he uses on his own for long periods of time. Ms. Robinson discusses how important it is for children to go outdoors every day and have opportunities to be active. She suggests some activities that Lee Ming can do with his mother or on his own. The parents work out a plan that will allow Lee Ming to be more active at home, while still respecting his father's need for quiet. Ms. Robinson realizes she needs to focus more on helping Lee Ming develop self-control and allocates time to teach him how to use materials appropriately. Within a few weeks, there is a dramatic change in Lee Ming's school behavior.

This example illustrates the importance of close communication between school and home in resolving problems created by different expectations.

Consulting with Parents About Special Needs

Parents are a teacher's greatest resource, especially for a child with a diagnosed disability. These parents have often spent years consulting with experts to diagnose the problem and find out the best strategies for promoting their child's growth and development. Teachers who welcome children with disabilities in their classrooms will gain the trust and support of their parents.

Get to know the parents' view of the disability, their current responses to the disability, their interpretation of the educational/medical counseling they have received, their membership in support/advocacy groups, their home goals for the child, their school goals for the child, and their views of key elements in their child's school success. It may take quite a bit of time to gather such extensive information from parents. Many have faced misinformation, prejudice, and undervaluing by professionals before they met you. Listen to their stories to learn how this family has coped with a disability. You will learn about the highs and lows of parenting this individual child. This information will help you formulate the best approaches to fully including the child in your classroom.

Because all staff who interact with the child may need specific information about the disability, you can facilitate parents' connections with other staff by helping to set up meetings or organize a time when all staff can get together. In addition to making sure current information is on file in the school office, remember to make necessary information available to all substitute teachers.

Including Families in the Classroom Community

Families are already part of your classroom community. Children do not enter into your classroom alone; they bring their families with them. Think about what children share at meetings, and what they are bursting to tell you when they arrive each day. Most often they share stories about family members, something that happened to someone they love, or a family event. Children need to see that their families are accepted in their school community.

Teachers convey this message by being open to what children share, by accepting their stories, respecting their concerns, and celebrating good news. This affirmation enables children to see the strong bond between their two worlds and to experience acceptance in both.

Teachers need to guard against being judgmental in responding to what children bring into the classroom about their families. Some of the experiences children share may be shocking and distressing: having a family member arrested or shot, or seeing physical violence in the home, for example. If your own discomfort leads you to say that those stories do not belong in school, you negate a part of children's lives. Thereafter, they may hide this part of their lives and lose their sense of belonging at school. Teachers can help children by being good listeners and responding to how the child is feeling: "That must be very upsetting. I'm glad you're safe."

Just as children share family stories at school, they also talk about school experiences at home. The meetings you have every day, in which children talk about topics that are of interest to them and participate as members of a community, give children information that they can take home and share with their families. Sharing information reinforces the link between home and school.

To make families an integral part of your classroom community, consider these suggestions.

- At the beginning of the year, display pictures of children and their families on a bulletin board as a focus of study. If photographs are not available, have children draw pictures of their families. Children can conduct interviews, draw and write stories, and have discussions about all kinds of families, even those that may not exist in your class. Read some of the wonderful children's books on families and encourage children to borrow them to share with their own families.

- When you conduct parent meetings or an open house, arrange the chairs in a circle as you do for all class meetings. You can model the way you conduct meetings with the children: greeting everyone, reading a morning message, going over the agenda, asking if people have anything they want to share, and involving everyone in the discussion.

- Encourage family members to enrich your curriculum by sharing their own talents and special interests with children. The notes you send home to invite their participation can be reinforced through informal communication. If possible, try to arrange the schedule so that choice times take place when family members are available to help.

- Use class projects that focus on the community or on different kinds of jobs to provide opportunities to involve family members in the classroom. Children might visit their parents' places of work or invite members of their family to school to be interviewed about their jobs.

- Think of activities for families who can't come to school (e.g., making phone calls, collating papers, sending in the snack). Acknowledge their contributions by describing how they have helped the class.

- Plan a special workshop on social problem solving so that parents can learn about how this works in your classroom, and how they can help their children handle anger and conflicts non-violently at home.

- Invite family members into the classroom to read to the class, bring a special object to share, or contribute to a class newsletter. Show appreciation for their contributions by having children write thank-you notes.

- If your school has a home-school liaison, you can ask that person to follow through with a particular family whom you have difficulty contacting.

Families want to experience belonging to a community as much as children do. The best schools truly serve the community around them. This sense of community can begin in your classroom.

Reinforcing the Classroom Structure

The structure you create in your classroom—by organizing the physical environment, designing the schedule and routines, and involving the children in establishing rules for classroom life—helps children develop responsibility and a sense of their own competence. Reinforce this structure constantly so that children know what is expected of them. Parents can be your best allies in making the structure work.

Explaining Your Classroom Structure to Families

To support the classroom structure you create, parents must understand what you expect and why, and how they can be helpful to their child. At an open house, parent meetings, or parent conferences, you can explain the various aspects of structure. Weekly bulletins and newsletters give you an opportunity to provide a little bit of information at a time and to reinforce what you previously shared in person. Older children can help present this information to their families.

In explaining your classroom structure to families, select topics critical to the success of your classroom. The suggestions that follow may prompt ideas of your own.

- Make a map or floor plan of your classroom. Attach a simple explanation of how it's organized, why you label materials, the purpose of shared materials, and how children help to maintain the classroom. Invite parents to contribute furniture or materials you may need such as computer paper, beautiful "junk" for collage and construction, collections for sorting and counting, books, plant cuttings, cooking utensils, a fish tank, shelf, or rug for the meeting area.

- List the rules you developed with the children and explain why you include children in this process. Discuss how you help children remember them, how children remind each other, and how you re-evaluate together when rules are not followed.

- Give each family a copy of the daily schedule and highlight the times you need volunteers most. Discuss why children need a snack mid-morning. Ask for contributions if this is appropriate.

- Share your list of jobs, how children identified the jobs needed, and the importance of everyone having a job each week. Invite parents to share what jobs their children have at home.

- Demonstrate how you introduce materials to children so that they learn to respect and take care of them.

- Explain how children can catch up if they are ill and miss several days of school.

- Share a list of board games that help children develop social, reading, and math skills. (This is especially appreciated during the holiday season.)

- Discuss the importance of going outdoors, even in cold weather, and the need for children to dress appropriately. You might suggest having a box in the classroom for extra mittens, sweaters, hats, and scarves for children who forget these items. Families are often willing to donate outgrown or extra clothing for this purpose.

- Describe the structure of choice time and the reasons it is valued by children and teachers.

Parents often say that their children do not talk about what goes on in school. When asked, "What happened in school today?" they respond with a shrug or "Nothing." The more information parents have about the daily program, the easier it will be for them to frame specific questions and get a response that can lead to more conversation. For example, families that understand your structure might replace the question above with something like, "What did you do at choice time today?"

A Structure for Homework

Often, homework becomes "homewar" and the results can be disastrous. Children may not understand what they are supposed to do and fail to complete the assignment. Some parents do not know how to help and may feel incompetent or frustrated. Others may just do the homework for their child. It's important to think about why you assign homework, what you expect, and to help parents so they can help their children successfully complete assignments.

Why do teachers in the primary grades assign homework? In addition to reinforcing skills and concepts learned at school, homework reinforces and strengthens the school-home connection. When children do schoolwork at home, parents learn about the curriculum and can talk to their children in a meaningful way about what they are learning. Another reason for giving homework is to teach children responsibility and good work habits. When teachers plan homework thoughtfully, it can achieve these positive outcomes. Here are some suggestions for informing parents about homework.

- Explain (and repeat if necessary) that it is **your** responsibility, as the teacher, to be clear in assigning homework. If parents find that their child doesn't understand what to do, they should send it back unfinished and let you know. An important goal is to make homework a successful experience.

- Make homework assignments age-appropriate. In first and second grade, children begin to develop a pattern regarding homework: taking work home, doing it, and bringing it back to school. For many, it's best to give assignments that involve family members, such as reading together or counting the number of windows in the house. Send home a brief note explaining the requirements. Allow enough time for the assignment in case parents are not available in the evenings. By third grade, children can be encouraged to do their homework independently, to develop consistent habits about when and where they do homework, and to keep track of their papers.

- Limit homework to between 15 and 30 minutes, depending on the child's age. Let parents know that if it's taking more time, their child can stop. Parents should write you a note about it. Reassure them that you will help the child if needed.

- Establish a schedule for sending homework. For example, let parents know that every Monday and Wednesday their child will bring home a work folder and their homework will be due two days later. You might first discuss the convenience of this schedule at a parent meeting. Parents may prefer having a weekend to work with their child on something like spelling.

- Make suggestions that will help parents develop their own structure for supporting homework. These might include: establishing a consistent place in the house to do homework, preferably a quiet place; turning off the TV; keeping incomplete homework in a designated place; posting a schedule on the refrigerator as a reminder of when homework is due; keeping completed homework in a backpack the child takes to school each day; reviewing homework with the child; signing the homework folder each week.

To reinforce the guidelines about homework and to promote good communication, some teachers have found it helpful to use a consistent system, such as the one described in the following letter to parents.

September 13, 1999

Dear Families:

Today marks the beginning of regular homework assignments for the class. On Mondays children will have spelling work and on Wednesdays a math assignment.

I select spelling words from each child's journal writing. This week I have only identified three words for each child; eventually the children will have five to seven words per week to study. Every Monday the children receive a card listing their spelling words. The homework will be to write a sentence for each word and underline the spelling word.
(Don't worry if other words in the sentence are misspelled. We will correct them in class.)

The math homework assignments will usually be some problems to solve based on something we've been working on in class.

All of the work will be contained in a red folder, which I hope you will help your child remember to bring back to school after completing assignments. Establishing a routine for time, place, and care of homework is important for third graders.

Thank you for your support.

Sincerely,

Supporting Children's Learning

One of the most important messages we give children is that they are competent learners who are acquiring a great deal of knowledge about the world around them. When children's families understand the curriculum and value the skills being developed, children receive positive messages about their growing competence.

It's extremely important to explain your instructional approaches to parents. For example, if you encourage children to invent their own spelling using their best knowledge about phonics when they are writing stories, it is a good idea to prepare parents for this or they may question whether their child will ever learn to spell correctly. Similarly, if you are encouraging children to count on their fingers as one strategy for solving math problems, you will want to let parents know that they need not discourage this practice at home.

Topics for long-term studies come to life when children take home what they are learning at school or when they bring to school what they learn at home. Homework assignments can focus on interviewing family members about what they know about the topic under study. Families can be invited to join investigations and contribute their ideas. Here are some examples of ways that children can include their families.

- While studying the neighborhood, children might ask their families where they shop and why.
- During a science study about food spoilage and mold, children could ask family members to predict what will happen to foods left out of the refrigerator.
- Children can invite family members to come on a trip.
- While studying inventions, children can interview older relatives or neighbors about the types of machines they had as children in their homes.
- While working on surveying and graphing information in math, children can select a question and survey family members about their preferences or opinions.

Long-term studies involve many discussions with children about what they already know about a topic, and what they want to find out. The charts that you develop during these discussions can be typed and sent home to share with families.

Dear Families,

The third graders of Room 312 are beginning a study about life in our town one hundred years ago. We will be visiting many of the town's landmarks and studying old photographs and maps. The children have discussed what they know about our town's history and what they want to find out. Here's what they said.

We think we know:
- There were only dirt roads a hundred years ago.
- Some of the buildings on Main Street were already built.
- There were no TVs back then.
- The bridge that crosses the river wasn't built but there was a ferry.
- There were no cars; people rode horses and used carriages.

What we want to find out:
- How many people lived here?
- Where were the schools and what were they like?
- Were there telephones a hundred years ago?
- When was the bridge built?
- Where did people go if they were sick?
- Before the mall was built, where did people go shopping?

The children will be interviewing you and other relatives to find the answers to their questions.

Sincerely,

A proven approach to involving families in promoting their children's reading skills is to have children read school books at home. This type of program leads to improved communication among children, family members, and teachers as well as substantial gains in reading skills. Here's how one first grade teacher began such a reading program with her class.

Programs where children read to their parents every night have been implemented in many schools in the United States and in England. Because the child is reading to the parent, parent literacy skills are not an issue. The results have been very positive. Children's reading ability improved dramatically and parents became more involved in their children's school life without having to come to school (Nurss, Huss, and Hannon 1993).

Some teachers have a book backpack program. Children choose from a variety of backpacks that are organized by topics. For example, they may check out a backpack about dogs with books like *Clifford*, *The Diggingest Dog*, or *Harry the Dirty Dog*. In addition there will be a notebook where children can write a statement or draw a picture about the story. This serves as a "book review" for other children who check out the backpack. Teachers may also include a book or magazine article for parents.

Parents do not have to be well-educated to make a difference. "The motivation and impetus for learning begins in the home," says Beverly Langford Thomas, Executive Director of the Head Start Program in the District of Columbia Public Schools. "It's not a set of skills. It's the values, desires, determination, and belief that it can happen." Ms. Thomas cites the experience of a colleague, now a professor at Johns Hopkins University, whose mother was concerned that he and his brother were clowning around too much in elementary school. The mother

---

Dear Families,

Your child is learning to read! Beginning this week, I will send home books for your child to share with you. Each book will be sent home in a plastic, sealable, storage bag. This is to help protect the book and to serve as a reminder to return it by the date listed on the card. You can help your child develop responsibility by finding a place at home to keep the book.

Shared reading experiences are an important part of our reading program. You will see many signs that your child is using new skills in reading. For example, notice if your child:

- Uses different strategies in trying to read new words
- Attempts to self-correct if something doesn't sound right or make sense
- Retells a story

Your encouragement will help your child see that reading is important. If you have any questions, please let me know.

Sincerely,

required the boys to read to her every night, and to write weekly book reports for her. They didn't know at the time that their mother could not read. What they learned from her was that reading was valued in their home.

Involving Families in Assessment

Earlier, we described how parents can help you learn more about their child. Through personal contacts, and by asking specific questions about the child, you can gain valuable insights. This information, along with your observations of the child, provides a comprehensive picture of the child's abilities. Involving families in all phases of the assessment process can promote mutual understanding, generate a joint commitment to achieving the goals for each child, and keep parents informed about any concerns.

Promoting Mutual Understanding

Teachers cannot assume that parents understand how children's work is assessed at school or the teacher's expectations for work quality. When papers come home with invented spelling, reversed numbers, or incorrect math problems, it can raise concerns that a teacher is not teaching children the "correct" approaches or valuing right answers. Even if you share your approaches during back-to-school night, you may find that it helps to remind parents of when and how you evaluate children's work. It is valuable to you as well as to children and their families to be clear about your expectations and methods for evaluating work.

Take time to explain any of the following approaches you use in your classroom:

- when you correct spelling and when you do not;
- how children edit one another's work and what they learn from this process;
- when you expect work to be perfect, when you do not, and why;
- why children are encouraged to count on their fingers or use manipulative materials in doing math;
- how you mark children's papers and what the marks mean; or
- why you don't use red pens to correct work or give stickers as rewards.

The portfolios of children's work provide a rich resource for sharing both the quality of a child's work and progress over time. Parents can contribute samples of their child's work to the portfolio—work that you might otherwise not have seen. Portfolios give parents a better understanding of the topics and projects the class is studying and allow parents to ask specific questions about their child's work in your classroom. Particularly for parents who are not entirely comfortable speaking in English, portfolios do not rely on words and therefore provide concrete evidence of your curriculum content and how their child is learning.

Involving Families in Establishing Goals

One of the primary purposes of assessment is to establish realistic goals for children in order to plan instruction. Parents will want to know your goals and how you plan to help their child achieve them. By involving parents in the process of formulating goals and identifying strategies that will help the child, you will find that you have strong allies in achieving these goals.

Ms. Woodburn is having her first conference with Nancy's mother, Ms. Fowler. She describes how one of Nancy's goals for herself this year is to write longer stories, and asks Nancy's mother what she hopes Nancy will learn in second grade. Ms. Fowler says, "I'm concerned about her spelling." Ms. Woodburn responds, "I feel that it is an important goal for Nancy as well. Nancy and I will come up with words each week from her writing, make a list, and these will be her spelling words for the week. She'll have some time to study them in class, but it will help Nancy if you can practice them with her at home as well."

Keeping Families Informed

Parents often want to know how their child measures up to the school's expectations. Is their child achieving at grade level? Does the teacher have any concerns about their child? A comprehensive approach to assessment linked to your curriculum allows you to convey an accurate picture of the child's progress and to discuss any concerns either of you have. All parents have a right to know this information and feel reassured when they learn that you have a plan for helping their child if there is a problem.

In any given year, you may have children whose progress is of particular concern to you and/or the parents. You may suspect that a health problem, a hearing loss, poor eyesight, or a learning disability is impeding the child's progress in your class. If you have established a relationship with the parents and have discussed each of your concerns, parents are likely to be open to suggestions that they have their child examined by a specialist. Problems identified early can often be corrected or addressed before the child experiences too many failures.

Don't to wait until the end of the year to let parents know if their child is not progressing according to your expectations. Nothing is more upsetting to a parent than learning that there is a problem when it's too late to address it. Sharing any concerns early in the school year allows teachers and families to work together on behalf of the child right from the beginning.

Families in Need of Special Services

For some families and in some communities, it may be especially challenging to establish close, trusting relationships on behalf of the children. The children who need the most help academically and socially often live in impoverished and unstable home environments. A concern voiced repeatedly by teachers of young children is that they are increasingly being called upon to "do it all." They feel that many of their children and families have complex needs that must be addressed before successful learning relationships can be established.

Community-based family support programs that link the adults as well as the children to formal agency services and informal community support can help teachers in their efforts to reach out to families in need. Providing new immigrant families with information about how the school and social services systems work, preferably in their own language, can involve teachers, families, and members of the community in joint support efforts.

Most family support programs work in partnership with parents, or other significant adults in the child's life, to build the family's capacity to respond appropriately to the developmental needs of its children. Program staff acknowledge and address the contexts in which families live, appreciating and valuing each family's community, culture, individual traditions, values, and lifestyles. The process of establishing trust and creating positive communication is particularly difficult when families are accustomed to an adversarial relationship with schools or community services.

In communities where school-home collaborations have been the most successful, the schools have taken an active leadership role. A cadre of teachers or an active principal has taken the initiative to personally create effective partnerships. These partnerships often include services such as: school-based medical and dental services, drug and alcohol abuse counseling, family crisis counseling, child care, parenting classes, employment training and counseling, and transportation. Services are provided at the school site or near the school.

An increasing number of schools, and almost all those receiving Title I funds, have a home-school liaison. This staff person is often in the best position to work with the principal and the community to explore how most effectively to acquire more family support services. Currently there are federal and state grant opportunities as well as private foundation funding possibilities. An essential first step is for teachers and administrators to make the decision that they want to work more closely with their most vulnerable and challenging students and families.

Closing Thoughts

Teachers and families share the same goals and therefore the responsibility for building a partnership that brings the child's school and home life together. The teacher must take the initiative for making this a positive partnership. Using the eight approaches to working with families described in this chapter will enable you to learn more about the children in your classroom, build a classroom community, reinforce the classroom structure, and both support and assess children's learning. Teachers who take time to build a partnership with each child's family have gained critically important allies in creating exciting classrooms and confident students.

References and Resources for Building a Partnership with Families

Beecher, R. M. 1985. Parent Involvement and Reading Achievement: A Review of Research and Implications for Practice. *Childhood Education* 62:44–49.

Benard, Bonnie. 1999. From Research to Practice: The Foundations of the Resiliency Paradigm. In *Resiliency in Action*. Edited by Nan Henderson, Bonnie Benard, and Nancy Sharp-Light. Gorham, ME: Resiliency in Action, Inc., 5–9.

Benson, Peter L., Judy Galbraith, and Pamela Espeland. 1998. *What Kids Need to Succeed.* Minneapolis, MN: Fire Spirit.

Berger, Eugenia. 1991. *Parents as Partners in Education.* New York: MacMillan Publishing Co.

Bickart, Toni S., Judy R. Jablon, and Diane Trister Dodge. 1997. *What Every Parent Needs to Know about 1st, 2nd & 3rd Grades*. Naperville, IL: Sourcebooks, Inc., and Washington, DC: Teaching Strategies, Inc.

Carnegie Foundation for the Advancement of Teaching. 1988. *The Conditions of Teaching.* Princeton, NJ: Carnegie Foundation for the Advancement of Teaching.

Coates, Grace Davila, and Jean Kerr Stenmark. 1997. *Family Math for Young Children.* Berkley, CA: The Regents of the University of California.

Comer, James. November 2, 1989. Keynote address at National Association for the Education of Young Children Conference. Atlanta, GA.

Hale-Benson, Janice. 1986. *Black Children: Their Roots, Culture, and Learning Styles.* Baltimore, MD: Johns Hopkins University Press.

Henderson, Anne T., Carl L. Marburger, and Theodora Ooms. 1986. *Beyond the Bake Sale: An Educator's Guide to Working with Parents*. Washington, DC: National Committee for Citizens in Education.

Henderson, A. T., and N. Berla, eds. 1994. *A New Generation of Evidence: The Family Is Critical to Student Achievement*. Washington, DC: National Committee for Citizens in Education.

Hymes, James. 1974. *Effective School-Home Relationships*. Sierra-Madre, CA: California Association of Young Children.

Lightfoot, Sara Lawrence. 1978. *Worlds Apart: The Relationships Between Families and Schools*. New York: Basic Books.

Liontos, Lynn Balster. 1992. *At Risk Families and Schools Becoming Partners*. Eugene, OR: ERIC Clearinghouse on Educational Management, University of Oregon.

Lynch, Eleanor, and Marc Hanson. 1992. *Developing Cross-Cultural Competence: A Guide for Working with Young Children and Their Families*. Baltimore, MD: Paul H. Brooks Publishing Co.

Nurss, Joanne R., Rebecca Huss, and Peter Hannon. 1993. American Parents Hearing Children Read: Trying a British Approach. *International Journal of Early Childhood* 25 (2): 20–26.

The Report of the Carnegie Task Force on Learning in The Primary Grades. 1996. *Years of Promise: A Comprehensive Learning Strategy for America's Children*. New York: Carnegie Corporation.

Storti, Craig. 1989. *The Art of Crossing Cultures*. Yarmouth, ME: Intercultural Press.

U.S. Department of Education. 1994. *Strong Families, Strong Schools: Building Community Partnerships for Learning*. Washington, DC: U.S. Department of Education.

Walking, H. F. 1984. Families as Partners on Educational Productivity. *Phi Delta Kappan* 65:397–400.

Weinberg, Pamela. 1990. *Family Literacy and the School: How Teachers Can Help*. New York: New Readers Press.

Web Sites:

U.S. Department of Education's Partnership for Family Involvement in Education. http://pfie.ed.gov

Parent Soup. http://www.parentsoup.com

National Parent Information Network. http://www.npin.org

Teaching Strategies, Inc. http://www.teachingstrategies.com

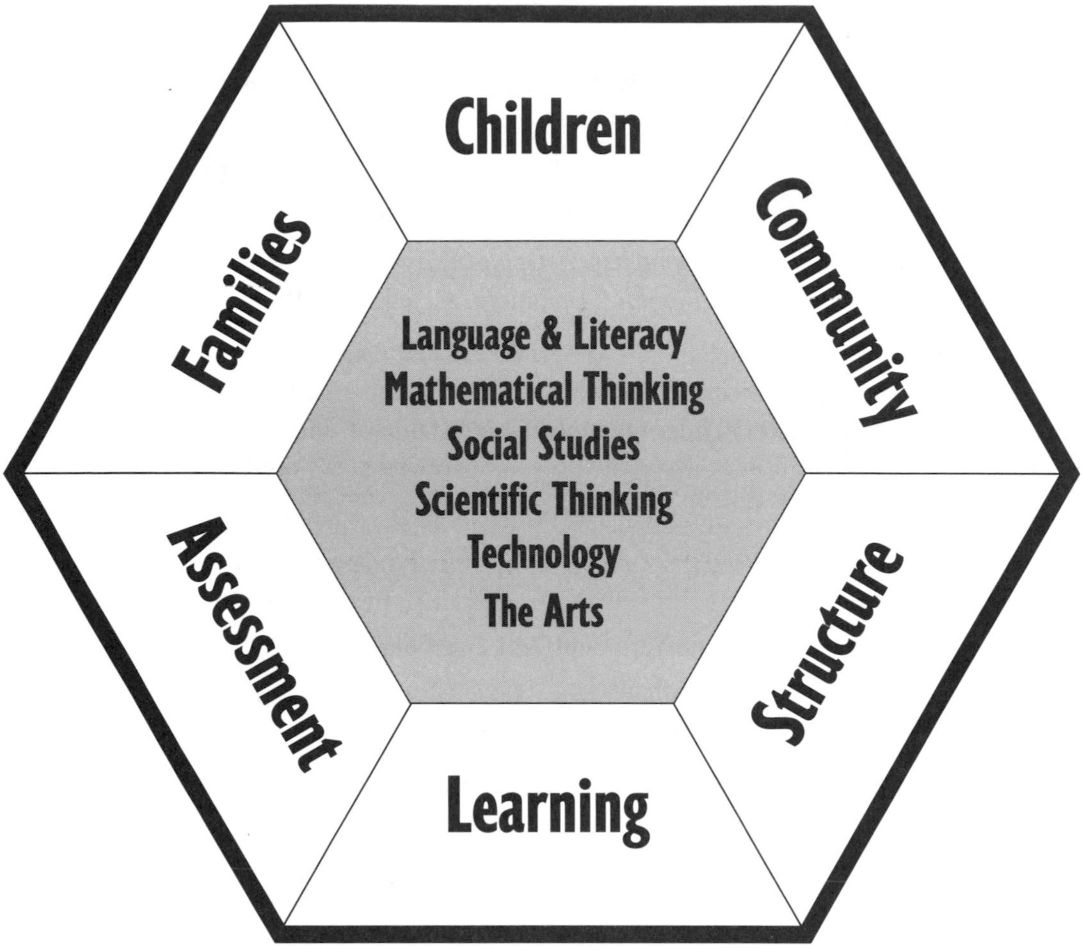
Children
Community
Structure
Learning
Assessment
Families
Language & Literacy
Mathematical Thinking
Social Studies
Scientific Thinking
Technology
The Arts

PART TWO

Introduction to Part Two

art Two of *Building the Primary Classroom* presents the content that is taught in the primary grades. It shows how language and literacy, mathematical thinking, social studies, scientific thinking, technology, and the arts are taught within the framework of six strategies.

The six strategies described in Part One make the subject matter of the classroom come alive. Knowing your children helps you plan where to begin, which materials to choose, and what questions to ask. The classroom community that you create enables children to work in small groups, to share supplies, and to feel safe taking risks. The structure you establish enables children to work independently because they anticipate the day's events, understand classroom rules, and know how to find, use, and put away materials. The approach to guiding children's learning helps children construct their own understanding within each subject area. The approach to assessment offers you many ways to find out what children are learning so that you can modify instructional approaches in order to address individual needs. Involving family members in homework and class projects that call for real-life application of skills and concepts enhances children's learning.

The chapters in Part Two are not meant to provide everything a teacher needs to know within a discipline; they offer a way to think about each subject area. The overviews of content and specific skills in each subject reflect child development research and national and local standards. These chapters show how concepts and skills are taught not only in the context of long-term studies or regularly scheduled work times, but also by taking advantage of teachable moments. The sample resources listed at the end of each chapter offer additional ideas about how specific activities can best be incorporated into your approach to curriculum.

As you read each of the subject chapters in Part Two, you will notice that children are having discussions in meetings, working in small groups to conduct active investigations, and representing their learning in a variety of ways. Teachers provide children with daily opportunities to reflect on their learning. The classroom doesn't change with each subject area. The framework remains constant and it is this framework that enables teachers to make learning meaningful for children.

LANGUAGE AND LITERACY

anguage and literacy skills are central to communication and to learning. Communication includes the ability to obtain information, clarify concepts and feelings, and convey ideas in ways that others understand. Learning involves reading for understanding, enjoying literature, and experiencing the power of putting ideas into print. Whenever we talk on the telephone, read the newspaper, write a letter, use electronic mail, discuss books and movies, or find out what time a store opens, we use language and literacy skills.

Young children come to school with a wide range of experiences and ideas about language and literacy. In infancy, they are surrounded by the sounds of language; they babble and adults respond, including them in conversations. Children see print all around them: they notice that cars come to a halt at the big red STOP sign; they see labels and signs in the supermarket; they listen to story books being read; they follow directions on the computer screen. Children also use writing as they play. They pretend to write grocery lists, messages, and letters. Teaching language and literacy means building on these early experiences in ways that convey our confidence that all children can learn to read, write, and express their ideas effectively.

An important goal in the primary grades is to help children see that language and literacy learning has a purpose. When children acquire language and literacy skills as part of meaningful activities, they see connections between what they are learning and their everyday lives. Classrooms can be places where listening, speaking, reading, and writing are integrated into all activities. Children can learn and use these communication skills on a daily basis.

Children Acquiring Language and Literacy Skills

Teachers who surround children with books, give them interesting reasons to write, and use meetings for in-depth discussions make language and literacy experiences a vital part of classroom life. Consider the following examples of classrooms in which teachers provide purposeful experiences for children.

*In a **first grade,** Ms. Wallen reads several "how-to" books to her class to introduce them to expository text. She encourages the children to write their own how-to books. They identify a range of topics, including "All About Riding Scooters" and "How to Bake Cupcakes." After making a list of ideas for their books, they interview their classmates for additional ideas. The children record the suggestions in their writing folders.*

Ms. Wallen models a specific type of writing for the children to support their growth as writers. She allows time for discussion and peer interaction. After listening to and talking about books that exemplify the "how-to" genre, the children are eager to become authors themselves. Because their knowledge is valued, they want to communicate it. Each child makes an independent choice about what to write. Through activities such as these, the children practice reading, writing, speaking, and listening.

*In a **second grade** classroom, Mr. Sanders and the children are gathered in the meeting area. They are discussing how each character in the stories they have read has a major obstacle to overcome. Mr. Sanders suggests that each child spend a few minutes jotting down ideas about how a particular problem was solved. When the discussion resumes, they notice similarities in the solutions and chart them, making three categories. The first column lists stories in which a miracle occurs. In the second, a new character enters the story and saves the day. In the stories listed in the third column, the characters consistently solve the problems on the third try.*

Mr. Sanders encourages the children to talk about the problem-solving aspect of each story. He models an organized way for children to record their ideas. Group discussions help the children clarify their thinking about the stories and learn strategies for analyzing story content and visually representing their ideas.

*A small group of **third graders** reads Charlotte's Web in a literature group. The teacher opens the discussion by asking, "What do you think about these characters?" Peter comments that he likes the character of Templeton, the rat. Others agree. Ms. Weiner suggests that they find some examples of how E.B. White describes Templeton. The children thumb through their individual copies of the book to find favorite selections about Templeton.*

In this classroom, the children eagerly discuss literature they have read together. The teacher guides the discussion so that each child participates—either sharing information or offering an opinion. The children are aware of the purpose of their work and therefore highly engaged in the process.

Language and literacy teaching is exciting for both teachers and children in these classrooms. The teachers emphasize what children *can* do, rather than what they don't know. The teachers foster social interaction because it is a vital part of language and literacy learning. They know that children learn from one another as well as from books and adults. They plan experiences that expose children to the joy of listening to and reading good literature and engage children in making discoveries about books as a source of information, about writing as a way to share experiences, ideas, and information, and about talking and listening as important ways of learning. When children have choices in their reading and writing selections, they are more likely to become self-directed learners. When they are properly motivated, they can then be taught skills to help them become more effective communicators.

Goals for the Language and Literacy Curriculum

Many children today have poor communication skills. Perhaps this results from hurried lifestyles, too much TV, and fewer opportunities to play informally with peers. Whatever the reasons, it is important for children to learn the art of conversation, experience the pleasures of storytime, and enjoy the satisfaction of being listened to when they have something to say. In addition, children need strong language and literacy skills if they are to function as productive members of society in the 21st century.

Recognizing this need, many organizations have proposed standards and position papers describing what the language and literacy curriculum should emphasize in the early grades. The National Council of Teachers of English, the International Reading Association, and the authors of the *New Standards Primary Literacy Standards* advocate an expanded view of the language and literacy curriculum. These organizations urge educators to broaden their thinking about teaching language and literacy, and to think in terms of lifelong goals. These are the goals.

- Clarify ideas and feelings.
- Communicate ideas and thoughts with others, orally, in writing, and through visual representations.
- Use literacy skills to obtain information from print and nonprint materials.
- Develop an appreciation for literature and writing.

An understanding of the value of these goals helps guide instructional decisions.

Clarifying One's Own Thoughts and Feelings

Putting complex ideas and emotions into words leads to a deeper understanding and clarity of thinking. Because children are capable speakers before they are writers, discussing ideas before writing them is often beneficial. For beginning writers, teachers may take dictation from the children, then read aloud what the children have said.

When children articulate their feelings and put their ideas into print, they recognize how much they know about a subject. Teachers provide support by suggesting that children continue writing, even after they think they have said everything. When encouraged to write more, they often learn more.

> *Ms. Tyler overhears a group of third graders having a heated argument about which combination of baseball players would make the best team. She proposes that the children list their ideas for teams and explain their choices, including each player's merits and weaknesses. Following their writing, the children share their work. After presenting his proposal to the group, Pavel exclaims, "I really do love baseball!"*

Putting their thoughts and feelings in words enables children to make sense of events in their lives. A child who reads a story about someone who has moved to a new home, may better understand her own feelings about a move her family is about to make. She may discover a phrase or passage in the story that describes her own emotional responses. Reading that one character writes letters to former classmates, she might decide to do the same. Personally connecting to a story in this way can help a child to overcome difficult feelings.

Communicating Ideas and Thoughts with Others

Because language and literacy learning affects how we communicate ideas, thoughts, and feelings, it is both personal and social. When something important happens, we phone our closest friend and share it. When we observe a terrible accident, we talk about it with anyone who will listen. When our best friends relocate, we are eager to receive a letter, e-mail, or phone call so that we can learn about what they are doing. It is natural for people to want to communicate with others.

When children have words to describe their feelings, they can cope more effectively with what is happening.

> *"I know you miss your mother while she's in the hospital," says Mr. Jenkins to Amelia. "She misses you too, and she probably wonders what you're doing at school. Why not write her a letter to tell her about the project we've been working on? I bet it will make her feel better just to read something you wrote for her."*

Children who can read and write about their experiences, express ideas clearly, and listen to the responses of others are equipped to take control of their learning. For this and many other reasons, communication skills are powerful.

Using Literacy Skills to Obtain Information

Children's school experiences should be connected with real-world tasks. Opportunities to ask questions, listen for information, read, write, and use CD-ROMs and the Internet as a way to make discoveries lead children to appreciate the reasons for having a repertoire of literacy skills. Children learn to use literacy skills to obtain information when they have interesting problems to solve and when they want to pursue answers to their questions. Their natural curiosity leads them into situations that require the use of language and literacy skills.

> *After doing research on hurricanes, Carly wants to find out more about weather. She learns how meteorologists measure rain and decides to conduct an experiment about rainfall by setting up a rain gauge outside the classroom. The class gets involved in estimating and measuring how much water will be collected each time it rains. Carly uses computer graphics to write a report on rainfall and shares her report with the class. Her classmates decide to continue the research by tallying monthly rainfall. They also e-mail a school in another part of the country working on a similiar study. They make graphs and compare their data about rainfall.*

Children use literacy skills to connect with people—near and far, real and imaginary, current and historical. Reading and writing biographies give children access to intriguing people—those they know and some whom they may never meet.

> *After reading a biography of Jackie Robinson, Marisa decides to write a biography about an athlete of today, Michelle Akers, who is on the U.S. Women's National Soccer Team and was its leading scorer. In the process of doing the research, she learns that Michelle Akers has chronic fatigue syndrome and has testified before Congress about the disease. Marisa admires Akers for overcoming this disability and for trying to help others with the same condition.*

Teachers can help children recognize their ability to reflect on events in history and make personal connections to them.

Developing an Appreciation for Literature and Writing

Children who are read to, who enjoy the sound of poetry, who learn to love stories and books, and who are given opportunities to write are motivated to become readers and writers themselves. Teachers cultivate a love of reading in children in many subtle ways. Holding a book in a particular way while reading, sharing a tidbit about the story to pique children's interest, reading with great expression and enthusiasm, all convey to children the value and excitement of books. Encouraging children to write their own stories, recording their observations of a recent snowfall, or reading them a funny e-mail message from a friend help to foster their appreciation for written communication.

Children develop an appreciation for literature and writing by listening to and reading books that are full of surprising language and fascinating plots. Stories that reflect children's cultural backgrounds and home life help them see how books relate to personal experience.

> *Hallie browses through the bookshelves in her classroom library, trying to find a book for quiet reading. She discovers the book* A Chair for My Mother *by Vera Williams. "Look!" she says. "This book has a mother, a grandmother, and a girl living in the same apartment—just like me!"*

Books can encourage children to bring their personal experiences to the classroom where they can write about them. Once children begin to identify with story characters, they also vicariously experience the lives of many different people, not just those like themselves.

With these broad goals in mind—clarifying thoughts and feelings, communicating ideas and thoughts with others, using literacy skills to obtain information, and developing an appreciation for literature and writing—it is evident how all aspects of the language and literacy curriculum are integrated. Talking about ideas and books helps children expand their vocabularies. Language is intricately woven into reading and writing. Children who are given extensive opportunities to write are simultaneously learning to read. Their writing is enhanced by what they read in books.

Components of the Language and Literacy Curriculum

Children must learn to listen with understanding to what others say. They must also learn to express their ideas articulately. Of course, children must develop the abilities to comprehend what they read and write with increasing accuracy and clarity. The skills of language and literacy, so necessary for communicating and learning, are organized into four components:

- listening
- speaking
- reading
- writing

Many national standards as well as state and local standards include components of viewing and visually representing (NCTE/IRA 1996). The profound influence of the media on our lives has compelled educators to recognize that children need guidance in learning how to critically examine movies, TV commercials, infomercials, and documentaries, as well as the extensive material available over the World Wide Web. Dramatic advances in technology also enable children to represent their learning visually in new ways beyond the traditional oral presentations, writing, and drawing. Children can produce multimedia written and graphic presentations, computer graphics, photography, and physical performances that demonstrate what they have learned and how.

Thus, visual language can be added to written and spoken language as a component of the language arts. However, because we present viewing and visual representations as a key part of learning in all the content areas (see Chapter 4, Guiding Children's Learning), we have not repeated that information here.

Each of the four components listed above includes particular skills for children to learn during the primary grades. The following chart provides an overview of the language and literacy curriculum.

Overview of the Language and Literacy Curriculum

Components	Children Learn to:
Listening	<ul><li>Listen for meaning in the ideas of others (e.g., in conversations and discussions)</li><li>Listen with understanding to stories (e.g., discuss what happened; identify problems and solutions)</li><li>Follow directions</li><li>Reflect on and relate relevant personal experience to what is heard</li><li>Listen to other points of view (e.g., take turns and respond)</li></ul>
Speaking	<ul><li>Speak easily to convey ideas (e.g., in conversations, in small or large group discussions, during play)</li><li>Ask and answer questions (e.g., differentiate between questions and statements)</li><li>Use language for a variety of purposes (e.g., self-expression, play, questioning, humor, drama)</li><li>Use language in imaginative ways</li></ul>
Reading	<ul><li>Sustain interest in reading activities</li><li>Understand and interpret information from a story</li><li>Use a variety of strategies to construct meaning from print (e.g., context cues, visual cues, prior knowledge)</li><li>Use a variety of strategies to figure out unknown words (e.g., letter-sound relationships, meaning, pictures, syntax)</li><li>Make logical predictions about stories (e.g., guess what will happen)</li><li>Respond to literature in a variety of ways (e.g., act out a role, draw a picture, make a diorama, keep a reading journal)</li><li>Select different kinds of books for a variety of purposes</li></ul>
Writing	<ul><li>Use writing to convey meaning for a variety of purposes (e.g., persuasion, humor, description, feelings)</li><li>Recognize conventions of print (e.g., use of capital letters, punctuation, grammar, spelling)</li><li>Compose stories or other text with a main idea and logical progression</li><li>Reflect upon and revise writing (e.g., edit for style, content, conventional spelling)</li><li>Sustain interest in writing activities</li><li>Develop legible handwriting</li></ul>

Weaving these components into learning experiences for children is the teacher's task. Because the components are interrelated, there are many ways to guide learning.

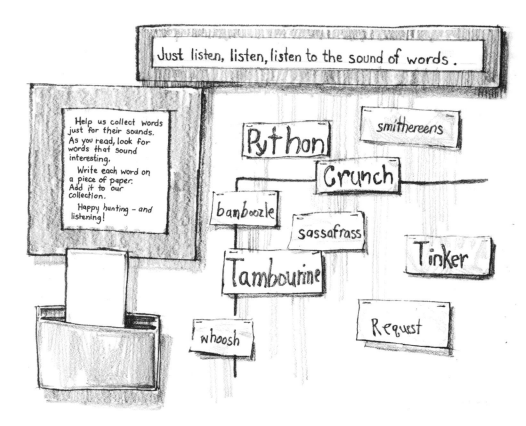

Listening

Listening skills involve hearing what has been said and relating it to personal knowledge. Children develop listening skills when they have opportunities to:

- participate in a discussion and respond appropriately;

- follow oral directions, first with one or two steps, then with more;

- repeat increasingly complex messages to a third person;

- concentrate in an effort to understand what is being said and ask questions or make relevant comments;

- receive descriptive, positive feedback about what good listening looks like (e.g., "I noticed that you were looking right at Mindy when she was talking.");

- receive clear feedback about the results of good listening (e.g., "Your question shows how much you learned and what else you want to know.");

- comment on similarities and differences between two books; and

- listen carefully for interesting language in books.

Children develop listening skills when there is something worth listening to and when they have good listening behaviors modeled for them. Teachers model listening behaviors by looking at someone who is talking, by asking questions, making comments, facilitating discussions, and taking turns.

Teachers can also help children recognize how words sound and how they make us feel. Some passages in books make us cry and some make us laugh. A classmate may say something that is comforting or hurtful. Teachers can encourage children to become observant about the tone of language. It is not just *what* words we hear but *how* the message is conveyed that affects our ability to listen.

> *In a second grade classroom a teacher helps Irene to think about how she makes a request. "I'm going to ask Julian if I can borrow his scissors. I'm trying to decide how to do it. Which one do you think he'll say yes to?" says Ms. Brown. "GIVE ME THOSE SCISSORS!" or "May I borrow your scissors for just a minute? I'll bring them right back."*

Children know they are being heard when they receive an appropriate response to what they share. When their classmates are attentive, they experience both the emotional and physical effect of being heard. When they provide that kind of support to others, they become good listeners. Children become more aware of listening behaviors when these skills are discussed. Meetings provide many opportunities to practice and discuss listening skills and behaviors.

Speaking

As children become better listeners, they develop more sophisticated speaking skills. Speaking skills include the ability to convey ideas and questions in discussions and conversations, and to use language for a variety of purposes. Children develop and demonstrate speaking skills when they:

- participate in discussions by communicating their own thoughts and feelings;
- describe what they are doing or thinking in response to open-ended questions and thought-provoking comments;
- ask questions that are relevant to a story;
- make up word games, riddles, poems, and songs;
- use imaginary language and new vocabulary in stories or skits they write, read aloud, or act out; and
- present an oral report or read a story they have written.

Children may need help organizing and expressing their thoughts. When they are encouraged to talk about their experiences and use new words, they are better able to incorporate those words into their permanent vocabulary. As children refine their vocabulary and describe events more clearly, they gain greater control over a conversation.

During a discussion of a class trip to a vegetable packaging plant, Bernard, a first grader, describes how the people worked together to get the tomatoes packed. He says, "You remember, they were all in a row and each person had just one job to do." Ms. Harris, his teacher, says, "Bernard, that's a great description of an assembly line. When people work like that they work on an assembly line." Later that day Bernard builds in the block area. He constructs a factory with an assembly line. He says, "Put these block people in a row along that long block. They are going to work on the assembly line to get those veggies out to the city!"

In addition to learning vocabulary, children can learn that there are different styles of communication. We talk to family members, to doctors, to teachers, and to one another in the classroom or on the playground with different voices, depending upon the relationship and where we are.

With experience, children become aware that communicating clearly takes time, skill, and patience. Listening and speaking skills are fostered in many ways throughout the day and are an integral part of reading and writing activities.

Reading

For children to be competent readers by the end of third grade, teachers must encourage an appreciation of spoken, written, and visual language, create an environment that promotes language development, and teach children the skills and strategies they need to comprehend written materials and decode the English language. Children develop reading skills when they:

- are read to every day;

- read appropriate texts (both in content and reading level);

- read a variety of print materials (e.g., stories, poems, songs, charts, signs);

- discuss what they have read and heard;

- develop a sight recognition of frequently used words;

- make predictions about text, summarize what they have read, and draw inferences;

- receive instruction about the sound structures of letters and words;

- attend to spelling-sound correspondences and common spelling conventions;

- learn new vocabulary;

- experience a print-rich environment with many opportunities to read—alone, with a partner, in a small group, or with the whole class; and

- write every day (e.g., journals, stories, reports, lists, messages, e-mail, letters).

During the primary grades, teachers can introduce children to a wide variety of reading materials: animal stories, mysteries, fairy tales, science books, poetry. Teachers can help children discover that books can be sad, humorous, puzzling, and enjoyable. By reading and talking about a variety of books, children learn that books can make us laugh and cry. Books can be scary and informative. Books can take us to places not yet explored.

Often children like to hear and read books over and over again. Sometimes books on a particular subject inspire children to seek more information or make something.

> *Ms. Snow, the school librarian, notices Jaime checking out his fourth book on woodworking and says, "You must really like carpentry." "I do," replies Jaime, "My grandfather loves it. I'm trying to learn as much as I can so that the next time I visit him, he'll be really surprised. He promised me that I could help him build a bookshelf."*

Children who enjoy reading reflect on the ideas in stories and often talk with their friends and families about what they are reading. Children can be encouraged to respond to books they have read together with classmates by doing projects.

> *After noticing the map in the front of* My Father's Dragon *by Ruth Gannett, a second grade class decides to make a study of books with maps. They find as many books with maps as possible. Next, they write a group story that involves following a map of their school to solve a mystery.*

Reading can offer a greater understanding of the world. First graders read non-fiction books about the local animals they are studying. Second graders hear stories about how families from many cultures live and work. They learn about the similarities and differences among people. Third graders read the newspaper to find the latest information on a proposed new city playground.

How Children Learn to Read

Everyone agrees that learning to read is essential for children in the primary grades. There has been much disagreement and misunderstanding, however, about the best ways for teachers to support young readers. Fortunately, recent syntheses of research of the last twenty years make it easier to understand the necessary elements of a high-quality reading program and to appreciate what has been learned from advocates of a *whole language* approach and from those who advocate that *phonics* is key.

When teachers foster an appreciation of spoken, written, and verbal language, and create an environment that promotes language development, most children begin to see themselves as readers and writers. Motivation is a central factor in becoming literate. The *whole language* perspective toward teaching language and literacy is built on this principle.

The whole language philosophy emphasizes creating a classroom environment that integrates learning and promotes communication skills all the time. Instead of focusing on the parts of language such as letter sounds or word recognition as a prerequisite to reading, children actively read and write across the curriculum, and in the process, learn particular skills, including letter-sound relationships, or phonics.

Phonics, of course, is one of many strategies readers use to figure out unfamiliar words. Traditionally, phonics has been taught through the drill and practice of associating letters and their sounds. However, a major finding of the National Research Council's Report, *Preventing Reading Difficulties in Young Children* (1998) is that children need *phonological awareness*, the ability to hear the sounds of language, and *phonemic awareness*, the ability to distinguish the smallest units of sound in speech. These are key ingredients in the development of literacy that have not been addressed sufficiently by educators. The Report notes that phonics instruction requires that children already know about the sound composition of words. Therefore, teachers must first increase awareness about the sounds of our language before children can benefit from phonics instruction.

Children are said to have attained phonemic awareness when they understand these concepts.

- Language is made of sentences.
- Sentences are made of words.
- Words are made of individual sounds.
- Sounds can be manipulated to make new words.

Current research indicates that phonemic awareness is one of the most powerful predictors of future reading success (Adams 1990; Stanovich 1986, 1994). Phonemic awareness is not the same as phonics. Phonemic awareness is oral; phonics connects the speech sound with the written symbol. Children who are phonemically aware can do these things.

- Create rhymes.
- Blend sounds together to make a new word.
- Tell how many sounds are heard in a word.
- Break spoken words down into individual sounds.
- Substitute, add, and delete sounds in spoken words.

Children in preschool, kindergarten, and the primary grades develop phonemic awareness by playing with language through songs, stories, and rhymes in social settings (Yopp 1992). If a child does not demonstrate phonemic awareness by mid-first grade, then further evaluation and intervention is required. When intervention occurs early in the primary grades, children have a good chance of overcoming their reading difficulties.

A Balanced Program of Instruction

Learning language is a process in which children first become aware of how, where, and when people listen, speak, read and write. Then they have multiple opportunities to explore in each of these areas before finally becoming competent users of all of these skills. Educators now speak of *emergent literacy* as a way of recognizing that language and literacy development is a process that begins with a baby's first awareness of language and continues with the child's early attempts at reading and writing. Children have to know the purposes and pleasures of reading to be motivated to learn the skills involved.

Beginning readers first must recognize that print tells a story and has a message. Evidence of this understanding occurs when children engage in these behaviors.

- Listen with interest to stories read aloud.
- Notice that the labels on shelves identify things.
- Write notes to friends.
- Make signs for block buildings.

The underlying goal of reading instruction is for children to read for meaning. Once they know that print conveys a message, they are ready to learn the strategies that readers use to make meaning out of text. The English language is particularly challenging; spoken English is based on syllables (5,000 different ones) and written English is based on an alphabetic system in which individual letters combine to form a spoken syllable (National Research Council 1998, 22). Further complicating learning, the same letter can have multiple sounds, making it difficult to develop rules for sound-symbol relationships.

Successful readers must attend to the sound structure of words, develop knowledge about print, and become familiar with basic purposes and mechanisms of reading in order to make meaning out of what they read. An instructional program that is balanced attends to all aspects of reading development and assesses individual needs carefully. Teachers guide children to develop strategies for reading at increasing levels of comprehension.

> The challenge for teachers is to help children develop a repertoire of flexible strategies for solving words while reading for meaning. In fact, to read means to use graphic symbols (letters clustered into words) embedded in continuous text. Children may know enough about the written code to recognize letters and words in isolation, and this is useful. However, to read for meaning they must be able to decode words strung together in sentences, paragraphs, stories, and informational texts. And, they must be able to relate the words in one text to other texts they have read. Further, the more texts they read, the more the phonological and visual information becomes available. Through repeated readings, the reader has more attention for the way words look and is able to learn more about phonics and word patterns (Fountas and Pinnell 1996, 164).

In sum, teachers must be knowledgeable about reading instruction and be able to recognize the individual needs of children as they learn to read. Many children learn through a rich literacy environment, ongoing instruction, and multiple opportunities to read and write every day. Others, particularly those with language-based learning disabilities, need more direct systematic instruction. All readers use multiple sources of information to make sense of unfamiliar words.

How Children Learn to Use Cueing Systems

Marie Clay (1991, 1993) has written extensively on the sources of information people use to make sense of unfamiliar words. She describes three cueing systems:

- meaning cues
- structural or syntactic cues
- visual cues

Meaning Cues

When readers use their understanding of the text to figure out a word they don't know, they are using meaning or semantic cues. Children who use their memory of experiences in everyday life to read a previously unknown word are also using meaning cues.

> *Ammar pores over a book on spiders. He looks for information on how spiders catch their food. He comes to the sentence, 'Some spiders catch insects by throwing a silk net over them.' He reads, "Some spiders catch bugs by throwing a silk net over them." His teacher, Ms. Swanson, says, "Ammar,* bugs *does make sense in that sentence. You know that spiders eat bugs. Let's look closely at that word. Does the word* bugs *start with an 'i'? What word could that be?" "Insects," says Ammar proudly.*

Structural or Syntactic Cues

Many children enter first grade with a strong sense of the structure of language or what sounds right. They intuitively know the grammatical structure of sentences. When they make use of this knowledge about the forms of our language to read an unknown word, they use structural cues. This can be observed when a reader replaces an unknown word with the same part of speech for that word. For example, a young reader may read, "I can ride a car," instead of "I can ride a bicycle." She has replaced a noun with another noun.

Visual Cues

When readers see a word in print, immediately recognize it, and say it out loud, it is called automatic word recognition. Children who rely on remembering whole words, without sounding them out, are known as sight word readers. They use the visual cues of the letters to read the word.

Children also use visual or graphic cues when they recognize individual letters, groups of letters, and the sounds represented by the letters.

> *Six-year-old Miriam looks at the sentence, "Here comes the school bus." She reads, "Here comes the school b-b, sss, bus." Ms. Fay says, "Miriam, you are looking closely at that word and thinking about what letters are there and what they sound like. Good for you. You read that new word."*

A strong reading program provides opportunities for children to increase their sight word vocabulary and phonetic awareness by using books that specifically support reading development. Knowledge can start with individual letters and expand to letter combinations and the sounds represented by those letters.

Learning to Self-Monitor and Self-Correct

Competent readers use these cueing systems as a "network of. . . strategies. . . to attend to information from different sources" (Clay 1991, 328). Because these strategies take place in the reader's head, they are difficult to observe and difficult to teach in isolation. We get better at using them through experience. As Fountas and Pinnell explain, ". . . modeling and showing is insufficient. The future swimmer must get in the water" (Fountas and Pinnell 1996, 149). Learning how to read requires the student to "get in the water," that is, to read regularly and often in order to experience how to use the cueing systems to self-monitor and cross-check (Clay 1991).

Teachers can help children to become aware of the strategies they use to puzzle out new words. When teachers foster independence and self-confidence, children can figure out words they don't know. With each attempt, children learn to ask themselves if what they read makes sense, if it looks right, and if it sounds right. If it does, they continue reading. If it does not, they should try again. Children use cueing systems to self-correct. They may ask themselves, "Did what I just read make sense?" (meaning), "Did what I just read sound right?"(structure), or "Did what I read look like what I said?" (visual).

As you read with children, carefully observe their reading behaviors and use of cueing systems. Tell children what you see them doing so they become aware of their own strategies and thus increase their reading independence. After you have labeled the strategies for them, it is appropriate to ask children how they figured out an unknown word.

> *Gabriel, a first grader, reads a book about pets. When he comes to the sentence, Here are the puppies, he says, "Here are the dogs. No, I mean, here are the puppies." Ms. Wilson says, "That was great reading. How did you know to change dogs to puppies?" Gabriel responds, "At first I thought it was dogs because the picture kinda looks like dogs, not puppies. Then I noticed the word was long and it had a lot of p's so then I knew it was puppies."*

There are many ways to weave reading experiences and direct instruction into the classroom day. These will be discussed later in the section on organizing the language and literacy curriculum.

Writing

Young children learn to write by writing. Most first graders have some idea of what writing looks like and understand that meaning is contained in print. When children scribble, draw, and pretend to write, the writing process has begun.

Most children have a natural desire to write because they want to belong to the adult world of literacy. They learn the value of writing by seeing adults write for a reason. When you send a note to the office, fill out a form, or write a reminder note to yourself on the blackboard, you show children that writing serves a purpose.

To become effective and powerful communicators, children must believe that they have something important to say and that their thoughts and experiences are worth recording. When children are motivated to write, they will struggle through the process of presenting their ideas. They are more willing to work at making their thoughts as clear as possible.

> *Jane, a second grader, complains about how the school play yard is always full of litter. The yard is used for a flea market on Sundays and it is not always cleaned by Monday morning. Jane reports this to her teacher who suggests that she make signs to ask the market workers to clean up after themselves. Jane interviews her classmates for appropriate slogans. When she makes her signs she uses bright colors so they won't be missed. To Jane's delight, it works! There is great improvement in the condition of the yard.*

How Children Learn Writing Skills

Children need many opportunities every day to write for reasons that make sense to them. Research on children's writing demonstrates the obvious: the more you write the better you get. When children have reasons and opportunities to write in all areas of the curriculum, including math, science, and social studies, their overall literacy development improves (Dickinson and DiGisi 1998).

Teachers can incorporate a variety of writing activities in their classrooms to show the range of purposes for writing, and to give children more opportunities for success.

Children use writing to **convey meaning** when they:

- use a message board or mailbox to send notes to classmates or the teacher;
- make signs for their block constructions;
- label drawings;
- make lists;
- write a report about something they have studied in science or social studies;
- write in a journal or notebook about a feeling, an event, or an observation;
- conduct an interview and record the information gathered; or
- write to explain their understanding of a math problem.

Children develop awareness of the conventions of print and learn the **mechanics of writing** when they:

- edit their writing for use of capital letters, punctuation, and grammar;
- underline the words in their writing that they think are misspelled;
- read their writing aloud to hear where the punctuation belongs and add the missing punctuation;
- re-read their writing and find an omitted word; or
- find and correct misspelled words.

Children learn to **compose stories** or other text when they:

- choose the topics they want to write about; or
- draw upon personal experiences for ideas.

Children learn to **revise and change their writing** as they:

- read a text they have written, decide a detail is missing, and add it;
- experiment with the arrangement of sentences and phrases;
- work on their writing over time and make changes along the way;
- revise their writing by taking out unnecessary information; or
- read their writing to classmates and get suggestions for improvement.

The Link Between Reading and Writing

Writing and reading are inextricably linked.

> During writing, the child constructs words (a building-up process) while composing and then writing a text. During reading, the child takes words apart (a breaking-down process). Combining reading and writing activities allows the child to coordinate and use both processes (Fountas and Pinnell 1996, 165).

As children become more accomplished writers, they notice how authors carefully craft their books. And, as children become more proficient readers, they notice the conventions of print. They begin to use punctuation in their stories. Exposure to varied and interesting literature improves children's writing. Similarly, providing children with opportunities to become aware of and imitate a number of writing forms helps them appreciate what they are reading.

> *Mr. Jackson picks up the basket containing a number of poetry anthologies. He reads several poems and then responds to a child's request to hear a poem he read the day before. After finishing, Mr. Jackson says, "We've been reading and talking about poetry for a while. What are some of the things that you've noticed?" Lia raises her hand and says, "Some rhyme and some don't." Dana adds, "One poem had a line that was repeated three times." Joey says, "Some poems talk about two things and say how they're different." Mr. Jackson writes down the different ideas children identify*

and suggests that everyone try writing a poem. Equipped with models of poems to think about and discussion to draw on, the children set to work.

To guide children as readers and writers, we must be aware of the different skills they need in spelling and handwriting.

How Children Learn to Spell

When spelling is taught as part of an integrated approach to language and literacy, children see spelling as a tool for writing and not as a prerequisite. Learning how to spell is integrated into children's writing through opportunities to write about something that is personally important. By incorporating writing, and therefore spelling, throughout the school day and in all subjects, children learn to spell the words they need.

Many teachers and parents wonder how spelling skills can possibly develop if children are encouraged to write using *invented, phonetic,* or *temporary* spelling to get their ideas on paper. Actually, as soon as children learn some letters, they should use them in their writing, doing their best to write words, parts of words, and sentences. Children may begin by using a variety of letters, using the same letter over and over again, or they may use many letters in a random order. Young writers may not hear or use all the letters. "Went" may be recorded as "wnt" and "dog" as "d" or "dg."

> *Ms. Santos wants to encourage William, a first grader, to write. "William, you really noticed many details about our guinea pig in order to draw this picture. Now slowly say the words that go with the picture. Listen closely for the sounds in those words. Put down the letters that you hear. Do the best you can. When you're finished you can read it to me."*

Such invented or phonetic spelling promotes awareness of the sounds of speech and letter-sound/sound-letter relationships. Children use what they are learning about letters, sound, and spelling patterns as they write. Teachers who observe children's development as writers can use their observations to guide their teaching of reading skills.

In addition to thinking about sounds, teachers encourage children to write a word the way they think it looks. This enables children to use what they already know about words they have seen in their environment. Many times children will remember a place where they have seen a particular word before and go back to find it. Children use their visual memories of words that surround them in books, posters, wall charts, and signs, and incorporate those words into their work.

The National Research Council Report makes clear " . . .that the use of invented spelling is not in conflict with teaching correct spelling" (1998, 7). Spelling instruction can support children in learning or confirming their knowledge about the sound structure of English. They benefit from instruction about short, regular words, learning the spelling and the meanings of prefixes, suffixes, and word roots, and learning about spelling patterns. In second grade, such instruction should be evident in children's own writing (National Research Council 1998, 212).

In addition, direct spelling instruction can take the form of discussions about unusual, tricky, or hard-to-remember words.

> *A third grade class gathers in the meeting area. Two columns of words are written on the chalkboard in front of them. The first has words that have the long a sound represented by -ay, the second by -ae. Michael raises his hand and says, "While I was reading I noticed the word rain has the long a sound but we don't have a column for it. I think we need an -ai- list."*

Children will begin using vowels after they understand that words have vowels. Teachers highlight this concept by showing children how longer words have more letters. Gradually children make the connection between word length and syllables and the fact that each syllable has a vowel.

Through observation, experience, direct instruction, and reminders, children apply the spelling system of our language. They become more skillful in identifying both the separate sounds in each word, and the letters and groups of letters representing those sounds. Encouraging children to use invented spelling does not mean they are never expected to learn and use standard spelling. As they study particular words and spelling patterns they should be expected to incorporate standard spelling in their writing. Explaining this process can reassure family members.

> *Ms. Ward keeps a sample of her second graders' work to share with families at conferences. When Jessica's mother expresses concern over seeing a number of stories with words that were not spelled correctly, Ms. Ward points out how Jessica's spelling is developing. She focuses on the word* phone. *Over a month it changed from* fon *to* fone *to* phone. *She explains that Jessica is not only learning the rules about spelling, she is gaining confidence in her own abilities as a writer.*

As in all areas of guiding learning, teachers need to be excellent observers to know just when a child is ready to learn something new. Although some spelling lessons can be taught to the entire class, spelling lessons are likely to be most effective when they respond to individual needs and are taught individually or in small groups.

How Children Learn Handwriting Skills

Neat and legible handwriting makes writing a more effective and accurate communication tool. It's easier for the writer to read what has been written, and ensures that the reader gets an accurate message. When children copy their own words neatly, they also improve their spelling skills because, as they record the word, they form a clear visual picture of it in their minds.

In the primary grades, children's fine motor skills are still developing and, therefore, forming small letters can be a difficult task. Close observation of children's skills will help you to recognize what an individual child is capable of attempting.

Some schools choose to teach manuscript letters in first and second grade and cursive in third grade. Other schools have adopted a combination of manuscript and cursive (the D'Nealian method) to make the transition into cursive easier.

Teachers can support children's acquisition of handwriting skills as part of the writing and reading program. Talk about handwriting as you write. Anything posted in the classroom that is written by the teacher should be neatly written in the same manuscript form that is expected of the children. In a third grade class where cursive is taught, the morning message can be written in cursive.

To combat the tedium of handwriting practice, many teachers keep it in the context of meaningful writing. Children can concentrate on letter formation when they write stories that are important to them. In reviewing a story, the teacher might ask a child what letters were difficult to write or to read.

> After Ms. Allen talks with Eduardo about his story, the two of them scan the text together. "Eduardo, are there any words you had a hard time reading to me?" asks Ms. Allen. "Yes" says Eduardo, "This one, the word car. The a looks like an o and an i because I didn't write the two parts touching." "Yes, I see what you mean. I think that would be a good letter for you to spend some time practicing. What do you think?" says Ms. Allen. "O.K., so other kids can read my story," says Eduardo.

Following this conference, Eduardo might practice letters in a handwriting book or on paper designed to help children learn neat penmanship. In this way, he is in charge of his learning and is invested in writing legibly.

Organizing the Language and Literacy Curriculum

Having read about the research on reading and writing and the many ways children acquire language and literacy skills, you may now be wondering how to implement best practices in the classroom. The six strategies you read about in Part One (page 5) provide the framework for promoting language and literacy learning in your classroom.

Because you know your children as individuals and developmentally, your awareness of their interests and skills allows you to provide the kinds of experiences most suitable for them. Already your class meetings support language and literacy development. During these times, children can practice listening and speaking skills and hear new vocabulary and ideas.

Language and literacy learning can be infused into the classroom in many ways that make guiding children's learning in this area a continuous process. Consider how to incorporate different aspects of language and literacy instruction as part of long-term studies. During work times you teach and practice specific reading and writing skills. Teachable moments also contribute to children's learning.

The structure of your classroom influences literacy learning as well. A good place to begin is by creating a classroom environment that promotes literacy.

Creating an Environment for Literacy

Children make the connection between language and print when teachers use print strategically throughout the classroom. Children see that print serves a purpose when it is used to support and explain the organization and routines of the classroom, and when print is an integral part of everyday activities and experiences.

Using Print for Classroom Organization and Routines

A natural way to create an environment for literacy is to use print in the classroom organization and to clarify routines. Some examples of print used for these purposes include: labels for materials, attendance charts, job charts, weekly schedules, and daily messages.

Labels for Materials

In Chapter 3, Establishing a Structure for the Classroom, we discussed labeling children's cubbies or lockers and all the storage containers in the room. Labels assist children in locating and using materials independently. In this way, children see a practical purpose for print.

Labels may be a combination of pictures and words. By second grade, the label might just be a word and could be made by the children themselves.

Attendance Charts

A convenient way to record daily attendance and help children make sense of print is to have attendance charts. Teachers can record children's attendance in various ways. Some suggestions follow.

- Take a photograph of each child on the first day of school and have children write their names on the reverse side of the photo. Place the photographs in a clear pocket chart that is attached to the classroom door. Each morning as children arrive, they flip the signed side to show the photo. When the photo shows, it means the child is in school. When a name shows, it indicates the child is absent. At the end of each day, children flip the photograph to show their written name, indicating they have gone home for the day.

- Mount library book pockets or index cards on tag board. Write each child's name on the book pocket and also across the top of the index card. Children simply flip the index card to indicate they've arrived in the classroom. The cards could have first names early in the year; last names could be added later.

- Take attendance using a class list on a clipboard. One child checks the name of each child who is present and makes a list of children who are absent.

- Have children sign in each day on a chart. This also serves to keep track of children's handwriting development.

When children take attendance, they learn to read the names of their classmates. The delegation of jobs and tasks to children makes teachers' lives less tedious and creates an environment where children see the importance of reading and writing in their daily lives.

Job Charts

Another way to include print in the environment is to post job charts. (See page 144.) Children use them to keep track of their job responsibilities for the week. These charts may have pictures and words, or only words. Children can generate a list of possible jobs for the classroom such as sweeping the floor, handing out snacks, watering plants, and serving as class messenger.

Schedule and Morning Message

Children want to know what their activities are each day. They feel more secure when they know what to expect. Posting a daily schedule meets this need and lets children use text in a practical way.

In addition to the schedule, which remains fairly consistent from week to week, you can write a morning message each day. Reading the daily schedule and the morning message as part of the first meeting of the day can become an important classroom ritual that helps children make the transition from home to school.

There are many ways to write a morning message so that children look forward to figuring out your system. Leave out a word and have the children try to spell the missing word. Color code special words you want to talk about or use colored chalk or markers to make a pattern.

In first grade classrooms, the morning message is often simple, including sight words that children use in their reading vocabulary. Repetitive phrases allow children to read the message successfully.

```
Hello.
Today is Monday.
We will play a new math game.
We will eat lunch at 12:00.
We will go outside after lunch.
```

In second grade the morning message can be more complex. Longer sentences and new vocabulary turn message reading into an interesting lesson, such as the spelling of ordinal numbers from one to ten, or a discussion about the use of descriptive phrases.

```
Good morning on a brisk, windy day.
Today is the sixth day of October.
At one o'clock we will go downstairs
to interview our principal, Ms. Smith.
Think about a question you would
like to ask her about her job.
```

Because third graders are more competent readers and understand what each of these topics means, the morning message can be written as a schedule.

```
11/7/98

Greetings!
Schedule highlights:
Gym - 10:30 a.m.
Projects - 1:00 - 2:30 p.m.

Later today we'll be discussing
frogs and toads. Let's think
about some of the differences
between frogs and toads.
```

This morning message ends with a statement relevant to a curriculum topic the teacher plans to explore with the children that day. Other examples might be: "Let's think about what makes a number odd or even." "Let's brainstorm some ideas about why December 21st is the shortest day of the year." Statements can also relate to classroom management such as, "Let's think about some reasons that we walk in a line in the hallways."

Using Print in Classroom Activities and Experiences

In addition to these organizational uses for print, teachers help children acquire language and literacy skills by using print in the environment as part of every activity. Teachers use experience charts, children's messages and signs, word walls, and children's work.

Experience Charts

Many elementary school teachers use experience charts. Preparing these charts with the children is an excellent way to document their ideas on a subject, thus clearly connecting spoken words with print. A group discussion at the beginning of a study often focuses on two questions: "What do you know about (the topic)?" and "What do you want to find out?" Charts can be developed to list the questions children want to ask a visitor, class members' favorite read-aloud books or favorite authors, or even favorite TV shows. In deciding whether to prepare an experience chart, ask yourself, "Will we want to read this information again?" If the answer is "yes," it's a good time for a chart. When experience charts are posted around the room, children can use them as a reference, find words needed for writing, and practice their reading.

You may want to record exactly what children say when you first begin to write experience charts each year. Later on, you can adjust for grammar and structure as children feel more comfortable in the classroom community. When children's language is written down, we show that we value what they say. They see their language recorded for future reference.

Imagine that your class is about to set up a frog environment in a glass tank. You invite the children to the meeting area where you have chart paper and colored markers. At the top of the chart is the sentence "What Do We Know About Frogs?" You pose this question to the children and as they share their ideas, you list them next to their names.

> *Marie — Frogs are green.*

> *Pavel — Frogs like lily pads.*

> *Bailey — Baby frogs are called tadpoles.*

By recording the children's names along with their statements, they can find their names and read the sentences they contributed. In second grade, you might simply write the children's initials. Such charts are also useful records for purposes of assessment.

> *K.S. — Frogs eat worms.*

> *A.T. — Frogs get oxygen through their skin.*

During such an activity a child may contribute an idea or suggestion that you know is incorrect. If this happens at the beginning of a study, record the idea as stated by the child. This is a research opportunity that may lead your children to re-evaluate and then record newly learned information. At the end of a study you might ask some extension questions before recording the children's ideas.

- Can you say more about that?

- Can you say the same thing in a different way to see if it still makes sense?

- Tell us about how you learned that.

- I'm not sure I agree. Would you like some help to figure it out?

These responses provide an opportunity for the child to self-correct and for the teacher to better understand what the child is thinking.

Two children may have conflicting information. Record both ideas and say, "You both have some good ideas. Let's read some books and do some research to see what else we can discover." In this way, both ideas are respected and the child with the incorrect information now has the opportunity to self-correct. The self-correction process is a powerful learning experience. Once children discover their errors, have them write the correction directly on the recording sheet. Children can also cross out their initial statements.

In third grade, when children have greater reading competence, names and initials are not needed to read the chart successfully. A group language experience chart may be written in paragraph form.

Charting activities naturally involve writing as well as reading. They also model handwriting and spelling at the same time. By thinking out loud as you write, you model that people think about spelling. They think about making a clear sentence. They think about what is being said. Depending on the age of the children, you can encourage them to help you sound out the words as you write them down. Older children may be encouraged to make some charts on their own as part of small group projects.

Messages and Signs

Children love to send and receive messages and make signs. When you make this part of the work of your classroom, you respond to children's interests and give them a goal for reading and writing. There are many ways to do this.

- Create a message board with special paper for message writing and provide opportunities during the day for children to write messages. (With the proper computer equipment, modem, and wiring you can do this online.)

- Establish a post office system with daily or weekly deliveries (mail boxes can be made from coffee cans, milk cartons, or plastic shoe pockets).

- Ask children to make signs to identify their displays (art, blocks, puzzles) or to make rules (Do Not Disturb).

- Provide time and materials for this kind of writing to take place.

Word Walls

Another way to include print in classroom activities and experiences is to designate a word wall in the classroom. This is a space for high-frequency words and is updated regularly with the children. Depending on the age group, the wall may contain sight words that the children are learning for reading or basic words they need for their writing. It may include words that are alike (similar beginnings or endings) or different or interesting patterns that children have noticed.

> One day a group of Ms. Ritter's third graders were helping each other spell the words could *and* should. *Michael said that his older cousin taught him a way to remember how to spell those words. He said, "* o u l d *stands for 'Oh you lazy dog.' That helps you to spell* could, would, *and* should." *The children suggested that these words be added to the word wall next to the phrase "Oh you lazy dog."*

Children's Work

When children's work—their writing, art, and constructions—is displayed with signs and labels, teachers send a message that work is valued. By placing the work where children can see and discuss it, teachers make it possible for children to observe, read, and talk about each other's work. Including print in the environment makes the point that reading and writing is a part of all aspects of our lives. In this kind of environment, language and literacy learning can be integrated into long-term studies quite naturally.

Promoting Language and Literacy through Long-Term Studies

In chapters 9 and 10, Social Studies and Scientific Thinking, we describe in detail how language and literacy activities are a natural and necessary part of all long-term studies. Finding materials for children to look at, read, and talk about is one of the steps in planning a long-term study. When children want information on a topic that interests them, they have a reason to listen, speak, read, and write. Here are some examples of how language and literacy skills can be applied to several different long-term studies.

A class that is studying the nearby **river** might:

- create a chart detailing what they know and what they want to know;
- interview the parks department employee responsible for that section of the river;
- read about river life in books, on CD-ROMs, on the Internet;
- write research reports about the animals that live in or near the river;
- keep charts about the salinity of the water at different times and places; or
- have many group discussions about what they are learning.

The investigations of children studying **immigration** may lead them to:

- listen to or read books about people who came to this country as immigrants;
- discuss stories about moving with family members and neighbors;
- write about a time they went to an unfamiliar place; or
- use the computer to write a script for a play about the experiences of children's ancestors.

When children explore the **neighborhood** around the school, they might:

- write letters to the city department responsible for pothole repair;
- publish the recipes for school lunches;
- interview the various workers in the school; or
- discuss plans for a school-wide recycling project.

As children learn about **animals** they can:

- keep a science journal of observations about the class pet;
- read about an animal of their own choosing;
- prepare an oral report about their animal;
- work with a classmate to design models of their animals; or
- write a detailed description of their animal.

A study of a **construction** site near the school can lead children to:

- make lists of what they know and what they want to find out;
- read books about construction and different kinds of machines and tools;
- write about their own homes;
- keep a journal of observations about the construction site;
- write instructions for making something;
- interview the job supervisor;
- interview the family member of a classmate who works in construction;
- make up words to their own work songs; or
- make a list of safety rules for their woodworking table.

While language and literacy activities will happen as part of long-term studies, planned work times for reading and writing also need to occur daily.

Planning Work Times for Reading

Work times are those scheduled times during the day when you plan particular language and literacy activities. Sometimes teachers work with the whole class, reading a chapter book aloud. At other times, children work in small groups as they read or discuss a book. Sometimes children work alone on their reading. Teachers move from group to group or child to child, asking questions, or teaching something directly.

There are many opportunities throughout the week to provide children with reading experiences and instruction. These four types of reading work times can help children explore:

- reading aloud;

- shared reading;

- guided reading; and

- independent reading.

Reading Aloud

Reading quality literature aloud every day to children—especially material that children may not yet have the skills to read on their own—is a powerful way to encourage children to become readers. By listening to good books, children learn that reading is a pleasurable activity. Listening to stories is also a way to provide reading instruction because it:

- introduces children to the characteristics of various types of literature;

- extends vocabulary;

- lengthens attention spans;

- creates an atmosphere of pleasure related to language and books;

- provides children with literary models of writing that can influence their own writing;

- helps children become familiar with different story structures;

- allows children to focus on language and story without the work of reading; and

- provides a jumping off point for science and social studies topics.

Children learn that the printed page can have many voices as they listen to various types of written material. The sound and tone of a passage depend on the type and purpose of the story, article, essay, or poem. A chapter in a non-fiction book about ducks will sound very different from a story book about ducks. Familiarity with the different voices of books is particularly important for children in the upper grades because they have to read and comprehend more complicated texts independently. This task is made easier when children have listened extensively to non-fiction read aloud. Teachers can provide the base for identifying a selection's purpose and voice by varying the materials that they read aloud to children.

Select Good Books

You can extend your collection and include all types of books by using the school and public libraries. Some teachers make a point of reading from a fiction book, a non-fiction book, and a book of poetry each day. Many teachers keep a stack of wonderful brief books on hand to read at transitional times. For example, when there are a few minutes before the music teacher arrives, you can read a book that is based on a song. Poems work well at transition times, too.

Read picture as well as chapter books. Picture books can be finished at one sitting. They can be used as examples for discussions about story development, settings, and openings, as well as for descriptive language, rhymes, and phonics. Reading chapter books aloud exposes children to more detailed story lines and introduces fluent readers to new authors.

Read Every Day

Try to set aside at least one long block of time every day to read and enjoy long stories and chapter books with the children. Some teachers read aloud following the lunch/recess period or at the end of the day. Think about additional shorter periods when a short story or poem might be read. For example, some teachers make poetry a part of their morning routine. A poem is read just after everyone has been seated and prior to discussing the daily schedule.

Model How a Competent Reader Reads

When you come to a passage in a book that is particularly beautiful or surprising to you, take time to stop and share your reactions with children. In this way you show children that the language and vocabulary in books is something to notice and talk about. Children see how competent readers respond to books.

Because each class of children has its own unique personality based on the individual children in that class, the group will often come to prefer a specific type of book, author, or illustrator. The books selected to read aloud can reflect this preference. Children may begin to learn about the style of a particular author or illustrator. Conversations about style can form the basis for discussions about ways to communicate ideas through books, and can also inspire children to look for books by these writers on their own.

Shared Reading

Shared reading occurs when children read books, songs, poems, or other printed material as a group. Like reading aloud, this activity builds community and allows for discussion and instruction. Shared reading differs from reading aloud in that children are verbal participants in the process of reading.

The shared reading experience sounds a bit like a reading chorus. Everyone reads together, though the teacher's (or child leader's) voice stands out. In this environment, even the most cautious reader can join in without feeling uncomfortable.

Don Holdaway, a New Zealand educator, suggested to teachers that they enlarge favorite books and poems and read them along with the children (1979). Making the print large and displaying the material on an easel makes it possible for everyone to see the print and the illustrations as you read the words together. *Big books* are now available from many publishers.

Beginning Readers

Shared reading is an important way to teach beginning readers basic reading skills. By pointing to each word as it is read, the teacher helps children to:

- follow along as the teacher reads;
- understand that we read from left to right and from the top of the page to the bottom;
- identify exactly where a word is located on the page; and
- extend sight vocabulary.

Favorite books, poems, and songs are read again and again in shared reading in response to the interests of the group. In addition to the big books that are available commercially, you can make big books for children to illustrate, or groups of children can make their own. Poems and the lyrics for songs written on chart paper or oak tag can be used for shared reading times. The readings presented in this manner and repeated throughout a school week become part of the children's reading repertoire. Children can then read them on their own. Through the re-reading of books, children extend their sight vocabularies.

Books that are particularly good for shared reading are repetitious, cumulative, predictable, contain common sight words, and use rhyme.

- *Repetitive* books repeat certain words or phrases. An example of a repetitive book is *The Gingerbread Man* where the passage, "Run, run as fast as you can, you can't catch me, I'm the Gingerbread Man," is repeated. Children listen for this part and join in when they hear it.

- *Cumulative* books add a new line on each page while repeating the previous line. *This Is the House That Jack Built* is an example. "This is the cat, that killed the rat, that ate the malt, that lay in the house, that Jack built." Children use their memory of the story and the repetition of each sentence to predict what text will be on the next page.

- *Predictable* books have stories that help emergent readers think about what they are reading by anticipating the words they may encounter on the next page. The teacher might ask, "What do you think will happen next?" modeling the question children need to ask themselves as they read. *The Three Little Pigs* and *The Three Billy Goats Gruff* are examples of predictable books.

- *Sight word* books use and repeat certain words. In addition to the familiar Dr. Seuss book, *The Cat in the Hat,* a repetitive book such as *Have You Seen My Cat?* by Eric Carle can also teach sight words. In this book, a little boy is searching for his cat. He asks the people he meets throughout the story, "Have you seen my cat?" When the cat that they direct him to is not his, he responds, "This is not my cat." These sentences are repeated again and again. A teacher might focus on a specific word, asking children to clap each time they hear it.

- *Rhyming* books or poems use rhyme to help children learn a spelling or word pattern. Teachers can write poems in large print on chart paper and highlight specific words or parts of words. For example:

Down! Down! by Eleanor Farjeon

Down, down,

Yellow and **brown,**

The leaves are falling

All over the **town.**

After reading the poem a few times to enjoy the beat, sound, and image, the teacher then uses the poem to teach a skill by asking, "What do you notice in this poem?" The children may point out a number of things such as color words or that some words look the same. They may notice that some words rhyme. The teacher selects one of their observations to comment on. For example, she might say: "Look closely at the end of the rhyming words.

What letters do you see? Can you think of any other rhyming words that rhyme with down?" The class generates a list of other words in the *o-w-n* family. Sometimes the teacher has a plan to teach a specific concept. In this case, she might say, "I notice that a number of words end with *o-w-n*. Can anyone find one of those words?"

Using these types of books during shared reading times enables teachers to teach reading strategies that children will use as they read independently. Because children will be at different levels in their reading skills, sometimes these strategies should be taught to a small group rather than to the whole class. Particularly after the whole class has enjoyed a big book, the teacher can work with small groups teaching different skills with the same text. One group may focus on rhyming words, another on a particular letter-sound relationship, another on predicting what will happen next.

Fluent Readers

Shared reading experiences also remain appropriate for more fluent readers. Shared reading experiences for fluent readers can serve many different purposes. Consider these ideas.

- Enlarge a poem on an overhead projector to demonstrate how in poetry, each word is chosen carefully and unusual words are often used. Children may also begin to memorize poems, building another important skill.

- Use a big book to discuss techniques authors use to depict a character or setting. Children can be encouraged to look for those techniques in their own reading and apply them to their own writing.

- Use a non-fiction big book to teach children how to read for research purposes. Readers who are fluent reading fiction may need support and guidance to read more complex non-fiction material.

Shared reading offers multiple opportunities to teach lessons valuable to all. It is also a chance for children to respond in different ways. Some children may be ready to notice that words are separate from other words, while others may be collecting sight words they recognize. Teachers take their cues about what to teach, based on the children's observations. Shared reading times can occur daily for different lengths of time, depending on children's attention spans and needs.

Guided Reading

Guided reading occurs when the teacher meets with a small group of children to observe reading behaviors and provide specific instruction. The books children read in guided reading groups must be chosen carefully so that children can read them with the strategies they currently have available, but also offer a few new things to learn. The teacher's assessment of reading skills is key, since the goal is for children to be able to read independently for meaning. Observing children's reading needs and interests helps the teacher decide what texts to select and what to teach.

Guided reading groups can be formed for different reasons. Sometimes a group of children is ready to learn a similar skill. At other times, a group forms around a common interest. Guided reading instruction topics might include a particular reading strategy, an author's writing style, or a literary technique. The teacher then selects a book that will best respond to the topic, and offers multiple copies to the group.

Whatever the purpose for forming the group, a guided reading group time is likely to have four components (Fountas and Pinnell 1996, 2). The teacher:

- introduces the text to the group;

- works briefly with individuals in the group as they read to themselves;

- selects particular items to teach or discuss after the children finish reading the book, if short, or a section, if it is long; and

- may work with the children to develop a follow-up activity or project.

Introduction

The purpose of the introduction is to interest children in the book and give them a frame of reference that may help them in their reading. It is a conversation not a directed lesson. While potentially difficult or unusual words might be shown to children and explained in the context of the story, this is not a time to practice reading lots of new words in isolation. If there are too many words the children can't read independently, then the text is too difficult.

Reading Time

As children read independently, the teacher moves from child to child. The teacher might ask a child to read a small section out loud to evaluate how the child solves the problem of an unfamiliar word or to guide a child in using picture clues to double check on a strategy. The notes a teacher takes during this time may become the basis for specific teaching at another time.

In the past, round-robin oral reading would have been part of this group time, but this is no longer a recommended practice (Opitz and Rasinski 1998). In addition to being a source of worry for many children as they wait their turn, round-robin reading can inhibit comprehension as children listen to slow-reading classmates. This leads to inattentive behavior from bored children. Nonetheless, oral reading skills are important and require practice. There are other ways to build these skills. Children can read a familiar text to a partner, prepare skits or plays, and read and recite poetry to the class.

Lesson Time

After reading time, the teacher calls the group together to teach the particular lesson planned, for example, about a particular reading strategy, how compound words work, the author's use of alliteration, or techniques for building tension in a story. Children also need opportunities to comment on what they have read and relate their personal experiences to the text.

They learn best when they can respond to the text in a group discussion. The teacher is a participant, using the ideas children bring to guide the conversation and extending children's thinking. This is very different from a recitation, where the teacher asks a question and is looking for the right answer. In a discussion the teacher acts as a facilitator, helping children work together to construct meaning (Gambrell and Almasi 1996).

Follow-up Activity

Finally, depending on the interests of the children and appropriate next steps, the children may do a project or activity that extends their understanding of the text or is a way to share the text with the class.

> Ms. William's second graders spent some time discussing the directions for how to shine shoes properly in The Chalk Box Kid by Clyde Robert Bulla. As a follow-up activity, they decided to write directions for making a peanut butter and jelly sandwich and then try out their directions to see how they worked.

Other responses might include writing, art work, skits, songs, dances, and, of course, reading related books. Sometimes responses are shared with the whole class.

Flexibility in Guided Reading

Flexibility is essential to guided reading. In the beginning of the school year, you choose the reading books and assign follow-up projects that support the goals you have set based on your observations of children. As the children become familiar with the routine and learn what is expected, they may choose the discussion topics and the projects they do to respond to the text. You can gradually begin to give children choices about the nature and order of reading activities. With fluent readers you may put together a collection of books that all address a specific goal. Children can select the particular book they want to read.

Groups should not remain static. As each strategy, interest, or reading behavior is taught and observed, the group can disband and children can become part of new groups. Multiple copies of books with a varying range of difficulty will permit children to form what some teachers call book clubs or literature groups, based on their interest in a specific book.

Personal Response in Guided Reading

Another aspect of guided reading, whether teacher-led or child-initiated, is the opportunity to talk about how books make us feel. In the following example, Ms. Bischof, a second grade teacher, plans to have children discuss their reading and relate their personal experiences to the story and characters in a book. She selects *Frog and Toad Together* by Arnold Lobel because the children are eager to read a "chapter" book. Unlike most chapter books, which are longer and more difficult for early readers, the books in the *Frog and Toad* series have short stories at a reading level appropriate to the children in this group.

> *Ms. Bischof joins a group of six readers at a table. She explains that she has six copies of a chapter book for them to read and talk about together. After giving out the book, she asks if anyone is familiar with the Frog and Toad books and encourages several children to comment on what they like or don't like about them. She gives the children folders to store their individual copies of the book and asks them to place the books inside. To prepare them for the story, she invites the children to talk about their friendships. Several children share stories about their friends. Ms. Bischof lets each child who wants to talk do so.*

> *After this introduction, the children take out their copies of the book and read the first story, "Spring," independently. As they do so, Ms. Bischof circulates from child to child, having each child read a short segment aloud to her. She listens for how they decode, how smoothly they read, and checks on strategies that have been taught previously. She notes her observations on a clipboard.*

> *Bringing the group back together for a discussion, Ms. Bischof asks: "What did the story make you think about?" The children don't respond. After another pause, she tries again: "We started out by talking about friends. Did anybody notice anything about friends in the story?" Ralph says, "I have a calendar in my room like the one in the story." Julie says, "The story reminds me of how my sister's alarm goes off and she wakes me up."*

Ms. Bischof feels that this was a good beginning for her and the group. She recognizes that the children's responses, though not relevant to her questions, were related to details in the story. By listening carefully to what the children tell her, she is getting to know them. Through this experience she helps children understand that they can talk about the ideas in books and that everyone can make a personal contribution to the discussion. Over the next few days, Ms. Bischof can encourage children to read the remaining chapters in *Frog and Toad Together*, use their reading strategies, and make a personal connection to the story.

Teachers often want to know how they can give this level of attention to a small group. What are other children doing during this time? Sometimes while the teacher works with a small group, other children may be doing different reading or writing activities that don't require teacher involvement. They may be working on drawing responses to a book, reading with partners, studying spelling words, reading or writing quietly. Or it may be a choice time when the other children are playing math or other board games, doing puzzles, working on a computer, or listening to stories on tape. Teachers generally try to schedule guided reading times with small groups three times a week.

Independent Reading

Independent reading time gives children an opportunity to relax and enjoy books without the direct involvement of a teacher. The purpose of this special time is to let children choose their own reading materials and read quietly.

For independent reading to be successful, the classroom should be filled with a variety of reading materials—magazines, joke books, adventure stories, biographies, sports books, books related to long-term studies in science or social studies—at different reading levels. It doesn't matter if children choose books that you feel are too easy for them or books they have read before.

In first grade, when many children have not yet had an experience with independent reading, teachers may need to set the stage for this time of the day. Begin by explaining to your class that this is a time when everyone will spend a quiet time with books. Have children choose a handful of books. Ask them to pick a spot in the classroom where they will be comfortable. Explain that once this time starts, they will not be allowed to get up and move around the room, as this can be distracting to other readers. At first you may observe first graders flipping through the books so casually that they barely seem to be looking at the illustrations, much less the words. Once they understand your expectations for this time of day, they will relax and get into the books. During this time you might hear some children say, "I'm finished with my books. What do I do now? May I get more books?" Respond based on your knowledge of the child. You may say, "Sure." Or you may say, "Look through your books again. See if you can find or read something you didn't notice in the first reading." In this way you can help some children increase their attention span for reading.

The length of time you allocate for independent reading should be consistent with children's abilities. Early in the year, first graders may only manage ten to fifteen minutes of independent reading. By third grade, you may be able to extend the time to thirty minutes a day. Take some time yourself to read at this time of day. When teachers read with concentration, they demonstrate that they also love books, giving children a model to imitate. Many teachers use independent reading time to have individual reading conferences with children.

Planning Work Times for Writing

In addition to daily opportunities to write across the curriculum, work times for instruction and practice should be scheduled at least three or four days a week. These activities provide a structure for thinking about and planning writing instruction (Fountas and Pinnell 1996):

- shared writing;
- interactive writing;
- writing workshop (or guided writing); and
- independent writing.

Shared Writing

In shared writing, the children talk and the teacher writes. When developing experience charts with children, teachers model a way to convert oral language into print. They also model how writing can be a tool for recording information that is needed for a particular purpose. The charts developed during shared writing should contain useful information that will be referred to over the course of several days or weeks, such as lists of supplies needed for an activity, a recipe, a things to do list, tips on remembering to bring homework back to school, etc.

Interactive Writing

Interactive writing, as the name implies, involves more joint composition than shared writing. This writing process demonstrates the connection between oral and written language and shows how helpful it can be to talk something through before writing it down. For example, a first grade class might write a story or poem together based on a text that has been read to them. Older children may also be the scribes. In this kind of writing activity, the teacher has a plan for calling attention to particular aspects of writing, such as how to listen for sounds to figure out how to spell a word, or how to use punctuation effectively. Interactive writing projects may take several days or weeks to complete.

Writing Workshop

A formal guided writing experience, often called *writing workshop*, is the cornerstone of a balanced writing program because it enables children to construct individual (or partnered) pieces of writing on topics of interest to them. The teacher provides "guidance, assistance, and feedback" keeping track of the specific skills children need to master (Fountas and Pinnell 1996, 35).

The concept and design of writing workshop was developed by Donald Graves (1983) and Nancy Atwell (1987). The format is designed to give children ownership and control of what they write (Calkins 1994). They are encouraged to see themselves as authors who make decisions about their writing, such as the topic, the genre, and the audience. During these guided writing times children use prior knowledge and their experiences and ideas as the basis for their writing, providing teachers with rich information about children's lives and their thinking.

The basic elements of writing workshop are a directed lesson, writing time, teacher and/or peer conferences, sharing time, revising, editing, and publishing. Many teachers adapt these elements to meet the needs of the children they teach. Research reports, fiction writing, essays, poetry, letter writing, etc., can all be incorporated into writing workshop.

Directed Lesson

The first five to ten minutes of the writing period are a directed lesson designed for the whole class. The meeting area is a good place to gather children for the lesson. Many different topics can be discussed in these lessons, including qualities of good literature, how to generate topics, word usage, and management issues. A lesson might be devoted to a discussion of saying things in different ways as this second grade teacher did.

> *Ms. Picard writes the following sentence on the easel:* Jack goes to the store. *She asks the children to think about how to develop this sentence so that it includes more descriptive language. The children come up with these ideas:* Jack walked slowly down the shady street to buy a drink at the store. Jack ran excitedly past his friends to find his father at the store. *They discuss how, by adding details and descriptive language, they could change the meaning of a simple sentence.*

A third grade teacher using a lesson to focus on the qualities of good literature might initiate a discussion about how authors write the setting of a story.

> *Mr. Shelton reads a number of passages from different books to show how different authors describe a setting. The class talks about how one author lists the particular objects located in the setting while another uses descriptive language, setting a tone that makes the place seem scary.*

Another lesson might be devoted to the different approaches people use to write. Some like to talk about their ideas with friends, others write first and then think out loud with others. Children can be encouraged to think about what helps them write, and to share their ideas with the group. Teachers can also share their observations of the children as part of a brief lesson. "I've observed that Betsy reads through the pages that she wrote the day before so she knows just where to begin each day. See if that approach helps you."

Brief lessons prior to writing time are the best way to teach the mechanics of writing. For first graders this might mean putting spaces between words and writing from left to right. A third grade teacher might emphasize the use of quotation marks. Teachers present a concept in many different ways. This is how a second grade teacher used a series of lessons to teach punctuation.

> *On Monday, Ms. Venable shows the children different ways writers end a sentence (period, question mark, or exclamation point) by displaying a set of sentences on a chart. On Tuesday, the class searches for periods, question marks, and exclamation points in a big book. On Wednesday, a child who has used these marks in a story she has written shares part of it on a chart. On Thursday, Ms. Venable models some personal writing in front of the children, stressing the necessary punctuation.*

Management issues are also an appropriate subject for lessons. When you first introduce writing workshop in your classroom, you may want to use this time to talk about how children get the materials needed for writing, as well as how to brainstorm ideas. Topics that may need reinforcement are cleaning up properly at the end of writing time and not interrupting a writing conference.

Writing Time

Following a short lesson, the children get the materials they need and spread out around the room to write. Many teachers encourage children to begin by writing about things they know about—the time they fell off their bike, the first time they needed stitches, or what it was like when their new baby sister came home from the hospital. Sometimes children write about worries or sad events—how they saw somcone attacked in their neighborhood or when their gerbil died. They choose their own topics so that their writing is of interest to them—telling about something they know about. Children usually work on their own, but occasionally they may write with a friend. Some children will have lots of ideas for writing time. Others may need encouragement and extra time to think. You may have to reassure them that their own experiences are worth writing about.

The way that story writing begins changes as children grow and develop as writers. Young children often start by drawing a picture. As they add details to the drawing, they describe the picture in greater detail. Thus, the story is created verbally along with the drawing. The next step involves drawing the picture and writing the story. At first, just a few words may be used even though the oral story uses elaborate vocabulary. As children become accustomed to invented or phonetic spelling, increase their written vocabulary, and see their invented spelling accepted, they will use more and more print. Children may plan their story by starting with a drawing, or by discussing the story plan with their peers and teacher. Gradually, children do more and more of their planning mentally.

Children talk and exchange ideas as they write. Their conversations are rehearsals for what they will write. However, some children have difficulty concentrating with discussion going on around them. To address this, teachers define a time for silent or quiet writing. Five or ten minutes is designated as "no walking and no talking" time. It may come at the beginning of writing time to set a tone for the period or it may come at the end to help children wrap up their work for the day.

Once writing workshop has been underway for several weeks you will find that children will be at different stages in the process—some will be listing new ideas, some will be working on initial drafts, some will be editing and revising, and others will be proofreading. The organizational and management systems you develop for writing are very important. Some teachers have children compose drafts that are stored in individual pocket folders. Other teachers have children do all their writing in notebooks. Many teachers encourage children to use every other line so reading and editing is somewhat easier. The resources described at the end of this chapter offer many practical suggestions for managing children's written work.

Conferences

Writing time offers teachers the opportunity to circulate and have conversations with individual children about their writing. Conferences can be a very intense time for teachers. This is where you offer individual guidance, assistance, and feedback as you check in with many children, and observe different writing levels and styles simultaneously. You must respond spontaneously to each child. You think on your feet and meet many needs at once. However, despite these multiple demands, conferences are also a special opportunity to connect positively with children and share information important to them. The observations you make during conferences can be the basis for some of the directed writing lessons.

Here are some suggestions for effective conferencing.

- Begin by asking general questions: "What are you working on?" "How is it going?" "Tell me about your work."

- Keep the child's work in the hands of the child and kneel down or sit at the child's level to show respect for the writer.

- Although you may notice many things to discuss or teach the child after looking over the piece, choose just one thing to respond to, trusting that the child will learn that one thing.

- Listen to what children tell you about where they are struggling or where they would like help, and teach to that point.

- Develop a shorthand system of notetaking to keep track of the conference. This helps you keep a record of whom you conferred with so you know which children to make time for next. The notes are also useful for assessment purposes.

As children gain confidence as writers and seem able to help one another, peer conferences may be added in addition to teacher-child conferences. Children are usually better able to help each other when they have a format to follow. Teach children to be specific when asking for help. You can model how to do this by offering ideas.

- "Did I tell enough about the accident?"
- "I don't know how to end this story."
- "I'm not sure I can tell where all my sentences end."

This way the helper is more likely to give the specific help that is needed. As children gain practice with this process, they will become more successful. Use lessons to teach children how to conduct peer conferences.

Sharing

Writing times often close by gathering children in the meeting area to have them share their work. Sometimes a child celebrates by reading a finished piece or a wonderfully constructed sentence or paragraph. At other times, teachers select a child who has successfully incorporated the lesson in his writing as a way to reinforce the lesson. Alternatively, children share to get answers to specific questions or problems such as "How should I end my story?" or "I need help with a title."

Of course, in order for sharing to be successful, children have to learn how to make comments that are constructive and respectful. You can model questions and comments for children and also have several lessons about the kinds of questions and comments to make. The work you have done to create a classroom community facilitates children's willingness to take risks such as sharing their work with their peers.

You may find that you have to guide the group to respond to the question and refrain from making unrelated comments. Teach them how to make specific comments: "I like the way the ending surprised me," is a much more helpful comment than "I liked your story" or even "I liked your ending," because it lets the author know exactly what was effective.

Revising

Once writing workshop is an established part of the schedule in your classroom, you may want to expand its scope. As children gain confidence in their writing, they will be able to revise some of their work. Revision may include adding information, deleting unnecessary information, and making sure ideas are conveyed clearly. As teachers confer with children, they can help them extend and elaborate upon their ideas. The ability to re-read a piece and decide if and how changes should be made shows real growth in the development of a writer.

First graders can be expected to make minor changes in their work toward the end of the year. Second and third graders may be ready for the following revision suggestions.

- Read through your piece and find one part where you could add more description.
- Re-read your writing to see if it makes sense. Is there anything you can change to convey your ideas more clearly?
- Think of a book that reminds you of what you are writing. Look it over and see if you get any ideas you could add to your piece.
- Experiment with a new beginning or ending for your piece.

Editing and Publishing

The editing process begins by having children look over their writing to find one or two mechanical errors. For example, children might first review for periods, or underline a few misspelled words and correct those that are on their personal spelling list.

There are many ways to work on editing, particularly with older children. Some teachers put an editing checklist in the back of each child's writing folder. As a child demonstrates that a skill has been learned, it is added to the checklist as something the child is now responsible for as an editor. It also provides a record of a child's progress for assessment purposes. Before children present their writing to the class, it is expected that they will have used their checklist. The following is an example of an editing checklist.

Malcolm's Editing Checklist	
9/17	My ideas are clear.
10/2	Each sentence ends with correct punctuation.
10/9	Each sentence begins with a capital letter.
10/12	The word *I* is always capitalized.
10/21	Names begin with capital letters.
11/3	I know the difference between *where* and *were*.

After children have done some editing, the teacher can do a final edit. Talk with the class about how editing is done by real publishing companies and explain your editing role in that context. Children may be able to do some rewriting depending upon their age and the length of their writing. Parents are often willing to type children's edited work for publication and to help put books together. Some children may be able to type drafts or final copies on the computer. By third grade, most children can be expected to make final drafts.

Teachers find that writing workshop is more productive when children know they have sustained writing times about four times each week for about one hour each day. This gives you time for a brief lesson, writing, conferences, and some sharing. It takes time to build the routine so that it fits into an hour, and initially, some portions may be missed or expanded.

In the example that follows, Ms. Capalongo's second graders will begin writing workshop. As you read, notice how the meeting, work time, and sharing all reveal opportunities for open-ended exploration and learning.

> *During the lesson, Ms. Capalongo asks: "What do you think makes a good story?" Some of the children's responses are:*
>
>> *"Something exciting happens."*
>>
>> *"It's scary."*
>>
>> *"It makes you laugh."*
>>
>> *"It's unpredictable and fun."*
>
> *Ms. Capalongo tells a brief story of her own in which she recalls getting a flat tire at the worst possible time. She then asks the children: "Who has a story in which something unpredictable happened to you?" Two children share anecdotes. Then she asks: "Who can remember something that happened to them that was scary?" Several children respond with memories.*
>
> *Now that she has set the stage, she says: "You all have great stories to tell. Some may be funny, exciting, or scary. Others may tell of accidents or something sad. We are ready to get started. Take a minute to make a plan for what you want to write."*
>
> *Ms. Capalongo dismisses the children a few at a time. They get their folders from milk crates they use for storage and settle in at tables.*

What you see in this example is evidence that Ms. Capalongo has established a structure for writing workshop. The children know where to get the supplies they need and where to go to pursue the task. Ms. Capalongo has built a community in the classroom and uses meetings as a forum for instruction, discussion, and sharing of ideas and experiences. Because the routines are predictable, children are relatively independent. At the same time, they work cooperatively.

While children write, Ms. Capalongo is able to confer with individuals and observe children working. Based on what she sees, she constructs a plan for the week's lessons. In addition, she uses her conference times to learn more about individual children and to suggest that the children talk with one another about their writing. Finally, she thinks about which children will read their writing at the sharing meeting.

Expanding the Focus of Writing Workshop

Since writing workshop is key instructional time, teachers consider what curriculum content should be taught and how. Thus, specific writing times may be directed toward poetry, letter writing, essays, and research reports related to social studies or science topics. The section that follows discusses specifically how you might incorporate research-writing opportunities. You can use this model of presenting examples of a particular style of writing and then have children write in this style with a purpose they deem important in mind.

Research Reports

Introduce research writing in a directed lesson by presenting examples of several books about a topic (e.g., raccoons or bridges). You can show that each book is different because each author had a different focus. One may write about the life cycle of the raccoon, another about how and where raccoons live. Someone writing about bridges might have conducted detailed investigations of different kinds of bridges, another researcher might have studied the traffic going over and under different bridges.

The next step is for you and the children to collect resources. Make sure that books are available at different reading levels. Information can also be gathered by making observations on trips, and collecting data from films, over the Internet, on CD-ROMs, videos, and pictures. Children can also interview people who have direct experience with the subject.

Critical to the research writing process is looking for information in a focused way. Have children begin by writing the questions they want to answer so they can look for specific information. If children have their own questions to provide the framework for their report, they don't need teacher-made outlines. Research writing can and should be a collaborative process where children help one another find information and share knowledge they have acquired. Writing times can be used for children to take notes and write and revise drafts. Children can use meetings to share works in progress as a way to receive feedback from their peers.

Independent Writing

In a classroom where writing of all kinds is encouraged and materials for writing are always available, you are likely to see children writing for many purposes all day long. Many teachers encourage children to keep journals or notebooks.

Children's journals are a private place to write about anything they want to share with the teacher. Journals may be used to jot down ideas for stories, complain about friendships or homework, comment about something that happened in the class, or keep a list of things noticed. Teachers can encourage all kinds of journal writing. Sometimes children keep separate math journals to record their thinking about new or developing concepts. Science journals may record observations. Literature journals may document reactions to books or poetry.

Writer's notebooks are often used to help children see that they can get ideas for writing all the time. Notebooks are the place to write down interesting words they have noticed or to describe something unusual that has just happened that they don't want to forget. Older children may be asked to use their notebooks to describe an image or picture.

Some teachers use notebooks or journals for writing homework assignments, particularly for second and third graders. Writing assignments can follow up on class lessons or expand on something the child was working on in class. For example, if the class had written an observation piece in class, the assignment that night might be to do another observation piece, or to stretch the one that the child began in school. Children can also be encouraged to write about whatever they would like. Some teachers find that it is helpful to develop a list with children of possible writing ideas and write them in the back of each notebook. Here is an example.

> Writing ideas:
>
> Memories
>
> Interview a family member
>
> Make lists
>
> Observe something carefully and describe it
>
> Think about how you feel and describe your feelings
>
> Notice the sounds you hear and write about them
>
> Think of phrases that you like that you have heard
>
> Write about a particular dream
>
> Your special wishes
>
> Describe something in detail
>
> Write about a favorite character in a book
>
> Write about a scientific question you would like to know more about
>
> Describe the work a parent or adult friend does every day

Using Teachable Moments

All of these planned reading and writing activities and discussions ensure that children will have concentrated learning opportunities every day to increase their language and literacy skills. In addition, there are many other spontaneous things you can do to enrich their learning.

Reading and writing opportunities occur naturally throughout the day. When teachers seize these moments, children see the varied purposes of reading and writing. Teachers can engage children in reading the morning message or daily schedule. They can engage children in using their reading and writing skills by creating an environment that encourages these activities. Here are some easy-to-implement ideas.

- Use message boards for children to write notes to the teacher and to one another.

- Create graffiti boards (with rules about what is appropriate) for spontaneous writing.

- Establish pen pal or e-mail relationships between children in different classes.

- Provide suggestion boxes for children to register their concerns. When children notice a problem in the school (e.g., another garbage can would keep litter from spilling), they can write to the custodian or the principal about the problem.

- Develop job charts that children read to know about their responsibilities.

If these approaches to guiding learning in language and literacy are new to you, consider where to begin. It's probably best to try one thing at a time. Many teachers find it helpful to begin with scheduling a read-aloud time every day as a way to link community building with language and literacy instruction. Consider the listening, speaking, reading, and writing activities you already provide in your classroom and think about what other ideas described in this chapter you are ready to try.

Closing Thoughts

Language and literacy experiences for children are most successful when they capitalize on children's inherent motivation to communicate—to listen, speak, read, and write. Children learn these skills most naturally in the context of social interactions. Effective teachers seize the many opportunities throughout the school day to have children apply language and literacy skills in an integrated way across the curriculum.

References and Resources for Language and Literacy

Adams, M. J. 1990. *Beginning to Read: Thinking and Learning About Print*. Cambridge, MA: Massachusetts Institute of Technology Press.

Avery, Carol. 1993. *…And With a Light Touch*. Portsmouth, NH: Heinemann.

Calkins, Lucy McCormick. 1994. *The Art of Teaching Writing, New Edition*. Portsmouth, NH: Heinemann.

Calkins, Lucy McCormick. 1991. *Living Between the Lines*. Portsmouth, NH: Heinemann.

Clay, Marie M. 1991. *Becoming Literate: The Construction of Inner Control*. Portsmouth, NH: Heinemann.

Clay, Marie M. 1993. *An Observation Survey of Early Literacy Achievement*. Portsmouth, NH: Heinemann.

Cunningham, Patricia. 1991. *Phonics They Use: Words for Reading and Writing*. New York: Harper Collins.

Cunningham, Patricia, and Richard Allington. 1994. *Classrooms That Work: They Can All Read and Write*. New York: Harper Collins.

Dickinson, David K., and Lori Lyman DiGisi. March 1998. The Many Rewards of a Literacy-Rich Classroom. *Educational Leadership* 55 (6): 23–26.

Fisher, Bobbi. 1996. *Inside the Classroom: Teaching Kindergarten and First Grade*. Portsmouth, NH: Heinemann.

Fisher, Bobbi. 1995. *Thinking and Learning Together: Curriculum and Community in a Primary Classroom*. Portsmouth, NH: Heinemann.

Fountas, Irene C., and Gay Su Pinnell. 1996. *Guided Reading: Good First Teaching for All Children*. Portsmouth, NH: Heinemann.

Gambrell, Linda B., and Janice F. Almasi, eds. 1996. *Lively Discussions! Fostering Engaged Reading*. Newark, DE: IRA.

Gentry, J. Richard, and Jean Wallace Gillet. 1992. *Teaching Kids to Spell*. Portsmouth, NH: Heinemann.

Graves, Donald. 1983. *Writing: Teachers and Children at Work*. Portsmouth, NH: Heinemann.

Harwayne, Shelley. 1992. *Lasting Impressions*. Portsmouth, NH: Heinemann.

Holdaway, Don. 1979. *The Foundations of Literacy*. Portsmouth, NH: Heinemann.

International Reading Association. 1998. *Phonemic Awareness and the Teaching of Reading*. Position Statement. Newark, DE: IRA.

International Reading Association and the National Association for the Education of Young Children. 1998. *Learning to Read and Write: Developmentally Appropriate Practices for Young Children*. Joint Position Statement. Washington, DC: NAEYC.

International Reading Association and the National Council of Teachers of English. 1996. *Standards for the English Language Arts*. Newark, DE: IRA.

National Center on Education and the Economy and the Learning Research and Development Center, University of Pittsburgh. 1999. *Reading and Writing Grade by Grade: Primary Literacy Standards for Kindergarten through Third Grade*. New Standards. Washington, DC: National Center on Education and the Economy and Pittsburgh, PA: Learning Research and Development Center.

National Center on Education and the Economy and the University of Pittsburgh. 1997. *Performance Standards*. New Standards.

National Research Council. Burns, M. Susan, Peg Griffin, and Catherine E. Snow, eds. 1999. *Starting Out Right: A Guide to Promoting Children's Reading Success*. Washington, DC: National Academy Press.

National Research Council. Snow, Catherine E., M. Susan Burns, and Peg Griffin, eds. 1998. *Preventing Reading Difficulties in Young Children*. Washington, DC: National Academy Press.

Neumann, Susan, and Kathleen A. Roskos. 1998. *Children Achieving: Best Practices in Early Literacy*. Newark, DE: IRA.

Opitz, Michael F., and Timothy V. Rasinski. 1998. *Good-bye Round Robin: 25 Effective Oral Reading Strategies*. Portsmouth, NH: Heinemann.

Pinnell, Gay Su, and Irene C. Fountas. 1998. *Word Matters: Teaching Phonics and Spelling in the Reading/Writing Classroom*. Portsmouth, NH: Heinemann.

Routman, Regie. 2000. *Conversations*. Portsmouth, NH: Heinemann.

Routman, Regie. 1990. *Invitations*. Portsmouth, NH: Heinemann.

Routman, Regie. 1996. *Literacy at the Crossroads*. Portsmouth, NH: Heinemann.

Short, Kathy G., and Jerome C. Harste with Carolyn Burke. 1996. *Creating Classrooms for Authors and Inquirers*. Portsmouth, NH: Heinemann.

Stanovich, K. E. 1986. Matthew Effects in Reading: Some Consequences of Individual Differences in the Acquisition of Literacy. *Reading Research Quarterly* 21:360–407.

Stanovich, K. E. 1994. Romance and Reality. *The Reading Teacher* 47 (4): 280–291.

Taberski, Sharon. 2000. *On Solid Ground: Strategies for Teaching Reading K-3*. Portsmouth, NH: Heinemann.

Yopp, Hallie. 1992. Developing Phonemic Awareness in Young Children. *The Reading Teacher* 45:696–723.

Mathematical Thinking

We use mathematical thinking to solve problems every day. Each time we consider how many gallons of paint we need to paint the kitchen, whether fifteen dollars will pay for the groceries in the cart, or how the furniture will fit into the moving van, we use mathematical thinking skills to organize information, compare amounts, and see relationships. Learning the concepts and language of mathematics—more, less, equal, a fraction of, multiples of, and so on—helps us to plan, calculate, reason, and communicate solutions to problems.

Children use mathematical thinking skills long before they come to school. They compare who can jump higher or ride bikes faster; they divide a pack of M&Ms among friends; they notice the patterns on the wings of a butterfly. Therefore, a logical way to teach mathematical thinking is to build on the skills children have, encourage them to use these skills purposefully, and plan experiences that promote learning new skills while solving problems like those encountered in daily life. When children are given opportunities to develop their own understanding of mathematics by applying skills to real problems, they are likely to become successful mathematical thinkers and to continue to use these skills outside the classroom.

Teachers may need to alter the way they think about mathematics and their role in teaching it. The environment that focuses on answers must be changed to one that focuses on the thinking process itself; teaching how to solve problems is much different from teaching how to get answers (De La Cruz 1994, 1).

This approach to teaching mathematical thinking encourages educators to ask, "How can we provide mathematical experiences that not only teach basic computational skills, but also help children develop the thinking skills necessary to solve real-life problems?"

Children Becoming Mathematical Thinkers

What takes place in classrooms where children develop numeracy—where they learn and use math skills purposefully? Consider the examples that follow in which children pursue investigations of mathematical problems.

*In a **first grade class**, several children make collections of* threes, *while others find stories of* threes *in the class library. Around the room, an assortment of collections are assembled including three buttons, three coats, three shoes, three red cubes, etc. Using a calculator, two girls add with three and record: 3+3=6, 3+3+3=9, 3+3+3+3=12, 3+3+3+3+3=15. Several children roll dice (some with dots and some with numerals) to see how many times they get the sum three or the number three. The book collectors find* The Three Billy Goats Gruff, The Three Little Pigs, *and* The Three Bears. *Two children record themselves singing, "Three Blind Mice," and then write in their journals different combinations to make up three mice (e.g., 1+2, 1+1+1).*

These children explore the concept of quantity by investigating many ways to construct the number *three*. They experiment with ways to use the number *three* to make larger numbers and find the number *three* in another context. The teacher recognizes that playing games is a useful way to explore numbers (and learn facts) and encourages the use of dice, card games, and board games. Opportunities like this for meaningful investigations help children develop an understanding of how numbers are used.

*In a **second grade class**, children investigate the concept of time. One boy uses a stopwatch to measure the length of time it takes to copy a ten-piece pattern block design. Using jars, tape, and sand, others construct sand-clocks that measure one, two, or three minutes of time.*

These second graders explore the concept of time using a variety of materials. Rather than simply teaching children to tell time, the teacher extends children's thinking by encouraging them to investigate the passage of time and to make and use tools to track time.

***Third graders** explore two- and three-dimensional shapes. After a work time spent exploring the shapes of different objects (e.g., windows, bookshelves, wastebaskets, boxes, pipes, funnels), they focus on the cube. Using a variety of strips of paper with markings to indicate six squares, one group experiments with folding them to see which strips will form a cube. Some can and some cannot. Over the course of several days, they write in their math journals about which shapes could be folded to form a cube, which could not, and why. Another group uses geometry software on the computer to create cubes of various sizes. Other children use art materials to draw different sized cubes, exploring and representing the number of sides viewed from different angles.*

As children engage in these activities, they think about the properties of three-dimensional shapes, visualize or develop mental images of the shapes, and become much more precise in their understanding of geometric relationships. The teachers in each of these classrooms guide explorations of math concepts in order to help children become mathematical thinkers. The children apply basic skills to real situations that are both appealing and appropriate for their age level.

The focus of the math curriculum is not only on arithmetic, but also on measuring, sorting, classifying, problem solving, geometry, probability, and number sense and operations. The problems presented to children may not be solved in one day; they are encouraged to stay with problems over time—to experiment, learn from their mistakes, and try again.

Children recognize changes in the math curriculum. Marilyn Burns and Bonnie Tank (1988, 1-2) asked a group of third graders how they would define mathematics. Their responses focused on numbers rather than the purposes of math.

> *"It's when you add two numbers."*
>
> *"It's odd and even."*
>
> *"Yuk!"*

These same third graders were then given extensive opportunities to solve real problems and to think and reason mathematically. Later, when asked again about mathematics, they responded very differently.

> *"I think about thinking because you have to think when you do math."*
>
> *"When I think about mathematics I think about looking at money when I go to 7-11 and adding how much there is. About subtracting a special year from 1987 to find out how long ago it was."*
>
> *"When I think about mathematics I think about learning and deciding if I should keep rolling the dice or if I should keep my score in the game of pig."*

To become thinkers and problem solvers, capable of understanding and making an impact on today's complex world of invention and technology, children must have experiences that spark their interest and curiosity, integrate their learning, and help structure their thinking. Teaching mathematics to achieve these goals means providing activities that challenge children to think for themselves, and solve problems together.

Goals of the Mathematics Curriculum

New approaches to the teaching of mathematics have evolved from the *Standards* first developed by the National Council of Teachers of Mathematics (NCTM) in 1989 and revised in 1998. These *Standards* (1989, 1998) strongly encourage teachers to create a classroom environment where children can be active learners who seek answers to interesting problems. The revised document reflects a greater emphasis on doing mathematics—that is, the activities children do to learn and practice the math curriculum. The activities involved in doing math help teachers make sure that the content at each grade level is actually understood by children. This means that children focus on problem solving, reasoning and proof, making connections, and communicating and representing mathematical knowledge and information throughout the curriculum. We describe these processes before considering the specific content of the math curriculum.

Becoming Mathematical Problem Solvers

Knowing how to solve problems is the top priority. Fortunately, children's natural curiosity uncovers mathematical problems. To solve problems, children need a repertoire of problem-solving strategies. First, children must comprehend the problem. In order to solve it, they have to interpret what it means and make a plan to solve it. By sharing and watching others, they learn that there are often many ways to solve a problem as well as different strategies—and some are more efficient than others. Experiences using manipulative materials, drawing pictures, discussing, dramatizing, trying different methods, and looking for patterns help children learn to use these strategies and discover new ones. With practice, children develop the confidence and perseverance to tackle the problem again when their first attempt fails.

To acquire the strategies and the flexibility needed to solve problems, teachers create a wide range of opportunities for children to work—individually and in small groups—on open-ended problems, as illustrated in the following examples.

> *A pair of first graders works with Cuisenaire Rods. They have been challenged to find as many ways to "build 10" as they can. One child builds as the other records. They take turns doing these jobs. Later several pairs talk with each other and share their recordings about how they solved the problem.*

> *A bag of marbles is presented to a group of four children, and they are given these clues:*
>
> *1) There are more than 6 marbles in the bag.*
>
> *2) There are only three colors.*
>
> *3) There are 4 blue marbles.*
>
> *4) There are half as many green marbles as blue ones.*
>
> *5) There is one more red marble than blue marble.*

The children are asked to figure out how many marbles are in the bag, and how many there are of each color. As they work together to solve the problem, the children come up with different solutions and learn to work cooperatively as team members. To extend this activity, the children rearrange the number of marbles and make up riddles of their own (Burns 1988).

Solving real problems enables children to learn that problem solving is a process that takes time, effort, and good communication. Children gain confidence as mathematical thinkers by creating and solving problems they believe to be important.

Learning to Reason and Prove

While learning to reason and prove may sound like a project for older children, primary grade children naturally try to "make sense of their world" (NCTM 1998, 137). As they discover new ideas, they compare them against what they already know. Noticing and tracking patterns or making rules about what makes a number odd or even requires logical thinking. With experience, children learn to defend their reasoning and prove that their arguments make sense.

Charles and Demetrios argue about how many hours are in one week. Charles tries to mentally add 24 seven times but gets confused. He gets two calculators from the shelf. They decide that Demetrios will add 24 seven times and Charles will multiply 24 by 7. After comparing answers, they describe their findings in a class meeting.

Elizabeth wants to make a life-size drawing of herself. The teacher asks, "How can we determine the size paper you will need?" Elizabeth asks her friend Sally, who is the same height, to lie on the floor. She uses a piece of string to measure Sally. Then Elizabeth and the teacher use the length of string to cut a sheet of brown paper the right size.

When we encourage children to discover and explain their own solutions to real-life problems, they begin to see themselves as capable mathematical thinkers.

Children love to explain things—why one object is heavier than another, why the shiny red marble speeds down the track faster than the dull blue one—and to justify their reasoning. The ability to reason mathematically begins when children make a statement and then try to explain their reasoning. To cultivate this skill, teachers ask children to explain, justify, and demonstrate how they arrived at their explanation.

Second graders demonstrate mathematical reasoning and proof when they tell which of the 32 attribute block pieces is missing from the set. They say, "I know that a small, blue, diamond is missing because there are four small squares, triangles, and circles, and only three small diamonds." Giving children opportunities to figure out and then explain their solutions teaches them that mathematics is not just a collection of numbers and symbols, but a language that makes sense.

Learning to Make Connections

Children learn to make connections when they can see how mathematics relates to their own lives. Teachers can facilitate this. On a trip to the grocery store, children might notice that products are boxed or canned in containers of many sizes and shapes. The contents of each package are weighed to determine their cost. The items are classified by their food type. The checkout computer reads each product identification code and then totals the final cost. Sharing these observations extends children's learning and encourages more observations.

Children come to value mathematics when they see how it connects to everyday experiences:

- as they classify a collection of rocks by attributes;
- as they use a computer to play games involving numbers, logical thinking, spatial sense, or money;
- as they compare the size of buildings in a study of the neighborhood;
- as they create and identify shapes in their artwork; and
- as they recognize patterns in books (e.g., *The Very Hungry Caterpillar, Ten-in-a-Bed, The Three Little Pigs, The Doorbell Rang*).

In each case children learn that mathematics is a useful and important part of their lives, rather than simply a study of numbers isolated in a textbook.

Learning to Communicate Mathematically and Make Representations

To communicate mathematically, we have to know the language of mathematics. When children talk about and reflect on what they think and do in math, they (and their teachers as well) gain a better understanding of what they are learning. Language—spoken, written, and visually represented—helps children clarify their thinking and structure their ideas. Using the language of mathematics, children learn how to communicate with signs and symbols, thus translating the word problem or the math experience into a new form.

> *A third grade class decides to make a map of the schoolyard. They want to show the location of each piece of play equipment and the distance between each one. They measure using meter sticks and a metric trundle wheel. The children communicate their findings by plotting a map, representing distances by number, and play equipment with symbols described in a key.*

> *A second grader has chosen to study black bears as part of the class's study of forest animals. He discovers in a book that black bears are six feet tall. After measuring a length of rolled paper that is 6 feet long, he draws, cuts out, and paints a Black Bear. His sign says, "Black Bears are this big—6 Feet!"*

Children can be encouraged to communicate mathematically and represent their thinking in a variety of ways.

- Draw their description of a problem or a solution.

- Build a model to represent a solution.

- Explain how they solved a problem.

- Dramatize their understanding of a problem or a solution.

- Listen to the ways other children solved a problem.

- Keep written journals about what they are learning or doing in math.

- Work with a partner or in small groups to create and solve problems.

- Invent and teach math games to each other.

- Create graphs from data collected from e-mail pals.

For children who are not very verbal, or whose primary language is not English, communicating ideas in writing, drawings, or actions gives them additional opportunities to demonstrate their competence.

Keeping the process goals in mind—becoming mathematical problem solvers, learning to reason and prove, learning to make connections, learning to communicate mathematically and make representations—will help you prepare a learning environment in which children pursue productive and interesting mathematical activities. As children gain confidence in their abilities as mathematicians, they will assume more responsibility for their own learning.

Components of the Mathematics Curriculum

Children need skills in specific areas to help them think mathematically. As defined in the NCTM Standards, the mathematics curriculum for Pre-K–12 should address the following concepts:

- number concepts and operations
- patterns, functions, and algebra
- geometry and spatial relationships
- measurement
- data analysis, statistics, and probability

The following chart provides an overview of the specific skills children are expected to acquire during the primary grades.

Overview of the Mathematics Curriculum

Components	Children Learn to:
Number Concepts and Operations	• Read, write, and compare whole numbers (by building numbers with materials, counting children) • Use counting strategies (counting on, counting backwards, counting in groups) • Use whole number operations (adding, subtracting, multiplying, and dividing) • Use the calculator to perform number calculations or to check computations • Show understanding of place value (100s, 10s, 1s) • Show understanding of fractions as parts of a whole (halves, thirds, fourths) • Estimate to compute reasonable/approximate answers to problems
Patterns, Functions, and Algebra	• Recognize attributes (shape, size, color, thickness, texture) • Recognize patterns (in nature, school, books, with numbers and shapes) • Make, copy, and extend patterns • Make predictions about patterns and apply rules • Sort, classify, and compare objects and groups of objects • Order materials/objects • Describe relationships using language (larger, smaller, heavier, darker, etc.)
Geometry and Spatial Relationships	• Recognize and name shapes according to attributes • Classify shapes according to attributes • Compare shapes using mathematical language • Develop a sense of spatial relationships and use descriptive language (above, below, beside, to the left/right of, inside, outside, on top of) • Recognize and explore properties of two- and three-dimensional constructions

At first glance, it may seem overwhelming to consider including so many different components in the math curriculum. As you read the definitions of each component and think about the examples, notice how often the components are interrelated. Most of the examples showing children's activities address multiple skills and span more than one component of the math curriculum.

The charts in each of the following sections illustrate examples of a continuum of learning and the progression of children's thinking in first through third grades. Based on your knowledge of the children in your class each year, you can make decisions about the kinds of experiences children need and where you should begin. It is normal for the children in any one grade to be in many different places on the continuum.

Measurement	• Estimate quantities (measurements, weights, elapsed time, volume)
	• Estimate and measure using non-standard units (about 3 hands long, 6 cubes long) and standard units (inches, feet, yards, centimeters, meters)
	• Use words to describe and compare measurements (longer than, twice as long, area, perimeter, volume)
	• Use standard instruments for measuring (scales, cups, rulers, meters, yardsticks)
	• Use time-related words in daily vocabulary (days, hours)
	• Tell time and make judgments about time (relate activities to the passage of time)
	• Recognize and understand coins and bills
Data Analysis, Statistics, and Probability	• Collect, report, and describe data (e.g., daily temperatures, hair color, type of shoes, food preferences)
	• Ask questions about data
	• Create charts and graphs that illustrate and organize data
	• Read graphs and draw conclusions ("What can you tell from this graph?")
	• Make predictions based on data

Number Concepts and Operations

The study of number concepts, sometimes called number sense, and number operations, what we call arithmetic, has traditionally been the central focus of the elementary school math curriculum. Learning number facts (3+4=7 or 7x8=56) and doing the four basic operations (+, -, x, and ÷) occupied a major portion of class time and were the basis upon which mathematical ability and achievement were evaluated. Number concepts and the use of operations are vitally important to the development of mathematical competency. However, the definition of number concepts is broader than simply performing the operations. Understanding number concepts requires three levels of understanding:

- number, e.g., the meaning of 4;

- the relationships between numbers, e.g., three is less than seven, twenty is 2 x 10; and

- the effects of operations on numbers, e.g., if you add two numbers you get a larger number.

Children learn arithmetic as they acquire an understanding of the meaning of numbers. Given opportunities to experience number symbols (7+4=11) linked with real-life activities (7 boys and 4 girls make 11 children), they begin to connect the mathematical symbols with real situations (who is here and who is absent). In fact, children begin constructing a sense of number in their highchairs as they finger three Cheerios, popping them into their mouths—one, two, three—their first counting lesson. And as they ask for more, they begin to discover the relationships between numbers: 5>3 Cheerios (five is more than three Cheerios). Throughout the primary grades, continuous real-life experiences with counting, relating, estimating, connecting, grouping, and interpreting numbers help children develop a solid understanding of number concepts.

Teachers can learn about children's number sense when they challenge them to create equations using various operations to equal 8. Some solutions might be:

8=24÷3	8=(3/4 of a dozen)-1
8=1/2 of 16	2+4+2=8-0
8=the time I go to bed	8=yesterday's date
8=+15-7	8=3+3+4-2

8=the number of children who sit at my lunch table

Children need extensive opportunities to count, group, and manipulate numbers before they can see how the placement of a number relates to its value. When asked what the "3" means or stands for in the numeral "30," most young children seem bewildered because they only understand that "3" means three things, and that "30" means thirty things. Although children can memorize that one column is for *the tens* and the other column is for *the ones*, meaning is not developed until children can see numbers both as a specific quantity and as a representation of an idea. Exploring numbers with real materials (e.g., manipulatives, classroom objects) enables children to make discoveries about numbers as symbols.

Games provide a wonderful opportunity for children to practice and reinforce number concepts independently of the teacher. Dice games, dominoes, playing cards, and board games can involve counting, finding sums, recognizing equivalent values, and figuring out number relationships.

Opportunities to explore number concepts often arise spontaneously in the classroom.

Ms. Whitson introduces a new painting activity to her first graders—tray painting (see page 117). She explains that there are four trays available for use. After discussing how the paint, brushes, and clean-up system will work, she asks, "How many children can work at a time?" Eager to work with their own trays, the children decide that only four children can paint at a time. She asks how many children are present in class today. When the children answer, "18," she asks how many painting groups there will be so everyone gets a chance to paint today. The children give various estimates. Then they spend a few minutes working alone or with partners, using chalk on the board, paper and markers, unifix cubes, or mental calculations to determine the solution. Each group explains how it decided on a strategy and came up with its answer. They agree that they need four groups of four and one group of two.

Exploring Number Concepts and Operations

Skills	A Primary Grade Continuum: Ways Children Might Demonstrate Skills		
Understanding whole numbers	• use numbers to identify quantities: count 10 plastic bears and write the number 10 • recognize the relative size of numbers: 2 is less than 6, 18 is more than 9	• recite numbers to 100 or more; keep track of how many days of school have passed and read the number on the number line • read and write numerals to 100 with a specific purpose in mind: record scores in a card game	• read and write numerals to 999: track mileage on an odometer • recognize the relative size of larger numbers: 600 is more than 500, 801 is less than 810
Using counting strategies	• count objects in a group pointing to each object as it is counted • count on: make a set of 7 cubes from a set of 4 cubes by adding 3 to the original set rather than starting over from 1	• count backwards from numbers 100 to 1 • see multiple ways to count a group of 50 objects, by 2s, 5s, 10s	• count on or backwards mentally: add 17+9 by adding 17+10 and subtracting 1 • count in groups: by 25s, 100s, 500s
Using estimation with computation	• find solutions to problems: each of three children can have 3 or 4 candies if there are 11 candies in all	• solve problems using knowledge of place value: 22+35 is about 50 because there are 5 tens	• check calculator solutions by estimating: 584 is too large for 10x52, and therefore recalculate
Developing an understanding of whole number operations	• use strategies (manipulatives, fingers, learning doubles, drawing a picture) to figure out 5+2=7 • solve real problems: there are 5 children who want to work at this table and only 3 chairs, how many more chairs do we need?	• use objects to show that 5 groups of 3 are 15 and 3 groups of 5 are 15 • use strategies to add and subtract: number families, 6+3=9, 9-3=6; doubles +1, 8+8=16, 8+9=17	• use repeated addition, number families, or understanding of multiples to solve multiplication and division problems • use knowledge of the distributive property to calculate 6x12: 6x10=60, 6x2=12, 60+12=72.

Estimating quantities	• look at a group of objects and decide: the quantity is less than 50, more than 20, nearly 30	• look at containers of objects and use estimating strategies: there are 5 objects in the first row, count by 5s to estimate the number in all	• regularly use words such as: about, near, approximately, in between, around
Developing an understanding of place value	• count quantities of objects by grouping them in tens and ones • count on from ten: 10 objects, add 3 more without beginning at 1	• use groups of objects to play trading games: chip trading with red, blue, yellow, and green chips • calculate the value of two 2-digit numbers: add 23+45 by showing 2 tens sticks and 4 tens sticks make 6 tens sticks plus 8 units (ones), or 68 altogether	• calculate the value of two 2-digit numbers using sense of tens and ones: 26+27= 40+13=53 • describe a 3-digit number in several ways: use base ten blocks to show 132 as 1 flat, 3 rods, and 2 whites, or 132 whites, or 13 rods and 2 whites, or 12 rods and 12 whites
Developing an understanding of fractions	• share a banana with a friend by splitting it into two equal parts • compare fractions: know that 1/2 of a group is more than 1/4 of the group and use the words "half" and "quarter" accurately	• identify equal parts of a whole object as 1/2, 1/3, or 1/4: see an apple sectioned into 4 equal parts, and ask for 1/4 • show and compare 1/2, 1/3, and 1/4 spatially: given three pieces of 4 inch paper, can fold one to show two equal parts, one to show three equal parts, and one to show four equal parts	• name equivalent fractions: in cutting a pie into 1/8s, discover that 4/8 is equal to 1/2 • label fractional parts with pattern blocks: if the yellow hexagon is one whole, then the blue diamond is 1/3, 2 blue diamonds=2/3, the red trapezoid=1/2
Using a calculator	• explore the different keys on the calculator • add 25+21+27 to find the total number of children in all the first grade classrooms	• use the +, -, x, and ÷ keys to solve number problems • use the + key and then use the = key repeatedly to add the same number	• play number games: assign each letter a numerical value and calculate the value of names and words; collect $1.00 words

Children learn about fractions as they share or trade cookies or negotiate deals: "If I eat half of my peas, may I have dessert?" The child splits the pile of peas evenly, one to eat, one to leave, etc. When teachers introduce fractions and operations with fractions in school, it helps to build upon this understanding. Teachers can talk about fractions as children build with unit blocks, as food is distributed at snack time, during cooking projects, and as materials are distributed.

> *Ms. Robinson has desks organized in groups of 4 in the classroom. When she begins a unit on fractions, the children sit at their desks and talk about each person's desk as part of their table group. Two desks in a four person grouping make up 2/4 of the group, three desks are 3/4 of the group.*

When children have many opportunities to explore and solve problems using manipulatives and real-life experiences, they construct and explain their own solutions. In the process, they develop understandings about numbers and operations.

There has been much discussion about whether young children should use calculators before they have a secure grasp of number facts. Calculators are an essential tool in the classroom, just as they are in our homes and offices. Through the use of calculators, children can solve more complex problems with larger numbers. However, calculators should not replace the need to learn and become fluent with basic math facts. Teachers have the responsibility to choose when and how calculators should be used. When making a decision to use a calculator for an activity, think about whether it will help or hinder a child's mathematical thinking.

Patterns, Functions, and Algebra

Patterns are repetitions (such as stripes on a shirt or lines on a leaf), sequences (spring, summer, fall, winter), and relationships (3, 6, 9, 12 are multiples of 3). We find patterns all around us in the organization of numbers, nature, and events. An understanding of patterns is required for much higher level work with numbers, geometry, and data analysis. When children see patterns operate as rules, they can begin to understand functions. For example, if children discover that if one object is five inches long, two of the same objects are 10 inches long, and three of the same are 15 inches long, and build a model to describe this pattern, they are beginning to work with the concept of functions. While it may seem surprising to talk about algebra as part of the curriculum for young children, every time we ask children to *count on* we ask them to use algebraic reasoning. By helping children notice patterns, and consider functions and algebra as a way to look for the relationships between things, we help them make connections, organize information, and solve problems.

Seeing the first three pyramids made from inch cubes, Ernesto constructs a fourth pyramid based on his understanding of the relationships between pyramids 1, 2, and 3.

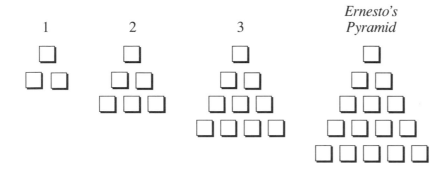

To understand patterns, children have to be able to identify or classify the specific attributes of the pattern, and describe the relationships between its parts. For example, in the number pattern, 1, 3, 5, 7, 9, 11,..., children identify that the numbers in this set are *odd* or that every other number is skipped. Children gain an understanding of patterns when they have opportunities to identify, create, and extend patterns using many different types of materials.

We also find patterns in the stories we read and the songs we sing. Learning about patterns will help children in all areas of the curriculum—mathematics, language and literacy, science, social studies, technology, and the arts.

Exploring Patterns, Functions, and Algebra

Skills	A Primary Grade Continuum: Ways Children Might Demonstrate Skills		
Identifying patterns and rules	• describe a pattern made with blocks: red-blue-red, or A-B-A-B • notice patterns in a shirt or in a song	• examine number patterns in a hundreds chart • see patterns in nature: stripes on a snake, lines on a spider web	• use an understanding of patterns to solve a problem: the rule is +6 for these numbers -6, 0, 6, 12, 18, ?, 30, 36
Creating patterns, using rules	• organize color tiles in a row by color: red, red, blue, red, red, blue • make circular designs connecting the beginning to the end using a pattern, such as a string of beads	• make patterns in more than one direction • make a number pattern using one rule: 12, 10, 8, —, 4, —, 0 (subtract 2)	• make line, circle, or area patterns using specific information: create an area pattern using 3 colors and 24 tiles • make a number pattern using two rules: multiply by 2, subtract 1
Extending patterns, using algebraic reasoning	• hear a snap, clap, click, click pattern and determine that a snap comes next • see a pattern in a Pattern Block design and be able to continue it	• say 15, 20, 25, 30, after hearing 5, 10… • plan for daily events: tell the sequence of tomorrow's events, based on a predictable pattern	• continue a pattern that repeats itself as well as grows: 1, 2, 1, 3, 1, 4…
Describing relationships	• sort and classify objects by similarities and differences and talk about their size, shape, color • order a group of objects according to size, quality, texture, or weight: describe a collection of balls organized from largest to smallest	• sort, classify, and describe objects in more than one way: first by shape, then by size • sort by given attributes: a set of large, plastic triangles, and tell how sorted	• compare two or more objects or numbers; explain that even numbers come in pairs, odds are a pair plus 1 • learn and explain tricks for multiples: 9s table increases by one in tens column, decreases by one in ones column: 9, 18, 27, 36…or the sum of the digits is 9

Geometry and Spatial Relationships

Experiences with geometry and spatial relationships are another way for children to organize and explore their world. Just as activities with numbers and patterns help children make connections and solve problems, experiences with geometric concepts and skills in the classroom lead children to develop an appreciation and understanding of the geometric world. Children begin to recognize the importance and use of a right angle in the building of houses and rooms. They laugh at the thought of a doorway built with angles of less than 90 degrees.

Geometry was once considered an enrichment unit to be explored if time permitted. Math professionals and educators now recognize that geometry is a critical component of the math curriculum. Children naturally explore the shapes and structures they see around them. In the primary grades, studying shapes and exploring properties of shapes requires work with numbers, measurement, and data analysis. Beyond the math curriculum, spatial sense is necessary for understanding maps, building structures, and planning designs.

The study of geometry challenges children to solve problems through investigation, experimentation, and exploration—strategies necessary for mathematical and scientific thinking. There are many excellent manipulative materials—geoboards, tangrams, pattern blocks, and geometric solids as well as graph paper and computer software tools—to help children develop an understanding of geometry. As children talk about shapes, draw pictures, create computer programs that draw shapes, and write about their knowledge, teachers can use these communications and representations of problem solving to assess children's understanding and plan instruction.

Exploring Geometry and Spatial Relationships

Skills	A Primary Grade Continuum: Ways Children Might Demonstrate Skills		
Learning about the attributes of geometric shapes	• explore the parts of shapes and how they are constructed: build a rectangle using straws and clay • investigate geometric solids: roll cylinders and spheres, stack cubes and boxes	• use geometric language to describe shapes and spaces: a rectangle has 2 short lines, 2 long lines, and 4 angles • begin to classify shapes by attributes: squares, rectangles, and diamonds are all four-sided shapes	• match, reproduce, describe, and name shapes: all triangles have three sides, some are tall and thin, others are short and fat • classify shapes by specific attributes: some triangles, rectangles, and squares all have right angles
Comparing and transforming shapes	• build shapes using other shapes: use two small tangram triangles to build a parallelogram, a square, and larger triangle • sort and classify shapes: make three groups of shapes (one with no straight sides, one with five sides, one with two long sides)	• recognize similar and congruent shapes: match similar shapes noting the only difference is in their size • recognize that different shaped containers can hold the same amount of water, even though the tall thin glass looks like it holds more than a short fat one	• notice differences in geometric solids: one pyramid has a square base, the other has a triangular base • analyze and classify shapes, compare number of sides, angles, lines of symmetry
Exploring spatial relationships	• explore ways to fill an area: use pattern blocks and put 5 diamonds or 10 triangles into an outline of a flower • experiment with containers: discover relationships between the amount of sand in a cylinder and in a cube of equal height	• construct shapes following specific rules: make a square on a geoboard that touches only 8 nails and put a triangle inside it • investigate symmetry: place a mirror on a pattern block design, showing the line of symmetry	• solve area problems: fill a space using square color tiles to find out how many will cover the area • build reflections: use the same pattern blocks to construct the other side of a 4-piece design

Measurement

Measurement activities encourage children to practice and integrate many different mathematical thinking skills. They make decisions about which tools to use and which strategies will work best. If they want to measure the classroom, for example, they might first decide whether to use their feet, Unifix cubes, a ruler, or a trundle wheel. When children compare their heights and figure out that Jeffrey is 2 inches taller than Scott is and 1 inch shorter than Laurel, they are using computation strategies.

> *Ms. Singer's third graders go to the schoolyard with stacks of containers to use in the sandbox. Many children crowd into the sandbox and begin to work. Castles and tunnels, mazes and gardens, highways and skyscrapers appear, some made by hand, others molded from the metric containers. They add water to fill moats and swimming pools. Laughter and excitement fill the air. Later, after the children have had time to explore freely, Ms. Singer directs them to a more formal measurement task. They use a variety of tools to measure their sand constructions.*

The children in this example are using the language of measurement: castles and skyscrapers are *tall*, moats are *deep*, gardens need *area*, water is *heavy*, and mazes and highways cover a *distance*. Next they begin to compare objects that have similar measurable attributes (e.g., "Look, my skyscraper is taller than your castle.") Measuring by comparing two objects is a necessary and normal step that children take before they start to measure with standard or non-standard units because it helps them focus on what they are measuring. Children quickly learn, for example, that it doesn't make sense to say, "My highway is longer than your skyscraper." Children need many opportunities to investigate and discuss the attributes of an object that are measurable.

Once children have the concepts and language of measurement, they begin to use a variety of materials or tools when confronted by a measurement problem.

> *Some children want to know whether the maze or the block highway is longer. They quickly see that they can't lay them out beside each other to compare their lengths. Instead, they solve the problem by using string to measure each length, then comparing the length of the strings.*

Often in second grade, and usually by third, children want more information about what they are measuring. They begin to question how much water fills that cup, or how much the box of sand weighs. At this time they choose standard units of measure to determine the measurement (e.g., the cup holds 1/2 a liter of water, the box of sand weighs just under a kilogram).

Exploring Measurement

Skills	A Primary Grade Continuum: Ways Children Might Demonstrate Skills		
Measuring with standard and non-standard units	• estimate length, height, or weight using a non-standard measure: guess that a new pencil is 6 paper clips long	• use non-standard units to determine length, weight: measure tables with links or pumpkins with string	• determine difference in weight between two objects: the piece of coal is ten blocks lighter than the piece of marble;
	• trace a partner's body and measure with Unifix cubes, arm lengths, or hands	• measure a specific item with a variety of tools: a chalkboard is 5 inches long and 13 cubes long	• explore the concept of perimeter: measure perimeter of a cylinder, a house, a dog pen
Using measuring instruments	• use a balance scale to determine which of two objects is heavier or lighter	• begin to link measures to familiar references: 4 hamburgers weigh about a pound, a notebook is about a foot high	• choose the best tool to measure: a trundle wheel to find the length of the playground instead of a meter stick
	• recognize the use of standard measuring tools such as ruler, scale, and thermometer and use the language that matches the tool	• use common instruments for measuring: scales for weight, cups for volume, thermometers for temperature	• use a measuring tool as a reference: find the distance around a can by first using a string and then measuring its length
Using estimation with measurement	• use a measurement tool to check an estimate: use a pan balance to find that 4 raisins weigh the same as a pebble	• use strategies to estimate space, objects or time: use Unifix cubes in stacks of 10 to measure the length of the classroom	• use strategies to estimate: one cupful holds 25 beans, the jar probably holds 6 cupfuls, so, the jar holds between 100 and 150 beans
Developing an understanding of time and time-related skills	• read, use, and discuss the information on the calendar: notice that days, weeks, and months follow a pattern	• experiment with duration of time: write name 20 times in one minute	• order events of the day, week, or year: start school in the fall, after winter holiday study mammals, science project due in two weeks
		• tell time on digital and analog clocks	
	• make reasonable estimates for amounts of time: it takes a second to throw a ball, and an hour to bake a cake	• order daily events: wake up at… go to school at… have dinner at… go to bed at…	• discuss a time line with understanding: order personal events on a time line

Data Analysis, Statistics, and Probability

Should a shoe store stock more Velcro or more lace-up sneakers for children? If I roll two dice, what sums will occur most frequently? When we gather information, we collect data. When we answer these questions we analyze data using knowledge of probability and statistics. A probability is a number that expresses the likelihood that something will happen. For example, the weather forecaster tells us there is a 50% chance of rain tomorrow. Statistics is the area of mathematics that helps us organize, describe, and interpret information so we can solve problems or make decisions. For example, by reading a graph we can figure out that second graders this year have more brothers than sisters, and all but two brothers are older than their second grade sibling.

Children begin to explore the fields of probability and statistics when they roll dice, make predictions about which sums will occur most frequently, and record the results. They may conduct surveys to find out about favorite foods or keep records about whose turn it is to do a certain job. They frequently ask questions that can be used to explore this aspect of mathematics.

> *Ms. Chavez's class wants to plan a sledding party after the first snowfall in December. She asks the children to think about which month has the most snow. After collecting information from the almanac, the class decides to plan its party in the month of February because February had 15 snowy days last year and 13 the year before, whereas January had only 8 last year and 10 the year before.*

When children have opportunities to collect data and explore statistics and probability, they learn how numbers express the likelihood that something will happen. These experiences help children understand their world and think about such things as their chances of getting chicken pox or the risk involved in bicycling. Further, the challenges presented by probability problems interest children, making numbers fun and relating them meaningfully to many aspects of their lives.

Exploring Data Analysis, Statistics, and Probability

Skills	A Primary Grade Continuum: Ways Children Might Demonstrate Skills		
Collecting, describing, organizing, and recording data	• create graphs with real objects: place shoes (e.g., velcro, tie, or buckle) on a large square grid to find out the most popular shoe type • record data: use a tally system to find out how many want bananas or how many want apples for snacks	• set up graphs in 1 to 1 correspondence with objects: line up data on a picture graph showing the colors of lunch boxes, one box to each number • conduct surveys and collect data: favorite foods, pets, siblings	• create graphs using pictures, bar, pie, or line form • graph data found in other curriculum areas: use a bar graph to show how many children in the class have read books by particular authors
Reading graphs and drawing conclusions	• notice patterns and describe relationships on a graph: guinea pigs seem to prefer apples over oranges • answer questions or solve problems using a graph's information: name 3 leaves that only have 1 point	• observe and describe data collected over time: find how many rainy days in October • compare information on a graph: talk and write about which category has more, less, the same, equal, not equal ($>, <, =, \neq$)	• notice and read graphs: use a weather graph from a newspaper to examine varying temperatures across America • find information on many types of graphs: pictograph, line, bar, and pie
Making predictions and developing arguments	• make and test predictions of simple possible outcomes or actions: if we keep this plant in the dark for more than a week, it will die • predict, then test which of 2 different colored crayons will be drawn most often from a paper bag	• make a prediction based on general knowledge: when you flip a coin, "heads" won't appear every time • predict an outcome and test it: roll 2 dice 50 times and predict which sum will occur most frequently	• invent and graph probability experiments: predict, then use a spinner with 4 colors to test which color is most likely to be selected • determine whether a prediction can be made from a sampling: the majority of first graders have one sibling; the majority of children in the whole school also have one sibling

Organizing the Math Curriculum

Teachers need a plan to address all the components of the math curriculum in a way that will make sense to children. Planning should be guided by the principles we outlined in Chapter 4, Guiding Children's Learning. Learning experiences must be purposeful for children and must be integrated with one another and with what children already know. Communication is central to all learning, and children need time to explore concepts and return to them over and over. Knowing that children construct knowledge by investigating, representing, and reflecting on their learning dictates the kind of experiences that will enable children to become mathematical thinkers. These experiences may take place as part of a long-term study, a work time, or in the context of a spontaneous teachable moment.

Promoting Mathematical Thinking through Long-Term Studies

When children are challenged to solve a problem that interests them, they are motivated to apply what they have learned and to learn new skills and concepts. That's why it is so effective to provide opportunities for children to work on particular math skills that arise naturally as part of long-term studies. Social studies or science projects enable teachers to integrate learning across many content areas. While a particular study is not likely to incorporate all the math skills that you want to teach at any given time, there are many components of mathematical thinking that naturally fit into the work of a long-term study.

A long-term study of a nearby **river** offers opportunities for a multi-age class to conduct first-hand investigations. In the process of studying the river, many mathematical questions arise for children to explore. Children might:

- measure the temperature of the water;
- count the different kinds of trees or plants growing along the bank; or
- graph the numbers of different kinds of animals they observe living in or near the river.

Some mathematical investigations that arise when a third grade class studies **immigration** might lead children to:

- make and read historical time lines;
- use necessary dates to calculate how old people were when they came to this country;
- conduct a survey to find out where their ancestors came from and when they arrived in this country; or
- figure out the size of the ships people traveled on and crowd into a space that size.

A study of the **neighborhood** around the school can be geared to all children six to eight years old. It is relevant to the children's lives and their investigations can continue after each school day. In the context of this study children might:

- count buildings, hydrants, windows, trees, etc.;

- notice patterns on buildings, in nature;

- make graphs showing different forms of transportation in use;

- estimate the number of people likely to pass a certain spot in a certain period of time;

- set up a store similar to one in the neighborhood, and buy and sell goods.

Animals appeal to most primary age children. Studies of local animals, whether they are squirrels and pigeons, lizards and armadillos, or bears and otters, are a good starting point. Children could:

- make life-size representations of the animals, using measuring materials to get the right size;

- compare the number of young each animal produces;

- compare the size of the males and females of the species;

- figure out how many children it would take to weigh as much as a particular animal;

- make time lines showing stages of maturation.

Long-term studies can address objectives in many subject areas while children explore interesting content. In Chapter 4, pages 175-81, we describe a series of steps for planning a study. One of the steps described charts that a teacher might make to help focus a study and find ways to integrate learning in many content areas. The following example shows how one teacher used a chart to help him think about the components of the math curriculum and how they could relate to his social studies project.

> *Mr. Fuller's second graders will study the construction site across the street from the school. An eight-story college dormitory is under construction, and he has contacted the supervisor of the project. The uncle of one of his students is a worker at the site. As part of his planning for this study, Mr. Fuller considers how he can incorporate mathematical investigations into the project.*

Study of a Construction Site

Math Component	Activities
Number	• Make time lines to indicate different stages of construction • Notice patterns in building design to explore multiplication • Count supplies and materials
Patterns	• Examine blueprints for patterns • Observe patterns in brick design • Estimate amounts of supplies and materials • Make estimates about size: windows, doors, number of bricks needed to make different sections
Geometry	• Investigate the use of different shapes used in building design
Measurement	• Study ratio by exploring the blueprints and an actual section of the building • Measure the size of a brick and the number of bricks required for a particular wall • Design and build a model of the dormitory under construction
Data Analysis, Statistics, and Probability	• Make graphs of the number and kinds of workers • Examine the job schedule charts the supervisor uses; make a comparable job chart for the classroom • Make predictions about when different stages of the project will be completed

After he makes the chart and thinks about how much measurement work the children can do in connection with the study, Mr. Fuller decides to begin the school year exploring non-standard measurement. He hopes children will then begin to recognize the value of standard measurement in construction. With this as his starting point, he then plans math work times to teach other math concepts and skills outlined in his curriculum guide.

When children are involved in studies that hold their interest, they often generate ideas for exploration that you may not have considered. Sometimes children want to solve a problem but don't yet have the skills to do so. If children conduct surveys and want to tabulate results, but lack the math skills, what are their alternatives? They may come up with strategies of their own to do the counting; they may use calculators, or you may decide to teach a particular skill because the children want to use it as a tool. Math work times can be designed to fit into the needs of a study or they may be designed to explore what children know and what they need to learn.

Planning Math Work Times

Most teachers schedule time for particular math activities every day. Sometimes math work times are used to introduce new materials, a new concept, or a game to the class as a whole group. At other times children work in small groups to explore a problem using a variety of materials. A teacher may work with one group while the others work independently. There are also times when children write in journals about their math learning or share their discoveries in a meeting.

In the following example, Ms. Herman is interested in finding out about the children's knowledge and use of basic number facts, and more important, their understanding and use of the language of mathematics. Knowing that the children need to be active, she chooses an activity that will engage the children in spilling nine large lima beans painted red on one side, white on the other. They will record their observations.

The activity offers many possibilities for mathematical thinking and for children to practice and discuss their ideas. By asking open-ended questions that challenge children to think, analyze, reason, and prove their theories, Ms. Herman will pursue the process goals of mathematical understanding as well as help children learn number facts.

With the whole class seated in a circle in the meeting area, Ms. Herman spills beans from the cup. This is what happens:

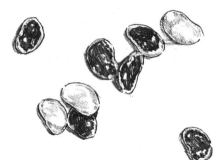

The children see the spilled beans and the following discussion takes place:

Teacher:	**Children:**
"What do you see?"	*"I see 9 beans, two colors, three chipped."*
"What do you see?"	*"I see 6 red ones and 3 white ones, and some beans are touching."*
"Do you see anything else?"	*"I see that they are not all the same size beans."*
Ms. Herman spills the beans a second time.	
"What do you see now?"	*"I see 9 beans, 4 red and 5 white."*
	"I see one more red than last time."
	"I see the same 9 beans."
	"No, they are not the same 9 beans, they are different, there is one more red one."

Teacher:	Children:
"What might happen when I spill them again?"	*"I think 2 reds, 7 whites."*
	"I think 3 whites, 6 reds."
	"I think 8 white, 1 red."
"Why do you think this?"	*"Because the red side is heavier because it is sprayed red and the heavy side will fall down faster."*
"Let's see what happens this time."	

Ms. Herman spills the beans a third time and gets 5 red and 4 white beans.

Teacher:	Children:
	"If you spill them again, I think that it won't be 5 red, 4 white."
"Why?"	*"Well the last spill was 5 red, 4 white, and you don't ever get the same thing two times in a row."*
"How do you know that?"	*"It hasn't happened yet. You've NEVER spilled the same thing twice."*
	"I bet if you let ME spill the beans, I'll get all reds," says one child. "No, that's impossible," says another.
"Why is that impossible?"	*"There is always one bean that won't do what the others do. Let ME have the beans and I'll show you."*
"What other questions do you have?"	*"What happens if you spill 10 beans?"*
	"What if you spill them from way up high?"
	"What if you don't shake them in the cup?"
	"What if you use little beans?"
	"What if you spill them one at a time?"

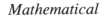

This communication between the teacher and the children shows how children can develop mathematical knowledge when the teacher sets up an interesting problem and poses open-ended questions that encourage children to think. The children are now ready to undertake investigations of their own. They will work with partners to spill their own containers of beans and record their findings. While they work, the teacher will talk with groups of children about their explorations. She knows that sufficient time must be allowed for this activity or the children will be frustrated.

As a way of involving families in this project, Ms. Herman has the children conduct probability experiments at home using nine pennies. She sends a note home with the children asking family members to work with their children to record how many heads and tails are shown each time the children *spill* the pennies.

Dear Families:

Our class is exploring number combinations. We hope you can help us with this project by conducting penny experiments with your child at home. You will need nine pennies. Each night next week, please spill the pennies (your child knows how to do this). Together, using the attached record sheet, record the number of heads and tails you get after spilling the pennies ten times. We will compare the results in class. Make sure your child brings the record sheet to school on Friday.

Thank you for your help with this activity.

Sincerely,

In the activity with the beans the teacher can observe what children are learning as she walks about the room and talks with them. Here are some examples of the kinds of mathematical learning taking place.

- *Number sense*—finding all the number combinations for 9 beans (eg., 1+8, 8+1, 7+2, 2+7, etc.).

- *Basic number facts*—seeing and recording number combinations that add up to 9.

- *Probability*—spilling the beans 30 times and recording which combination occurs most frequently.

- *Data collection*—having all the children spill their 9 beans 30 times, then recording all the data to observe the findings.

- *Graphing*—representing the data on charts and organizing it to show the findings visually.

- *Reasoning and proof*—proving that 9 beans can never be 5 red, 5 white; proving that white beans do not come up more often because the red side is heavier; proving that the height from which the beans are dropped does not affect the outcome.
- *Mathematical relationships*—devising a way to use the bean-spilling experiment to explore subtraction (e.g., spilling 9 beans and subtracting the red ones from nine, so the white ones will always be the answer!).

A simple activity with beans was planned by the teacher in order to focus on basic number facts and language. In the process of their investigations, children reveal their knowledge of other components of mathematical thinking. As the children work together, the teacher is able to assess their learning—writing quick anecdotal notes on a clipboard to help her remember what children know and what they can do.

Mathematical problem-solving opportunities, such as the one described above, enable children to construct their own knowledge. When children try to solve real mathematical problems, they are more likely to see a purpose to their learning and ask questions that lead to further learning. Ms. Herman's math lesson enables the children to investigate, represent, and reflect on what they are learning, as outlined below.

How Children Investigate Mathematical Problems

As they investigate math problems, children engage in several processes:

- observing
- seeing connections
- making predictions
- reasoning and using logical thinking
- hypothesizing and arguing
- questioning

The children observe as they look carefully at the spilled beans and describe what they see. They make connections as they notice that different numbers of beans are red or white, or that the second time there is one more red bean and one fewer white bean. Ms. Herman asks the children to predict what might happen the next time. They explain why they think something will happen and devise hypotheses to explain their predictions. She asks questions and the children ask questions. Knowing that all children do not engage in each element of the process all the time, Ms. Herman will build these elements of investigation into future learning experiences.

How Children Represent Their Learning in Mathematics

Mathematical conversations, as well as writing, drawing, building, or creating charts and diagrams, help children clarify their thinking. They also give the teacher information about what they understand and where they need additional support. Ms. Herman creates the structure for children to represent their learning in several ways. This helps her to evaluate how children's thinking changes and gives the children a record of their project. Ms. Herman provides worksheets for the children to record how many times each combination appears, as well as worksheets for them to record their homework with pennies. Some children make drawings of all the possible combinations. These are displayed around the room.

Opportunities for representation can be built into many mathematical activities by providing:

- meeting times for discussions;

- bulletin board space for children's designs and writings about math;

- meaningful worksheets that challenge children to record findings;

- *lab* books or math journals for recording ideas and drawings that represent the process used during an activity;

- a *save and share* table that displays constructions, designs, and inventions made by the children;

- a record of the questions children want to try to answer as part of a project; and

- space to showcase mathematical discoveries (e.g., the patterns in the hundreds board).

How Children Reflect on Mathematical Thinking

In the example with the beans, Ms. Herman has several meetings to discuss findings and generate some new questions. She also builds several opportunities into the work times for the children to reflect upon their learning. At the end of each day's math time, the children record their thoughts and observations in their math journals.

When children are encouraged to share the strategies they use to solve problems, they learn to value the process of finding answers. Other opportunities for reflection are designed to have children think about what they learned. When children look at the bean recording sheet and write down one discovery they made or write about something they now understand that they didn't before, they are learning to be reflective thinkers.

Teachers can ask many kinds of questions to help children think about problem-solving strategies. However, reflecting on mathematical thinking, while valuable, can be overdone! Not every work time or lesson has to have a reflection assignment built in; think about where and when it is appropriate, useful, or interesting.

Teaching Math through Play

Math games offer a variety of experiences for children to practice winning strategies and number facts. By incorporating time for games in the course of the day or week, you can make sure that children get the practice they need. Dice, playing cards, and board games can be introduced to the whole class or to small groups during a math work time. (See the section on games in Chapter 3, pages 113-14.) New games soon become part of children's repertoire and therefore an option for choice time as well as for math periods. If oak tag, stickers, or other materials are available, children can invent their own games as well, and challenge others to play them.

Planned work times ensure that children are exposed to a certain number of math skills and concepts, and most teachers find that beginning the day with a plan is crucial. In addition, teachers can increase the opportunities for math learning by infusing math concepts into everyday activities and allowing for the unexpected, spontaneous learning that naturally emerges.

Using Teachable Moments

Sometimes the best teaching occurs when it is least expected. A question comes up, a special class is canceled, or you discover your clock is ten minutes fast and you have to fill the time. You can use these opportunities to engage children in mathematical thinking and thereby demonstrate the usefulness of mathematics and challenge children to apply what they are learning.

Taking attendance in the morning offers practice in number concepts: "How many children would be here if everyone were in school today? How many are missing?" When you write the daily schedule, plan a calendar, or organize materials, you can include patterning. Talking about the time of day or how much time you have before something else happens incorporates measurement into everyday events. Children can estimate how long it will take to do something or go somewhere. When you read a book, there are possible connections in looking for patterns of behavior, noting the ages of the characters, thinking about the time of year, and predicting outcomes. Keep these activities from becoming rote by changing them frequently.

If you have a repertoire of *math moments* to draw upon, you will find it becomes easy to infuse mathematical thinking into many parts of the day. At transition times, for example, rather than simply asking children to form a line, or wait in line until everyone is quiet, use math as a way of accomplishing the task. Here are some examples.

- Have children count off to form work groups and have signs on the tables so children can quickly form their groups (e.g., if you have 21 children and you want groups of 3, have the children count to 7 and then start over until everyone has a number between 1 and 7).

- While the children are in line say, "I'm thinking of a number between 5 and 50. Raise your hand if you want to guess what number it is." As children guess, give them hints: "10 is too low." "44 is too high."

- Have children announce their place in line using ordinal numbers: first, second, third, etc.

- Ask the children to organize themselves into various shapes: a square or a triangle; or have them form two parallel lines or two perpendicular lines.

Understanding the components of the math curriculum and the routes (long-term studies, math work times, and teachable moments) that teachers can take to guide children's learning, makes it possible to organize an approach for each year. Mapping your math curriculum on an annual basis ensures that you will address all the components at some time during the year. Even though plans invariably change, advance planning reminds you to collect and organize the materials needed, and helps you think of ways to include math learning with other subjects.

Since most skills and concepts in mathematics relate in some way to one another, the sequence of skills and concepts can be flexible. For example, should measurement or number sense be taught first? In order to explore and discover the concept of measurement, children need to have number sense, yet to have number sense children need to understand the value of numbers which can be gained through measuring. Since math skills are interrelated, you don't have to be locked into a set timetable for teaching math. You can teach math skills and concepts in a way that fits best with the rest of the curriculum and the interests of the children.

In planning the math curriculum schedule, you may want to keep these things in mind.

- Plan your long-term studies in social studies and science first and consider what math activities can be incorporated into the study.

- Start with a unit that gives children many opportunities for success, individual expression, and creativity and that gives you a chance to assess individual needs.

- Weave number work and problem solving throughout each topic of study.

- Focus on one area (e.g., patterns, number sense, measurement, etc.) for about a month.

- Be flexible about changing the order of skills taught if you want to use them as part of a social studies or science theme.

- Think about the components of the math curriculum as a spiral in which you return again and again to the concepts of each.

No one has to reinvent the wheel, nor does a teacher need to feel, "I can't teach this way because I'm not creative," or "I've never understood machines." Texts, manuals, and catalogs can pave the way to expert mathematical teaching with manipulative materials. The manuals that accompany tools such as calculators discuss at length how to use them and how to teach children to use them. For the use and applications of the computer in the math curriculum, coordinate with a media specialist if one is available, or read about evaluating software in the chapters on Establishing a Structure for the Classroom and Technology. The wealth of resources now available can augment your program and inspire your thinking about each of the components of the math curriculum.

Closing Thoughts

If children are to use the tools of mathematical thinking to solve problems, then the classroom environment has to encourage children to explore and question. Engage children in the process of solving problems to learn the value of using strategies and pursuing problems over time. Skills are learned as part of the process, not as ends in themselves. When children solve real-world problems, they engage in mathematical reasoning and thinking and construct their own knowledge of mathematical relationships. They become mathematical thinkers.

References and Resources for Mathematical Thinking

Apelman, Maja, and Julie King. 1993. *Exploring Everyday Math*. Portsmouth, NH: Heinemann.

Arithmetic Teacher. Monthly math magazine. Reston, VA: National Council of Teachers of Mathematics.

Baker, Ann, and Johnny Baker. 1991. *Raps and Rhymes in Math*. Portsmouth, NH: Heinemann.

Braddon, Kathryn L., Nancy J. Hall, and Dale Taylor. 1993. *Math through Children's Literature: Making the NCTM Standards Come Alive*. Englewood, CO: Teacher Ideas Press.

Burns, Marilyn. 1992. *About Teaching Mathematics: A K–8 Resource*. White Plains, NY: Cuisenaire Company of America.

Burns, Marilyn. 1992. *Mathematics and Literature (K–3)*. White Plains, NY: Cuisenaire Company of America.

Burns, Marilyn, and Bonnie Tank. 1988. *A Collection of Math Lessons: From Grades 1 through 3*. New Rochelle, NY: Cuisenaire Company of America.

Charlesworth, Rosalind, and Karen K. Lind. 1999. *Math and Science for Young Children*. Albany, NY: Delmar Publishers.

Copley, Juanita. 2000. *The Young Child and Mathematics*. Washington, DC: NAEYC and Reston, VA: NCTM.

De La Cruz, Yolanda. Spring 1994. Considerations in Teaching Mathematics to Young Children. *ACEI Focus on Early Childhood* 3.

Fosnot, C.T., and Maarten Dolk. 2001. *Young Mathematicians at Work: Constructing Number Sense, Addition, and Subtraction*. Portsmouth, NH: Heinemann.

Kamii, Constance. 1989. *Young Children Continue to Reinvent Arithmetic: Implications of Piaget's Theory, 2nd Grade*. New York, NY: Teachers College Press.

Kamii, Constance. 1985. *Young Children Reinvent Arithmetic: Implications of Piaget's Theory*. New York, NY: Teachers College Press.

National Council of Teachers of Mathematics. 1989. *Curriculum and Evaluation Standards for School Mathematics*. Reston, VA: NCTM.

National Council of Teachers of Mathematics. October 1998. *Principles and Standards for School Mathematics*. Discussion Draft. Reston, VA: NCTM.

National Council of Teachers of Mathematics. 1991. *Professional Standards for Teaching Mathematics*. Reston, VA: NCTM.

Richardson, Kathy. 1999. *Developing Number Concepts: Counting, Comparing, and Pattern*. Book 1. White Plains, NY: Dale Seymour Publications.

Richardson, Kathy. 1999. *Developing Number Concepts: Addition and Subtraction.* Book 2. White Plains, NY: Dale Seymour Publications.

Richart, Ron. 1994. *Making Numbers Make Sense.* Menlo Park, CA: Addison-Wesley.

Smith, Susan Sperry. 1997. *Early Childhood Mathematics.* Needham Heights, MA: Allyn & Bacon.

TERC. 1998. *Investigations in Number, Data, and Space.* Cambridge, MA: TERC and Menlo Park, CA: Dale Seymour Publications.

Thiessen, Diane, Margaret Matthias, and Jacquelin Smith, eds. 1998. *The Wonderful World of Mathematics: A Critically Annotated List of Children's Books in Mathematics.* Richmond, VA: NCTM.

University of Chicago School Mathematics Project. 1998. *Everyday Mathematics.* Chicago, IL: Everyday Learning.

University of Illinois at Chicago. 1997. *Math Trailblazers.* A TIMS Curriculum. Dubuque, IA: Kendall/Hunt Publishing Company.

Welchman-Tischler, Rosamond. 1992. *How to Use Children's Literature to Teach Mathematics.* Richmond, VA: NCTM.

Whitin, David J., and Sandra Wilde. 1995. *It's the Story That Counts: More Children's Books for Mathematical Learning, K–6.* Portsmouth, NH: Heinemann.

Whitin, David J., and Sandra Wilde. 1992. *Read Any Good Math Lately? Children's Books for Mathematical Learning, K–6.* Portsmouth, NH: Heinemann.

Web Sites

The 100th Day of School Web Site

http://users.aol.com/a100thday/index.html

This web site was created by Joan Holub, illustrator of the book *The 100th Day of School* by Angela Medearis (Scholastic), to encourage and enhance 100th Day celebrations in schools.

Aunty Math

http://www.dcmrats.org/AuntyMath.html

This site provides an every-other-week math challenge for grades K–3. Students with questions or suggestions can e-mail Aunty Math directly, and a Tips for the Current Challenge page provides suggestions for modifying or extending each problem.

Children's Trade Books in Math

http://www.luc.edu/schools/education/csimath/zbib.htm

This is a selected bibliography of available books for kids that teach and reinforce math concepts. The site is organized by topic: number operations, money, large numbers, geometry, algebra books, miscellaneous.

Developing Educational Standards—Math

http://putwest.boces.org/StSu/Math.html

An annotated list of Internet sites with K–12 mathematics educational standards and curriculum frameworks documents maintained by the Putnam Valley Schools in New York.

Elementary Math Problem of the Week

http://forum.swarthmore.edu/elempow/

Elementary Math Problem of the Week from the Math Forum is designed to challenge elementary students with non-routine problems, and to encourage them to verbalize their solutions. In conjunction with its companion project, Visiting Math Mentors, solutions submitted from students are answered.

Family Math Home Page

http://theory.lcs.mit.edu/~emjordan/famMath.html

This site provides information on how to implement a family math program in your school.

Helping Your Child Learn Math

http://www.ed.gov/pubs/parents/Math/

An online book from the U.S. Department of Education for parents of Kindergarten–8th grade students (5–13 years old) that describes activities that parents can do with their children.

KIDLINK in the Math Curriculum

http://www.kidlink.org/english/general/curric3.html

KIDLINK activities can be used across curriculum areas. Teachers can sign up to be a part of math projects linking classrooms across the country and the world.

The Math Forum

http://www.forum.swarthmore.edu/

This site, hosted by Swarthmore College and funded in part by the National Science Foundation, includes interactive projects such as Ask Dr. Math, Elementary Problem of the Week, as well as an extensive Forum Internet Resource Collection.

NCTM Standards Online

http://www.nctm.org

This is the website of the National Council of Teachers of Mathematics and contains information about the NCTM Standards.

TERC

http://www.terc.edu

TERC is a nonprofit research and development organization that focuses on mathematics and science teaching and learning. It is funded by the National Science Foundation, the US Department of Education, and private foundations. Their web site includes a complete description of projects divided into four categories: Math, Science, Research, and Tools for Learning. TERC developed *Investigations in Number, Data, and Space,* a standards-based curriculum funded by the National Science Foundation.

SOCIAL STUDIES

9

Social studies is the study of people—how people live, work, get along with others, solve problems, and are shaped by their surroundings. Drawing upon the disciplines of history, geography, economics, political science, and sociology, children investigate topics to learn about the world around them and to appreciate the importance of culture and heritage. They build upon their growing knowledge about themselves, their families, and their communities to make sense of this new information.

Children learn about social studies before they come to school and as part of everyday life in the classroom.

> The knowledge and understanding that students already have about life come from the social and cultural communities in which they live and learn both inside and outside of school. These understandings form the platform upon which they currently stand and from which they will launch themselves into the future. The curriculum then must always be connected to as well as go forward from the students' life experiences (Short and Burke 1991, 34–35).

When the classroom functions as a community, children learn first-hand about responsible citizenship: how to make choices; how to accept different points of view and different ways of thinking; how to treat others with respect and develop tolerance. They gain basic knowledge about living in a democracy where all individuals have rights and responsibilities to their community, and where all people can express and feel proud of their cultural heritage. Children also acquire social studies knowledge in the context of a long-term study. Topics that interest children lead them to ask questions, actively investigate issues, and make connections between what they are learning and their daily lives. In the process of their investigations, children learn how to be researchers and they become experts on topics related to everyday life.

Children Exploring Social Studies

How do primary grade teachers make social studies come alive in the classroom so that children are motivated to learn? The following examples from three classrooms show how children explore topics in social studies.

*A **first grade class** is studying the topic of "Families." The teacher, Ms. Wong, encourages the children to bring family photographs from home, engages the children in discussions about their families, and reads stories and poetry about families. The class writes letters inviting family members to be interviewed about where they grew up and the kinds of work they do. Some interviews are done by sending e-mail messages to parents at their work sites. The children draw and paint family portraits, create family trees, and make maps and blueprints of rooms in their houses. Children make graphs about numbers of people living in their household, and chart on a world map where their family members were born, including themselves, their parents, and grandparents.*

To study their families, these first graders are engaged in first-hand research, collecting data by observing, interviewing, reading, and talking. They gather information about size and configurations of families, how family members earn a living, the roles of family members today and in the past, what is eaten for meals, and how holidays are celebrated. Their constant interaction and exchange of information and ideas expands their knowledge and broadens their understanding of family structures. Ms. Wong encourages the children to think about similarities and differences among their families. The children have many opportunities to represent what they are learning and to reflect on new understandings.

*Ms. Bannon's **second grade class** is investigating bridges as part of its study of the local community. At a meeting, she asks the children what they already know about the three bridges in their town and what they want to find out. Their first trip to see one of the bridges provides them with some answers to their questions and generates new ones. Following the trip, the children reflect on what they observed: boats on the river, factories along the shore, and the elaborate construction of the bridge. Some children decide to build a model of the bridge and others to paint pictures of scenes on and around the bridge. A few children go to the library to find books about how bridges are built while others find pictures of famous bridges on the Internet.*

During this study of their community, Ms. Bannon knows that the children will learn about rivers, bridges, transportation and travel, industry, history, economics, and geography. She has created a framework for the study and lets the specific direction come from children's interests. By first providing the children with opportunities to express what they know and what they are curious about, Ms. Bannon generates interest in the study and encourages the children to take responsibility for their learning. By approaching the study of community through a topic that is in the children's immediate environment, trips can be used as primary sources of information. The children review their questions and consider new ones prior to each trip. In this way, Ms. Bannon establishes a clear purpose for the children's research as well as a procedure for collecting new data. Follow-up activities, such as drawing, building, painting, writing, graphing, and discussions enable children to represent and reflect on what they are learning.

*As part of its study of local history, Mr. Lucas's **third grade class** collaborates with residents at a senior citizens' home. They make regular weekly visits to the home for eight weeks. During the first two visits, children interview their senior partners about their childhoods. The children decide to create written and illustrated biographies of their partners. During a class discussion following one visit, Kian remarks that since he has been going to the seniors' home, he has observed that only a few places in town have ramps for wheelchairs. His distress, expressed with the passion typical of eight year olds, is shared by his classmates. Responding to their concern and interest, Mr. Lucas temporarily shifts the curriculum plan. He asks the children to think about ways they can learn more about this problem. The children decide to conduct a survey of the town for wheelchair accessibility. Based on their findings they will decide what action to take.*

Mr. Lucas has designed a study in which children interact with the elder citizens of the community. Many children in the class either have no living grandparents or their grandparents live far away from the community. By establishing relationships with senior citizens, Mr. Lucas knows children can learn first-hand about the history of their community. He also wants children to gain understanding and empathy for the older people in the community. He uses Kian's concern as the catalyst to help the children become more aware of and involved in community issues.

In each of these classrooms, social studies learning is active, purposeful, and connected to real-life issues and experiences. Children study topics in depth and become experts. Rather than simply reading about families, communities, and local history in a textbook, their questions about the world around them serve as the basis for exploration and research. Trips, interviews with people, artifacts, e-mail, the Internet, videos, films, and books are used as sources of information that allow children to acquire conceptual understandings as they develop the skills involved in conducting research.

What Children Learn

The social studies curriculum is a blend of content and process. The content comes from the many disciplines that contribute to social studies. Because young children construct knowledge by expanding upon their own experiences, much of this content is centered in the child's own world, the family, the local, and then the wider community. The process involves learning how to be researchers, critical thinkers, and active members of a classroom community as they acquire specific skills.

Many organizations have recommended standards and curriculum guidelines that address social studies, history, civics, geography, and economics. Such documents include *An Overview of the National Standards: History, Basic Edition* (1996), *Charting a Course: Social Studies for the 21st Century* (1989), *Geography for Life, National Geography Standards* (1994), *National Standards for Civics and Government* (1994), *Expectations of Excellence, Curriculum Standards for Social Studies* (1989), and *Reaching Potentials: Transforming Early Childhood Curriculum and Assessment*, vol. 2 (1995). States and local school districts also have content standards. Some recommend that children learn specific facts; others articulate broad concepts that children should understand at various grade levels.

This is an overwhelming amount of material for teachers to integrate in a meaningful way. Remember that primary grade children learn best when their explorations of social studies begin with their immediate environment. For example, they can learn more about maps by making maps of their rooms at home or their classroom, their school, and then their neighborhood, than by memorizing maps of the world. Before studying American or world history, they can study their families, communities, towns, or cities to learn about how people function in groups and communities. Social studies instruction should build on children's natural curiosity to explore the world around them.

By engaging in long-term studies on topics of interest to them, children learn about themselves, others, and their community. They learn how people live and work and begin to explore culture and heritage. Actively researching topics allows children in the primary grades to develop critical thinking skills such as identifying problems, observing, questioning, gathering and analyzing information, debating ideas and opinions, and drawing conclusions. And by participating in a classroom community, children learn what it means to live in a democratic society where respect for others and freedom of speech are preserved and responsibility is shared.

Components of the Social Studies Curriculum

You may have very specific requirements for social studies content in your local school district. We have found that broad concepts underlie social studies content in the primary grades and can help you to organize any social studies content. The value of thinking in terms of broad concepts is that it will allow you to help children make connections. Once children begin to understand these concepts in relation to their own immediate and familiar experience, they can apply them to studies of the larger world. The broad concepts of social studies can be grouped under six components:

- human similarities and differences
- basic human needs
- human interdependence
- rights and responsibilities
- people and the places they live
- people and the past

The following chart outlines what children might learn in social studies by participating in a classroom community and studying topics that address these components. An understanding of each of these components and the ways in which children can investigate topics can be very helpful to teachers in organizing the social studies curriculum.

Overview of the Social Studies Curriculum

Components	Children Learn to:
Human Similarities and Differences	• Recognize common and unique human characteristics • Identify similarities and differences in family structures, lifestyles, ways of communicating, customs, and habits • Recognize instances of bias • Compare and appreciate similarities and differences in cultural heritage
Basic Human Needs	• Recognize basic needs for food, clothing, and shelter (safety, security, belonging) • Recognize that money and other forms of economic exchange may be used to obtain goods and services
Human Interdependence	• Describe roles in families and communities • Describe how people depend on one another for goods and services • Recognize the need to make decisions about how to use resources • Describe the kinds of work people do and the skills and tools needed to perform these jobs
Rights and Responsibilities	• Identify the need for rules at home and in school • Participate in group decision making for the common good • Recognize how laws protect rights and property • Recognize reasons for leadership and cooperation, and methods of group decision making such as elections • Talk about and use strategies for solving problems and resolving conflicts
People and the Places They Live	• Identify ways the environment shapes our lives (e.g., in terms of transportation, housing, jobs) • Recognize the effects of climate on the way people live • Identify ways people get from place to place and ways they transport goods and information • Identify ways people rely on environmental resources • Identify some ways people affect the environment • Recognize that maps are symbols for actual places • Make maps and use simple mapping symbols
People and the Past	• Demonstrate some understanding of chronological time (e.g., the sequence of their own lives and that of family members) • Explore the concept of change (e.g., by studying themselves, the school, neighborhood, nature) • Recognize the influence of one's heritage on present day living • Recognize that human life is continuous (e.g., by developing intergenerational relationships)

Human Similarities and Differences

Recognizing and respecting differences in gender, race, ethnicity, religion, ability, age, family composition, and lifestyle is an important component of the social studies curriculum. Children can begin to understand and explore human diversity through opportunities to see events and ideas from the perspective of others.

They learn about human similarities and differences by sharing information about themselves and listening to what others have to say. When teachers are willing to relate stories from their own lives, children feel more comfortable about telling their own stories. These sharing times often lead to interesting discussions about social issues. As children read and listen to stories about other people, study photographs, watch videos, take field trips, and work on projects, teachers can encourage them to recognize and appreciate similarities and differences. Some of these differences include how people express emotions, the size and composition of families, the types of houses people live in, what they eat, and the kinds of work they do.

Learning about similarities and differences helps children recognize and appreciate diversity in thinking, feeling, and acting, and promotes understanding of the many different influences that shape people's lives. When children see that the way they and their families conduct their lives is valued, they gain confidence and self-esteem.

Basic Human Needs

Children investigate how people go about their daily lives by first examining their own actions and then gradually researching how their families and other community members live. They begin to see that basic physical and social needs—safety, security, food, clothing, and shelter—are consistent among all people, regardless of when and where they live. Children can consider the difference between people's *needs* and *wants*. These questions might stimulate thinking about basic needs.

- What do each of us need to live?

- How do we get what we need?

- What happens if we can't get what we need?

- What are some things we have but don't actually need?

As they get older, children compare their actions and behaviors in daily living to those of people who lived long ago and those who live in other places. While basic needs are universal, the ways in which different people meet them vary. This understanding occurs gradually as children study many different topics over the course of several years.

Human Interdependence

Children in the primary grades are interested in how people work together to get what they need. The concept of human interdependence includes understanding how people depend on others to accomplish tasks, how they divide labor and share responsibility, and how they exchange goods and services.

As children explore how goods are produced and services performed, they learn about the world of work and acquire an appreciation for the different jobs people perform. Children can investigate these types of questions.

- Who provides our families with the goods and services we need?
- How do people work together to produce goods and services?
- Who produces them?
- How do we pay for these goods?
- What are the services needed by our community?

Whether the study involves a food store, a construction site, immigration, or communities long ago, children can examine how people get what they need and how they accomplish goals through interdependent relationships.

Rights and Responsibilities

For children in the primary grades, fairness, individual rights, and adhering to rules are issues of great significance. As their sense of justice and fairness grows, they are ready to consider the reasons for establishing rules.

In a classroom community children develop first-hand knowledge about rights and responsibilities in society. They learn how respect, cooperation, and responsibility are essential to community life. When they help to establish classroom rules that ensure the safety and protection of each member of the class, they learn why communities need rules and laws. Classroom jobs give children a chance to do tasks that maintain the community and to learn that all jobs are important. Opportunities to engage in group decision making and social problem solving help children become responsible citizens. They can also talk about how they work together in the classroom and what responsibilities each person has to contribute to the common good. Discussions such as these can lead to greater understanding about the use of limited resources, issues of fairness, and how decisions are made in a democracy. Children can then begin to understand how the larger community works together to make decisions, establish rules, and elect leaders.

People and the Places They Live

How people's lives are shaped by their physical environment is an important social studies concept. Children in the primary grades can begin to explore the relationship between people and where they live.

- How do the physical features of our location affect our lives?
- How does climate affect how people live?
- In what ways do the natural resources that are available in a particular locale influence the types of houses people build or the foods they eat?

Children in first grade can explore the answers to questions such as these in the context of their own environment. By age eight, children can begin to compare their own ways of living to how people lived in the past and to how they live in other places.

As issues related to the use of the world's resources are of increasing concern, the topics explored in social studies can help children develop an appreciation for natural resources and their importance to human life. In the primary grades, children begin to learn about how people use (and abuse) the environment. For example, they might investigate how houses are built, how water is used, or how factories dispose of waste. Opportunities to raise their own questions and to express their concerns will encourage children to see how preserving the environment is important to their lives.

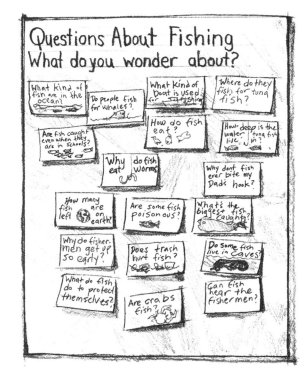

Another aspect of understanding people and the environment is learning how locations are recorded symbolically on maps. For young children, this means making real maps. Constructing models and block buildings of real places is one way children make maps. Drawing maps of real places—the classroom, the school, a room in their house—increases children's understanding of how to represent location using symbols. In addition, children can explore different types of maps and globes.

People and the Past

An important reason to learn about the past is that it connects us to our heritage. Who we are is in part a reflection of the history of our families. Where our parents, grandparents, and great-grandparents lived and what they experienced influences our values, ways of interacting, and how we interpret events.

Young children do not learn best about the past through stories of who came on the Mayflower. Such an approach begins too far in the past and will most likely not represent the families of children in your class. Instead, understanding the past begins with an examination of children's personal life histories. Writing personal narratives about memories of being younger, making family scrapbooks, and constructing personal time lines fosters a beginning understanding of history. Interviewing family members about their childhoods leads children to realize that they are a part of a history and helps them develop an appreciation for their heritage.

As children begin to develop a sense of the passage of time, they can also explore the concept of change. They have changed since they were infants, preschoolers, and since last year. They can explore how the school building, facilities, and equipment have changed since the school was constructed or what changes have taken place in their classroom. Stores in the neighborhood may have closed and new ones opened; there may be a new subway or bus line, or a new parking area nearby. The landscape outside the school may change with the seasons.

Children gain an increasing appreciation for change and the passage of time by hearing and reading stories of growing up at another time period. They can relate their own experiences to those of other children and begin to appreciate how life would have been different if they had lived during another time period. How did people communicate without telephones or write without computers? What did they do for entertainment and news before television and radio existed? How did families get food without supermarkets and cook without gas or electric stoves? When children make up skits, put on costumes, and recreate scenes from long ago, they begin to acquire an appreciation and understanding of history.

Skills for Social Studies Inquiry

The skills children acquire as they investigate social studies topics teach them how to be researchers: to raise questions, seek information, and think critically about what they discover in their investigations. Researchers go through a process using the following skills.

- Ask a question or identify a problem.
- Gather information.
- Analyze information.
- Draw conclusions.

Ask a Question or Identify a Problem

Researchers begin any study by identifying what they already know about a topic and what questions they want to answer. Articulating knowledge and asking questions helps them to focus their thinking. Sometimes an investigation begins because a problem has been identified: "There isn't any supermarket in this neighborhood," "There's too much garbage in the street," or "There are too many car accidents on this corner." This prompts children to ask why.

Gather Information

Having identified the problem and their questions, researchers determine the best approaches to obtaining answers: making on-site observations (trips), interviewing experts, reading books, watching videos, studying artifacts and maps, and so on.

The process of conducting first-hand research involves the same detective skills used by anthropologists and archaeologists. Children learn how to look closely at an object or an event under study and pick up clues to help them answer their questions. Teachers guide children in using research skills to find answers to the questions that interest them.

Ms. Frisher's third grade class is studying the history of New York City. To find out what New Amsterdam was like, they examine old photographs and maps. They discover that the area where their school is located was originally farm land and that New Amsterdam was located in lower Manhattan. On a walking tour of this area, the children note that the names of many streets are Dutch. In a class discussion on their findings, they debate whether the names of streets represent Dutch surnames or whether they are Dutch words that have specific meanings (such as the type of stores that existed at the time). "How could we find out?" asks Ms. Frisher. "We could look up the words in a Dutch/English dictionary," suggests LaShon. She and Carly go to the school library and return empty handed. "This school doesn't have a Dutch dictionary," they report. "We could call some book stores to find one," suggests Carly. Several children comb the yellow pages, discovering a listing for foreign book stores. They phone numerous stores before finding what they need. "How about the Internet?" suggests Curtis. Ms. Frisher helps Curtis and Kelly use a search engine on the computer to seek the information they need.

Analyze Information

A central part of conducting research is classifying and comparing findings, which children do when they discuss topics under study. In daily meetings, teachers guide children to talk about aspects of a study and help children to think critically about the information. Discussions also help children clarify their thinking. Because social studies involves learning about people, many questions have no single answer. As children debate ideas and hear different opinions, they learn that reality is a blend of multiple perspectives—each person's view of reality has merit.

Draw Conclusions

After getting information from many sources, sharing their own views, and hearing other points of view, children are ready to make sense of what they have learned. They can construct a logical understanding of a topic. This sometimes leads them to want to take action—to write to the corporate head of a food chain, to voice concerns to the Sanitation Department, or to mount a campaign for a stoplight.

Children who have had opportunities to conduct first-hand research on social studies topics begin to internalize both research and critical-thinking skills. When the teacher introduces a new topic, these children are ready to talk about what they know and what questions they have. They begin to think in categories: workers, equipment, animal life, stores, vehicles. They have lots of ideas about ways to investigate the topic and how to show what they are learning. Children who develop these process skills in the early grades are learning how to learn, a skill they will use throughout their lives.

How One Topic Can Address All Components and Skills

Each of the six components (broad concepts) of the social studies curriculum can be addressed in the context of a good social studies topic. Rather than focusing on a particular component, it is much more practical to focus on topics for studies that will allow children to experience these central concepts over and over during many different investigation experiences (just as they do in science). Similarly, a rich topic enables children to use all the process skills as well.

To illustrate how a topic might address several components of the social studies curriculum, let's consider a long-term study on "How People Communicate." During this several-month-long study, children could explore communication in relation to themselves, their families, and their local community. They might take trips to the telephone company, a local newspaper, a local radio station, and the post office. They might invite a sign language teacher, a computer technician, a web site manager, or a television producer to visit the class. Some children might write and broadcast a weekly radio show over the school's intercom system; others could publish a weekly newspaper. Depending on the age and interests of the children, the teacher could address all components of the social studies curriculum as outlined next.

To explore **human similarities and differences** children could:

- collect interview data about how different members of their families communicate with friends and relatives (e.g., visiting in person, talking on the phone, sending letters, e-mail, and faxes);

- explore different languages spoken in their homes and by people they know;

- learn some sign language;

- compare ways people of different ages communicate; or

- compare today's methods of communication to those used in the past and in other places.

To consider issues related to **basic human needs** children could:

- discuss how people communicate their needs and feelings;

- identify ways to call for emergency help; or

- investigate different ways people use communication to get food, clothing, and housing.

To relate the topic of communication to **human interdependence** children could:

- study various local workplaces providing communication services (e.g., telephone company, local radio station, neighborhood newspaper);

- consider how people have to work together to perform their jobs within various communications industries; or

- conduct interviews with people who work at a public radio station to find out how they get money to operate (e.g., fund raising, contributions, subscriptions).

To think about **rights and responsibilities** related to communication children could:

- have a discussion about rules people might need for public and private communication;
- review classroom rules for discussions;
- discuss rules for using the Internet and e-mail safely and responsibly; or
- discuss the concept of freedom of speech.

To explore how communication is linked to **people and places** children could:

- compare newspapers from different cities and towns;
- consider why some people have satellite dishes;
- investigate how people in different places communicate in emergencies;
- correspond with children in another area of the country or world using e-mail; or
- interview people who use pagers and cell phones to find out why and when they use them.

To examine how communication relates to **people and the past** children could:

- interview their parents and other older family members to find out what methods of communication they used as children; compare these methods with those used today;
- research inventions related to communication; or
- read biographies of inventors of various methods of communication.

In order to investigate these topics children begin by asking many questions and gathering information from multiple sources. As they collect materials, make observations, develop charts and displays, work on reports, and have discussions, they analyze their information. And as they prepare projects and final reports they draw conclusions. In the process they gain a deeper understanding and appreciation for their world. They come to appreciate the complexities of everyday life. They ask *why* and *how* questions about their immediate, familiar environment. When children are given opportunities to think critically about their world in the primary grades, they are likely to apply these skills and understandings to future learning and living.

Organizing the Social Studies Curriculum

To address the content of social studies and support the development of critical thinking and research skills, teachers organize curriculum in two ways. First, they make social studies a part of everyday life. Second, they select topics for long-term studies that will engage children and hold their interest.

Making Social Studies Part of Everyday Life in the Classroom

In the United States, a long-term goal of education is to teach children how to be members of a democratic society in which individuals have rights, obligations, and responsibilities. Acquiring the values that underlie a democratic society—respecting oneself and others, and accepting responsibility for the community and the environment—is the foundation for learning about group membership.

Everyday life in the classroom can be a powerful textbook for the social studies curriculum. In this setting children can acquire skills in human relationships and learn about respect and diversity. The approaches teachers take to help children know one another and to build a classroom community are part of social studies.

Knowing the Children

Learning about children in the class and helping children learn about one another is the basis for building a primary classroom and the beginning of social studies. Children learn about the individual qualities of their peers by:

- conducting interviews and surveys about one another;
- sharing personal experiences;
- exchanging greetings in many different languages;
- preparing snacks that reflect their home cultures; and
- creating displays in the classroom that reflect their own interests and family life.

Building a Classroom Community

Children learn about responsible group behavior by participating in a classroom community. Group discussions about classroom concerns foster acceptance and respect for others as children recognize that different people have different opinions and different ways of thinking and expressing themselves.

Ms. Hall, a first grade teacher, is concerned about Angela, who has been the target of some ridicule and rejection. After trying to deal with the problem on an individual, as-needed basis without success, Ms. Hall decides to discuss the problem at a class meeting. She talks with Angela's parents about the plan and they agree. She then talks with Angela and asks if she wants to be present at the meeting. Angela decides she would rather not participate.

Ms. Hall starts the meeting by saying, "I feel the need for all of us to work together to solve a class problem. I've noticed that Angela is treated differently from other members of our class. I wonder if other people have noticed this." Every hand in the class shoots up and the children are all eager to share their ideas. Because interest in the topic is so strong, Ms. Hall allows every child to speak. "It seems as if all of you have noticed the same problem I have," says Ms. Hall. "Let's see if we can think of some things we can do to help Angela and all of us to feel more comfortable in our class. I'll write down your ideas so we can discuss them." After the list is made, Ms. Hall says, "This is a good list of ways we can help everyone feel comfortable in our class. I'm going to post this list so we can all remember." In the weeks following the meeting, Ms. Hall notices an improvement in how children relate to one another and Angela seems happier.

A sensitive teacher can guide children to think about problems in daily life and consider solutions. In this way, children begin to see how individuals can make a difference and contribute to making the world a better place. It is not enough to operate a classroom in a democratic manner with decision making based on elections. Researchers have found that democratic meetings without a "spirit of cooperative community" become a place where children focus on their "narrow self-interest" (Lickona and Paradise 1980). When shared values and goals are articulated, then "participation in decision making improves moral reasoning and prosocial behavior" (Berman 1997). As teachers work to build a classroom community, they foster children's social studies learning by:

- encouraging participation in group decision making;
- involving children in establishing and evaluating rules;
- giving children opportunities to express opinions in a public setting;
- using meetings as a forum for children to listen to the ideas and opinions of others;
- having meetings and using role plays to discuss conflict resolution;
- comparing class rituals to those in various cultures;
- discussing differences in ways that people communicate;
- encouraging children to respect differences in general;
- teaching children how to work collaboratively with classmates and/or work with partners in a younger class;
- conducting polls and elections; and
- helping children to respect public spaces by doing daily jobs to keep the classroom neat.

As valuable as a classroom community is for teaching social studies lessons, children also need opportunities to conduct first-hand research on topics that interest them. Long-term studies provide the vehicle for social studies explorations.

Selecting Topics for Long-Term Studies in Social Studies

In the process of participating in a long-term study, children become experts on topics that engage their interest. If the topic is appropriate, children understand the purpose of what they are learning. They are able to raise relevant questions and to go about finding answers. In the process of their investigations, children use and refine the skills they are learning in other subjects. They become researchers who know how to seek out information, think critically about what they observe, and share information with others.

The first step in planning a study is to select an appropriate topic. The six components of the social studies curriculum provide a wealth of ideas. It's not possible to plan an in-depth study on more than two or three topics in social studies in any given year, so how do you choose?

Teachers select appropriate topics by considering children's developmental abilities, their interests and experiences, as well as the resources in the community. A teacher's interest in the topic is also essential. Your enthusiasm (or lack of it) will have a profound effect on the children and on your own level of satisfaction.

Developmental Considerations

Too often developmental considerations have been misunderstood. For example, in the past, in an effort to build on children's personal experiences, the curriculum focused on self, family, and community in an oversimplified way. Self, family, and community became the curriculum content itself rather than the framework used to understand content. Seefeldt (1997) describes the typical social studies curriculum: K—the home and neighborhood; 1st grade—the community and community helpers; 2nd grade—the United States; and 3rd grade—people in other lands. What was lost was that a study of self, family and community is not a continuum of content. Children should not simply study "self," then "family," and so on. Rather, children this age continually think about how what they are learning applies to themselves, to their families, and to the larger community. They make connections based on how they see themselves and their families operate in the world. This is how they learn about needs, relationships, similarities and differences, the continuity of life, and interdependence. Well-understood developmental considerations should be a primary factor in selecting appropriate topics for studies.

Children's thinking and learning changes over time. First graders, for example, tend to be egocentric in their thinking; they rely on their own personal experiences as their frame of reference. What they can see, touch, and hear captures their attention. For them the idea of community is best understood in terms of the family unit, and then the school. Studying families for first graders means focusing on their own families:

- researching what their families eat and trying some different kinds of food for snack;
- listing the stores where their families shop, visiting them, and then building models of those shops with blocks or boxes; and
- recording and defining the jobs their family members do and visiting them at their workplaces or inviting them to the classroom to find out more.

Following these personal investigations, first graders can begin to compare their own personal experiences with what others do.

Second and third graders, gradually able to think about what is not in their immediate experience, continue to relate their learning to what is familiar. For example, if they are beginning to understand about different jobs, why people work, and the interdependence of goods and services in their own communities, they will be motivated to investigate the types of jobs that exist in a different environment or in the past. Children living in rural settings can study the city and vice versa. By third grade, a study of families might involve learning about immigration and genealogy, expanding children's thinking beyond their own experience in terms of time and place.

How children learn about human interdependence provides another example of developmental differences. First graders can study how people work together to accomplish goals in their families, in school, or in a particular industry. By second grade, children's thinking abilities have expanded so that they can investigate multiple services provided within the city, comparing how each is accomplished. By third grade, children might compare services available in the community today with what was available in the past. As children get older, the need to use the self as a point of reference becomes less pronounced. These evolving abilities are outlined in the chart below.

How Thinking About Self, Family, and Community in the Primary Grades Influences Instruction

Developmental Considerations	First Grade	Second Grade	Third Grade
Degree of Egocentricity	Must have direct relation to the self	Can be vicarious, yet familiar	Can move beyond personal experience both in time and place
Area of Study	Self, family, school, neighborhood, immediate city or town	Immediate community, state, and country	Other cultures and/or other eras
Degree of Complexity	Basic concepts are applied to familiar groups	Multiple concepts can be applied to familiar groups	Multiple concepts can be applied to unfamiliar groups

Other developmental considerations are also important. For example, some curriculum materials (Hirsch 1991) call for teaching first graders to color and learn from maps of the world and to learn to use cardinal directions: north, east, south, west. However, a map is an abstract symbol and a map of the world is a picture that represents artificial land distinctions called continents. Because six year olds need concrete experiences before abstract concepts become meaningful to them, you can conclude that learning about continents does not fit our construct of a topic that allows for meaningful and relevant social studies learning.

Similarly, since many six year olds, and some sevens and eights, are still not totally comfortable with directionality—for example, they can't always identify their left or right arm consistently—learning about north, east, south, and west are abstractions that may not make much sense to them. Using the rising and setting sun to teach directions presents additional problems. It requires us to give false information (the sun doesn't really go down). In an effort to simplify, teachers may find themselves saying, "north is up or at the top of the page, south is down," etc. This may allow children to answer specific questions for a test but it does not contribute to real understanding of maps or directions.

There are ways, however, to give children experiences with maps and directions that are meaningful and appropriate. Children can use blocks to show how the classroom is organized and then transfer that information to graph paper. They can map the route from the classroom to the recess area and show how traffic flows. When lining up there are opportunities to discuss who is in front of (or behind) whom and to talk about how many right and left turns it takes to get to the lunchroom. Cardinal directions can be introduced as another language to use in reading maps, using a compass, and talking about directions.

Children's Interests and Experiences

Topics that inherently interest children will be more likely to engage their attention over time. Most six year olds tend to be interested in work—who does it and how. They readily focus on the particular—the workers in the apple orchard or the sanitation workers. Seven year olds' curiosity is often captured by systems—how things fit together. For example, what are the various services provided within the community, or what are all the different methods of transportation used in the city? Eight years olds begin to wonder about the past—how things that are familiar to them looked long ago.

Children's interests also grow out of their life experiences. If children live in a rural community, a study of subway systems is not relevant to their experience. However, after first learning about transportation methods where they live, they can consider what possibilities exist elsewhere and why. Children are usually interested in significant current events. For example, following a local flood or earthquake, children are likely to be curious about related topics.

A study that begins with a familiar, tangible project will be more likely to grab children's interest. For example, in a study of trash, you may begin by asking children to keep track of what goes into a particular wastebasket each day at home. After making comparisons between the contents of different household trash containers, children can then think about who picks up the

Questions about Golden Gate Park

1. How big is it?
2. Is it the biggest park in San Francisco?
3. Who owns the park?
4. What did it look like a long time ago?
5. How do you grow grass? How long does it take to grow grass?
6. Is there a place to eat in the park?
7. How many rats are in the park?
8. How many playgrounds are there?
9. Who built Golden Gate Park?

Thinking About Golden Gate Park

trash, where it goes, and how it gets there. They may compare which rooms produce the most trash, what different households consider trash, or the difference among household, school, and industrial trash. Eventually, children may consider how different places dispose of their trash or what people did with their waste before municipal sanitation departments existed.

Relying on the Immediate Environment

Selecting social studies topics that take advantage of the resources available in your school's environment is practical and meets the criteria outlined in the preceding chart. A study of a park is meaningful if there is one close by for children to visit. A study of dairy farms is an excellent way for children to learn about food production and distribution—if children can visit one. A study of a construction site enables children to learn how buildings are built, who builds them, and what materials are used—if the children can take repeated trips to check the progress of an actual building project.

The concepts children learn in social studies can be explored through a wide range of topics. Think about places in or near your school where children can see workers on the job, goods being manufactured or distributed, or various forms of transportation. Your immediate environment can be your textbook for social studies.

Questions to Consider and Sample Topics

A good social studies topic is one that allows you to plan a wide range of experiences so that children can learn by investigating, representing their knowledge, and reflecting on what they have learned.

To identify opportunities for **investigation,** ask yourself these questions.

- What do children already know about the subject?
- Can the children conduct first-hand observations?
- What artifacts are available for children to observe (photographs, blueprints, site documents)? Are there collections to be gathered?
- Can the children conduct interviews?
- Can the children take trips to conduct first-hand investigations?
- Are there experts on the topic who can visit the classroom?
- Are there read-aloud books available on the topic?
- Are there books available that children can read independently?
- Do I have access to videos or filmstrips related to the study?
- Are there songs that relate to the subject?
- What open-ended questions that encourage investigations will I be able to ask as part of this study?

To identify opportunities for children to **represent** their learning, ask these questions.

- What art projects lend themselves to this study (drawings, paintings, collages)?
- Can the children build models as part of this study?
- Will children be writing interviews? What else can they write?
- Are there opportunities to make charts, graphs, or maps?
- Can children do skits or plays related to the subject?

To identify opportunities for children to **reflect** on what they are learning, ask these questions.

- Can children keep a learning log or journal as a way to record what they are learning?
- How can children return to their questions and assess whether or not they have found answers?
- When will time be allocated for children to reflect on their projects related to the study?

The following is a list of sample social studies topics for children in the primary grades.

Our School

Houses in the Neighborhood

Stores and Services in the Neighborhood

Buildings in the Community

Public Buildings in the Community

Roads and Bridges: Who and What Travels on Them

What's Underground in Our Community

Factories Along the River

Bridges and Tunnels

Transportation

Food: From Origin to Table

Waterworks

Garbage and Sewage

Recycling

How People Communicate

Family Histories

Recreation Places

Organizations in the Community

Use this list as a starting point and add topics that you, as well as the children, will enjoy.

Making the Best of Inappropriate Curriculum Guidelines

What does a teacher do when the curriculum guidelines, based on local district standards, require teaching subject matter that is less than appropriate for the children you teach? For example, in some areas K–4 standards require that by the end of 4th grade children should be able to locate the seven continents. While this might be a reasonable expectation for the end of fourth grade, in order that children absorb this information, the curriculum has been organized so that children study Africa and Antarctica in Kindergarten, North and South America in first grade, Australia in second grade, Asia in third grade, and Europe in fourth grade. The problem is not the expectation, but the process used to get there.

The benchmark may require children to read and understand maps. This skill can begin to be developed in Kindergarten by extensive play with blocks and block building. In first grade, children could make maps of the classroom and then use milk cartons and other materials to construct dioramas of the neighborhood. By third grade, children work on map skills as they study a map of the subway system and take a trip on the subway.

If, however, you are required to teach content that you know is inappropriate, there are ways to think about adapting the content so that children can focus on some important concepts and be researchers. First grade teachers, for example, required to have children study Japan or China, can focus on daily life. They begin the year by having the children examine their own daily lives—the different types of homes they live in, the routines of their school days, the similarities and differences in the foods they eat, etc. They study geography as well. If they live in a city, they study city life, including jobs, public transportation, and recreational facilities. Then, using literature and videos, children can compare city life in a foreign country to city life as they know it. By carefully exploring daily life and drawing comparisons with children's own experience, it is less likely to perpetuate the simplistic stereotyping that can occur with more superficial studies.

Allocating Time for Social Studies

To ensure that social studies is included in the curriculum, teachers must allow time in the daily schedule. Meetings are the forum for many lively discussions on social studies topics. Time is also needed for trips, project activities, and work times.

Meetings

Discussions about issues related to community life or a social studies topic take place daily. Meetings are used to introduce a study, to plan investigation and representation activities, to bring back information following activities, and to exchange new ideas.

The initial questions that children pose in the introductory meeting for a study form the basis for their ongoing investigations. Throughout the study, teachers use meetings to review the list of questions children have generated and to discuss what they have found out and what they still want to know.

Trips

Try to plan at least one or two trips related to each topic of study. If the topic relates to what is in the immediate environment, taking trips is a manageable endeavor. For example, in a study of the school building, a trip may simply be a walk to another floor of the building. If children are studying a river or the local park within walking distance of the school, several trips can be planned to conduct investigations.

When you plan a trip, it is a good idea to visit the place by yourself first. In this way, you can plan how to focus children's investigations and, at the same time, determine logistics for the trip. Then spend some time preparing children for what they will see. In a meeting, you might ask children what they think they might see. Have children reflect on the questions they have listed and consider which ones might be answered on the trip. Following the trip, children can discuss what they saw and plan how they will represent what they learned. Rather than waiting until the end of the study to take the trip, plan the outing early on so that children will have first-hand experiences that they can draw upon.

Using clipboards or trip boards helps children organize what they see on a trip. Trip boards are pieces of cardboard on which paper is stapled so that children can record what they find out on their trips. When children have a convenient way to record impressions and information, they can refer to their notes when they return to the classroom.

Project Time

If possible, try to schedule several large blocks of time (an hour and a half) each week for children to immerse themselves in projects related to a social studies topic. During this time, children can work in small groups on projects such as building a model, writing a report, painting a mural, making graphs, constructing maps, or preparing a play.

Large blocks of time are needed for projects because children often have to get set up, talk and negotiate with one another, complete tasks, and clean up. It is sometimes helpful to allow fifteen or twenty minutes on the day before a scheduled project time so that children can do some of their planning.

Work Times

In addition to meetings and project times, schedule work times for social studies or integrate social studies content into work times for other subjects in these ways.

- Use writing workshop times for research writing about a social studies topic.
- Read aloud from a chapter book related to the topic.
- Conduct surveys, collect information, and make graphs related to information about the topic during a math work time.
- Read from informational books with a partner.
- Use a math time to design scale models and maps.
- Use choice time for children to pursue independent interests related to the social studies topic.

Appropriate topics and time to explore concepts in depth enable children to see relationships between their own life experiences and the events, people, and places they are studying. Social studies explorations provide opportunities for teachers to help children learn to value what takes place in their own communities every day and to understand the complexity of the work people do. Without these opportunities to learn social studies content, children could easily take for granted many of the systems and people that make communities work.

A Long-Term Study in Action: Our School

In Chapter 4, Guiding Children's Learning (pages 175-181), we outlined the steps for planning long-term studies. Here we show how a teacher uses these steps to think through and plan a long-term study on "Our School."

Selecting a Topic

Ms. Lourdes teaches a first and second grade multi-age class. Using the guidelines for topic selection, she decides that a study of the school is appropriate for her class for the following reasons.

- The topic is relevant to children's lives. Because the school is familiar to her students, Ms. Lourdes is certain that they will be able to offer ideas when she asks them what they already know about the school. Their interests and questions will shape the direction of the investigation experiences she devises.
- Resources and materials are readily available. Ms. Lourdes can use trips as a primary method for children to gather information. Everyone in the building is an expert; there are many opportunities for interviews.

- The topic permits children to think, question, and solve interesting problems through active investigation. Children's work will include designing research questions and seeking answers by taking trips around the building for first-hand observations, conducting interviews and surveys to collect data, and having discussions to share information with one another.

- What children learn from this study can be applied to future living and learning because it is practical and fundamental to any study of community workers. Main ideas include:

   —many different people are needed to run an institution;

   —workers need a range of skills and responsibilities to do their jobs; and

   —workers use a variety of tools and machines to accomplish their jobs.

- The children will also learn basic research skills, which can then be used in their subsequent investigations of community workers. These skills include:

   —thinking about what is already known about a subject;

   —deciding what questions will be explored;

   —planning and conducting interviews;

   —taking notes during trips or when visitors come to the class; and

   —reviewing site documents (e.g., in their school study these might include employee handbooks, time sheets, and job descriptions).

- The topic addresses curriculum objectives. The school district's curriculum guide calls for a study of community workers. The school study will be the first of several places where children can investigate the work of people in their community.

- The topic can be explored in different ways over an extended period of time.

Confident that her topic is a good one, Ms. Lourdes moves on to plan the next steps.

Getting Ready for the Study

Having selected a topic, Ms. Lourdes makes a brainstorming web. Her categories include: places, people, equipment, and activities. She has been teaching at the school for several years so she is already quite familiar with her subject. However, she takes a preliminary walk around the building, looking at it from a child's perspective.

She makes a chart of ideas about how the study can address objectives in math, science, language and literacy, technology, and the arts. She considers having the children study how water gets into the building as part of a science study. This decision will wait until the study is well underway and she has assessed the children's interests.

Ms. Lourdes considers some open-ended questions and discussion starters that she can direct to the whole group.

- What are some of the different kinds of work done in this building?
- Let's think about the different kinds of machines in use in our school.
- Let's brainstorm a list of all the things we could count in this building.

Materials that she collects include books, poetry, and a poster of a one-room schoolhouse. She speaks with school personnel (cafeteria and custodial workers, secretary, principal, resource teachers, librarian, audiovisual specialist) to find out if they are willing to be interviewed by the children. She also sets up a visit to another school so that the children can make comparisons. In addition, she arranges for the children to communicate by e-mail with children in a school in another part of the country. Both classes will study their schools and the children will exchange information and e-mail messages about what they are learning.

Introducing the Study to the Children

Ms. Lourdes knows that an essential part of introducing a study is generating the children's interest. She does this by putting a few books around the room and hanging the poster of a one-room schoolhouse. On another wall is a blueprint she has found of their school building. She begins the first meeting by asking children to brainstorm a list of all the people who work in the school. Then she asks them to look around the room for clues about what they will be studying. She follows with the set of questions that begin all studies.

- What do you already know?
- What do you want to know?
- How can we find these things out?

She takes the class on the first trip for an overview of the building and uses the opportunity to teach them how she expects them to use trips to gather information. This includes both research techniques such as thinking in advance about what will be seen, or how to keep track of what is observed, and considering ways to document what is learned. Following the trip, she asks the children if they have new questions as a result of looking at the school through an investigator's eyes.

Inviting Families to Participate in the Study

Two of the parents in Ms. Lourdes' class attended schools in other countries where their experiences were very different from those of the children. One other parent is a junior high school principal, and another a teacher in an older grade. Ms. Lourdes decides to have the children interview members of their families about their school experiences. She will then suggest inviting family members to come and share their experiences and perspectives with the children.

Listening to and Learning with Children

Ms. Lourdes arranges for the children to take trips around the school building with a partner and in small groups with a parent volunteer so that they can conduct interviews and surveys. Their destinations are based on the questions generated by the children. For example, the children want to know the total number of classrooms, children, workers, pets, and public spaces. They take trips to observe the different types of bulletin boards, doors, and windows in the building. They visit the custodian, the librarian, and the cafeteria workers to find out about the jobs these people do, the skills they have, and the machines and tools they use. They interview the secretaries, teachers, principal, and children in different grades.

Children record and represent what they learn throughout the study. They recreate the school using blocks and make maps of different locations in the school, including the classroom, the hallway, and eventually, each floor of the school. They draw and paint scenes from the school. Based on the interviews, children document their findings in various forms. Counting and surveying experiences are used to make graphs and charts as records of the information collected. In the process of doing these activities, Ms. Lourdes talks with them about what they have learned and how they want to express it.

Ms. Lourdes begins every new investigation activity with a meeting in which the children collectively brainstorm what they want to know, what they wonder about, and what they anticipate finding out from their investigation. Afterwards, the children gather again to reflect on what they have found, comparing their predictions with their discoveries. As children work on projects, Ms. Lourdes invites them to share their work with one another. By doing this, children give one another valuable feedback, often making useful suggestions. In addition, Ms. Lourdes lets the children critique one another's work, rather than encouraging them to rely entirely on her evaluation. In this way, she finds out about the children's shifting interests. She can continually assess what they are learning.

Concluding the Study

Children are proud of becoming experts on a subject. Telling others about what they have learned serves many purposes, including clarifying thinking and recognizing accomplishments.

Based on prior experience, Ms. Lourdes anticipates that the children will be enthusiastic about all the information they collect about the school and will want to share it with other classes. She will ask the children how they want to share their knowledge. In previous years the children have shared by:

- making a presentation for another class in the form of a TV talk show;
- writing an article for the school newspaper; and
- having an open house for parents.

Ms. Lourdes has outlined a logical plan for her study of the school based on the developmental stage of the children, their interests, and local resources. She may adjust her plans depending on the interests of the children or local events.

Closing Thoughts

When social studies is presented well, it enables children to acquire the tools to become successful learners. As children pose questions, conduct research, engage in discussions, and present their findings, they learn to think critically and make connections between what they are learning and their own lives. In-depth studies of topics close at hand give vitality to the familiar, and encourage children to go beyond the superficial in their research efforts. They become experts on everyday happenings and build an increasing understanding of people, places, and events. Participating in a classroom community teaches children respect for others and the environment, as well as group living and decision making. It gives children a sense of pride in their own heritage.

References and Resources for Social Studies

Alleman, Janet, and Jere Brophy. 2001. *Social Studies Excursions, K-3*. Portsmouth, NH: Heinemann.

Berman, Sheldon. 1997. *Children's Social Consciousness and the Development of Social Responsibility.* Albany, NY: State University of New York Press, 129.

Gamberg, Ruth, Winniefred Kwak, Meredith Hutchings, and Judy Altheim with Gail Edwards. 1988. *Learning and Loving It: Theme Studies in the Classroom.* Portsmouth, NH: Heinemann.

Hirsch, E. D. 1991. *What Your 1st Grader Needs to Know.* New York, NY: Bantam Doubleday Dell Publishing Group, 86–96.

Jorgensen, Karen L. 1993. *History Workshop: Reconstructing the Past with Elementary Students*. Portsmouth, NH: Heinemann.

Katz, Lilian G., and Sylvia C. Chard. 1989. *Engaging Children's Minds: The Project Approach.* Norwood, NJ: Ablex Publishing.

Lickona, T., and Paradise, M. 1980. Democracy in the Elementary School. In *Moral Education: A First Generation of Research and Development.* Edited by R. Mosher. New York, NY: Praeger, 334–5.

McDermott, J. Cynthia, ed. 1999. *Beyond the Silence, Listening for Democracy*. Portsmouth, NH: Heinemann.

Mitchell, Lucy. 1991. *Young Geographers*. 4th ed. New York, NY: Bank Street College of Education.

Seefeldt, Carol. 1997. *Social Studies for the Preschool-Primary Child*. 5th ed. Upper Saddle River, NJ: Prentice Hall.

Short, Kathy, and Carolyn Burke. 1991. *Creating Curriculum: Teachers and Students as a Community of Learners.* Portsmouth, NH: Heinemann.

Sobel, David. 1998. *Mapmaking with Children*. Portsmouth, NH: Heinemann.

Tunnell, Michael O., and Richard Ammon, eds. 1992. *The Story of Ourselves: Teaching History Through Children's Literature.* Portsmouth, NH: Heinemann.

Wolk, Steven. 1998. *A Democratic Classroom*. Portsmouth, NH: Heinemann.

SCIENTIFIC
THINKING

S cience is the search for ways to explain and understand the natural and physical world. Scientists are equipped with insatiable curiosity as well as the necessary tools for scientific investigation—the ability to observe carefully and without bias, to think logically and critically, and to reason. Conducting scientific investigations involves asking questions, gathering and analyzing information, and suggesting explanations that can be tested.

Scientific investigations can relate to straightforward questions such as why leaves change color, as well as more complex problems such as how did the universe begin or what is a cure for a mysterious disease. Regardless of the nature of the question, the core of scientific thinking is seeking explanations through systematic investigation of objects, phenomena, and living things. Critical to the scientific process is the belief that through investigation, one can begin to understand the physical and natural world.

Like adult scientists, children in the primary grades constantly seek explanations about their world. Eager to explore the phenomena they encounter every day—sound, water, light, motion, plants, and animals—young children touch, manipulate, look, and listen in order to form explanations for how the world works. Science curriculum in the primary grades is most effective when it builds on children's natural inclination to seek explanations and fosters their desire and willingness to seek answers to questions through active investigations. Nurturing children's sense of wonder—their interest and excitement in finding out about the world—is at the heart of the science curriculum in the primary grades. Teaching children how to think like scientists is its focus.

Children Exploring Science

The discipline of science is so vast that it would be impossible to identify a set of theories, concepts, and facts that all children should learn during the primary grades. For this reason, learning to engage in the process of scientific thinking is a more appropriate focus for the science curriculum. Any topic that addresses scientific knowledge—living things, earth and space, matter, and energy—can be a vehicle for teaching scientific thinking.

The examples that follow show how teachers plan experiences that allow children to use scientific thinking as they build knowledge of the natural and physical world.

*In Ms. Diaz's **first grade** classroom a study of small creatures is underway. The children have collected earthworms by searching in piles of decomposing leaves on the playground. They are interested in finding answers to questions such as, "Do earthworms have legs?" and "How do earthworms move?" Children work with partners using hand lenses to observe the movements of earthworms. They measure their worms with lengths of string. The children look for clues about how the worms move. They exchange discoveries about their observations. "My worm is a little rough. When it moves on my hand, it tickles," exclaims Peter. Teresa says, "I can't seem to measure mine. It gets small and then stretches out very long. It won't stand still." Ms. Diaz responds, "Peter, the tickling comes from the bristles on the worm. What do you think those bristles might be for?" And to Teresa she asks, "How do you think the worm gets bigger and smaller?" She suggests that the children make larger than life drawings of the worms so that they can document all the parts of the worm that might help the worm to move.*

Ms. Diaz has selected the topic of living things for children to investigate. The study, which she calls "Small Creatures," is interesting and accessible to her students. By taking children for a collecting walk and then giving them an opportunity to pose questions, she sparks their curiosity. She first guides their investigation by setting up opportunities for them to observe closely and study the creatures. She continually asks questions that encourage children to wonder, question, observe, and pose explanations. When children share their drawings during a class meeting, Ms. Diaz points out all the techniques children used to record their ideas on how worms move.

*As part of their study of motion, small groups of children in Ms. Thompson's **second grade** construct tubes, tunnels, and runs for different sized marbles. She challenges the children to build a pathway for the balls that will keep them in motion for as long as possible and cause them to change direction at least once. Children talk about their work as they test, observe, question, and pose explanations. Liz observes, "The higher we start the ball, the farther it goes." Ray asks, "How can we make the ball turn a corner? It keeps going in a straight line." Having tried several balls made of different materials, Jake concludes, "The metal ball works better than the glass marble. It bounces less." Ms. Thompson suggests that the children make drawings of their constructions so that they can share their findings at the class meeting.*

In this classroom children go about the process of scientific inquiry: they question, investigate, collect data, explain, draw conclusions, and describe findings. Their investigation is about energy and they are exploring important concepts: force, gravity, mass, momentum, and friction. Because they are curious to solve the problem posed by Ms. Thompson, and because they can experiment with real materials, they feel competent and purposeful about their work. They are actively engaged in solving a problem. They represent their thinking by building structures and drawing and writing about them. By sharing their ideas with each other, they clarify their thinking.

> *Everyone seated in Ms. Walker's* **third grade** *classroom meeting area has just finished listening to* In Shadowland *by Mitsumasa Anno. Children are busily sharing personal stories about having seen their shadows at various times. Ms. Walker asks, "What do you think makes our shadows appear?" The children discuss possible explanations. Then she announces that they will take a series of shadow walks on several days. She asks, "Do you think we will see our shadows? How can we keep track of when and where we see them? What tools do we need?"*

Ms. Walker uses a story to kindle children's interest in light and shadows. She encourages them to ask questions and consider possible explanations. To prepare them for the shadow walks, she has them think about how to conduct an investigation and how to record what they see. Throughout the study, children will record, measure, chart, and graph what they observe. They will measure their own shadows at different times of the day and graph the lengths. They will do this over the course of several days and make comparative charts. In this study, the children will explore important science concepts such as the many sources of light, how shadows are produced when light is blocked, and how shadow shape and size change depending on the position of the light source and/or object.

The teachers in these classrooms have set up learning experiences that trigger children's natural sense of wonder. While each child may take something different from these experiences, all children are engaged in scientific thinking. The teachers give children opportunities to use the process of scientific inquiry to solve problems and devise explanations. Children are encouraged to ask questions, conduct investigations, test explanations, and describe and revise conclusions. They will make discoveries and gain understanding through active and purposeful investigation. Their work involves their hands and their minds.

It is not enough to go from instruction where children are observers of the scientific process to instruction that involves children in doing science. Children must also think about what they are doing. As they explore, children must have experiences structured to encourage questioning, explaining, and evaluating.

What Children Learn

The science curriculum, like social studies, combines content and process. The body of knowledge embedded in the disciplines of biology, chemistry, physics, geology, earth science, and others is the content of the curriculum. The process involves knowing how to engage in scientific inquiry and to use scientific methods flexibly. Teaching children these process skills is an essential component of the science curriculum.

In recent years, scientists and educators have come together to define national standards for science education in such publications as *Science for All Americans* (1989), *Benchmarks for Science Literacy* (1993), and *National Science Education Standards* (1996). Together, these publications encourage an approach to teaching science that emphasizes understanding and connections, rather than simply the acquisition of facts.

They assert that an effective science curriculum:

- nurtures children's excitement and curiosity about the material world around them disposing them to use scientific skills, abilities, and attitudes.

- enables children to understand and use the processes of scientific inquiry, that is, to know how to go about the work of being a scientist.

- helps children develop an understanding of unifying concepts and processes in science while they acquire specific content knowledge.

Dispositions for Scientific Thinking

Scientists are curious; they ask questions about the world around them, and they believe that they can find answers to these questions through systematic investigation. A central focus of the science curriculum, therefore, must be to foster children's natural curiosity about the world around them. Curiosity is essential for scientific investigation. It is what motivates scientists to pose questions, identify problems, use logic and reasoning to consider solutions, construct investigations, analyze data, and form explanations.

Having an open mind is beneficial beyond the realm of science because we live in a diverse, dynamic, and complex society. Within the field of science, however, it is especially important to be open to new ideas. Very often great scientific discoveries are the product of unexpected experimental results: for example, Alexander Fleming discovering penicillin from mold. Flexible thinkers willingly revise their thinking as they acquire new information. Therefore, an effective science curriculum will encourage children to be open to new ideas.

Scientists, as well as experts in other disciplines, do not accept answers without first thoroughly evaluating data. It is also important for children to learn not to accept ideas and events at face value, but to analyze and evaluate them. This helps children move to a higher level of thinking. A good science curriculum, therefore, promotes appropriate skepticism. It encourages children to search for logical explanations and to recognize that theories must be supported by evidence. Children also can learn the limits of science—that we cannot answer all questions.

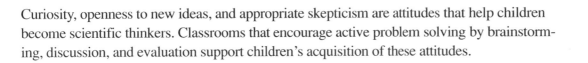
Curiosity, openness to new ideas, and appropriate skepticism are attitudes that help children become scientific thinkers. Classrooms that encourage active problem solving by brainstorming, discussion, and evaluation support children's acquisition of these attitudes.

The Process of Scientific Inquiry

An essential element of being a scientific investigator is knowing how to find answers to questions. Viewing science as a process of inquiry supports the most current understanding of how children learn best. Children make sense of the world by constructing knowledge, accumulating new information as they add on to what they already know. The best science instruction encourages the process of constructing knowledge through investigations.

Scientists conduct investigations in order to answer questions. Some investigations involve careful observation and descriptions; others involve classification; and some require experimentation. Scientists use tools to help them collect and analyze data. They use what they learn to construct explanations or answer questions. Communicating findings is an important part of the process because scientists want other people to repeat their investigations and confirm the results. Scientists are always comparing their findings with the work of others.

Asking Scientific Questions

Children are innately curious. Teachers can build on this natural inclination to ask questions by showing children that their questions are worthwhile and helping them to see how their questions can become the basis for investigation.

> *Ms. Nolan introduces a study of the moon to her class by reading* Owl Moon *by Jane Yolen. After the story, she asks the children, "What do you know about the moon?" Hector states, "The moon is out at night." Miyoko replies, "I've seen the moon out in the daytime too." Other children chime in with various points of view until finally, and with some frustration, Hector asks, "Ms. Nolan, isn't the moon out only at night?" She agrees that Hector's question is a good one and asks the children to suggest ways to find an answer. The children decide to watch the moon for a month. To encourage the investigation, Ms. Nolan prepares a recording sheet so that each child can observe the moon daily. On their recording sheet they can write down the time of day they see it and draw a picture of how it looks. For several days the children bring in the data they collect. When the children are unable to observe the moon because of overcast skies, Ms. Nolan shows them other ways to collect data. She brings in a newspaper to show the children that the time the moon rises and sets each day is documented in the newspaper. She shows them how to use the Internet to find the same information.*

Not every question leads to a meaningful investigation. What makes a question scientific is the possibility of finding an answer through careful and systematic investigation. The more opportunities children have to ask questions, the more they will learn to ask the right question at the right time. Often children ask questions that cannot be systematically investigated. For example, "Why do seasons change?" is a question that can lead to an interesting discussion and much speculation, but not directly to an investigation. Children can, however, investigate how the natural environment changes from one season to the next by observing and documenting what they see and then forming explanations for these changes, such as why trees lose their leaves.

Children's questions change as they gain experience and maturity. For example, a first grader might ask: "Why is there a filter in the aquarium?" A third grader who has had some experience with aquariums might ask, "How does this aquarium filter remove the dirt from the water?" Providing opportunities for children to answer their own questions enables them to connect previous knowledge and experience with new experiences. The increasing sophistication of children's questions comes as much with experience as with maturity. The third grader who has never had experience with an aquarium is just as likely as the first grader to ask the question, "Why is there a filter in the aquarium?"

Prior to any scientific investigation with children, allow time for them to ask questions. Sometimes their curiosity and sense of wonder is spontaneous, as in the example of a third grader who asks, "Which weighs more: snow when it's melted or snow when it's snow?" At other times, the teacher sets the stage for questions by presenting a problem. An example of this is a teacher who challenges the children to think about what type of ramp they would have to build in order to keep a ball in motion and change directions at least once.

Finally, effective science teachers encourage children to come back to their questions and see whether they have been answered. Posting the children's questions on charts helps to create an environment for inquiry. As investigations proceed and children raise new questions, these should be added to the lists.

Planning and Conducting Investigations

Investigations are carefully planned to collect the information or data needed to answer the question. Young children generate explanations and new ideas all the time. The more experience they have with scientific investigations, the more realistic and plausible their ideas become. The science curriculum comes to life in a primary classroom when children are encouraged to plan investigations to test their ideas.

Children in a first grade class collect seeds from oranges and lemons to see if they will grow into plants. Using soil and cups, they plant the seeds, water them regularly, and observe what happens.

In a mixed-age classroom of seven and eight year olds, the children are studying temperature changes. Seth predicts that an ice cube wrapped in aluminum foil and placed inside a plastic bag will stay frozen longer than an ice cube placed in the open air. He conducts an investigation to try to prove his theory.

10

Teachers can encourage children to think like scientists by getting into the habit of asking "what will happen if. . . ." questions. Ask children to think of situations about which they have some experience.

- What do you think will happen when we mix these two paint colors together?
- What would happen if we put this piece of clay into the water?
- Which technique do you think will be most effective for wiping the blackboards, a wet sponge or a dry cloth?

Challenging students to explain why they think something will happen helps them to make the connection between prior experiences and a new, but similar, event. When we ask children to predict about unfamiliar situations, they are likely to make wild guesses. Scientists develop explanations based on previous experience or knowledge.

Seeking answers to scientific questions can involve setting up a systematic test, gathering data, and then studying the results. Scientists conduct controlled experiments or *fair tests*. They decide on one factor to be tested and plan the test to measure that factor alone; all other factors, or *variables*, remain the same. The idea of a fair test is one that primary grade children can begin to grasp.

Children's understanding of the notion of *fairness* begins to develop in the preschool years. During organized games, children start to compare their own abilities with their peers'. By the time they reach first grade, many children have a solid sense of what fairness means. If asked to set up a fair running race between two students, most would agree that each runner would have to start at the same point and proceed over similar terrain. All conditions would have to be the same so that the variable being tested is the speed of the runner and nothing else.

> *Some children studying plants in a second grade class wonder what would make plants grow faster. Several children suggest trying fertilizer. Ms. Ruiz asks them to plan an experiment that might answer this question. Diana and Inez decide to add fertilizer to a set of pea plants. They measure the plants' growth and record this information in a table Ms. Ruiz designed on the computer. Ms. Ruiz asks them to think in terms of setting up a fair test. Inez sees that in order to test whether fertilizer makes a plant grow faster, she and Diana can't just observe a fertilized plant. Instead, they will need to compare a fertilized plant with an unfertilized plant. The children plan an experiment where both fertilized and unfertilized plants will be grown under the same conditions: the same light, temperature, humidity, soil, and pot size.*

Some children will grasp the idea of a fair test more readily than others. Rather than telling children to be sure they use a fair test, teachers can pose questions so that children recognize it for themselves. For example, Ms. Ruiz might have asked Diana and Inez: "How will you know if one plant is growing faster than the other? What will you need to do so that you can compare the growth of the two plants?"

Gathering Data

One of the most important ways that scientists collect data is through observation. From birth, we use our senses to learn about the world around us. Scientific investigation calls for refined observation—paying careful attention to detail and knowing when observations are relevant to the problem being explored. Learning to observe carefully also means relying on all of the senses and being able to choose and use tools for observation, such as a hand lens, microscope, or measuring device.

At first, children tend to rely on what they see. They often neglect information that their other senses can detect. Children who are developing more refined observation skills will notice details about appearance but will also use touch, smell, and hearing for more information. Teachers can promote children's observation skills by encouraging them to observe using all their senses.

- *Look:* discriminate size, color, shape, and position of object; count features; estimate length, volume, or weight and compare these to other known objects.
- *Touch:* determine whether objects feel rough, smooth, wet, dry, oily, scaly, heavy, light, bumpy.
- *Listen:* note the volume or the pitch of sounds and make comparisons with sounds such as falling rain or a crashing toy.
- *Smell:* describe how something smells and compare new smells to familiar ones ("It smells like lemons." or "It smells like trash.").
- *Taste:* identify terms such as sweet, bitter, sour, or spicy. (Tasting experiments should be carefully supervised.)

To help children observe details beyond those that are obvious, teachers can ask probing questions and offer tools such as magnifiers or simple microscopes. In order to gather data effectively, children need time to study objects and events carefully. This means providing extended work times as well as encouraging children to study objects over the course of time.

Constructing Explanations

Analyzing information and drawing conclusions are central to problem solving and occur in many subjects, not just in science. Children use these skills as they read literature, solve math problems, or create an art project. For young children, an important part of scientific investigation is thinking critically about what is happening. In science, a believable explanation depends on the support of evidence and logical thought. A scientist is aware that one can easily be influenced by one's preconceptions. Using evidence and logic minimizes the effect of personal bias in constructing an explanation.

Studying an object or event through observation and experimentation usually yields a great deal of information. Interpreting information means finding the significance of all the data that have been gathered. Too often, interpretation of data is left out of primary grade science activities. Instead, activities are planned more for entertainment, and children are not encouraged to think about explanations. To encourage children to interpret data and draw conclusions, teachers can ask children questions.

- Why is this happening?
- What does the evidence show?
- What really happened during the experiment?
- What did we find out?
- What new questions do we have now?

Careful analysis of data reveals patterns, relationships, or trends. The critical thinking skills of comparing and classifying are used to interpret these relationships. Comparing means judging the similarities and differences among observed objects or attributes. This skill is important during the process of classification. Classifying means organizing things into groups according to common characteristics. For example, to organize or group a collection of seeds into categories based on size, the seeds must be compared to see the range of sizes, then classified into categories accordingly. At first, children will use simple categories: things that float, things that are green, or things that are tiny. As they gain experience, they will be able to use more than one attribute to form groups: metal things that float, leaves that are green and don't fall to the ground in autumn.

In science, constructing an explanation requires at least three steps.

- Analyze the collected information or data.
- Form a generalization or explanation.
- Apply the explanation to other situations or problems.

Typically, the processes of interpreting data and drawing conclusions happen simultaneously for young children. As children gain experience, they begin to develop the more advanced skill of making generalizations and applying these to new problems. For example, in a class discussion about why snakes shed their skin, a second grader may relate information learned the previous year about hermit crabs. Past experiences are keys to a child's ability to analyze information and construct an explanation.

Communicating Findings

Science requires the ability to communicate clearly so that ideas and discoveries can be shared. Children can be encouraged to describe their findings and ideas both verbally (in discussions) and non-verbally (drawing or making a model). Reading and writing in the context of science investigations helps children see another important use for their growing literacy skills.

Keeping records of observations (descriptions, drawings, charts) is a common and useful way to track discoveries and communicate information. Children can write descriptions, make drawings, charts, and graphs to communicate information and express ideas. Depending on the child's ability and experience, communication might include a one-word caption for first graders or a short, three-sentence description from a third grader. Record keeping serves other purposes as well. When challenged to describe their thoughts, children become aware of what they know and do not know about a subject. Questions surface and ideas can be clarified.

Scientific observations and experiments provide many opportunities for children to talk with one another. As they talk, they use increasingly detailed language to describe, clarify, and explain their ideas to one another.

Unifying Concepts and Processes

There are common themes or ways of thinking that have applications across all the disciplines of science content knowledge and guide thinking about scientific observing, investigating, and the construction of scientific explanations (National Research Council 1996; Bredekamp and Rosegrant 1995; American Association for the Advancement of Science 1993). These themes include systems, models, and constancy and change.

Systems

We talk about systems all the time—ecosystems, transportation systems, the solar system, the human body as a system. Each system has an order and organization within it that helps us understand how the parts are connected and how these parts affect each other and the whole.

For primary grade children the important aspect of the theme of systems is to recognize that things are made of parts that influence one another as they work together. For example, what happens to the marble if a section of the ramp is removed, or what happens to the plant if it isn't watered for a week? They discover that if a part is missing, broken, or not connected properly, there is an impact on the system. Children can begin to learn that there is an order to how things work and that things can be classified as a way to help us understand the parts and the order. For example, before trying to build something, it is often helpful to group all the parts.

Related to the theme of systems is the idea that the form of organisms in the natural world and the form or shape of objects made by humans each has a particular function. Form and function are interrelated. Primary grade children can learn about this concept as they study animals and plants. They explore how ducks' feet help them swim and different birds' beaks enable them to eat particular food. They learn that desert plants have tiny leaves and plants in areas that receive more rain tend to have large leaves.

Models

Scientists use physical, mathematical, and conceptual models to develop better understandings of how real things work. Models can be physical, three-dimensional representations of things, such as a model car, boat, or house. Or they can be two-dimensional representations, such as a drawing or a graph. Models allow people to look at something conceptually and discover relationships. Models also enable people to test out their ideas.

Children use models throughout all areas of the classroom. As they learn math they use manipulatives to represent numbers and groups of numbers. And learning to read and write involves manipulating symbols (or models) for sounds. Of course, young children naturally play with dolls, trucks, and other toys and use them to represent objects in the real world.

Primary grade children can learn to recognize how physical models may be the same as or different from real things. They may be a different size, lack some details, or are unable to perform all the functions of the real thing. As children use models they can begin to see how models can help us learn something about the real thing. As they conduct investigations, they may use models to experiment with design changes. When they report their findings with graphs, diagrams, and sketches, they see how using models increases understanding.

Constancy and Change

How things stay the same and how they change is a unifying concept in many disciplines as well as in science. Scientific thinking requires that we observe change (or the lack of it) and find a way to quantify or measure it and then describe it, looking for patterns and relationships.

Because measurement is an important mathematical task for primary grade children, they should be involved in thinking about and noticing change and evolution in many of their daily activities. They can use tools to measure how things change. After noticing that the water in the fish tank was at one level yesterday and today it's lower, a third grader might measure the water level with a ruler, and a first grader might use Unifix cubes or string.

Primary grade children should know that investigations can be designed to watch how things change and stay the same; that measurement tools can be used to monitor change; and that things change in different ways, such as size, weight, color, and movement. Older primary grade children can learn to manipulate changes in one feature of an object but not the other and to notice and record patterns in change.

These unifying concepts can be woven throughout the components of the science curriculum so that children become aware of the connections to be made.

Components of the Science Curriculum

Children need to develop knowledge in multiple areas to help them to think scientifically. In *Building the Primary Classroom*, we have organized the content of the science curriculum into three categories: life science, earth and space science, and physical science. Technology is addressed in the next chapter.

Overview of the Science Curriculum

Components	What Children Learn
Life Science	• the body of knowledge that includes big ideas such as behavior, needs of plants and animals, characteristics, habitats, and life cycles
Earth and Space Science	• the body of knowledge related to day and night, the moon and the stars, climate and weather, and the earth's surface
Physical Science	• the body of knowledge that includes the properties of substances and the relationship of the substance's properties to its purpose as well as the body of knowledge about light, sound, heat, motion, and electricity

The unifying concepts of Systems, Models, and Constancy and Change are embedded in each of these components.

Children build their understanding of science concepts slowly, based on their experiences with real materials and phenomena. They need to revisit these same ideas many times and in many ways in order to refine their understanding. Rather than trying to address a definitive list of *must cover* science topics, teachers can be more successful in teaching science by focusing on fewer topics in more depth.

The previously mentioned Standards documents as well as the books listed in the Resources section of this chapter can help you identify the important concepts within the topic you decide to study with children. If you are required to teach particular topics, these materials can help you think about how to organize instruction so that children can conduct scientific investigations in ways that are appropriate for their development and level of understanding.

While abstract concepts (e.g., condensation and evaporation, the atomic structure of matter, the conservation of energy) are key to a high-level understanding of science, all of science begins with direct observations of phenomena and noticing what happens to them. The topics children study in the primary grades should be connected to the world around them, that is, objects and materials that they can observe directly, describe, and find patterns in. Both *Benchmarks* (1993) and the *Standards* (1996), for example, describe how children should have experiences that enable them to learn that water disappears in an open container but not in a closed container. Rather than pushing for children to learn about evaporation and condensation, which are abstract concepts more appropriate for older elementary grade children, primary grade children can learn more by focusing on the size of the container, for example, the area of the uncovered portion, and whether " . . .using a fan to blow air over the surface of a container of water makes the water disappear faster" (National Research Council 1996, 125).

We have organized the three broad categories of scientific content knowledge into a series of charts. Each chart identifies science concepts appropriate for the primary grades (National Research Council 1996) and offers ideas of topics for investigation.

As you review the charts, keep in mind that it would be impossible for any teacher to try to address all of the topics listed. These charts are offered simply to show the range of possibilities for scientific explorations. At the most, you might explore three topics in depth during a given year. It is the process of engaging in scientific thinking and acquiring a deeper understanding of the big concepts, e.g., "all living things change and go through cycles," that are revisited year after year within the context of new studies.

Life Science

Concepts	Suggested Topics for Investigation
Plants and animals (organisms) have basic needs. Animals (and people) need air, water, and food; plants require air, water, nutrients, and light.	• ourselves • birds • fish and other aquatic creatures (e.g., hermit crabs, snails, frogs)
Each animal and plant has particular structures that serve different functions necessary for growth, survival, and reproduction.	• pets • insects and other small creatures • plants • mammals
Internal cues, such as hunger, and external cues in the environment, such as the amount of rainfall, influence the behavior of organisms.	• trees and leaves • terrariums • gardens
Organisms and their environments are closely connected. The world has many different environments. Particular environments support different animals and plants.	• habitats (e.g., puddle, playground, field, forest, desert, pond, lake, river, ocean) • strategies for survival (e.g., the turtle's shell, creatures who lay many eggs, animals who hibernate, camouflage)
All living things change and go through life cycles.	• egg to chick • caterpillar to butterfly • mealworm to beetle • baby to adult (humans and other animals)

Earth and Space Science

Concepts	Suggested Topics for Investigation
The sun, moon, stars, and clouds all have properties, locations, and movements that can be observed and described. The sun provides light and heat.	• day and night • the moon and its changes • seasons • shadows
Weather changes from day to day and across seasons. These changes can be measured and described. The Earth is composed of rocks and soils, water, and gases.	• water (e.g., water cycle, evaporation) • weather (e.g., clouds, forecasting, types of storms) • volcanoes and earthquakes • weather • erosion • rocks • land forms
The earth's surface changes over time due to the effects of water, wind, ice, and forces beneath the surface of the earth. Soils have different properties that affect how they support plant life.	• recycling and garbage • compost • plants and soil • dirt

Physical Science

Concepts	Suggested Topics for Investigation
Based on what they are made of, objects have distinct properties that can be observed such as size, weight, shape, color, and temperature.	• structures (e.g., houses, skyscrapers) • building materials (e.g., clay, bricks, woods, steel, cement) • construction • inventions • materials and their uses (e.g., rubber for tires, metals for cars, plastic for containers)
Objects react to other substances. Materials exist in different states—solid, liquid, and gas. Some materials can be changed from one state to another. The position of an object can be described by its relation to another object. The position can be changed through movement and the movement can be measured over time.	• balancing (e.g., weighing things, constructing block buildings, making mobiles) • solid objects (e.g., properties and uses) • liquids (e.g., flow, properties of liquids) • gases (e.g., air, steam) • boats • kites, balloons, planes • sinking and floating in water
Sound is produced by things that vibrate. The rate of vibration affects the pitch of the sound. Light travels in a straight line until it strikes an object. Light can be reflected, refracted, or absorbed by an object. Heat can be produced by burning, rubbing, or mixing one substance with another. Electricity produces light, heat, sound, and magnetic effects.	• light and shadows • mirrors • rainbows • color • solar energy • sound • hearing • musical instruments • water • ice • snow • inventions • balls and ramps • spinning things • machines • inventions • magnets • uses of solar energy • electrical devices • batteries and bulbs • lights in our city • inventions

Organizing the Science Curriculum

Teachers who are alert to the everyday opportunities to teach scientific thinking and who generate enthusiasm about investigating any of the topics suggested in the charts can make science an important part of their curriculum.

> The essence of science activity, and usually its starting point, is the encounter between the child and some phenomenon; some face to face interaction of children and things around from which they can learn directly through their own physical and mental activity (Harlen 1989, 6).

Many teachers do not feel comfortable teaching science. Their discomfort may come from the view that science is a set of facts and theories to be memorized or that it is a body of knowledge that is incomprehensible. Because discomfort sometimes leads to avoidance, science is often pushed to a back burner in primary classrooms. Periodically, children may read about a topic in a textbook or engage in clever science activities, but they do not undertake true scientific investigations.

To be an effective teacher of science in the primary grades, you have to be willing to think like a scientist as well as a teacher. There are countless opportunities to guide children toward thinking scientifically by making science a part of everyday life in the classroom and by engaging children in studying a topic that interests them (and you).

Making Science Part of Everyday Life in the Classroom

Science isn't a subject that just happens once or twice a week. Children can learn to think like scientists and recognize scientific questions in their everyday world when teachers use daily experiences to promote the skills of scientific inquiry. Daily experiences with objects, plants, animals, and weather provide children with opportunities to observe, think scientifically, and draw conclusions about the physical and natural world (Doris 1991). By making materials available, modeling scientific thinking, and responding to events that occur in the environment, teachers can make science part of everyday life.

Provide Space and Materials to Encourage Science Exploration

The classroom can be a laboratory for questioning, observing, predicting, and explaining on a daily basis apart from any particular study. By including materials that are interesting to explore as a part of the physical environment, teachers create a setting in which children spontaneously ask questions and conduct informal investigations.

Identify an Area for Scientific Investigation

Allocating space in the classroom for science gives children the message that it is important. The area will be inviting if it includes interesting materials. Displays can consist of books, newspaper articles, and magazines related to particular topics, creations made by children, and objects collected by the teacher or children. Tools for investigation and collections can be kept in a science area or displayed on a shelf or table. Materials such as colored pencils, markers, journals, and different types of paper should be accessible.

It is important to change the materials and the displays in the science area so that interest is constantly renewed. Introducing a new poster, a new book, or a new tool during a meeting is likely to encourage children to select the science area at choice time. You might also display pictures of scientists at work.

Provide Tools for Scientific Investigations

An important part of science is becoming familiar with the purposeful use of tools and beginning to recognize the ways tools relate to mathematical and scientific thinking. Some tools such as scales, measuring cups, thermometers, calculators, and rulers are for measuring. Other tools such as magnifiers, microscopes, and cameras aid observation.

Children will begin to understand the purpose of tools when materials are accessible to them. Displaying tools and materials in an organized way enables children to use them on a regular basis. Initiating interesting projects for children to work on and giving children opportunities to initiate projects gives them a reason to use tools for investigation.

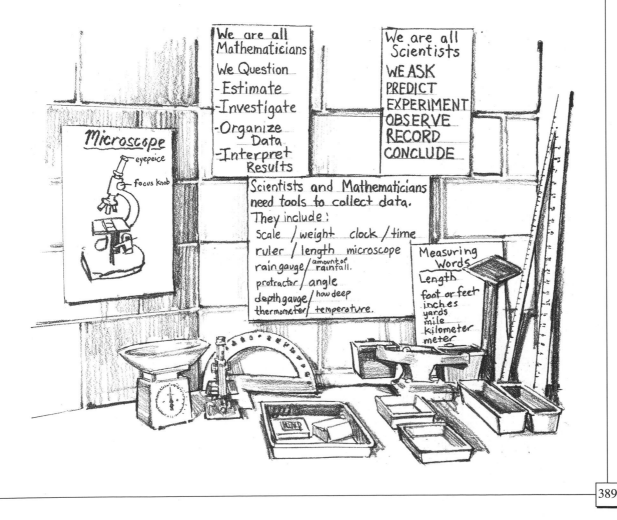

Opportunities to gather data over time are an important part of scientific thinking. You can encourage children to collect data over time by providing tools for recording information such as paper and pencils, colored markers, tape recorders, calculators, and computers. Weather charts and graphs, for example, can become a focus for scientific investigation when they are used to help children think about patterns of change in the environment and changes in the seasons.

Create an Invention Center

Inventing things is part of science and technology. (The Technology chapter has more on studying and creating inventions.) An invention center to inspire investigation could be a portable box of junk with a variety of materials such as corks, film containers, sponges, spools, balloons, straws, Styrofoam, springs, bottle caps, string, and scraps of wood. These materials can be collected by sending a written request home with children and by asking neighborhood merchants for interesting recyclable materials. Pose a challenge for children.

- Make something that spins.
- Create something that moves.
- Invent something that can move things up and down.

Children can be encouraged to draw and write about their creations.

Provide a Variety of Interesting Collections

Children can be inspired to sort and classify objects if the science area includes collections of leaves, flowers, seeds, magnets, marbles, sea glass, stones, or fabric scraps. These activities are more likely to occur if you organize the collections in bins with trays next to them on which children can sort and classify.

Provide magnifiers to encourage children to investigate objects carefully. Placing a sign that says, "What do you notice?" or "Find an interesting way to group these objects and record your method," can motivate children to begin their explorations.

Include Living Things in the Classroom

A tank for fish, hermit crabs, turtles, or a frog can be a catalyst for ongoing science discussions and observations. Class pets such as a guinea pig, rabbit, or bird also provide opportunities for children to conduct investigations while learning how to care for living creatures. Including plants in the classroom often sparks discussions about what they need to grow, when they bloom, and how to keep track of growth over time.

Model Scientific Thinking

Children are more likely to think like scientists when they interact with adults and peers who model this way of thinking. Your own enthusiasm and curiosity can be a catalyst for children: "I just can't wait to find out how this caterpillar is going to change and how long it's going to take." If you can't wait, the children will often feel the same way!

Share Your Observations

Teachers model scientific thinking by being observant and pointing out scientific events when they happen. For example, when water forms droplets on the classroom window, you might ask, "What do you think is happening here? What's causing the water to form beads?"

Teachers also share their interest in science by bringing objects from home. For example, a piece of bread with blue and white fuzzy mold is something we all have found in our homes at one time or another. Bringing it into the classroom might lead to interesting discussions and possible investigations. After letting children know where the bread was and how long it had been there, ask some questions.

- How can we find out what is growing on the bread?

- What might we use to see what is growing more clearly?

- What would happen if we left the bread out even longer?

Whether the discussion and possible investigations are initiated by the children or by you, the goal is to encourage children to be curious and consider cause and effect.

Encourage Children to Share

The way you respond to child-initiated topics can model scientific thinking. Many times children arrive on Monday morning with something they have found during the weekend or with a story of an event they witnessed. They might bring in shells, a nest, a small creature, or an independent project that they have created. By inviting children to talk about their experience or discovery and encouraging the others to ask questions, teachers help children think like investigators.

> *First grader Josie raises her hand during the meeting Monday morning and says, "Over the weekend I saw a rainbow." Ms. Douglas responds, "Mmm. Let's think about this like scientists. Tell us about what was happening when you saw it." Josie replies, "I was playing with my sister in the park." Ms. Douglas asks other questions including, "What colors did you notice in the rainbow?" and "What was the weather like? Was it raining? Was the sun shining?" After Josie shares some of her observations, Ms. Douglas says to the class, "Let's think about what causes rainbows."*

By using Josie's story about the rainbow as a focus for discussion and asking specific questions, Ms. Douglas conveys the message that paying attention to what is happening in the environment and sharing it with others is important. She uses this experience to extend children's thinking on the topic by asking questions and encouraging discussions.

Often something that a child brings in from home sparks others to try something out during choice time. Opportunities to link children's interests outside school with activities in the classroom helps children to make connections between home and school.

Respond Scientifically to Problems

The way you respond to problems that come up in daily classroom life is another way to model scientific thinking. If the water or power is suddenly shut off, you can demonstrate to children that such events require investigation. Simply posing the question, "I wonder why this is happening. How can we get to the bottom of this?" will most likely lead to an interesting discussion. When equipment fails to work, another opportunity for scientific thinking is available.

> *Ms. Arnold is about to show her class a videotape but the machine won't work. She says to the class, "Let's think about what we know. Is it plugged in? Is the power on? Do we have it on the right channel? Do we have the tape in?" The children help her check out answers to each question and add some of their own.*

By thinking aloud, Ms. Arnold models how to reason through a problem. She demonstrates that electronic devices are not objects to be afraid of, but rather objects that can be figured out if examined in a systematic way.

Responding to Events in the Environment

The location of a school automatically suggests a broad range of possible scientific investigations. Right outside your classroom window you might find material for ongoing observations.

- Track various types of birds that land on a bird feeder outside the classroom window to learn something about migratory patterns.
- Record monthly observations of one particular tree near the school, noting changes over time.
- Maintain a graph of temperature recorded at the same time each day over a period of several months.

Environmental events also suggest possible scientific inquiries.

- Explore the construction or demolition of a local building.
- Investigate the change of seasons.
- Track a space shuttle flight.
- Study the progress of a sick classroom pet.

A violent storm, drought, snowfall, fire, or earthquake can become the basis for a lively questioning and discussion period. Taking a walk after the snow to observe how it fell, its texture, and the effects of the wind can encourage children to note details and use descriptive language in discussion.

Like the social studies curriculum, science content will vary from classroom to classroom, depending on the age of the children and their prior experiences, the immediate environment of the school, and the interests of children and their teachers.

Selecting Topics for Long-Term Studies in Science

The topics you select for long-term studies in science engage children in the process of scientific inquiry and lead them to an increasing understanding of important science concepts. Because the focus of the science curriculum is on the process of inquiry, any of the sample topics suggested in the charts can become the basis for a long-term study. By studying a variety of topics in depth over the course of the primary grades, children return again and again to central concepts in science. The concept "organisms have basic needs," for example, might be studied in first grade by growing lima bean plants, in second grade in a study of insects, and in third grade during a study of mammals.

Strive to balance the science curriculum by choosing at least one topic that includes a life science study (e.g., insects, birds, plants), one from physical science (e.g., sinking and floating, things that fly, water, air, sound), and one from earth and space science (e.g., day and night, soil). This will provide children with a variety of materials to investigate and allow them to broaden their skills and knowledge of the world.

In selecting the topics you want to pursue during the year, think about what you would enjoy and what would interest the children you teach. Ask yourself what resources are available in your immediate area, and which topics will allow the children to conduct first-hand research and use scientific thinking skills. Because you can do only so much, you will also want to consider which topics provide natural linkages to other subjects you will be teaching. In this way you can alternate or integrate topics you plan to study.

Children's Interests

Without interest, motivation is likely to be absent. In first and second grades, children are often interested in topics related to their own experiences and environments. Studying living things or rocks gathered locally, their own bodies, and their pets is generally of greatest interest. By third grade, children typically have increased eye-hand coordination and like to design and create inventions, machines, structures, gardens, and musical instruments.

Make sure to leave some time during the year for child-initiated topics. A flexible curriculum makes the science program more interesting primarily because it results in changes from one year to the next. One year the curriculum might be paper airplanes, another year forest animals or recycling. When you proceed with a topic initiated by the children, you send strong messages to children: your ideas are important and together we can explore this topic to learn more. In addition, you show children that their curiosity has an important place at school and they can determine the direction of their own learning.

When children raise their own questions about a topic, they are likely to be motivated to search for answers. As you consider the timing of a particular topic, think about occasions or situations when related questions are likely to arise in the course of typical classroom discussion. For example, are there months when rain or lack of it are noticeable to children? A water study would be very effective at this point. Children are likely to raise questions about many seasonal changes. For example, the presence of seeds and fruit in early fall, and the formation of ice, snow, and frost in the winter are good starting points for studies of plants, water, and weather. Children's observations of shorter daylight hours might lead to a study of darkness, light, and shadow.

Availability of Resources

A subject comes to life for children when they can experience it in many different ways. Talking with a naturalist, looking at pictures, and reading through many books provide children with ideas for questions and discussions. In *Kids on the 'Net*, Jessica Morton describes how the children in her class corresponded with experts via e-mail during a year long study of birds (1998). Videos and filmstrips are other valuable resources. When resources such as books, experts, photographs, and charts and diagrams are readily available, planning science experiences becomes easier for teachers.

Some topics can be readily explored only during a particular season. Whether you plan to study ice and snow or grow plants, you'll want to consider conditions inside and outside the classroom. For example, if you plan to grow plants, warmer temperatures and more light in your classroom will help. Outside the classroom, there may be opportunities for children to observe the life or phenomena they are studying. Children will be more involved and motivated when they can, for example, see and collect insects from the outdoor environment of the school or neighborhood.

Opportunities for First-Hand Research

An important consideration in selecting a topic is whether it can be experienced directly and therefore offers opportunities for first-hand research. Young children learn best when they can actually touch, see, hear, and manipulate the objects or events being studied. Water, sound, insects, and plants are all topics that require simple and readily available materials. Materials for the study of rain forests, underwater sea life, or dinosaurs are less accessible for scientific investigation and require more dependency on the teacher for information.

Use of Scientific Thinking Skills

To help children go about the work of being a scientist, the topic should allow them to question, plan, and conduct an investigation, gather data, construct an explanation, and communicate findings. Not all topics lend themselves to the same kinds of investigation. Studying life cycles relies on direct observations over time to gather data. Other topics enable children to handle and manipulate the materials being studied (e.g., sound, motion, water). Still other topics require systematic experimentation where objects studied are compared: for example, product testing (determining which paper towels pick up the most water) or growing plants (testing to see the effects of different types of soil or environment). Consider the possibilities in the topics selected and strive for a variety of experiences through the year.

Linkages to Other Subjects

Coordinating plans for long-term studies in social studies and science helps children make connections. Integrating curriculum also makes addressing all subjects more feasible. Science and social studies may be integrated, for example, by studying transportation. Boats and harbors relate easily to a study of the properties of water, including buoyancy. An investigation of tools and simple machines can be integrated with topics such as the school, a supermarket, a construction site, or a study of a city long ago. A study of plants might be integrated with a study of early America. Some teachers alternate science topics with social studies topics, rather than trying to integrate them.

Here are some examples of ways in which science might be integrated with other subjects.

- While studying seeds and plants, organize math experiences around sorting, classifying, charting, and graphing.

- While studying the neighborhood in social studies, children can interview the people who work in the school, and link their work to machines that depend on electricity.

- While studying transportation in social studies, children can investigate tunnels and bridges in science.

Children learn best by having time for extensive exploration of a few topics during the year. Therefore, it is a good idea to resist the temptation to touch briefly on many topics. Two or three topics studied in depth will allow enough time for children to delve into a subject and to learn more than superficial facts.

Questions to Consider

In selecting a topic for science, an important consideration is whether or not it will enable children to learn by actively investigating, representing, and reflecting on their learning.

To identify possibilities for ***investigation,*** ask yourself these questions.

- Can the children observe first-hand the phenomena or objects for study (shadows, snow, living things, rays of light)?
- Can the children control the science process themselves, not just handle the materials or objects? In other words, can the children produce the phenomena by their own hands and vary what they do to effect change (DeVries and Kohlberg 1987)?
- Are materials available for experimentation (soil, seeds, water, cups, hand lenses)?
- Are any measuring tools necessary for the investigation (thermometers, clocks, stop watches, rulers, balance scales)?
- Are print materials available for children to read independently to find answers to questions (field guides, biographies of inventors or other scientists, informational books, charts, captioned photographs)?
- Are videos or filmstrips available that can provide additional information?
- Is there computer software that can be effectively integrated with the study?
- Is there space and are the facilities adequate for the type of investigation being planned (sun or grow-lights for plants, sink, space to store ongoing experiments)?
- Can the children take field trips to observe or collect?
- Can household materials be used?
- Can families be involved in the study?
- Who are the "local experts" who can be consulted on the subject?
- What connections can be made between the investigation and everyday life (water study is related to water use and pollution, freezing and melting, lunch box and thermos design)?
- What open-ended questions can be asked to encourage further thinking?

To identify opportunities for children to ***represent*** their learning, ask yourself these questions.

- Are there opportunities to make charts, graphs, or maps?
- Can children sketch and record observations?
- How will children's observations be systematically gathered (recording sheets, in folders, in journals)?
- Can children design and build models as part of this study?
- Can art projects (painting, drawing, collage, papier maché) or dramatic skits be incorporated into the study?
- Can children record their observations and discussions on video or audiotape?

To ensure that there are provisions for ***reflecting*** on learning, consider the following questions.

- At what points in the study could I have children make notations in their journals?
- Can I use meetings to encourage group reflection?
- What questions will I pose to encourage children to reflect on their learning?

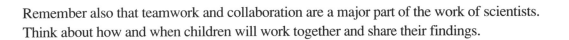
Remember also that teamwork and collaboration are a major part of the work of scientists. Think about how and when children will work together and share their findings.

A Long-Term Study in Action: Insects and Small Creatures

In this section we will show how Ms. Henry, a second grade teacher, thinks through the steps for planning a study on "Insects and Small Creatures."

Selecting a Topic

Ms. Henry wants to begin her science curriculum with a topic that will engage children in becoming researchers. Using the guidelines for selecting an appropriate topic, she decides on a study of "Insects and Small Creatures" for the following reasons.

- The topic addresses children's interests. Ms. Henry knows that many children are fascinated by and inquisitive about nature. Several children have brought insects and small creatures into the classroom to share or have pointed them out on the playground. She also appreciates the fact that some children are squeamish about bugs and will want to view them from a safe distance, at least at first.

- Resources are available in and around the school. Ms. Henry will begin this study in the fall when insects can be collected and observed outdoors. The school library has a number of resource books with detailed illustrations of insects and small creatures and a number of excellent story books. She has been collecting posters and pictures from magazines that she can display in the classroom and she has a collection of nature magazines the children can comb through.

- Children can conduct first-hand research, first by collecting insects and creatures outside the building, then by observing them closely. To continue the study, the children can set up environments for the insects in the classroom where the insects can be observed under magnifiers and microscopes.

- The study will foster scientific thinking skills. Children already know something about the topic and they will be able to generate questions to explore. They can compare different creatures and classify them. Creature habits can be studied over time, allowing children to predict, observe, and interpret data.

- The study provides natural linkages to other aspects of the curriculum. The children will make detailed drawings of the insects they are studying and label body parts. They will count body parts, categorize and graph types of insects, and note patterns in development. They will write about their findings in science journals, read stories and poems on small creatures, and pantomime or dramatize how insects move and communicate.

- The topic can be explored by children over time. Ms. Henry is alternating between science and social studies topics for long-term studies. Depending on the interests of the group, the study may resume in the spring.

The process of selecting the topic helps Ms. Henry begin planning what she needs.

Getting Ready for the Study

Ms. Henry begins by making a web on the topic of insects and small creatures. She identifies the following categories: body parts, ways of moving, environments, use of body parts, stages of development. This brainstorming activity gives her many ideas for planning. She looks through old calendars and nature magazines to find pictures. She collects books from the library and identifies poems she can teach to children. In preparation for the first collecting walk, Ms. Henry takes some preliminary field trips to see where the children will be able to find good specimens. She pulls out her box of beautiful junk to see what can be used to make insect cages and locates an empty fish tank that can be made into a terrarium.

Introducing the Study to Children

To generate interest in the study, Ms. Henry sets the stage by displaying some materials in the classroom. These include:

- photographs of spiders, butterflies, beetles, and bees taken from *Ranger Rick* and *Nature* magazine; and

- books and magazines about insects and non-insects from the school and community library.

Prior to the first class meeting about insects, Ms. Henry uses a choice time to work with a few children to set up a terrarium in the science area. In the terrarium, they place a few hardy local creatures including crickets, beetles, and a grasshopper. Next to it she displays large pictures of worms, beetles, butterflies, bees, and spiders. She puts several books related to the topic on the table with the terrarium.

At a class meeting Ms. Henry asks the children to look at the picture of small creatures on the bulletin board. She has them close their eyes and think about a time when they have seen these or other creatures. They discuss their thoughts and she records what they say on a chart. The children list many small creatures including some that are not insects, such as salamanders, worms, and slugs.

The next day during meeting, Ms. Henry records what the children already know about insects and other small creatures. She asks them what questions they have. Ms. Henry is careful to allow everyone's questions to be recorded and reminds the class that during a brainstorming session, questions are only asked, not answered. The process of charting what the children know and want to find out goes on for several days. For homework, children think about some additional questions. In this way Ms. Henry assesses children's prior knowledge of the subject and makes decisions about the pace and sequence of the activities of the study.

During a subsequent meeting, the children review their list of questions. They consider which of their questions can be answered by conducting observations and experiments. Ms. Henry places a star next to those that can be the focus of future investigations and asks the class to begin thinking of ways an experiment or observation could be organized. The children work in pairs to plan some possible experiments to answer the questions.

Listen to and Learn with Children

During the course of the study, Ms. Henry takes the children on many walks. Prior to the first one, she says, "Let's think about which questions on our list we could answer if we had a collection of small creatures to observe for a few days." In this way, she assigns a purpose for the walk outside. Ms. Henry talks with the children about ways to collect insects and other creatures without harming them.

During the first walk, children collect several ladybugs, a cricket, two worms, and a large beetle. Back in the classroom, Ms. Henry encourages them to think about whether the creature they found is an insect. She adds to the list of questions, "What is an insect?"

Children use the skills of inquiry—questioning, predicting, observing, experimenting, interpreting data and constructing explanations, and communicating their findings—as they create environments for their creatures and observe their behaviors over time. Ms. Henry encourages the children to make sense of the information they gather by analyzing it and drawing simple conclusions.

When children ask her, "Why is it that. . . ?" Ms. Henry responds with, "Why do you think it is that. . . ?" When children are working in pairs or groups on tasks, she circulates and asks questions to stimulate more careful observations.

- How many legs did you count?
- Does this creature have any eyes or ears? If not, what other structures do you notice that might help it sense what is happening around it?
- Is the outside of the body hard or soft?

As children investigate, Ms. Henry provides information about the characteristics of insects. She reads books explaining how insects are different from other small creatures. Ms. Henry invites a naturalist to come to the classroom to talk with the children about insects. She sends a letter home to parents asking if anyone has something related to the study to share with the class. She plans other activities that help provide facts and other information as children need them.

Throughout the study Ms. Henry has the children record their predictions, observations, and explanations of their investigations. They make labeled diagrams, charts, and graphs and they write in their science journals. As children make paintings, collages, and drawings of what they study, they continue to think about new information. Some children construct models of creatures; others build magnification boxes to study the insects more closely. Some children write stories using the knowledge they are acquiring about insects; others make a recording of insect sounds.

The children have numerous opportunities to reflect on their learning. They use their science journals to write about investigations and to reflect on what they have learned. Ms. Henry schedules two or three science meetings each week so that children can share their journal notes or show what they have made or drawn. Throughout the study, meetings are used for discussions of children's observations and discoveries. Meetings are also a time to record new questions.

Concluding the Study

Giving children a chance to apply the knowledge they have gained during their study by building a model, making a presentation, or building an exhibit helps them synthesize what they have learned and feel proud of the work they have done. A culminating activity provides closure for a study. Ms. Henry asks herself several questions.

- How will children share their various representations with others outside our class?
- What are some culminating activities for this project that will enable the children to share what they have learned with children in another class or with families (an exhibition, a book, a photo album, a TV talk show)?
- In what ways can the class share its knowledge about this topic with family members and members of the larger community?

The children decide they want to set up a Creature Zoo. They plan the exhibits, categorize the insects and small creatures they have been studying, and write up summaries about each creature to be featured in the display. Children from other classes and families are invited to visit the exhibit over a two-day period. Ms. Henry asks a parent volunteer to take photographs of the Creature Zoo. The photographs are organized by the children into a book about the project.

Ms. Henry intends to extend what the children learned during this investigation by introducing a study of life cycles. The children will observe the transformation of a caterpillar into a butterfly, letting it go when the weather is warm. They will also apply their knowledge of small creatures to a pond, as there is one located nearby the school. In this way, Ms. Henry can encourage her students never to view a study as really ended. As scientists, they will continue to observe insects and will question and wonder. They will be likely to share their interest with others. It's often this spontaneous sharing that students do months after a study that provides a teacher with the best source of assessment of children's learning, and with a way to measure the success of a study.

Closing Thoughts

Science in the primary grades can be an exciting and integrated part of classroom life. As teachers guide children in learning to think scientifically, they have many opportunities to make brainstorming, communication, math skills, and critical thinking relevant in the context of an investigation. Children who are used to brainstorming solutions to classroom problems will readily apply this skill to suggesting explanations for scientific problems. Working in groups and keeping science journals enables children to apply their communication skills. As children identify patterns, measure, estimate, and use logical reasoning in the context of a scientific investigation, they begin to see the connection between math and science, and they build a deeper understanding of the world around them.

References and Resources for Scientific Thinking

American Association for the Advancement of Science, Project 2061. 1993. *Benchmarks for Science Literacy.* New York, NY: Oxford University Press.

Bredekamp, Sue, and Teresa Rosegrant, eds. 1995. *Reaching Potentials: Transforming Early Childhood Curriculum and Assessment.* Vol. 2. Washington, DC: NAEYC.

DeVries, R., and L. Kohlberg. 1987. *Constructivist Early Education: Overview and Comparison with Other Programs.* Washington, DC: NAEYC.

Doris, Ellen. 1991. *Doing What Scientists Do: Children Learn to Investigate Their World.* Portsmouth, NH: Heinemann.

Hall, Jody S., with Carol Callahan, Pedie O'Brien, Helen Kitchel, and Patricia Pierce. 1998. *Organizing Wonder: Making Inquiry Science Work in the Elementary School.* Portsmouth, NH: Heinemann.

Harlen, Wynne. 1989. *Developing Science in the Primary Classroom.* Portsmouth, NH: Heinemann.

Hart, Craig, Diane Burts, and Rosalind Charlesworth, eds. 1997. *Integrated Curriculum and Developmentally Appropriate Practice.* Albany, NY: State University of New York Press.

Loucks-Horsley, Susan, et al. 1990. *Elementary School Science for the '90s.* Alexandria, VA: ASCD.

Morton, Jessica. 1998. *Kids on the 'Net: Conducting Internet Research in K–5 Classrooms.* Portsmouth, NH: Heinemann.

National Research Council. 1996. *National Science Education Standards.* Washington, DC: National Academy Press.

Rutherford, James F., and Andrew Ahlgren. American Association for the Advancement of Science. 1990. *Science for All Americans.* New York, NY: Oxford University Press.

Saul, Wendy, and Jeanne Reardon, eds. 1996. *Beyond the Science Kit: Inquiry in Action.* Portsmouth, NH: Heinemann Press.

Sivertsen, Mary Lewis. 1993. *State of the Art: Transforming Ideas for Teaching and Learning Science, A Guide for Elementary Science Education.* Washington, DC: U.S. Department of Education.

Strauss, Michael. 1995. *Where Puddles Go: Investigating Science with Kids.* Portsmouth, NH: Heinemann.

Whitin, Phyllis, and David Whitin. 1997. *Inquiry at the Window: Pursuing the Wonders of Learners.* Portsmouth, NH: Heinemann.

Building the

Primary

Classroom

TECHNOLOGY

Technology enables us to use our knowledge and resources to make changes in our environment and develop products to control it. Think about the incredible impact technology has had on society and scientific advances. The development of the telescope in the 17th century led to discoveries in astronomy; the steam engine and the cotton gin revolutionized transportation and agriculture; the airplane, television, and, of course, calculators and computers have enabled us to go places faster, see more, and access information, manipulate data, and design simulations in ways never before possible.

As long as there have been people, there has been technology. Indeed, the techniques of shaping tools are taken as the chief evidence of the beginning of human culture… Technology extends our abilities to change the world: to cut, shape, or put together materials; to move things from one place to another; to reach farther with our hands, voices, and senses. We use technology to try to change the world to suit us better. . . . But the results of changing the world are often complicated and unpredictable. They can include unexpected benefits, unexpected costs, and unexpected risks—any of which may fall on different social groups at different times. Anticipating the effects of technology is therefore as important as advancing its capabilities (Rutherford and Ahlgren 1990, 23).

The study of technology in the classroom involves helping children think about how things work, how problems can be solved by designing products or tools, and how something can be done better through new design or the use of tools. Studying inventions of the past and thinking about and creating new ones help children understand that people can invent new tools and machines that improve our lives. In particular, children can learn about and use computers and other high-tech equipment. These tools offer ways to enhance their learning while integrating and broadening the curriculum.

Children Learning About Technology

Technology activities include learning about inventions, exploring tools, making things, and using computers and other media for communication. These types of activities, integrated throughout the curriculum, can help children become comfortable with the role of tools in our lives. Here are some examples showing children learning about and using technology in many different ways across multiple content areas.

*Ms. Carter puts pulleys and gears at the invention table and challenges the **first graders** to figure out a way to build a machine that performs a task. The children decide what they want their machines to do. Melanie and Janaye work on their invention during three different choice times. On the third day, they proudly share their invention—a windmill-like model with moving arms, complete with gears, and a crank made out of self-hardening clay found among the art supplies. Zachary creates a make-shift crane using the pulley and discovers that it can lift a rock that weighs as much as a unit block.*

These children are learning about machines by creating them. They have been given ample space to work and a wide variety of well-labeled, well-displayed materials. When children invent, they learn about the processes and materials associated with invention. Invention activities can also reinforce children's learning in other areas of the curriculum. For example, children use mathematical thinking to consider the dimensions and shapes of objects they build. In the process of inventing, children take risks, experiment, produce, record, and share. They show persistence, engage in problem solving, and use tools as they think about how inventions of many kinds help people.

*A class of **third graders** is exploring biography as a literary genre. After reading a biography of Benjamin Franklin, the teacher challenges the students to take on the role of an inventor. Those who accept the challenge think of a desirable invention, research the Internet for similar inventions, create a plan for the product on paper, collect the tools and materials necessary, construct the invention, evaluate how it worked, and use the computer to write a news release about the invention for the class newspaper.*

In this example, the teacher connected technology and literacy. Research activities also reinforce social studies.

*Several **second graders** are using three classroom computers. On one computer, Sarah and Latitia record a collection of favorite class jokes for the school newsletter. When they finish, Jerome and Carlos will finish editing their script for a skit and print out the banners they will use as props. Michael and Alice use a software program that requires them to find the missing attributes in a pattern and create a creature that fits the pattern. Noah and Ursula are having trouble mastering their subtraction facts and each practices for ten minutes using software that provides immediate feedback. Johan and Marty compose and send e-mail to children in a second grade class in another state, asking if they would record information about* *how many pounds of paper their school collects for recycling each week. Maria and Adam use the World Wide Web to gather information on methods of recycling. They download pictures as well as information and will include these in their report to the class.*

The children have discovered that one tool, the computer, serves a variety of purposes. They use different programs to write, store data, work on mathematical problems, conduct research, and communicate over distance.

In these classrooms, children are learning about the purposes and uses of tools in history and in our lives. Computers are not used to take a break from the rest of the curriculum but are an integral part of many projects.

What Children Learn

When the technology curriculum is well planned, children have many hands-on experiences where they are involved in design projects and use computers, audio-visual equipment, and many other tools to create, communicate, and solve problems. The technology curriculum in the primary grades should build from children's interest in making things and figuring out how things work to using tools to help get things done.

New approaches to teaching technology in the classroom are advocated by the American Association for the Advancement of Science (AAAS) in three publications: *Science for All Americans* (1990), *Benchmarks for Science Literacy* (1993), and *Blueprints for Reform: Science, Math, and Technology Education* (1998). The National Research Council has developed content standards related to technology in its *National Science Education Standards* (1996). In addition, the International Society for Technology in Education has issued *National Educational Technology Standards for Students* (1998).

The result of this thinking about the nature of technology and its relation to other disciplines has brought consensus about what primary grade children should be doing. Children should:

- do technology projects as well as learn about technology as it applies to other curriculum areas;

- work with many different kinds of materials, learn about their properties and how they are suited to different purposes;

- use a variety of tools and develop understanding about the purposes and functions of these tools;

- explore the design process by beginning with a problem, designing, building, and evaluating a solution;

- understand the role of technology in "collecting, storing, retrieving, and dealing with information as well as in transmitting it" (AAAS 1993, 200); and

- use computers throughout the curriculum to manipulate and store information.

Components of the Technology Curriculum

Many states have developed standards related to technology based on the work of these organizations. Some states have chosen to include technology as part of science or mathematics standards or have integrated it into all content areas; other states have separate standards for technology. Whatever the structure, children should understand these concepts.

- Appreciate how people throughout history have used technology to understand, control, and change the world.

- Learn about and use tools for design.

- Learn about and use computers and other equipment.

Overview of the Technology Curriculum

Components	Children Learn to:
Appreciating Technology	• Demonstrate awareness of examples of technology and the concept of inventions (e.g., telephones, VCRs, can openers, toothbrushes) • Recognize that tools affect how people accomplish things and have positive as well as negative effects • Recognize that tools are made of parts that are connected in particular ways • Compare natural objects with objects made by humans
Learning About and Using Tools for Design	• Recognize that people can design and make objects to solve a problem • Identify a problem that can be solved with technology • Use the design process to propose and implement a solution, evaluate a product or design, and communicate the problem, design, and solution • Use tools to observe (e.g., magnifying glass), measure (e.g., ruler), make things (e.g., hammer, stapler), and communicate (e.g., tape recorder, audio-visual equipment)
Learning About and Using Computers and Other Equipment	• Recognize when and how a computer can be used • Use input devices (e.g., mouse, keyboard, digital cameras, scanners) and output devices (e.g., monitor, printer) to operate computers • Use the computer to communicate, collaborate, publish, and interact with peers, experts, and others • Use the computer to locate, evaluate, and collect information from many sources • Use computer tools (e.g., word processors, drawing programs, multimedia programs) to construct models, prepare publications, and produce creative works • Use computers to solve real-world problems and make decisions • Use laserdisc players, screen capture devices, digital cameras, scanners, graphics tablets, or other equipment as tools for investigation and representation • Demonstrate responsible use of technology, information, and software

Appreciating Technology

Because we are all daily users of technology, we often take it for granted. As primary grade children begin to explore the world around them, they can examine how technology is used in their homes, at school, and at family members' work sites. They can name the tools and machines they use every day and compare how tasks were accomplished before this equipment was available. They can investigate how people in different occupations use technology to do their jobs and, for older students, how jobs have changed over time.

When children study inventions, they perceive that people try to solve problems by creating devices that make work more efficient, or that make play more enjoyable. Making technology education a part of the curriculum encourages teachers to think about tools and to heighten children's knowledge of the history of technology, and the important role of tools in our lives. Children can understand how the tools of technology are important to the scientist, mathematician, engineer, architect, builder, graphic artist, and other workers.

Teachers can think about how to infuse learning about technology into many aspects of their curriculum by having children investigate the tools that are used in many areas. For example, when studying temperature, children can learn about the thermometer; when studying buildings, children can learn about the tools and machines that are used in the construction process; when studying the local post office or fire station, children can explore how computers help people get the job done.

Learning About and Using Tools for Design

By the time children enter school they are experienced users of technology. They ride in automobiles, use household utilities, operate wagons and bikes, use garden tools, help with the cooking, operate the television set, and so on. Children are also natural explorers and inventors; they like to take things apart and make things. School should give children many opportunities to examine the properties of materials, to use tools, and to design and build things. The task in these grades is to channel the students' inventive energy, to increase their purposeful use of tools, and to broaden their understanding of what constitutes a tool, such as a container, paper and pencil, camera, or magnifier (AAAS 1993, 44).

Technological design involves a process (National Research Council 1996, 137).

- Identify a problem.
- Propose a solution.
- Implement a solution.
- Evaluate a product or design.
- Communicate a problem, design, and solution.

Teachers engage children in thinking about problems or needs and then support their efforts to design a solution. There should be real purpose to children's design tasks whether it is "making a device to shade eyes from the sun . . . [or] comparing two types of string to see

which is best for lifting different objects" (National Research Council 1996, 137). These types of activities allow children to make choices. They must evaluate the effectiveness of different materials for making things. A material might be stronger, for example, but much harder to shape or cut (AAAS 1993, 188). As children think about and use tools in the design process, they come to appreciate that tools have different and special purposes; that tools help us to accomplish specific tasks; and that it is important to select the appropriate tool for the job.

Learning About and Using Computers

In just a few years, computers and connections to the Internet have come to be regarded as essential in every classroom. While we must not assume that computers alone will improve student learning, computers and computer-linked resources like the Internet are here to stay. It is important that teachers integrate this technology into the curriculum in ways that support meaningful and engaging learning.

The kinds of learning experiences children have on computers should enable them to:

- question, explore, create, solve problems, and make decisions;
- use computer programs to record information and publish stories on their own, with a partner, in a small group, or with the entire class;
- send and receive information, using e-mail as a vehicle to promote communication as well as reading and writing; and
- seek information, determine its usefulness, and draw conclusions or make generalizations about the information gathered (recognizing that teacher input is required to evaluate content for most children until third grade).

Obviously, using computers shouldn't change what you teach, in terms of content, collaboration, and communication. Rather, by building computer use into existing activities the technology can support worthwhile learning projects in the classroom. An important aspect of providing experiences that lead toward acquisition of these skills is to capitalize on the way computer use fits into building a classroom community. With computers, children can work in small groups to brainstorm ideas about the information needed and different ways to present it, to make decisions and draw conclusions about the information gathered, and to share their information with others.

We have discussed the importance of building a classroom community to help teachers address children's basic needs, promote their resilience to hardship conditions, teach the values of respect and responsibility, and foster their social and academic competence. Through technology, the walls of the classroom have come down and the community is much larger. Children can communicate via e-mail with people in other cities, states, or countries.

An equally important aspect of learning computer skills is to help children think about ethical behavior and responsibility. Children can practice behavior that demonstrates values important to us all—respect for ownership, privacy, and property. Here are some of the ways children can learn about these values related to technology.

Respect for Ownership. New technology makes it very easy to copy someone else's work from a web site or electronic encyclopedia and paste it into a report. You can initiate a discussion during a class meeting with a question such as "How would you feel if someone took something from your backpack or desk?"

Respect for Privacy and Confidentiality. You help children learn to respect the privacy of others' files, disks, and e-mail when you talk with children about respecting each other's private journals, and keeping secrets told in confidence. With the technology in the classroom, you can teach children to respect privacy by only opening e-mail or files that belong to them, or those they have permission to look at.

Respect for Property. In the classroom you talk about what materials are shared and which are personal. The same principles apply to technology. Children learn to care for actual hardware and software that all share. Other kinds of property—electronic information such as files and data—cannot be held in the hand, but are virtual property. You help children understand that erasing a friend's story from a diskette or changing the data on another person's project shows disrespect for another person's property. You can also help children to understand how a computer virus or worm can be spread and the precautions that need to be taken to prevent this from happening.

Integrating Technology Across the Curriculum

Just having computers in your classroom and being wired for the Internet will not necessarily enhance learning. What is important is how you use the technology. Think about the technology as another tool to help children construct knowledge. When technology is integrated into the curriculum and your instructional practices, children can acquire a deeper understanding of key concepts and are able to use technology to strengthen their understanding in language and literacy, math, science, social studies, and the arts. When planning how to integrate technology, think about the principles discussed in Chapter 4, Guiding Children's Learning.

Learning should be purposeful and relevant to children's lives. Is there a clear purpose in using the technology to enhance learning? Is this use of technology appropriate for the age of the children?

Meaningful learning is integrated. How can I integrate technology into the different subject areas? How can I incorporate technology in a natural way rather than as an add-on subject? What other kinds of supporting materials do I have available?

Communication is central to learning. How can I design activities that will increase communication and collaboration? How can I use technology to help children communicate with others outside of the classroom?

Learning takes time. How will I schedule time for online and classroom activities? How can I help children use productivity tools with any topic we are studying throughout the year?

Use what children know to build purposeful and meaningful activities. Knowing the goals for your technology curriculum will help you make decisions as you plan for long-term studies, work time in the content areas, and, of course, those teachable moments. There are some general principles for using technology in a meaningful way.

- Make sure the technology activity is appropriate for the child's age and ability level. Preview all software and Internet sites to make the most of instructional time.

- Link the technology activity to a child's experiences and interests.

- Begin with first-hand experiences and social interaction before using technology (e.g., learn how to read a thermometer and practice asking appropriate questions before asking e-mail pals about their climate or interviewing a meteorologist online).

- Guide children in developing a meaningful way to represent what they have learned (e.g., while studying a nearby river, insert photos of boats and ships taken with a digital camera into a report written using a word processor).

- Support children in planning and completing long-term studies that incorporate the use of technology.

Learning About and Using Technology in Long-Term Studies

When children work on long-term studies about topics of interest, teachers can think about how and when to incorporate technology learning throughout the study. What children do and learn will depend on what is appropriate at each stage of development.

A long-term study of the nearby **firehouse** offers many opportunities for **first graders** to think about technology. Children might:

- observe the tools, machines, and equipment used by firefighters—hoses, ladders, trucks, protective clothing;
- study how the warning sounds and lights on the trucks are made;
- find out how computers help firefighters pinpoint the location of the fire on a street map after receiving a 911 call;
- learn how to make a 911 call and what important information to report;
- list the number of false alarms vs. actual fires or medical emergencies that a station records in a week or month and share this information with children in another community;
- find out about the technology we can have in our homes to warn about fire and to put out fires (e.g., smoke detectors and fire extinguishers);
- find out who decides when and how to use each piece of equipment in fire-fighting situations;
- examine fire safety rules and fire-fighting equipment at school;
- discuss fire escape plans and routes at home and at school; and
- consider how fires were put out long ago before some of this equipment was available.

When a **third grade** class studies how **Native Americans** lived in their community long ago, they might use the overarching theme of how tools influence people's lives—how they build houses, hunt or grow food, cook, travel, and communicate. Teacher-selected CD-ROMs, as well as carefully selected sites on the Internet, could facilitate the research process. To explore this topic, children might:

- build a boat that floats and then compare the tools and materials they used with the ones that were available to the particular tribe they studied;
- identify how our lives today differ from those of Native Americans long ago as a result of particular inventions such as matches or refrigerators;
- communicate through e-mail with children who live on a reservation; and
- create a replica of a Native American village, keeping a record of the design process, and the pros and cons of using different materials.

Children studying a local **body of water**—a river, stream, canal, or bay—might investigate:

- how people transport goods;
- what tools are needed to analyze temperature, salinity, drinking water safety;
- when and how those tools were invented and how they influenced what we know;
- how water is used to produce power; and
- how bridges and tunnels are built.

They could share information or seek information with children in schools up or down river or living near a different body of water.

In Guiding Children's Learning, we described a process for planning a long-term study and integrating content from many subject areas. In the chapter on Mathematical Thinking, we showed a chart that a teacher made to think about how to integrate specific activities related to math into a study of a construction site. The following chart shows how that same teacher might incorporate technology learning into the study of the construction site.

Study of a Construction Site

Components	Children Learn to:
Appreciating Technology	• Observe and keep records about how each piece of machinery and tool is used—e.g., to lift, to dig, to communicate, to break apart objects. • Find out about protective gear that had to be invented to make this new equipment safe—e.g., ear guards for noise protection. • Explore several pieces of machinery in more depth to figure out their parts and how they are put together—e.g., dumptruck or ditch digger. • Compare how holes are made in the ground naturally, e.g., by the force of water, and various objects that could be used to dig holes intentionally—cups, shovels, motorized equipment.
Learning About and Using Tools	• Design and build a bookshelf for the classroom or a cage for the class pet. • Design and build a physical model of the building under construction.
Learning About and Using Computers	• Use a computer design program to illustrate blueprints or design a home. • Create a computer design of the classroom. • Use a spreadsheet program to keep track of the data collected related to the construction project. • Prepare a presentation on the study using the word processors, graphics programs, or multimedia applications. • Use a digital camera to take pictures at the site at different stages of the construction process and use the photos in a timeline.

Learning About and Using Technology During Work Times

While there may be selected weeks during the year when children investigate specific inventions or design and build things at an invention area or construction table, there can be opportunities throughout the year for children to learn about and use technology during specific math, language and literacy, music, art, science, or social studies activities.

- During measurement work in **math**, children can learn about rulers and thermometers as inventions. These tools enabled people to build accurately and use heat and cold safely. They e-mail children from around the world and make a graph of temperatures.

- As part of an ongoing **language and literacy** project, children can read books about tools and machines. Children might also write about their own inventions. They can use books about inventions on CD-ROMs to support learning to read.

- Children can design and build **musical** instruments and write music using special software on the computer and play it using keyboards equipped with MIDI devices.

- During an **art** activity using paint, children might explore how different brushes or other art tools create various effects. They can also explore the different shapes and widths of brushes on electronic paint programs.

- As part of **science** investigations, children can consider how the tools they are using— e.g., magnifying glasses, microscopes, scales—enable them to be better observers and data collectors.

- In **social studies**, children gain a sense of the past as they study toys from long ago. Grandparents visit the class and share toys from their childhood. The children compare toys from long ago with toys of today. They examine the gears on wind-up toys and learn how a battery turns on a switch. The teacher bookmarks a web site that allows children to take a virtual tour of a toy museum. Children draw a model of a new toy they would like to invent.

Using Teachable Moments to Incorporate Technology Use

Being aware of technology and its importance in the overall curriculum enables teachers to incorporate technology into many areas of classroom life. In Chapter 2, Building a Classroom Community, we describe the importance of class meetings in helping children learn to listen to one another, develop speaking skills, exchange information, share different points of view, as well as learn particular skills and content, and learn to reflect on their learning. In the examples that follow, teachers use video equipment to help the community-building process.

- A teacher uses a video camera to record several class meetings. The children then view the video on several occasions, once to help them think about how they could learn to take turns better, another time to evaluate whether they were really looking at the speaker, and a third time to generate rules for class meetings.

- After viewing a videotape of their clean-up time, a group of children decides to change the number of children assigned to specific jobs to even out the workload.

- A group of children videotape a skit they wrote, "How to Use Computers Responsibly" and share it with other classes.

- Children in classrooms in two different parts of the country ask questions about each other's life at school, via videoconferencing.

- A teacher encourages children who are hesitant about speaking up at meetings to read books and tell stories into a tape recorder and share them with younger students to gain confidence.

Making Computers Work in the Classroom

Because computers can be exciting additions to the classroom with their magic buttons, access to flashy pictures and information, and many bells and whistles, teachers should be particularly thoughtful about the purposes of these expensive tools and how they will best serve the children. If computers are an add-on to the curriculum, it will be almost impossible to find the time for some children to use them and others will use them to keep busy after their "real work" is done. When computers are a tool for learning, just as markers, pencils, paper, and books are, then children can use them in many classroom activities and all subject areas. Computer use must complement a well-planned curriculum.

As children enter the primary grades, many still focus on one attribute at a time. When children at this stage of development sit at a computer, they may only focus on the mechanics of the computer, such as clicking the mouse, and may miss the entire purpose of the activity. To be effective, technology activities should be designed around the developmental needs of the child.

Teachers have a responsibility to help children use their time well at the computer. Just as you preselect books that are appropriate for a child's reading level, you preselect sites on the World Wide Web. First and second grade students may look for information on the Internet as part of a small group activity with teacher assistance, while third graders can be expected to explore sites independently that have been previewed and bookmarked by the teacher.

There is so much information available at the click of a button that it is very easy to become entrenched in a technology curriculum that has been described as a mile wide and an inch deep. Time can be wasted just downloading information and pictures to make a poster pretty rather than learning something new, thinking about it, and using it to connect with other information. Careful planning and thinking about what you want children to know and be able to do will help you use instructional time at the computer wisely and efficiently.

E-mail can be used as a vehicle to interest children in the power of communication and give them another reason to learn to read. By typing in the word *e-pals* on a search engine on the Internet, you can find many schools and classes that are interested in communicating. Here's an example of how several classes connected through e-mail and learned about life in other parts of the country.

> *First graders read the book* Flat Stanley *by Jeff Brown. The book describes a boy who got smashed by a bulletin board and his family mailed him to visit a friend in California. For this project, each child drew a picture of Flat Stanley and wrote in a class journal about their own community. They mailed the pictures and journal to one or more schools in a different state. Before sending the pictures and journal, the class compiled an e-mail message to let the other school know Flat Stanley was coming. Every class that receives the message will do the same project writing about its own community. Children track Flat Stanley's travels on a large map.*

Becoming Computer Literate

If you are uncomfortable with computers, the best way to begin is to explore the computer on your own and gain experience with the technology. When you yourself are comfortable with computers it will be easier for you to guide children's learning. While schools or districts offer professional development opportunities with hands-on experience with computers, the time is often limited. If you have little experience with computers or are unfamiliar with the software you have been given, you may feel uncomfortable about having computers in your classroom. Talk to other teachers in your school; find out who knows about computers and software. Ask for a lesson. The children in your class, too, are often excellent resources.

In order to make good decisions you need to be familiar with the terminology. Computer ***hardware*** refers to the physical equipment, including the CPU or central processing unit, the monitor, keyboard, mouse, scanners, printers, zip drives, disk drives, CD-ROM drives, and digital cameras. The programs you choose to run on the machines are called ***software.*** Nowadays, most software comes on CD-ROMs. CD-ROMs, which look like music CDs, are disks that contain large amounts of information—equivalent to about 350,000 pages of text— in one place. For example, there are CD-ROMs that contain entire encyclopedias, the complete works of Shakespeare, and many multi-media, interactive games and puzzles. In addition, software programs can be downloaded from the Internet. A *shareware* program is one that is downloaded from the Internet but users must pay a fee in order to access the full program. Be aware, though, that just because software is free doesn't necessarily mean that it is a good program. Just as you evaluate other educational materials for effectiveness, you must also examine software.

Children's work can be saved on a:

- hard drive inside the CPU;
- floppy diskette;
- zip disk (which holds the equivalent of 70 floppy disks); or
- re-writable CD-ROM.

In addition, children's drawings, photos, or handwritten stories can be scanned and made into a computer slide show or an electronic portfolio.

The ***Internet*** is a vast network of more than 100,000 interconnected smaller networks in over 100 countries worldwide comprised of commercial (.com), academic (.edu), and government (.gov) systems. It has been dubbed the information superhighway because of the extensive amounts of information available on every subject. Through virtual reality on the Internet, children can walk through a museum or tour a hospital. They can see how scientists and technicians use virtual reality to build a car, perform an operation, or design a building.

In order to be able to access the Internet, your school needs an access provider, which can be a major online service (such as America Online) or any of a number of local, regional, or national Internet Service Providers (ISPs). Then you need a way to connect. Until recently, this connection has been a modem, which uses a phone line to access the Internet. More and more schools have become wired for the Internet with fiber-optic cabling or a cable modem service. Finally you need browser software (Netscape Navigator or Microsoft Explorer), which is normally supplied by your computer manufacturer or Internet provider. There is also browser software designed especially for children with a feature that filters inappropriate sites. Even when using the best filtering software, sometimes inappropriate sites may appear. Teachers should continue to preview and bookmark appropriate sites for children this age rather than letting them surf the net.

The ***World Wide Web,*** often used synonymously with the Internet, is actually only one part of the Internet. The Internet also includes newsgroups, chat rooms, and, of course, electronic mail, known as e-mail (the most commonly used application on the Internet). The World Wide Web became a center of Internet activity because of the great amount of information one could access in the form of Web pages via a Web browser, such as Netscape Navigator or Microsoft Explorer.

It is even possible now to connect to the Internet without having a computer! Devices such as WebTV enable you to connect a keyboard to a television set. One drawback to WebTV, though, is that you do not have the ability to download or print information.

Safety on the Internet

Millions of people now use the Internet to exchange e-mail, surf web sites, and participate in chat rooms. While ISPs generally do everything they can to provide a safe online experience, they cannot police everyone who uses their services. Once you are connected to the Internet, you're able to exchange information with people you don't know. Even though most people have positive experiences using the Internet, there are risks involved. Children, who are trusting, curious, and anxious to explore, can be the targets of crime and exploitation. Primary grade children should not surf the net without adult supervision. Some of the risks involved in using e-mail, the World Wide Web, or other online services include exposure to inappropriate material, harassment, or legal or financial consequences. Teachers using online features should discuss the following safety rules with children and post them by the computer.

- Never give out personal information such as your address, telephone number, parents' work address/telephone number, or the name and location of your school without your teachers' permission.

- Tell your teacher right away if you come across any information that makes you feel uncomfortable.

- Never agree to get together with someone you meet online.

- Never send a person your picture or anything else without first checking with your teacher.

- Do not respond to any messages that are mean or in any way make you feel uncomfortable. It is not your fault if you get a message like that. If you do, tell your teacher right away so that the online service can be contacted.

Making Decisions About Software

Many wonderful programs (software) that you can use with your children do not depend on the Internet. Whether or not children will spend their time usefully on the computer depends in part on the software that is available to them. To select good software, think about your goals and whether each package meets them. Try the software yourself to become familiar with the format. Demonstration software is often available on the Internet so that you can download and preview the application (program). Software can be expensive, so it's best to seek out some objective sources of information. Start by talking to other teachers or technology specialists in your school or district. Many school, community, or university libraries often have sample software or journals that review software. There are also Internet sites with reviews of children's software.

Some software helps children construct the correct answer following a mistake; some provides reinforcement if a child has difficulty. Other software lets children work together to solve open-ended problems and make discoveries. While drill work with paper and pencil can be tedious, some children make good progress practicing math facts or other repetitive tasks in interesting ways on the computer. Be aware that some of these programs may include violence, such as blowing up answers, and consider whether you think that is appropriate.

Make sure that you have a variety of software in the classroom that relates to how and what you are teaching in other areas of the curriculum. You also want children to have experience with many different kinds of programs. Consider this example.

A group of second graders learning about weights and measures are using tools to take apart old bathroom scales in the classroom fix-it center. They also use a software program called The Way Things Work *by David MacCaulay to see a model of a bathroom scale, hear an explanation of the scientific principles of how gears work, and find out about the history of the scale. The children later create different kinds of scales to weigh things in the classroom.*

Primary grade children should be exposed to word-processing programs. Some children, especially those with learning disabilities who have difficulty writing with pencil and paper, may be more comfortable writing on the computer. There are also inexpensive portable keyboards that can be used for word processing.

Many good drawing and painting programs are available for children. Look for programs that encourage originality, creativity, and inventiveness. Some drawing programs include clip art and a menu of backgrounds from which to choose. While this might seem to make it easier for children, it is less creative. Graphic tablets are another way to create original drawings and have them appear on the computer for editing or incorporating into a report or presentation.

The publications and web sites in the Resources section at the end of the chapter will help you to select software. The following questions and guidelines can help you conduct your own review of software packages.

Is the software age appropriate? The software should match children's skill levels. Is the material presented using pictorial representation or does it rely on abstract ability? Do picture icons represent ideas or directions so that children are likely to figure out what to do on their own?

Can children work independently? Look for software that children can use independently while still making choices. You don't want children to be trapped in a program they can't use properly and be unable to change or stop. Recognize that children will experiment with all the options. Make sure that the program will not lose anything.

Is the pace right? Children, like adults, become impatient with programs that take too long to do things. If the program takes a long time to load or too long for graphics to appear, children may lose interest. If the program moves too fast, children may get frustrated and give up.

Is the content open-ended? This is the heart of any review. If the computer is to be used as a tool for investigation, there has to be something to investigate. This means the process should hold children's interest and be worth exploring. There should be different ways to do things and several ways to go about solving the problem. Can the children's ideas be incorporated into the program?

Can children use the program in different ways? Because children are at different developmental levels, the better software products will allow you and the children to set varying levels of difficulty and to control features such as the speed of the program and the sound level. Children should be able to learn different things from the content as well.

Can children work together? Some programs encourage children to work with others to consider alternatives, make decisions, and alter the course. Children can make their own creations or design and build a project.

Does the program offer rewards for winning? Be wary of software programs that offer too many rewards, bells, or whistles. These types of programs usually focus on getting the right answer and are less concerned with the process.

Is the program free from bias relating to gender, culture, or handicapping conditions? Are both girls and boys portrayed in the software as problem-solvers? Is there stereotyping of roles or ethnic groups? Are there ways that children with special needs can use the program?

Can children succeed without elaborate instruction? Good software enables children to figure out what to do on their own, without excessive (or maybe any) instruction. Appropriate software helps children become less dependent on the teacher.

Will the software run on your computer? Hardware and software have to be compatible for programs to work properly. Check the requirements carefully before you purchase software.

In addition to the appropriateness of the software, other considerations should influence your choices as well. Find out what teacher-support materials are available and whether there are record-keeping functions for keeping track of children's work. There are some programs that enable you to create a separate desktop for each child using the software. While this allows you to custom design programs for each child and control access, it can discourage children from working together because each child has his or her own set of programs.

Children love to save their computer work and, when possible, take it to their next year's classroom. If your school is not on a network, you may want to consider putting individual work on a disk to be transferred to the computer in the next year's classroom.

Planning the Environment and Scheduling Time

For young children, the most appropriate place to use computers is in the classroom rather than a computer lab. When computers are accessible throughout the day, they can be used as part of many investigations or representation activities as appropriate. Try to arrange the space so that several children can work on the computer or computers at a time. If you can cluster multiple computers, children working on adjacent computers can collaborate and critique one another's work. Placing two or more chairs around a computer will encourage social interaction and problem solving.

There are many logistics to consider when setting up your computer area. Oftentimes the source of electricity or telephone jack will dictate the location of your computer area. Make sure that you can see the computer screen from other parts of the classroom, and that all of the basic supplies, such as diskettes and printer paper, are nearby. Locate the area away from water, art materials, or other things that might damage the computer, such as magnets.

If you have a child in a wheelchair, be sure to consider space and table height. At the end of this chapter, there are examples of assistive devices to ensure that all children have equal access to technology.

In most cases you will have few computers and many children. Some software exists that is intended to be used by a whole class using a projection device (e.g., Tom Snyder's *Decisions, Decisions* series). However, most computer projection devices are expensive. An alternative is to have a computer-to-TV connector that will allow the images seen on your computer screen to appear on the TV. If you are searching for information on a web site or reading e-mail with a group of children, viewing the information together can be helpful. You can also use this to introduce new software to the whole class. More often, though, children will work independently—alone, in pairs, or in small groups. Because computer use is usually a popular activity, teachers need a way to schedule children so that time on the computer is equitable.

You may find these suggestions helpful.

- Have children sign up for computer time.
- Organize children into cooperative groups for computer activities. Each student in the group can have a specific job such as text writer, calculator, graphics, chart maker, presenter, etc.
- Post a visual display near the computer to indicate who has or has not been to the area. After spending time on the computer, a child can move a clothespin with his name on it from a column labeled "No" to "Yes." When everyone has had a turn, move all the clothespins back to the "No" column.
- Have children place index cards with their names written on them into library pockets to indicate that they have used the computer.
- Ask children to place an object, such as a small flag or paper cup, on top of the computer monitor when they need help. Some children can be designated "experts" who can provide assistance for particular software programs.

Because you want children to be engaged in their work at the computer, some systems (such as a timer that rings after ten minutes) may undermine efforts to engage children in meaningful work. Balance is the key. Keep in mind that the computer is only one of many learning tools in the classroom. Children should not use it as their only resource.

Other Equipment

f course, computers are not the only high-tech equipment available for classroom use. You may find you have access to other equipment as well.

Laserdisc (Videodisc) Player. A laserdisc resembles a CD-ROM but is quite different. It produces high-quality video images and stores the equivalent of 5,000 floppy disks! Laserdiscs are *read-only,* which means that you cannot record information on them. You must have a laserdisc player rather than a computer to show them. Many laserdiscs come with a teacher's guide with preprinted barcodes. For example, if you have a laserdisc about weather and want to show children what a real tornado looks like, you simply pass a special pen over the barcode to access that segment.

Screen Capture Device. A screen capture device (e.g., "Snappy") allows you to connect a VCR to your computer and grab either a still shot or a short video clip and import it into a document or presentation.

Digital Cameras. Digital cameras, both still and video, have become more reasonably priced for classroom use. Some cameras store approximately 50 pictures in the unit before you download them to a computer through a cable. Other cameras use a floppy disk that you simply remove from the camera and insert into your computer. Digital cameras do not use film and produce instant results. Pictures can be stored on the computer and integrated into stories or other documents. Teachers can take pictures of children's 3-D artwork or constructions and use them as documentation in a child's electronic portfolio. In addition, relatively inexpensive videoconferencing cameras can be connected to the computer. Children can meet face-to-face with an expert on a topic or chat with children in another part of the world.

Scanners. Scanners, which work almost like a copy machine, can be used to turn children's artwork, writing, or photos into digital images. These images can be placed into documents created on a word processor, paint program, slide presentation program, or desktop publisher. Once the images are digitized, you can change their appearance using special software.

Graphics Tablet. A graphics tablet that is connected to the computer allows children to draw freehand with a stylus and see the image appear on the computer screen. Once the image is on the screen, children can use a paint program to color the image.

Using Assistive Technology

Assistive technology helps children with disabilities to communicate, learn, play, move about, and be as independent as possible. Often, such technology enables children to participate more fully in daily classroom activities. Not only is assistive technology beneficial, but it is also mandated by law for children with disabilities when appropriate. A child's IEP (Individualized Education Plan) will determine the need for assistive technology. Choosing the right assistive technology for a child is a challenging and complex task and usually involves the collaborative efforts of a team of professionals including the classroom teacher, occupational therapists, physical therapists, speech/language pathologists, and assistive technology specialists.

Assistive technology devices may incorporate simple tools such as switches to turn on a battery-operated object. More high-tech devices include alternative keypads, touch screens, speech synthesizers, and voice recognition devices. These special devices allow all children access to the world of technology.

Portable keyboards (such as AlphaSmart or Dream Writer) are an appropriate alternative for those students with disabilities who can type well enough to use a standard keyboard but for whom handwriting is not fast or neat. They are relatively inexpensive, are lightweight, and do not have a screen like a laptop. As children type a story, they view text on a small screen on the keyboard. Later the keyboard is attached to a computer and by hitting *send*, the text is transferred to a computer where it can be edited and printed.

Most important, assistive technology enables children with disabilities to participate in all classroom activities, whether it is writing a story or working on a long-term study.

Closing Thoughts

As technology becomes more important in our everyday life, we can offer children appropriate technology learning that will help them explore, question, and solve problems. We want children to appreciate technology through the study of inventions and tools, to engage in the design process by building things for a purpose, and to learn about and use computers and other equipment as part of many ongoing classroom projects.

References and Resources for Technology

American Association for the Advancement of Science, Project 2061. 1993. *Benchmarks for Science Literacy.* New York, NY: Oxford University Press.

American Association for the Advancement of Science, Project 2061. 1998. *Blueprints for Reform: Science, Math, and Technology Education.* New York, NY: Oxford University Press.

Healy, Jane M. 1998. *Failure to Connect: How Computers Affect Our Children's Minds—for Better and Worse.* New York, NY: Simon and Schuster.

International Society for Technology Education. 1998. *National Educational Technology Standards for Students.* Eugene, OR: author.

Morton, Jessica. 1998. *Kids on the 'Net: Conducting Internet Research in K–5 Classrooms.* Portsmouth, NH: Heinemann.

National Association for the Education of Young Children. 1996. *Technology and Young Children—Ages 3 through 8: A Position Statement of the National Association for the Education of Young Children.* Washington, DC: NAEYC.

National Research Council. 1996. *National Science Education Standards.* Washington, DC: National Academy Press.

Rutherford, F. James, and Andrew Ahlgren. American Association for the Advancement of Science. 1990. *Science for All Americans.* New York, NY: Oxford University Press.

Wright, June L., and Daniel D. Shade, eds. 1994. *Young Children: Active Learners in a Technological Age.* Washington, DC: NAEYC.

The following web sites review educational software for teachers and parents:

California Instructional Technology Clearinghouse
http://clearinghouse.k12.ca.us

Children's Software Revue
http://www2.childrenssoftware.com

SuperKids Educational Software
http://www.superkids.com

tech.LEARNING
http://www.techlearning.com

THE ARTS

The arts are a natural part of children's experience. Children love to design, make, and do things with materials and tools. They mix paints, pound clay, and build structures with blocks, cartons, or other materials. They solve problems when they plan a dance sequence, write a play, or design a mural. When children *do* art, they experience the joy of rhythm and music, and the satisfaction of using tools effectively.

The arts give children opportunities to reflect on and express their ideas and feelings in another language, one that does not rely on words and numbers. In addition, arts activities may come naturally to children because they allow children to relax and be playful. As children paint, design, construct, mold, sketch, weave, sing, dance, and act, they discover new things and integrate what they are learning about their world. For these reasons, including materials for the arts in the classroom and providing time for children to use them on a daily basis enriches the curriculum.

Some adults readily engage in creative activities. They may play an instrument, dance with a community group, or take photos and develop their own film. Perhaps they make all the gifts they give. If you are interested or talented in these ways, you are likely to be comfortable with your ability to incorporate the arts in your classroom. Many of us, however, are not dancers, or portrait artists, or musicians. We may feel uncomfortable about areas we think require special talents, and worry about not being "good enough" to teach these subjects. We say, "I can't draw well," or "I can't carry a tune." If you feel that you do not have enough time or talent to include the arts in your program, we hope that this chapter will help you see how they can become a natural part of your teaching.

Children and the Arts

The activities and projects that we label *the arts* are a means through which children construct knowledge, investigate, and represent what they are learning. Previous chapters illustrated how arts experiences are tools for children's learning in the other subject areas. In this chapter, we show how such experiences also give children knowledge and skills in the arts as disciplines in their own right.

The following scenes will seem familiar and could have appeared in other chapters. Read them here and see them through a new lens, a lens that views the arts as a crucial part of instruction.

> *Several children in Ms. Peters'* **second grade** *paint a mural depicting their trip to the apple orchard. Through this activity they relive the trip and recall many details. They experiment with the blue and yellow paint, mixing two primary colors to get just the right shade of green for the leaves. "Add just a dot more yellow, not a glob," says Jason excitedly. "Cool," says Monica. Ms. Peters suggests that they can make the leaves look shiny by adding liquid detergent to the paint.*

Mural making extends and reinforces what the children have learned about apple orchards, and simultaneously, provides an excellent opportunity for children to use painting as a way to represent and communicate their ideas. As they go about recreating a scene from their earlier observations, they develop understanding about color, line, texture, and perspective.

> *Mr. Cantor just finished reading aloud* Justin and the Best Biscuits in the World *by Mildred Pitts Walter. He asks, "What could we do that would give everyone a chance to show what they liked about this book?" The children brainstorm the following ideas: do a skit, create a mural of scenes, prepare biscuits, make dioramas. They talk about the kinds of ideas they want to represent. After agreeing on three projects, they divide into groups to plan how they will begin.*

This **third grade** teacher encourages the children to demonstrate their ideas in a variety of ways. In the process, they explore different forms of expression and gain a deeper understanding of content. A lesson conceived as a way to discuss the ideas and language in a book is enhanced when children can express their ideas creatively through arts-related projects.

When you include the arts, you expand children's repertoire of experiences. If you planned painting activities that were unconnected to what was going on in the classroom, you may now think about encouraging an arts activity connected to a social studies project. If you considered a field trip to explore neighborhood stores, think now about having children create a mural showing these stores. Drawing pictures in a journal to record science observations might now become part of a long-term project to collect data over time and analyze the results. As you become more familiar with different forms of creative expression, you and the children can learn about the materials, tools, techniques, language, and ways of thinking about each area of the arts.

The Role of the Arts in the Curriculum

n 1998, U.S. Secretary of Education Richard Riley said, "In this age of information when our economy is increasingly built on generating ideas, it is a serious mistake to shortchange our children's instruction in the arts" (Riley 1998). To prepare children to live in the 21st century, they need an education that builds persistence and production skills. At the same time, they also need to think imaginatively and creatively to generate the ideas Secretary Riley believes our economy is built upon. A well-developed arts education program can guide children toward these goals.

Interest in making arts education an integral part of the curriculum has prompted a number of groups to define a new way of thinking about education in the arts. The *National Standards for Arts Education* (1994) identifies the knowledge and skills in the arts that are important for children to acquire and describes how the arts can integrate all subjects and extend learning across the curriculum. The Task Force on Children's Learning and the Arts: Birth to Age 8 (1998) also developed a Position Paper on arts education.

The joint conclusion is that the arts are both important in their own right and tools for learning. The arts:

- foster learning experiences that hold the interest of children;
- encourage problem solving;
- stimulate understanding of other people's ways of living and culture;
- enhance non-verbal communication; and
- provide a way to develop competence in new arenas.

As disciplines, the arts are "a way of knowing" (CNAEA 1994, 8). Children can learn the vocabularies and techniques associated with the various art forms, as they sing together, create dances and songs, skits and plays, and visual art. They "learn in, through, and about the arts by actively engaging in the process of creating, participating in/performing, and responding to quality arts experiences, adapted to their developmental levels and reflecting their own culture" (Task Force 1998).

In this section we define the arts and show how they can extend and enrich learning in all other subjects.

Defining the Arts

The arts include the visual arts—painting, drawing, molding, sculpting, weaving, designing, and constructing—as well as the performing arts—music, dance, and drama. We believe the arts have the power to develop the thinking and imaginative abilities of children as they explore and learn about their world (Sautter 1994, 433). We do not believe that the arts are pleasant diversions from the core academic basics of schools. Nor should the arts simply serve as programmatic add-ons to fill out the school day. Both of those traditional ways of viewing arts education limit the purpose of the arts.

During the course of the school year children can become familiar with a variety of art media, including:

- painting and drawing (with crayons, markers, pencils, scratch-art panels, chalk, pens, watercolors, tempra paints, and acrylics);

- printmaking processes (stamping, etching, block printing, monoprinting, rubbing);

- modeling (using firing and non-firing clays, plasticine);

- assemblage and collage (connecting varied materials in two- and three-dimensional arrangements using glue, paste, tape, staplers);

- puppetry (using newspaper, papier maché, stick and felt finger and hand puppets);

- fiber arts and sewing (loom and off-loom weaving, stitching).

Other activities included in the arts are singing, dancing, creating skits and plays, and storytelling. Using video and audio equipment, computer drawing programs, and blocks also enhances the arts curriculum.

What Children Learn

When the arts become an integral part of the curriculum and instruction, children gain valuable skills and knowledge.

- They use a variety of media for communication and expression.

- They develop aesthetic knowledge and appreciation for many forms of expression.

- They solve problems using various media materials.

- They learn about the world around them through their senses.

- They develop an understanding of others and themselves.

As such, the arts constitute both a separate subject in the curriculum and a means to integrate other subjects. With this in mind, we will describe what and how children can learn in the arts. Then we will discuss how experiences in the arts enrich other subjects.

Using a Variety of Media for Communication and Expression

When teachers provide different kinds of materials and opportunities for expression, children with varying skills and talents will be able to find something of interest to them. How will they do this? To properly engage with the materials, children need time to explore them. They also need time to discover different ways to express their ideas and feelings and create their own representations. You can offer special choice times that allow for unstructured experimentation. The following are some examples of the kinds of media you might present and ways children can explore and express themselves.

- Paint with different sized brushes or sponges on different kinds of paper or wood.
- Model with clay, plasticine, papier-maché.
- Make collages using different textures.
- Find different ways to attach objects together to create three-dimensional constructions.
- Create a dance after hearing a new piece of music.
- Record sounds and talk about how they make you feel.
- Create a drawing that describes a mood.

Developing Aesthetic Knowledge and Appreciation

When children create, design, make, or perform—when they are artists—they gain an appreciation for the creative work of others as well as their own. As they figure out how to make things happen in a particular way, children develop a deeper understanding of color, line, shape, balance, pattern, rhythm, movement, and texture.

Each art form comes with its own vocabulary and offers its own learning experiences. For example, experiences with music give children opportunities to learn about rhythm, melody, aspects of pitch, loudness, and simultaneous sounds as well as the great variety of different kinds of music. When children dance, they learn about space, time, and dynamics; when they follow a dance routine, they evaluate how the movement expresses someone else's ideas. Children explore dramatic expression when they make up skits based on a known or imaginary story, role play how a problem could be solved, or watch plays and discuss the production.

Children can do many things to develop aesthetic knowledge and appreciation.

- Listen to many different kinds of music in the classroom.
- Attend concerts, dance performances, and plays.
- Examine the work of different artists and illustrators.
- Explore the way different structures are built.
- Play musical instruments or dance.

Solving Problems Using a Variety of Media and Materials

When we think about problem-solving opportunities for children, we tend to focus on mathematical thinking. But, when children draw, they solve problems too. Consider the child who is trying to draw a road and wants to show that one section is nearby and another is far away. As the child experiments, talks with friends, and looks in picture books, she solves the problem by using perspective. When children create and critique works of art, they consider multiple perspectives, recognize that there can be many ways to solve problems, and make choices among various approaches. The arts then, provide a way of developing problem-solving abilities.

Drawing, talking, modeling, writing, critiquing, and experimenting are effective ways for children to learn problem-solving skills while they consider choices and make decisions. Here are some examples of problem solving in the arts. Children can:

- decide how to make a sculpture from recycled materials;
- create scenery and props for a play;
- make up new words to a familiar tune to use in a report on a topic;
- create a computer program that makes stars appear randomly in different colors on the screen; or
- combine dance steps across the floor while changing level, direction, or tempo.

Learning About the World Around Them

The arts allow children to sharpen their abilities to learn through their senses. Sensory learning is important in view of recent brain research that indicates that each sensory experience creates connections between brain cells. Repeated experiences solidify these connections. Thus, the arts provide an excellent opportunity to help wire children's brains for successful learning. Consider these ways children use their senses in the arts.

- They use a variety of textures and materials in a sculpture.
- They pantomime various jobs of people in the community.
- They create sound effects for a class play using everyday objects.
- They imitate movements of different kinds of animals.

Develop an Understanding of Others and Themselves

As children learn about art in different cultures and eras, they become aware of people's lives, beliefs, and ways of expressing themselves. They also become better able to think about, understand, describe, and respect the origins of their own culture and environment. Here are some examples of what children might do as they develop this understanding.

- Create musical instruments used in different parts of the world.
- Learn dances that were popular in different eras in history such as the waltz, charleston, and jitterbug.
- Make crafts that children enjoy in other parts of the world.
- Dramatize a folktale from another country.

How the Arts Enhance Other Subjects

As noted earlier, experiences with artistic expression have appeared throughout this book as a means to express and enrich children's learning in all subjects. The following identify examples of how children might use the arts to support their learning in each subject.

In **math**, children can:

- use pattern blocks to reproduce patterns onto paper, using templates or stickers.
- design a pattern for a weaving and then weave it.
- illustrate word problems in a journal.
- make geometric sculptures with toothpicks, straws, popsicle sticks, or found objects.
- determine measurements for scenery and quantities of props needed for a play.
- use refrains of songs to explore other kinds of patterns.
- dance through the room covering as much space as they can and still return to their spot in 12 counts, 10 counts, 8 counts, and so on.

As part of **language and literacy** activities, children can:

- act out scenes from a story read aloud.
- make a tape recording of jump rope chants and rhymes and write the words on chart paper.
- create sound effects that go along with a poem or story.
- act out the story of a familiar song.
- create pictures using art techniques used by authors and illustrators, such as the torn paper pictures used by Leo Lionni.
- choreograph a dance that illustrates the traits of a specific character in a story they have read. Other children can guess who it is.

In **science**, children can:

- create skits about how animals communicate.
- dramatize a science observation: a butterfly emerging from a chrysalis, a chick from an egg.
- make tape recordings of sounds in everyday life: dripping water, a door closing, paper tearing, scraping fingernails.
- illustrate their observations in a science journal.
- investigate how tension affects range of movement by trying out different body movements in a tense and relaxed state.
- make a shadow play.
- make paper from different plants.
- design birds' wings for a play about birds.

In **social studies**, children can:

- sketch observations on a neighborhood walk.
- share dances or music they enjoy at home with their families.
- draw, paint, or make constructions to represent impressions from a field trip.
- make rhythm instruments, such as drums, bamboo sticks, and shakers, that might be used by people in other cultures.
- create a bookshelf or wooden box planter with woodworking materials to learn about construction workers, cabinetmakers, or builders.
- create costumes out of brown paper bags to act out some historic event.

These examples illustrate ways the arts can enhance children's learning. Consider what is most comfortable for you and ways you think both you and the children can experience success.

Arts Activities

I f you're still feeling a bit uncomfortable about using the arts in your classroom, this section describes a few activities to help you get started. We highlight skits and plays, murals, block building, and singing. Keep in mind that you can't offer everything at once or you and the children are likely to be overwhelmed. Consider also the time of day that best lends itself to something new.

Skits and Plays

Dramatic activities such as skits, role playing, and class plays bring out different talents in children. Some children are natural actors and love center stage; others like to stage manage or get involved in choosing props or creating scenery; some write scripts. In drama, children learn to think creatively, take risks, and use their imaginations.

Preparing skits and plays also allows children to practice social skills such as collaboration and problem solving. They share ideas and form new friendships. Drama projects can also be a legitimate extension of learning to resolve conflicts (through role plays) or exploring specific content in the curriculum.

Some drama activities are easy to promote in the primary classroom. Here are some ideas to explore.

- Ask children who have read the same book to choose a scene to dramatize for the class.
- Divide the class into groups of four to six children. Give each group a bag full of unrelated items (e.g., a toy telephone, a funny hat, a basket, two books, a pad) and have them create a short skit involving the materials and everyone in the group.
- Play "Charades" using book titles that the children know well.
- Ask groups to role play different ways to solve problems that occur at recess.
- Make time to share skits, plays, and puppet shows children have created during choice time, recess, or after school.

If you demonstrate that you value these endeavors, children will take them seriously and spend time on their productions, thus furthering their learning while they increase their skills.

Class Plays

Preparing and presenting a class play can be a wonderful culminating project related to a long-term study in social studies or science. Plays allow children to put their learning to use and share it. If they have had many experiences during the year in inventing skits, singing together, and perhaps even writing their own words to songs, you will have a good idea of how each child can contribute.

There are many different sources for class plays. Sometimes a play can be based on a book that has been a success in the classroom. If a book has been read over and over again, the children may know it by heart.

> *Ms. Taylor observes that her first graders love the book* May I Bring a Friend? *by Beatrice Schenk. Their enthusiasm leads to dramatizations; children act out the parts of different animals in the story. They talk about how a giraffe might walk and why the queen would frown about where the guests could sit down. The children are eager to perform these skits for their families and the other first grade classes at their school. Ms. Taylor talks with the children about what they would need to do and they generate a list: choose parts, make costumes, rehearse, make scenery, make programs. Rather than writing the script, Ms. Taylor encourages the children to continually practice their scenes. She helps them decide what changes they want to make until they are pleased with their play, and feel ready to perform it for an audience.*

Plays can develop from long-term studies, too. For example, a second grade class is studying birds. The children go on bird walks, keep records of the numbers and kinds of birds they see, draw pictures and make models of birds, learn about the size and shape of feathers and feet, learn where birds live and about their nesting habits, and so on. The teacher, Mr. Diamond, reads many stories about birds. One day he reads a modern folktale, *The Bird-Feather Rainbow* by Marc Gellman, that has many different kinds of birds in it (1989). The children love the story, which involves quarreling birds that won't help each other. Noting their interest, he proposes they turn the story into a play, which can be culminating activity for their long-term study.

Children can use their extensive knowledge of birds to become the characters they choose to represent in the play.

> *Mr. Diamond asks each child to make a list of the special characteristics of one of the birds. He adapts the story using the children's list of birds. The children decide to make costumes, which, of course, is very time consuming. First, the children design wings for the birds, then brainstorm to identify materials they can use. Several children make samples using coat hangers for the shape and tissue paper for the feathers. Another child makes a design with cardboard and aluminum foil. A parent volunteers to cut simple felt hoods in a variety of colors. Several children work with the parent to sew the hoods together and decorate them with tissue paper feathers. As the play begins to take shape, the children decide to add songs to the script. Because the class has spent time every week learning songs together, they have a repertoire of songs to think about using in their play. When the birds quarrel, they sing, "I'm Gonna Tell." When the Dove goes off after the Raven, they sing their own version of "I'm On My Way." At the end of the play, when all the birds learn to work together to make the rainbow, they change the words of "This Little Light of Mine" to "This Rainbow of Mine, We're Gonna Make It Shine."*

As you can tell, putting together a class play takes time. If you try to do a play and also try to keep up with everything else you usually do, you and the children will be exhausted rather than fulfilled. Instead, let the usual schedule go. Be reassured by all the learning that can take place when children work on a play: reading and writing (producing the script, program, and advertisements), problem solving (creating scenery and costumes), and collaboration (creating ways to include everyone in the play). Don't be afraid to ask for help when your class puts on a play. It's a wonderful way to involve family members, who can assist with making costumes, constructing scenery, or videotaping the play. Children love to watch themselves and you will learn from their comments as they watch. And, of course, all family members can participate as the audience for a play and join in the cast party to celebrate.

Murals

Making murals fosters collaborative work, allows teachers to guide and assess children's learning about particular content, and encourages the development of children's aesthetic understanding and appreciation. They explore concepts about light, color, pattern, size, shape, and variation—concepts that may also be explored in language and literacy, mathematics, social studies, and science. The process of creating a mural also requires that children plan and work together. They engage in research and express their understandings about a subject as they plan the mural. During the process, teachers have many opportunities to observe how children interpret what they have learned, solve problems, resolve conflicts in an everyday context, and how they talk to and learn from one another.

Each mural project will be different, as you involve children in planning, designing, creating, and sharing the project. If you have not done much painting in the classroom, you may be concerned about how to start. As a rule of thumb, give children time to use paints during choice time and make sure you have procedures for set-up and clean-up as described in Chapter 3, Establishing a Structure for the Classroom, pages 116-118.

Planning the Mural

Once you and the children have decided upon a mural project—based on something you are studying in social studies or science or as a response to a book the class read—plan on using several meeting times to talk about the scope of the mural, its size, and the materials needed. Murals can be painted, made from fabric and cutouts pasted on paper, or designed with grasses, shredded paper, sticks, or other collage materials. By planning together, children can make decisions about whether they want to use paint for an underwater scene, collage and cut-out materials for a desert landscape or river scene, or milk cartons and sticks for a three-dimensional city scene. Then the class can plan a system for collecting and organizing the materials.

Designing and Making the Mural

Once children have agreed upon the subject and materials, they can brainstorm how the mural should look. Younger children's plans will change as they work; older children are more likely to stick to an agreed-upon design. Several problem-solving design sessions may be needed to address scale, perspective, and specific content. As with other projects, the mural may be divided into sections, with different groups at work on different scenes (e.g., animals, fish, plant life, buildings, roads).

> *A class of second and third graders studying the Sonoran Desert in the Southwest wants to create a mural. The children research topics such as gila monsters, rattlesnakes, roadrunners, saguaro cacti, weather, and plant life. As they design and create the mural, each child contributes by drawing animals, plants, or land formations, depending upon what he or she has researched. The children talk to one another about the relative sizes of their cactus or kangaroo rat and make concessions based on new knowledge. Kim, who is an expert on the saguaro cactus, wants the season to be spring so her cactus can be in bloom. Hannah and Badr agree because they want to show the nesting areas where their animals lay their eggs in the spring.*

As children work they will reveal what they learned from their research and share this knowledge with one another. They may also share misgivings about their contributions. You may hear complaints ranging from: "I hate my animal" to "I can't draw that!" If the mural is big enough, children will have several parts to design and make. Children discover what they are good at and classmates will ask one another for help: "Let's get Eric to draw the flowers—he really knows how to make them look real." Because the children have a stake in the outcome, they work hard to make their sections go together. They mix their paint carefully to make sure the brown backgrounds blend together; they find ways to accommodate the different perspectives and adapt as the need arises.

Sharing the Mural

A mural is a record of the learning that has taken place in the classroom—an aesthetic expression of specific knowledge. In the process of exchanging information, children learn a great deal from each other. The child who is an expert on lizards works next to the child who knows all about plants. Although no individual child has researched all about the desert, the children as a group own the mural and absorb information from one another.

A mural can be shared with the larger community by inviting family members and other classes to view it and having children take turns explaining the various parts. Another option is to hang the mural in the hallway of the school with an appropriate title and written explanations.

Block Building

When primary age children have access to unit blocks, they can build elaborate structures that require joint planning and execution. As they talk about their designs, they form pictures in their minds, which they then try to communicate through language and with blocks. In the process of building, children negotiate, share, and role play, practicing the social skills needed to initiate and maintain friendships. Moreover, because blocks are designed in mathematical units, children learn about size, shape, weight, length, order, area, and number as they create structures. As their structures become more elaborate, they may begin to think like architects, considering design features, symmetry, and aesthetics.

In many schools, blocks are not a feature in the primary classroom. But, we feel there are significant advantages to block activities. (See pages 118-119.) Providing space for a block area, arranging blocks for use, providing pictures and challenges for block construction, and establishing procedures for their use, all send messages to children about the importance and value you place on blocks.

Involve the children in the organization and rules for the block area. Use these suggestions to stimulate children's interest.

- Hang pictures of various structures and bridges in the block area to inspire building.

- Keep measuring tapes and recording sheets in the area for children to measure the dimensions of their buildings.

- Place a scale in the area that could be used to compare the weights of different unit blocks.

- Teach a fraction lesson in the block area, and then have children work on fraction problems using blocks.

- Use blocks to begin a study of mapping. Have the children work in small groups to create the shape of the room and the furniture in the classroom with blocks.

- Post a written challenge in the block area (e.g., How long an extension bridge can you build? or What kind of structure can you build using only triangles?).

After children have had these or similar experiences, you may feel ready to use block building as part of a larger study.

A group of second graders is studying the community around their school. They go on several neighborhood trips, first to focus on the businesses and stores in the area, and then on the community services available. Pictures, discussions, and graphing projects follow each trip. Some children use the block area to build models of the various places they visit.

Ms. Simpson holds a meeting to plan a project connected to the study. The children decide to build a model of the neighborhood including some offices, stores, and community service buildings. They agree that blocks can be used to create certain structures and that milk and juice cartons will be used for others. The children make decisions: they will work with partners because there isn't enough room for every student to have his or her own building; they will write letters to families asking for donations of milk and juice cartons in different sizes; they agree on which buildings will be built by whom.

During the next week, the children work on their block community at different times of the day. In addition to the groups responsible for the structures, other groups form to build roads, stick figure people, and trees. Children make signs designating various spaces and buildings. While children are working in the block area, Ms. Simpson is assessing their understandings and planning ways to extend the study.

Here are some suggestions for you to try with your class.

- Consider the space available and find a way to protect the structures children build.
- Introduce blocks and block building to the class and develop rules together.
- Allow the necessary time for clean-up.
- If there is a problem, brainstorm some ways to solve it with the children.
- Value the children's work and have discussions about it. Allow the children to share their work with the others in the class.

Singing

When children and teachers sing together, they develop a special camaraderie. Singing becomes a ritual that the class does together in distinct ways and at special times. It can lighten up the dreariest day. Singing can also extend children's learning—when the songs you sing relate to particular subject matter—and promote musical awareness and appreciation—when you call attention to rhythm, harmony, verses, and refrains.

Even if you are one of those people who "can't sing one note on key," you can still bring singing into your classroom. Figure out what you are comfortable doing. If this is an area in which you might need some support, here's what you might do.

- Borrow tapes or records of folk songs from friends and the library.

- Bring in a tape recorder and music tapes that inspire everyone to sing along.

- Brainstorm with the children and list the songs you all know.

- Make charts with the lyrics of favorite songs. Children can take turns pointing to the words.

- Team up with a teacher who is especially skilled in this area.

- Encourage children to lead the class in song.

During their study of a nearby river, one class learned river songs such as: "Roll On Columbia," "River of Dreams," "Way Down Upon the Swanee River," "Down By the Riverside," "Peace I Ask of Thee Oh River," "Old Man River," and "Erie Canal." Another class studying the harbor and ocean vessels learned some different songs: "Blow Ye Winds in the Morning," "'Twas Friday Morn," "The Sinking of the Reuben James," and "The John B. Sails."

You can find songbooks in libraries or ask a music teacher to guide you to source material. Family members who come from different parts of the world and other cultures can often be excellent resources for new songs. There are songs to be found on every subject from friendship to garbage. A group involved in a clean-up project around their school took to chanting the Pete Seeger song "Garbage" as they advertised the recycling campaign for the school.

Linking the Six Strategies to the Arts

The six strategies presented in Part One of the book allow you to create the kind of classroom in which projects in the arts are exciting as well as manageable. In turn, each of the strategies is supported by work in the arts.

Knowing the Children You Teach

All good teaching begins with knowing about child development and the unique qualities of each child. Teachers look for the strengths that will help each child experience success. Providing a range of activities and projects allows every child to excel. One child might compose a song for a skit, while someone else writes the words. Another child may design the scenery for a class play. These may be the children who have not been the most eager mathematicians or readers. When they can show their talents in other ways, they develop self-confidence and often begin to improve their skills in other areas as a result.

Because the children in your class change each year, you will most likely change the focus of activities as well. Some years you will have singers who learn all the words to the songs you teach and want to sing them over and over again; other years the dramatists take over and skits become the preferred activity.

When children have time to make, design, and build things, you can learn about their needs and promote their emotional, social, physical, and cognitive development.

- Emotional development addresses children's mental health and well-being. Many children today live with fear and anxiety because of such stresses as a difficult family situation or neighborhood violence. Emotional release and comfort can come from using drawing tools, paint, clay, and building materials. Self-worth is fostered when children create objects that are appreciated by others and proudly displayed in the classroom.

- Social skills are essential for children to become competent learners. When children plan a puppet show, work on a mural or at the computer together, they learn to share their ideas and opinions, listen to others, take turns, and work together to achieve results.

- Physical development is enhanced when children have various opportunities to use both small and large muscles. Children build their fine motor skills when they guide a pair of scissors or staple and bolt construction materials together. They refine eye-hand coordination as they thread a needle or hammer nails to create a three-dimensional structure.

- Cognitive development is encouraged when teachers provide multiple ways for children to learn. Children create music, work with the visual-spatial world, and apply their knowledge productively. Arts activities give teachers and children the ways to "represent these other intelligences" (Oddleifson 1994, 447). Projects provide children with various ways of communicating. When teachers emphasize only verbal and written skills, they ignore how powerfully messages are delivered in other ways.

As you come to know the children better by observing their work on projects in the arts, you can make decisions about ways to enhance each child's growth and development. Instructional decisions about how and when to guide learning can then be based on what you know about a particular group of children.

Building a Classroom Community

When you have daily meetings, help children to relate positively and work collaboratively, and teach them to solve social problems, you are building a classroom community where it is possible for children to create, design, and make things. By the same token, these kinds of activities are natural community builders. As children work together, they talk about what they are doing and share ideas. They benefit from working in a group and begin to understand how to make a contribution. They learn to appreciate one another's talents and seek out the class experts for help.

Meetings are a natural focus for discussions about projects—planning them as well as sharing the results. When children have been involved in creating with art supplies, building materials, and tools as part of their natural work in the classroom, they enjoy brainstorming about what kinds of projects they would like to do. With practice, children can generate the ideas that are needed. You can get them started.

- Let's think about what we can make or do connected with our study of the neighborhood.

- How can we design something to show all this information?

- Now that we know so much about_____, let's consider ways to show it.

- Are there several different ways to show our ideas about_____?

When children work together on projects they are engaged in community building. The community becomes a safe place to take risks.

Establishing a Structure in the Classroom

Without a clear structure in the classroom, the kinds of activities we describe can easily be overwhelming. If the physical environment of the classroom is clearly organized with places for painting supplies, for creating structures or inventions, for using blocks or other building materials, for rehearsing skits or songs, then children know where to find what they need and how to use it. As you think about resources to make available, consider that the way you display materials reflects their importance.

How materials are introduced to children helps to ensure their appropriate use. The message to be conveyed is that materials are used for important purposes. Children also need clear expectations for behavior. That's why teachers develop routines for setting up painting trays, for identifying the number of children who can work in a particular area, and, of course, for clean-up. It is worth taking the time in the beginning of the year to create and practice these routines so that the children can work more independently later.

The work children generate as they use materials can be displayed prominently. When you take care to arrange children's creations beautifully, the message is clear—this is important and valued work. You can talk with the children about design principles and plan together how to use classroom space for displays.

Guiding Children's Learning

Young children learn best when they are actively involved rather than listening to someone talk. They develop understanding and competence when they have experiences that enable them to figure things out for themselves. Artistic experiences and materials can help children to think for themselves, express original ideas, explore and discover new information, and explore and discover new relationships.

The four principles discussed in the chapter on Guiding Children's Learning apply to planning activities in the arts as well.

(1) Learning is purposeful and relevant.

(2) Meaningful learning is integrated.

(3) Communication is central to learning.

(4) Learning takes time.

Teachers *make learning purposeful and relevant* by encouraging children to answer questions of interest to them and helping them make connections between what they are learning and what they already know. When teachers offer open-ended experiences with materials— rather than with adult-made samples, patterns for tracing or "coloring-in," or commercial activity sheets—children are able to explore, create, and make their own products. They learn that it is appropriate to have their own feelings and views about a work of art, a particular piece of music, or a book. With this growing confidence in their own abilities, children approach the arts in purposeful ways.

The second principle is that *meaningful learning is integrated*. When children engage in projects using the materials and tools of the arts, they are experiencing an integrated approach to curriculum.

Cameron wants to build a model of the type of longhouse in which the Piscataway Indians of Maryland lived. Having researched the topic, he knows what a longhouse looked like and the materials the Piscataways used to build their homes. He asks Ms. Swann what he should use. Together they go to the building table and the supply closet where leftover scraps and other materials are stored in buckets and bags. As they examine the items, ideas begin to form: "This rough piece of wallpaper would work as the dirt floor," says Cameron. "I've got some leftover grass from my Easter basket at home that looks like grass. I'm going to bring it in to use for a grass mat." "Could you use real sticks and dirt for the roof, or would these popsicle sticks work better?" asks Ms. Swann.

This example shows that you don't have to plan all details in advance. What you can do is demonstrate your readiness to approach a problem and your conviction that it can be solved.

The third principle is that ***communication is central to learning***. As children participate in creating and making things in the classroom, teachers can influence their growth and development by responding to their work and engaging them in conversations about what they are doing. How teachers use language and how they respond to children's efforts conveys important messages.

- I am interested in what you are doing.
- I want to hear your ideas.
- I respect your way of saying and making things.

Children need approval, permission, assurance, support, and encouragement from adults to inspire them to create and express their ideas and feelings. Here are some suggestions.

Describe what you see. "I see so many different shapes in your painting." "You made your picture symmetrical. How interesting to see the same things on both sides of the paper." "I notice a lot of spaces to look through on all sides of your sculpture."

Talk about the process. "It looks as if it was really hard to make all those boxes stay together." "How did you create so many new colors when you only started with three?" "How did you decide which scene to act out for the class?" "Did you think of the melody first or did you write the words first?"

Ask open-ended questions to get children to think and respond. "What do you notice about the shapes in your painting?" "What were you thinking about as you built that tower?" "What do you think you could use to keep that tower from tipping over?" "Is there a different sized brush you can use to get to all those little places inside your sculpture?" "What can you do to show that the character is only pretending to be angry?"

Encourage and support continuing efforts. "You solved that balance problem in your building!" "You just discovered a new way to make a stitch with needle and yarn. Would you add it to our stitch frame so that other people can learn something from you?" "That's a great discovery you just made about our new graphics program. How can we record it so others can use it also?" When children are engaged in arts projects you can also model very important interactions by helping children ask for feedback on their products.

Encourage children to evaluate their own work. "Which drawing material—the chalk or the colored pencils—did you find worked best in showing the life cycle of the butterfly?" "Which did you enjoy the most—acting in the play or designing the scenery?" "How would you do this project differently next time?" "Would you describe how you figured out how to write the words to go with the music?"

Help children articulate the feedback they want. "Do you want the class to comment on the story as a whole, or do you want the group to give you advice about the ending?" "Would you like us to tell you what we liked the most in your dance?" "Do you want to tell us how your movable sculpture works?"

Finally, ***learning takes time***. Activities that involve children in designing and making things require lots of time because the process is as important as the product. For significant learning to take place, children need to come back to their work and be able to make changes based on new discoveries. For these reasons, it is helpful to schedule several large blocks of time each week (one to two hours at a time) when children can invest themselves in project work in the arts. Additional time for children to return to their projects can be found during choice times.

Assessing Children's Learning

Assessment involves observing children regularly and collecting samples of their work in order to plan instruction and evaluate children's progress. When children paint or draw, make up skits, or create a structure to show what they have learned, you have the opportunity to observe and question them as they go about their work. The physical products they create can become part of a portfolio. If arts activities are a regular part of classroom life, you are likely to have many examples of children's thinking over time. The special talents of individual children are likely to be expressed as well.

You may have to train yourself to look for things you might not have noticed before. For example, try to look for increased detail in children's artwork, and how they use space and color to express ideas. Note which children are willing to try an art form they are not yet good at. When children feel safe taking risks and experimenting with materials, they may later be willing to try different approaches to solving other problems in reading, writing, or mathematical thinking.

Art projects provide many opportunities to assess the process of learning. In creating scenery and props for a play, children have to think about multiple solutions to problems, make a plan, change their ideas or build consensus within a group, and stay with a task until it is completed. Many important life skills can be practiced as part of these art projects.

Your knowledge about children and what they are learning will be richer and more comprehensive with these kinds of observations.

Building a Partnership with Families

Family members can help you extend your comfort level with certain projects. The grandparent who paints, the guitarist, or the costume designer may add to the experiences you are able to offer.

When children create in the classroom through the visual arts, music, dance, or drama, you have many things to share with families to further the school-home partnership. In these activities, children demonstrate directly what they are learning. Family members may be more interested in joining the class for special culminating activities because they are aware of the scope of the studies.

Closing Thoughts

The arts are a means through which children construct knowledge, investigate, and represent what they are learning. They are also subjects in their own right, with content, materials, and tools that children must understand in order to be knowledgeable and productive adults. The arts are integrally linked to each of the six strategies for building the primary classroom.

References and Resources for the Arts

Bland, Jane C. 1958. *The Art of the Young Child.* New York, NY: Museum of Modern Art.

Blecher, Sharon, and Kathy Jaffee. 1998. *Weaving in the Arts: Widening the Learning Circle.* Portsmouth, NH: Heinemann.

Consortium of National Arts Education Associations. 1994. *National Standards for Arts Education.* Reston, VA: Music Educators National Conference.

Gardner, Howard. 1982. *Art, Mind, and Brain: A Cognitive Approach to Creativity.* New York, NY: Basic Books.

Gellman, Marc. 1989. The Bird-Feather Rainbow. In *Does God Have a Big Toe?* New York, NY: Harper Collins.

Heinig, Ruth Beall. 1992. *Improvisation with Favorite Tales: Integrating Drama into the Reading/Writing Classroom.* Portsmouth, NH: Heinemann.

Hirsch, Elizabeth, ed. 1996. *The Block Book.* 3rd ed. Washington, DC: NAEYC.

Kelner, Lenore Blank. 1993. *The Creative Classroom: A Guide for Using Creative Drama in the Classroom, PreK–6.* Portsmouth, NH: Heinemann.

Klugman, Edgar, and Sara Smilansky. 1990. *Children's Play and Learning.* New York, NY: Teachers College Press.

Lord, Lois. 1958. *Collage and Construction in Elementary and Junior High School.* Worcester, MA: Davis Publications.

Oddleifson, Eric. 1994. What Do We Want Our Schools to Do? *Phi Delta Kappan* 75 (6).

Riley, Richard. November 10, 1998. New Arts Assessment Shows Few Opportunities for Most Students; Riley Says Education Essential. U.S. Department of Education. http://aep-arts.org/highlights/riley.html.

Sautter, Craig R. 1994. An Arts Education School Reform Strategy. *Phi Delta Kappan* 75 (6).

Task Force on Children's Learning and the Arts: Birth to Age 8. 1998. *Position Paper.* Washington, DC: Arts Education Partnership.

Task Force on Children's Learning and the Arts: Birth to Age 8. 1998. *Young Children and the Arts: Making Creative Connections.* Washington, DC: Arts Education Partnership.

A

N

O

P

Z

Building the

Primary

Classroom

Notes

Building the

Primary

Classroom

Building the

Primary

Classroom

Building the

Primary

Classroom

Notes

Building the

Primary

Classroom